# AUTOMOTIVE ENGINE FUNDAMENTALS

**Frederick E. Peacock**
*Indiana Vocational Technical College*

**Thomas E. Gaston**
*Purdue University*

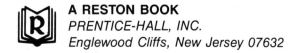

**A RESTON BOOK**
*PRENTICE-HALL, INC.*
*Englewood Cliffs, New Jersey 07632*

Library of Congress Cataloging in Publication Data

Peacock, Frederick E
   Automotive engine fundamentals.

   Includes index.
   1. Automobiles—Motors—Design and construction.
I. Gaston, Thomas E., joint author.   II. Title.
TL210.P35     629.25    80-12324
ISBN 0-8359-0276-5

10  9  8  7  6  5  4

Printed in the United States of America

# *Dedication*

The authors, acting jointly, dedicate this book to their wives, *Frieda* and *Dorothy*, two special people whose understanding, patience, and support endured through the many months of research and writing.

Acting individually, the authors also wish to extend their dedication to include some people whose influence—though exerted long ago—is found on every page.

Mr. Peacock's dedication is to his Father, *Bill Peacock*, who advised him always to spend his life working at what he enjoyed. "Only if you enjoy what you are doing," the senior Mr. Peacock told his son, "will you do it well."

Professor Gaston's dedication is to *Clarence and Thurston Gaston*, the Father and Uncle who, together convinced him early in life of a truth that he hopes to share with readers of this book: Even an ordinary man, with sufficient diligence and dedication, can do extraordinary things.

# Contents

# Acknowledgments

This book, like the technology it deals with, is not the creation of any one or two minds. Its authors know, perhaps better than a casual reader *can* know, that an automotive text, like automotive technology itself, is always the product of an intricate pattern of social cooperation among individuals who are often unknown to each other and separated by time, distance, and technological specialization.

Among these unnamed contributors, in the present instance, must be the several instructors who taught us, the scores of students whom we have ourselves instructed over the past decade, and the numerous colleagues with whom we have often discussed technical and instructional problems. Our gratitude to these people is not at all lessened by the fact that we find it impossible to name them here or detail exactly the important contributions they have made to this book.

However certain individuals and organizations have contributed in tangible ways that we are aware of. We would particularly like to thank Mr. Leland Koch for his excellent photography and Mr. Dennis Boyd for his fine drawings. Both gentlemen incurred personal inconvenience in order to keep their considerable talents at our disposal during the writing of this book. Our debt to them is great.

The following organizations also extended courtesies to us, largely through the agency of the individuals named. We would like, therefore, to thank them for helping us make this text as accurate, as complete, and as informative as possible.

AVCO—Lycoming Division
R. B. LeMar

Balance Technology, Inc.
Franklin E. R. Rensler

Champion Spark Plug Company
Automotive Technical Services
Dan M. Lane

Chrysler Corporation
Howard V. Hendricks

Cincinnati Milacron, Inc.
John A. Edgar

Cross-Fraser
Division of the Cross Company
John D. Borseth

Dana Corporation
R. F. Draughon

Ford Motor Company
L. H. Lee
D. A. Haines

General Motors Corporation
Chevrolet Division
D. R. Harrig
GMC Truck & Coach Division
Keith J. Pitcher
Harrison Radiator Division
T. S. Siuta
Service Section
R.L. Neal

Indiana Vocational Technical
College—Muncie
Dennis Gaddis

International Molybdenum
Corporation
S. A. Wright

McQuay-Norris, Inc.
Michael P. Josvanger

Motor Vehicle Manufacturers
Association of The United
States, Inc.
William D. McLean, Ph.D.

National Institute of Automotive
Service Excellence—NIASE
Virginia I. Andrews

Peugeot Motors of America, Inc.
Andrew Stuckey

Purdue University Aviation
Technology Department
Dick Carton

Sealed Power Corporation
George Wickstrom

Stirling Power Systems
Joseph E. Tyson

TRW Replacement Division
N. J. Musil

Volkswagen of America, Inc.
Herbert W. Williamson
Frederick Bologna

Wallace Murray Corporation
Schwitzer Division
Max E. Rumbaugh, Jr.

Winnebago Industries, Inc.
Harry Prestanski

In every case, the people named gave us significant and timely help with enthusiasm and good cheer. They helped to make the writing of this book the pleasure that it was.

*Frederick E. Peacock*

*Thomas E. Gaston*

# Preface

We feel, as authors that our own backgrounds give us an exceptionally good understanding of the students who will read this book. Between us, we represent a son of a mechanic, a father of a mechanic, a former student of automotive technology, and a long-time instructor of courses in automotive engines. So we know personally many of the young people who are now embarking upon careers in automotive technology. We find them to be, in general, bright, inquisitive, and ambitious. They are more than willing to work hard in order to learn those things which they know to be related to their own interests. But they demand directness and practicality and become impatient with unnecessary vagueness or pretentious complexity.

We tried, in writing this book, to respect these commonsense values of our readers. To do this, we were careful to avoid two particular weaknesses often found in similar texts. First, we sought to eliminate what one authority calls COIK writing. COIK stands for "clearly only if known." Probably every instructor has, at one time or another, adopted a text which seemed clear to him, only to find later that his students were unable to absorb much from it. Often, the writing in such books is clear only to those who already know the material that is supposedly being taught.

We tried instead to address this book to the interested student on his own terms. Even complex points of theory are explained in simple readable language. When we felt that a homespun example or humorous anecdote helped to clarify a point, we were not embarrassed about introducing it. Our goal was always to convey to the student the genuine understanding of engine theory that he properly expects from such a text. We were more than willing to sacrifice a little stuffiness and professional dignity in pursuit of that goal.

The second pitfall we were determined to avoid was superficiality. It is comparatively easy to "simplify" a text by leaving out discussion of the more difficult concepts. But such a book, in our view, can make no real contribution to technological education. It is merely a training document, suitable only for guiding the rankest beginners through mindless exchanges of parts. A lasting career in today's rapidly changing technology, we feel, must be based on a complete understanding of basic engine theory. So this book is designed to arouse, sustain, and satisfy the curiosity that leads students to ask *why* things are as they are.

The students on whom we tested preliminary versions of these chapters more than met this challenge. Their responses confirmed in every sense our conviction that students recognize the value of thoroughness. They sensed, as we hoped they would, the fact that this fuller, more systematized knowledge will make it easier for them to think through novel problems for themselves. In this unpredictable period in the history of the industry, we think that students with this kind of training will be much less susceptible to technological unemployment.

For these reasons, it will be seen that this text—despite its emphasis on readability—is as technically accurate, as complete, and as theoretically sound as we could make it, given the practical realities surrounding our work. To the best of our ability, we have written the book that would have been helpful to us when we began our own training. We think students deserve such a text. And we feel sure they will profit from it.

# THE MODERN ENGINE:
# AN OVERVIEW

# 1

# Your Opportunities in Automotive Technology

The fact that you are reading this book suggests that you are seriously interested in the automotive service industry. Perhaps you picked up the book on your own, just to get an idea of what automotive technology is and what opportunities it offers. But most likely, you are reading it because it was assigned as part of your work in a course in automotive mechanics. Either way, that makes it a good bet that you are the kind of person who should be considering a career in automotive technology. People who are willing to do serious reading in good texts and to enroll for formal training in academic courses are the kind of people who have a future in the automotive service industry.

Today's automobiles are too complex, too expensive, and too important to our nation's survival to be serviced by untrained people. The day of the "grease monkey" has passed. The school dropout who starts "fooling around with cars" today is unlikely to learn enough on his own to qualify him to set up shop.

That is why some states have already begun to license mechanics. It is also why a national program of testing and certification of mechanics by The National Institute for Automotive Service Excellence is rapidly gaining public support throughout the country. And it certainly explains why the Motor Vehicle Manufacturers Association of the United States expresses its concern that the nation already faces "a shortage of well-trained, competent mechanics with good attitudes and work habits."

**Figure 1–1.** The testing and certification program of the National Institute for Automotive Service Excellence is one of many movements aimed at upgrading the quality of automotive service. *Courtesy of N.I.A.S.E.*

To the industry as a whole, this shortage of trained people presents a major challenge that government and business leaders are attempting to meet in a number of ways. To you, as a person just now choosing a career, the shortage has a special meaning. It means that if you get the in-depth technical training needed today—the kind of training this book provides—you can reasonably expect to find your opportunities in automotive service to be limited only by your own imagination, initiative, and ability.

The purpose of this first chapter is to give you some idea of how great, how varied, and how challenging those opportunities can be. But the person who makes the most of his opportunities in automotive technology must be able to work with his head as well as his hands. He must know what is going on in his industry, as well as what is happening at his workbench. That is why this book on engines begins with a brief look at the history of the automobile. We hope to make clear that the automobile as we know it today is not the creation of any one man. It is instead the sum total of countless different contributions by *thousands* of different people separated from each other by years and miles. Yet these people all worked together, sometimes without even realizing it, to give us the modern automotive engine.

It is not only possible, it is probable that some of the readers of this book will someday make their own contributions to this technology. We do not know, of course, whether you will be one of them. But we hope that you will at least accept that possibility, as you begin your study of automotive engines. Most mechanics, to be sure, never give crucial clues to automotive engineers, invent important tools, or develop revolutionary improvements in service procedures. But some do. And those who do are usually people who are able to see how their own work fits into the big picture. That is what you will get from this first chapter—the big picture.

**Figure 1–2.** Among the jobs available to those trained in automotive service are those of service manager, motor pool supervisor, and parts supply specialist.

## OBJECTIVES

When you have completed this chapter you should be able to:

- Explain why no one person can be said to have invented the automobile.
- Tell who Nicholas August Otto was and what he contributed to the modern automobile.
- Name two early competitors of the internal combustion engine and tell approximately when and why they lost out.
- Name five specific jobs that are open to a person thoroughly trained in automotive technology.
- Name five ways in which the automobile has influenced modern life styles.

## HOW IT ALL BEGAN

Almost no object in daily use is more familiar to us and more commonly taken for granted than the automobile. The number of cars in use in this country today equals almost half our population. If we count up such auto-related businesses as insurance, steel mills, and highway construction firms, we find that one-sixth of our people owe their jobs to the automobile. Over four households in five have at least one motor vehicle. More than half have either a second car, a pick-up truck, or a recreational vehicle in addition to the family car. How did all this come to be? Where did it start?

Would you say it started in 1678, when Ferdinand Verbiest, a priest serving in China, built the first working model of a steam-powered vehicle? Or did it start two centuries earlier in Italy, when Leonardo Da Vinci first tried to design such a machine? Or a century later, in 1769, when a French army officer named Nicholas Joseph Cugnot built a steam-powered "tractor" to pull cannons? These were all beginnings in a process of development that would lead, in time, to today's sophisticated automobile. But it is important to understand that they were only beginnings. Cugnot's first artillery puller, for instance, could only go about two miles per hour. To do that, it had to stop every few hundred feet to build up steam. On his second try, he reached the unheard of speed of five miles per hour. Unfortunately, however, he lost control of the vehicle, which ran off the road and was wrecked.

Such a small beginning could hardly be called the "invention" of the automobile, but it was a step towards it.

**Figure 1–3.**

A major contribution to automotive technology was made sixty years later by a man who was not even thinking about cars. The man was Samuel Colt, the American gunmaker. While others were following up on Cugnot's pioneering work with the steam engine, Colt began to manufacture his famous revolver using interchangeable parts in machinery. Without that pioneering technology, the automotive assembly line and the entire automotive service industry as we know them would be impossible. But neither the experts nor mechanically minded laymen fully appreciated the significance of Colt's achievement in the early and middle years of the nineteenth century. It would be another half-century before Colt's work would be applied to automobiles.

**Figure 1–4.** The Colt 45 revolver, "The gun that won the West." Its inventor, Samuel Colt, pioneered the technology of interchangeable parts in machinery. Fifty years later, Colt's techniques were adapted to automobile manufacture and service.

There were, however, three things that did excite those early experts: (1) the rapid development of the steam engine, (2) the electric motor, and (3) the invention of the internal combustion engine. During the last century these three kinds of power sources were drawn into a technological race. The first one to gain a decisive edge, in economic practicality, was destined to propel the millions of automobiles that would be built in the twentieth century. You know, of course, that the internal combustion engine won out over its competitors. But it is important to remember that, a century ago, this outcome was by no means certain. In fact, the steam engine and the electric motor both had such early leads that careful investors at the turn of the century considered the internal combustion engine "too risky" for their money.

## The Steam Engine

To understand how this could be, it is only necessary to look at how quickly Cugnot's steam-powered cannon mover was developed into a commercially useful vehicle. Cugnot's invention came in 1769, about the time of the American Revolution. Thirty years later—as Thomas Jefferson was about to become the third President—Richard Trevithick built the first steam-powered carriage in England. His was quickly followed by others in England, America, and on the Continent. The new technology flourished, particularly in England. In rapid succession came the development of the variable-ratio transmission, the hand brake, and the differential.

Meanwhile, the steam engine itself was being improved. By 1829, Sir Goldsworthy Gurney had taken a steam-powered stagecoach on a 200-mile round trip from London to Bath and averaged better than fifteen miles per hour. Soon afterward, English steam coaches, able to carry up to fourteen passengers at a time, ran regular routes in several parts of England. In fact, steam-powered vehicles were beginning to do rather nicely in England's highly competitive transportation industry.

So operators of the older horsedrawn stages joined with the newer railroads and convinced lawmakers to stifle the young upstart. In the name of "public safety," the Red Flag Act of 1865 was passed. This made it illegal to operate a "self-propelled" vehicle unless a man walked in front of it carrrying a red flag. At night, instead of a flag, he was to carry a lantern. Either way, the steam-coach could not go faster than the man could walk.

Since horsedrawn coaches and trains were free from this restriction, they were soon transporting virtually all the passengers in England. And without the profits from passenger fares, England's impressive new automotive technology was left without economic incentive. Little progress was made there until after the law was repealed in 1896.

**Figure 1–5.**  Long before the gasoline-powered engine became practical, fleets of steam-powered coaches like this one provided comfortable and dependable transportation to commercial passengers.

**Figure 1–6.**  England's Red Flag Act of 1865 required all "self-propelled" vehicles to be preceded by a flag carrier on foot. This unreasonable law made automobiles impractical and stalled English technology for almost a third of a century.

## The Electric Car

Meanwhile, the electric car was quietly making gains. As early as 1839, a Scotsman named Anderson had created a workable electric-powered vehicle. And by the 1890's, electrics were being mass-produced in most industrialized countries. In 1889, the Electric Cab Company of London, which had been given special permission to operate without red flags, had fifty taxicabs on the streets. American manufacturers in Boston, Massachusetts; in Des Moines, Iowa; and in Hartford, Connecticut, were soon turning out electrics. By 1900, almost 500 electric-powered vehicles were in use as taxicabs and delivery vehicles in New York City alone.

The electric also gained quick popularity with consumers. Ladies especially liked its quiet dependability. Even by today's standards its performance was not bad. In 1899, Camille Jenatzy, a Frenchman, captured the world's speed record for an electric by getting 65.23 mph (100 kilometers per hour). Electrics became popular for in-city driving. In the twenty years from 1896 through 1915, almost 35,000 electric cars were built in the U.S. by more than fifty different manufacturers. Only after the introduction of Kettering's electric starter in 1911 could gasoline-powered engines begin to match the convenience and dependability of the electrics.

**Figure 1–7.** The electric car gained quick popularity at the turn of the century. Ladies especially liked its cleanliness and dependability. *Courtesy of the Motor Vehicle Manufacturers' Association of the United States of America.*

## The Internal Combustion Engine

Because of a series of important developments in Europe about the time of the American Civil War, several experts had become convinced that the internal combustion engine was a realistic competitor of steam and electricity for automotive power. After earlier work by the Englishman Alfred Cecil, the first workable internal combustion engine was created in 1860 by the Frenchman, Jean Joseph Lenoir. Lenoir's engine was powered by a manufactured cooking gas, somewhat like natural gas. He used a spark from a battery to ignite the gas. At first, Lenoir's engine only powered pumps and machinery, but after two years he mounted a modified version in a crude vehicle.

Then, in 1866, the German Nicholas August Otto made the crucial breakthrough that led to the modern engine we know today. He designed the first four-stroke, piston engine. There is no reason for you to remember most of the names that we have mentioned in this chapter. They are included only to illustrate the point we made earlier: That no one person "invented" the automobile. But you should remember the name of Nicholas Otto. His contribution was so important that the four-stroke, five-event cycle used in most engines still bears his name. You will hear often of the "Otto cycle" as you study engines, and in the next chapter you will learn more exactly what it is. At first, Otto's engine did not use gasoline. Like Lenoir, he began by burning cooking gas. But by 1876, he put his four-stroke cycle to use in a gasoline engine, and the era of the modern automobile had begun.

**Figure 1–8.**   Nicholas August Otto, German inventor of the four-stroke piston engine. *Courtesy of the Bettmann Archive.*

The last third of the nineteenth century was a period of exciting progress in automotive technology. Except in England, where the Red Flag Act halted serious work, automobiles of all kinds improved rapidly. Otto's new invention was first used to power a car by his fellow German, Gottlieb Daimler, in 1886 and was first put in an American car by the Duryea brothers in 1893. Within ten years, gasoline-powered cars were being manufactured by Oldsmobile in volume, and the competition was heating up.

**Figure 1–9.** Soon after its introduction to the United States in 1893, the gasoline-powered car became a lower-priced competitor of the electric and the steamer. *Courtesy of the Motor Vehicle Manufacturers' Association of the United States of America.*

All this progress gave your great-great grandfather a lot to consider, if he set out to buy a car in 1910. Would he buy a steam-powered vehicle, an electric car, or an automobile with one of those newfangled gasoline engines? Each had its advantages.

The steam engine had an established reputation. It had been used in cars for over a hundred years and had reached a high state of development. Therefore, it was faster, more reliable, and more comfortable than its gasoline-powered rivals. It also had better acceleration.

Electric cars were more reliable than steamers and were simpler and cheaper to operate. While not as comfortable as the steamers, they were quite adequate. Why, then, would anybody buy one of those noisy, smelly, and balky gasoline-powered engines?

There were a number of reasons. The steamer and electric car both had important disadvantages. Electric cars all required some kind of battery. Even the best batteries were so heavy that much of their own energy output had to be used in just moving themselves. This greatly limited the amount of energy available to propel the rest of the car. Also, because the batteries had to be recharged frequently, electric cars were not suited to long trips or country driving. Steam cars, on the other hand, could go anywhere, but they could not be manufactured economically.

**Figure 1–10.** In great-great grandfather's day, a buyer who wanted performance and dependability might well prefer a steam or electric car to a gasoline-powered one.

Economy soon became the most important advantage of the gasoline engine. Manufacturers of internal combustion engines were the first to take full advantage of Colt's principle of interchangeable parts. Thus they could manufacture cars quickly and sell them for much less.

At the turn of the century, when gasoline cars sold for $300, Baker Electrics were $3,000 and Doble steam cars $10,000. In 1907, Henry Ford, who had already set a world's speed record of 92 mph in his "Arrow" racer, decided to exploit this price difference. Ford stripped his Model "T" of frills, set up an assembly line, and brought modern manufacturing techniques to the automotive industry. People literally waited in line to buy his black Model "T's" for $800. And when his Highland Park, Michigan, plant opened in 1913, he astonished the country with his ability to assemble a new Model "T" every 93 minutes.

By comparison, the manufacturers of the famous Stanley steam car only brought out 650 vehicles in their best *year*. This shows how decisively the technology of the internal combustion engine beat out its competition just after the turn of the century. Steam vehicles and electric cars soon faded into the past. Profits from the huge new market for gasoline-powered cars began to finance a succession of improvements and refinements that continues today.

**Figure 1–11.**   Henry Ford's Highland Park, Michigan, plant, opened in 1913, astonished the world by producing a new Model "T" every 93 minutes. *Courtesy of the Motor Vehicle Manufacturers' Association of the United States of America.*

All this progress is the result of a huge cooperative effort on the part of thousands of people in the industry. And among all those people, few indeed are more important than the trained mechanics who see to it that engines keep doing what they were designed to do.

## HOW THE AUTOMOBILE CHANGED OUR LIVES

Think for a moment about a simple, everyday occurrence: a suburban housewife stops off at a shopping center on her way to her job downtown. If you are like most people, you assumed as you read the preceding sentence that the woman was driving a car, though you were not told that. The automobile is so common today that we take it for granted almost every time transportation is mentioned. In this case, though, your assumption is correct. The woman was in a car.

How did you know? You probably reasoned that, since she lived in the suburbs and worked downtown, she almost *had* to drive to work. Again, you were right. That is why, back in 1890, none of this was even possible. Before the automobile, there were almost no suburbs to live in and no shopping centers to stop by. Suburbs and shopping centers, like the road that carries our housewife downtown, were built after the automobile began to change the way we live. They were built *because* the automobile made possible a complete change in our life-styles. Today there is almost nothing we do that is not influenced in some way by the automobile.

**Figure 1–12.** Suburbs, shopping centers, and superhighways are now taken for granted. They, along with many other things in daily life, are direct results of the automobile.

As people moved out of the cities, into their new suburban homes, they had to travel farther to work. So almost three million miles of paved roads had to be built for them (Figure 1–13). These modern roads make it natural for today's car owner to travel distances that would have staggered the imagination of the common man a century ago. In 1900, the average American seldom traveled more than 200 miles a year. Today our citizens average over 12,000 miles per year.

However, not all the changes brought about by the automobile have been blessings. Homeowners who moved to the suburbs often left behind them older houses that, in time, turned into city slums. And as the number of operating vehicles climbed into the millions new problems began to plague our nation (Figure 1–14). The exhaust from cars driven by thousands of commuters contributes daily to the air pollution in every large city.

The huge amount of foreign oil now being imported to fuel so many cars also worries some of our leaders. They fear that our national defense and our economy could depend too heavily on the goodwill of the oil-producing countries. A sharp increase in the price of oil was, after all, a major cause of the 1974 recession that at one point put three million American laborers out of work.

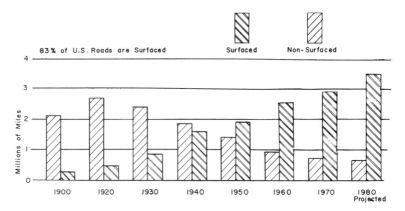

**Figure 1–13.** More than three and one half million miles of paved roads were constructed in the United States between 1900 and 1980.

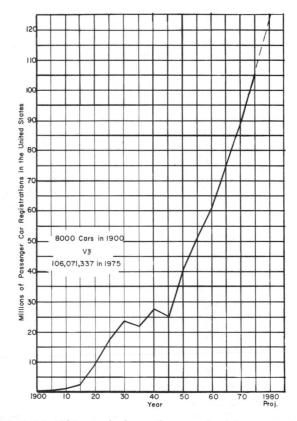

**Figure 1–14.** This graph shows the growth of the automobile industry in the United States between 1900 and 1976. Each block represents five million vehicles in operation.

This is why competition among car manufacturers is heating up again. The industry is in a complex and sometimes contradictory race to develop an engine that (1) decreases pollution, (2) increases fuel efficiency, and (3) maintains performance. You will learn more about this in Unit 3, when we try to take a brief look into the future.

Meanwhile, remember that you are seeing the impact of the automobile whenever you:

- Drive down a superhighway and see the hundreds of acres that have been paved in concrete:
- Pass a suburban housing development;
- Stop off at a shopping center;
- Drive cross-country on vacation;
- Read about such national problems as inner-city decay, pollution, and the energy shortage.

## OPPORTUNITIES FOR YOU

From this brief glimpse of the automotive industry—past and present—you should already be able to imagine some of the opportunities it offers. Though the shortage of skilled mechanics seems likely to continue for several years, huge amounts of money are involved in every phase of the industry.

In 1977, Americans spent $3,213 *million* for mechanics' labor alone. The parts used by those mechanics cost another $2,700 million. And the figures keep going up. (The 1977 total labor cost was up 12% over 1976.) As of July 1, 1976, there were 97,818,221 cars and 26,560,296 trucks in operation in the U.S. In 1977, vehicle owners spent an average of $26.59 per month per vehicle on maintenance. This is the money that will support the businesses and pay the wages of mechanics who are now in training.

The reader who learns what is written here will find that he has all the information necessary to do well in a Department of Transportation approved automotive curriculum. An engines course based on this text should prepare the student to take the National Institute for Automotive Service Excellence (NIASE) test for engine repair. It should also cover much of what he must know to pass the NIASE Gasoline and Diesel Truck Engine Test. These are important facts—they mean that training based on this text, properly conducted by a qualified instructor, will meet the highest standards of the trade.

It goes without saying that the student who completes this training will be qualified to work as a shop mechanic. Being a specialist whose services are needed in a wide variety of businesses, he can look forward to an unusual degree of employment flexibility and job security. Almost any new car dealership, garage, or industrial motor pool is a potential employer. So are any of the numerous dealers in farm equipment and recreational vehicles, not to mention small engine repair shops and other related businesses. Once on the job, the man with the right qualifications will also find opportunities for advancement. He may, in time, be promoted to service manager or placed in charge of the parts department. Or he may decide to leave and work for a parts supply house or go into business for himself.

The mechanic with a good head for business and the self-discipline necessary to save money may well look forward to owning his own service station. Or, with a larger investment, he can open a small, independent garage or franchised service outlet.

**Figure 1–15.** Some franchise service outlets are set up to help qualified people open their own businesses.

These latter opportunities, of course, require more than training in automotive technology. The owner of a small business must also have a basic understanding of management, bookkeeping, and finance. Much of this knowledge can be learned either on the job, by an energetic and ambitious mechanic or in part-time evening courses at a nearby technical school, community college, or university.

Sound training in automotive technology is, however, the essential first step. And for those who happen to be reading this book, there is no better place to begin than right here. Just take a few minutes to answer the review questions below to help you remember the important points in this introductory chapter. Then turn to the next chapter and start learning the basic principles of automotive engines. By then, you will be on your way!

## REVIEW QUESTIONS

1. Why is it that we cannot say precisely who invented the automobile?

2. What did Nicholas August Otto contribute to the development of the modern automobile?

3. What two competitors of the gasoline-powered car once enjoyed technological and commercial advantages over it? When and why did they lose out in the competition?

4. Name five ways in which the automobile has changed our life style in this country.

5. Name five specific vocational opportunities that are open to a person who is well trained in automotive technology.

UNIT

# 2

# How Engines Work: The Otto Cycle

Not long ago several journeyman mechanics were having coffee before work began in the service department of a local dealership. They had been talking of some of the new experimental engines that you will read about in Unit 3. Somebody wondered aloud if some new "Buck Rogers" kind of breakthrough could come soon. If so, would they, their training, and their skills suddenly be left behind? Could it happen that, by the year 2000, they would be as unnecessary and outmoded as yesterday's village blacksmith?

The mechanics talked, but the service manager didn't say anything. He just looked at his men. Beyond them he saw their well-equipped shop with its thousands of dollars worth of sophisticated test equipment. Only when somebody asked him directly did he give his opinion.

"I'm not worried a bit," he said. "All engines do the same thing. They're all made of levers and wheels and wires and pulleys. They're going to keep on making engines with levers and wheels and wires and pulleys. As long as they do, we can fix 'em."

We think that service manager had the right idea. He was reminding his mechanics that their knowledge of basic engine theory was certain to be of lasting value. With it, they could see how much all engines have in common. That basic understanding, he knew, could always be applied to any repair job on any engine, no matter what its design.

This chapter gives you that kind of basic understanding. Without it, a man may become a good parts-changer but never a mechanic. So it is well worth the time and effort it takes to learn these important concepts now. None of them are actually difficult. However, to use them properly, you must have precise definitions to some words that are often used loosely in everyday conversation. It is important to remember that, when you are talking shop, these words always mean *exactly* what you learn here.

As you begin to learn the basic vocabulary, you will also be learning how today's internal combustion engine fits into the whole family of engines. You will see that all engine types are, as that service manager said, different ways of doing the "same thing." And you will develop a general understanding of how internal combustion engines work.

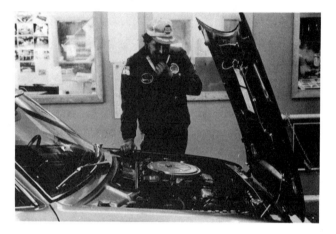

**Figure 2–1.** A mechanic with a sound knowledge of engine theory can soon figure out how any particular engine solves the universal problems of engine design.

## OBJECTIVES

After completing this chapter, you should be able to:

- Define the following terms:
  engine
  energy
  work
  BTU
  foot-pound
  thermal efficiency
- Name four essentials in the operation of all heat engines.

- Name and explain, in order, the four strokes and five events that make up the Otto cycle.
- Explain the working of a steam engine, using a diagram provided, and show how that engine uses the four essentials of heat engines.
- Explain how the working of an internal combustion engine employs the four essentials of heat engines, using a diagram provided.

---

# WORK AND ENERGY

Ask any fifth grader why we have engines, and he might tell you, "Engines do work for us." But what is work?

**Definition:** Work is done when a force on an object causes it to move.

*Remember:* In order to have work, there *must* be motion. In everyday speech, a layman might call it "work" to hold a heavy weight motionless on his shoulders. In mechanics, however, using energy is not considered work unless it produces motion.

One advantage of this definition is that it enables engineers to *measure* work. The basic unit of measurement for work is not the foot (meter), as in measuring distance. Nor is it the pound (kilogram), as in measuring weight. Instead, the basic unit for measuring work combines the measurement of distance and weight into a new unit for measuring movement. This new unit is the foot-pound (Newton-metre). Basically, *foot-pound* is a term that tells us how much (weight) can be moved how far (distance).

**Definition:** A foot-pound is the amount of energy needed to lift one pound one foot.

If you have ever worked with a torque wrench, you have already used foot-pounds to measure work.[1] The torque wrench is calibrated to account for the leverage supplied by the handle length and the exact lines of force used in tightening a bolt. But its basic unit of measure is equal to the foot-pound, the amount of energy needed to lift one pound one foot.

---

[1] Some experts distinguish between the foot-pound, as defined above, and the pound-foot, used in measuring torque. However, the amount of force used is the same; only the direction of force is different. In practice, the mechanic can safely consider the two terms synonymous.

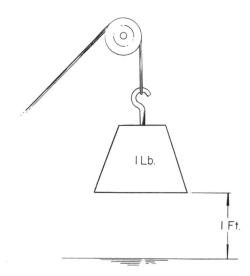

**Figure 2–2.**   The basic unit for measuring work is the foot-pound, the amount of energy needed to raise one pound one foot.

We have been defining work as a unit of *energy*.

**Definition:**   Energy is the capacity to do work.

It is no accident that energy and work are defined in terms of each other. Energy is the cause; work is the effect. Thus, energy is anything that is capable of causing motion. Figure 2–3 shows several common forms of energy. Each of these kinds of energy can, under the right conditions, be made to do work.

There is an important distinction to remember when thinking about energy. One kind of energy is found only in *moving objects*. When the moving cueball strikes the stationary eightball, the eightball also begins to move (Figure 2–4). Some energy has been transferred from one ball to the other. When the transferred energy causes the eightball to move, it is doing work. The energy in moving objects is called *kinetic* energy. You will see later in this unit that kinetic energy was put to good use in engines by the inventor of the flywheel.

Figure 2–5, however, introduces a second kind of energy— *potential energy*. The junk car on the bluff may not seem any different from the one in the valley, but it is. Remember, we defined energy as the ability to do work. Suppose Farmer Jones wants to move a heavy tool shed twenty-five feet towards the bluff. He could chain his tool shed to the nearer jalopy (Figure 2–6A) and topple the car over the cliff. The weight of the falling car would pull the tool shed for him. This should leave things as they are shown in Figure 2–6B.

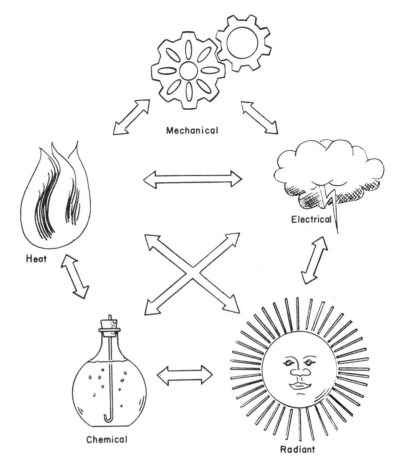

**Figure 2–3.** Though energy can neither be created nor destroyed, it can be changed from one form to another.

**Figure 2–4.** Kinetic energy can be transferred from one object to another. The cueball does work when it strikes the stationary eightball and starts it moving.

**Figure 2–5.** These two junk cars look very much alike. Yet the one on the cliff has more *potential* energy.

**Figure 2–6.** Shoving the car over the cliff turns its potential energy into kinetic energy and does the work of moving the tool shed.

In this case, the junk car has done work. Notice though that Farmer Jones could not have put the car in the valley to any such use. Only the car on the bluff had *potential* energy. Whatever forces brought that junker to the top of that cliff, in effect, stored potential energy in it. When he toppled the car over the cliff, Farmer Jones merely turned that potential energy into kinetic energy.

# IMPORTANT FACTS ABOUT ENERGY

This brings us to two extremely important facts about energy. First, energy can*not* be created or destroyed. Second, energy *can* easily be changed from one form to another. In fact, you change the form of energy every time you plug in a soldering iron or slow your car to a stop. The soldering iron turns electrical energy into heat.

But what happens to the kinetic energy in your moving car when you put on the brakes? Remembering that the disc brake rotors get hot may give you a clue. The answer is that the brakes turn the car's energy into heat.

That's just the opposite of what happens when you fire a pistol. In that case, the heat energy from the burning powder is turned into kinetic energy in the speeding bullet. From these examples you can see how common it is for energy to change form. But in all these exchanges the total amount of energy never changes—energy is neither created nor destroyed.

With the principles just explained, we can now understand what that service manager meant when he said that all engines do the same thing.

**Definition:**    An engine is a machine that transforms some form of energy into mechanical work.

Normally, the work output of an engine is used to drive another machine. Figure 2–7 shows three kinds of engines, including two that are not generally called engines. (The common technical name for such machines is "prime movers.") But they all meet our definition. They turn energy into mechanical work and power other machines.

A. Windmill          B. Steam Locomotive          C. Water Wheel at Waterfall

**Figure 2–7.** More commonly called *Prime Movers*, these machines actually meet the definition of an engine. They turn other forms of energy into mechanical energy and use it to do work.

The water wheel turns the kinetic energy in the falling water into mechanical power that drives an electrical generator. The windmill converts the kinetic energy in the moving air into mechanical energy that will power a water pump. And the steam engine turns the heat given off by burning wood into mechanical energy that powers the locomotive. Of the three, only the steam engine is of special interest to us.

The steam engine, like most other engines in widespread use, is a heat engine. The potential energy in its fuel is first turned into heat and then into mechanical energy. With the (somewhat questionable) exception of the electric motor, all engines ever used in cars have been heat engines.

## BASIC FACTS ABOUT HEAT

A basic understanding of heat is important to an understanding of engine theory. So let's discuss heat. You know, of course, that all matter exists in one of three states: solid, liquid, or gas. You may also know that the amount of heat in a substance is what determines its state. Put a pan of water in a freezer, remove some of its heat, and the liquid water turns to solid ice. But put that same pan of water on a stove, add more heat, and you can watch the liquid turn into a gas: steam.

All substances will do the same things if *enough* heat is added or taken away. The melted iron in steel mills and the liquid oxygen used in rocket engines are two examples. Iron, normally a solid, turns into liquid when it is heated enough. Oxygen, normally a gas, becomes a liquid when it is cooled enough. What causes this? And why is it important to the mechanic?

To answer these questions, let's think for a moment about solids, liquids, and gases the way scientists do. Scientists now know that all matter, regardless of its state, is made up of tiny electrical particles called electrons, protons, and neutrons. These particles are organized into larger groups called atoms. Atoms, in turn, are organized into still larger units called molecules. The force that holds these particles together in their patterns is the attraction between positive and negative charges of electricity. It is not important for us to understand exactly how those electrons and atoms are organized inside the molecule. But it is essential that we know that they are always in motion. So even though Figure 2–8 depicts molecules as if they were marbles, you should understand that "inside" each of those marbles is a complex pattern of electrical movement.

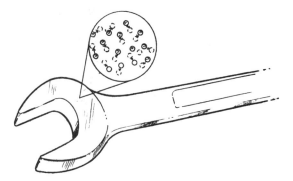

**Figure 2–8.** All matter is made up of atoms and molecules in almost constant motion.

It is convenient to think of molecules as marbles in that molecules are themselves in constant motion, and they move as units. Since the whole system of electrons and atoms moves together, you can think of it as a marble that can collide with other marbles. Actually, though, molecules are rapidly moving patterns of electrical activity. And what we call "collisions" are tiny, but violent, exchanges of electrons between molecules. Remembering all this, we can now consider how heat causes solids to melt and turn into gas. That knowledge will make it surprisingly easy to understand the theory of heat engines.

All matter, we said, is made up of atoms and molecules in motion. The *amount* of molecular movement, however, can vary a great deal. In solids, the molecules tend to bunch close together and more or less to quiver in place (Figure 2–9A). We can imagine them acting like iron filings, caught midway between the opposite poles of a magnet. Or we can think of them as people, standing close together in a crowd, listening to a speech. Every moment, somebody is shifting position or tossing his head, but nobody is going anywhere. There is very little movement and very little energy to be given off.

However, if we begin to heat up the solid, two things happen. First, the molecular action speeds up. Second, the molecules begin to bump into each other more often. They space themselves further apart so that they have a little room to move. By the time we have heated our solid enough to melt it into liquid, those molecules are no longer standing shoulder to shoulder. They are dancing in place, like people on a crowded dance floor. Every so often, one dancer jostles another. As each moves to give way, he bumps someone else, and so motion constantly ripples across the dance floor. That is the kind of molecular activity that is going on in the liquid in Figure 2–9B. It gives off some energy but not a lot.

However, if we keep heating the liquid until it boils, it turns to gas. This means that the molecules have spread very far apart. To do this they had to speed up their movement still more. The molecules in the steam above the tea kettle in Figure 2–9C are really banging into each other as they spread out. It is as if the dancers were hurrying to space themselves far enough apart so that they could do calisthenics. Only if they find enough room to allow everyone to do his own brisk exercises without bumping anyone else will things go smoothly. With this much activity, quite a bit of energy is given off.

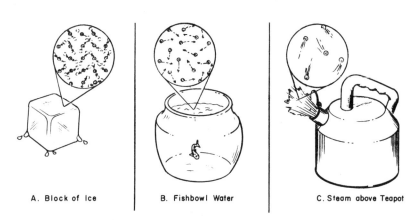

| A. Block of Ice | B. Fishbowl Water | C. Steam above Teapot |

**Figure 2–9.**    Molecules in a solid are close together and in limited motion (A). When enough heat is added to melt the solid, the molecules speed up their movement and spread further apart (B). If even more heat is added, the liquid will boil and turn to gas. By this time, the molecular motion is intense and the molecules are far apart (C).

## MEASURING HEAT

Heat, then, is a form of energy that exists in molecular activity. We already know that energy is normally measured in foot-pounds. So it may be surprising to learn that heat is *not* usually measured that way. This is because scientists had already worked out a way to measure heat before they realized that it *was* a form of energy. The standard unit for measuring heat is the British Thermal Unit (BTU).

**Definition:**    One BTU is the amount of heat energy required to raise the temperature of one pound of water one degree Fahrenheit.

BTU's and foot-pounds are both measures of energy, just as pints and gallons are both measures of liquid. Therefore, we could measure the same quantity of energy in either foot-pounds or BTU's. One BTU equals about 778 foot-pounds. Usually, though, we measure heat energy in BTU's and mechanical energy in foot-pounds.

## ESSENTIALS OF HEAT ENGINES

In these terms, the job of the automotive engineer is to turn BTU's of heat into foot-pounds of mechanical work. To do this, he must always have four things:

1. Heat or potential energy that can be converted to heat
2. A working fluid
3. An engine
4. An appropriate way of raising and lowering the temperature of the working fluid

Remember these four essentials. In the remainder of this chapter, you will learn how they apply to the two major kinds of heat engines.

All heat engines are classified as either internal or external combustion engines (Figure 2–10). In both types, fuel is burned to turn its potential energy into heat energy. That heat energy is then used to speed up the molecular motion in a working fluid. As you already know, speeding up molecular activity causes molecules to spread out. This means that whatever is being heated expands; it "seeks" more space. It is the force of that expansion that is turned into mechanical work.

## USING HEAT TO BUILD PRESSURE

There is, however, one important difference between what happens when a working fluid is heated inside an engine and what happens when water is boiled in a pot, as in Figure 2–9C. The steam from the boiling water is allowed to spread out in the air. But what happens in an engine is more like what would happen if we put a pint of water in a tin can, screwed on the lid and threw it into an extremely hot fire (Figure 2–11).

In that case, the molecules speed up their motion and try to spread out. But there is no room, so they soon start colliding violently. To return to our example of the people on the crowded dance floor, it is as if somebody suddenly turned out the lights and yelled, "Fire!"

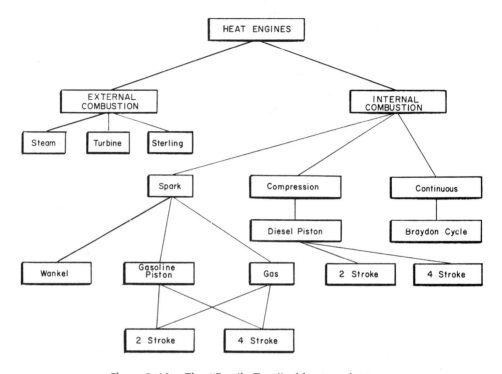

**Figure 2–10.**   The "Family Tree" of heat engines.

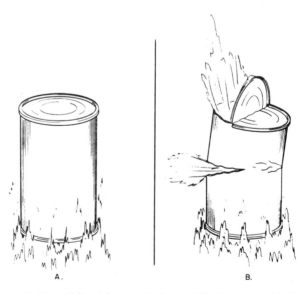

**Figure 2–11.**   If liquid is sealed in while heat is added, the colliding molecules have nowhere to go. As millions of molecules are sent hurling into the sides of the can every second, pressure builds up. Eventually, the lid will fly off or the can will burst.

The molecules are hurling about faster and faster like people in a panic trying to get out. They bounce off each other. They fly into the walls of the can and bounce back into other molecules. The molecules they strike are then sent hurling into the wall themselves. Thus the level of molecular activity increases. Pressure builds up inside the can. Soon millions of molecules are hitting the metal wall every second. When the water inside gets hot enough, either the lid pops off or the can bursts. That means something has moved. At that point, part of the heat energy in the can has performed work.

In a heat engine, of course, only one part of the expansion space is allowed to move. That moving part is linked to a series of levers and wheels which, in a car, carry the mechanical energy to the wheels. But notice that every heat engine must have a place to burn fuel and a place to let the heated fluid expand. Only as the pressure is being reduced through expansion can it perform work. Figure 2–12 shows how the process takes place in an external combustion (EC) engine.

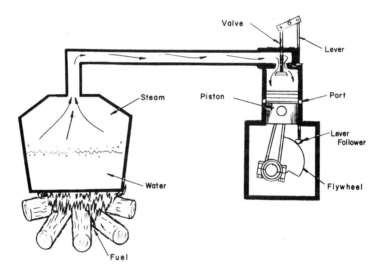

**Figure 2–12.**   A simple steam engine begins with a boiler, which is simply a larger, heavier version of the tin can in Figure 2–11. The boiler is connected to an expansion chamber with a movable floor. Instead of bursting the expansion chamber, the pressurized steam pushes down on the movable floor and does work.

## A SIMPLE STEAM ENGINE

Wood is burned outside the engine to produce heat. This heat is used to turn water into steam. When enough pressure has built up, the valve opens, and the steam is allowed into the cylinder. This cylinder serves as an expansion space. Its "floor" is a movable piston, which the pressure pushes downward in the cylinder. Thus, the pressure is not released at random as in the exploding can. It can only expand inside the cylinder by moving the piston. As the piston passes the exhaust ports, the steam escapes and relieves the pressure. Meanwhile, the weight of the turning flywheel gives it a tendency to keep on moving. Thus the flywheel has *kinetic energy*, which carries the piston on down as far as it can go and then up again. Lever A is linked to the flywheel, so that the intake valve opens when the piston is near the top and closes when the piston is near the bottom.

Figure 2–13 shows a better-designed and more realistic steam engine. However, the one in Figure 2–12, though simple, is adequate for our purposes. It can turn heat energy into mechanical work. Its work output can power another machine. So it gives us the first of our four essentials for heat engines—the engine. In the wood, we have the second essential: potential energy that we can turn into heat energy. The third essential, the working fluid, is the steam that moves the piston. The fourth essential is the means of controlling the temperature of the working fluid. The more wood we add to the fire, the hotter the water gets. Remembering how the essentials are put to work in this simple steam engine is a good way to organize our knowledge of basic engine theory.

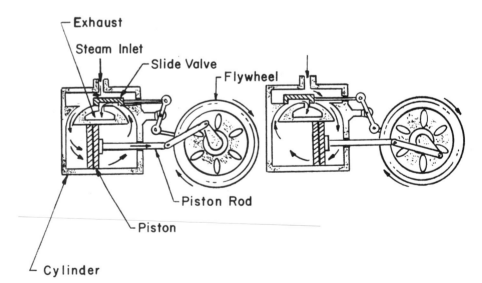

**Figure 2–13.** In this more realistic steam engine, a sliding valve makes every stroke a power stroke. By the time the piston has traveled as far as it will go in one direction, the valve has opened the inlet port on the other side. So compressed steam then pushes the piston in the opposite direction.

We must, however, be clear on two points about the meaning of the term *working fluid*. If we remember that work is only done when there is motion, the rest should be easy. The only part of the expansion chamber that moves is the piston. Hence, whatever moves the piston is the working fluid. A second point that sometimes trips up beginners is mistaking the word *fluid* to mean *liquid*. Technically, a fluid is any substance that can *flow;* so fluids include gases as well as liquids. In the steam engine, of course, the working fluid begins as liquid and is turned into gas. On the other hand, no internal combustion (IC) engine in use today uses any liquid as its working fluid. In IC engines the working fluid is always a gas.

# THE OTTO CYCLE

As you learned in Unit 2, almost all automotive engines built in the twentieth century have been "Otto-cycle" internal combustion engines. The Otto cycle is sometimes referred to as a four-stroke, five-event cycle. Like our simple steam engine, this most common IC engine generates power by forcing a piston downward in a cylinder (Figure 2–14). Each time the piston completes one up- or downward movement it has made one *stroke*. On each stroke, one of the five events of the Otto cycle takes place. And each stroke is named for the Otto-cycle event that it causes to happen. At the end of each stroke, there is one point where the piston pauses and reverses direction. This point, on the up stroke, is called *top dead center* (TDC). On the downstroke, it is *bottom dead center* (BDC).

## Intake Stroke

The piston is attached by a *connecting rod* to an offset section in a crankshaft (Figure 2–15). Attached to one end of the crankshaft is a flywheel. At the top of the cylinder are two valves (Figure 2–16). The Otto cycle begins when the intake valve opens with the piston near TDC. As the piston makes its down stroke, it creates a partial vacuum. This causes outside atmospheric pressure to force the fuel-air mixture from the carburetor into the cylinder. This *intake* stroke is the first event of the cycle.

## Compression Stroke and Ignition

The second event begins when the piston nears BDC and the intake valve closes (Figure 2–17). With both valves closed and the piston on

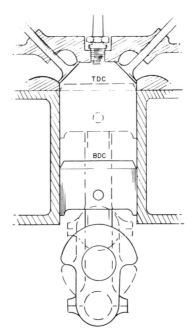

**Figure 2–14.**   The point at which the piston stops and reverses directions is called *dead center.* Each time the piston moves from top dead center (TDC) to bottom dead center (BDC) (or vice versa) it makes one *stroke.*

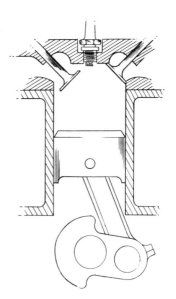

**Figure 2–15.**   The piston is attached to the crankshaft by a connecting rod.

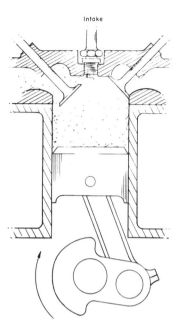

**Figure 2–16.** The intake stroke begins when the intake valve opens with the piston near TDC. As the piston moves down, a fuel-air mixture enters through the intake valve.

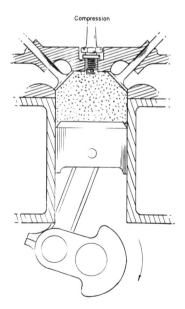

**Figure 2–17.** With both valves closed, the upstroke of the piston compresses the fuel-air mixture and heats it to a temperature near its ignition point.

the upstroke, the fuel-air mixture is compressed. You already know that heating a substance in an enclosed space speeds up its molecular motion and increases its pressure. What do you suppose happens when we simply crowd those molecules close together and increase pressure? Won't they collide more? And isn't that just another way of saying that the heat increases? As a matter of fact, the compressed gases inside the cylinder reach about 300° F (149° C) when the pressure reaches its maximum of 200 pounds per square inch (PSI). Raising the temperature about 150° F (66 ° C) more would cause them to explode. We could easily do this by compressing them more. (You will see in Unit 3 that this is essentially what is done in Diesel engines.) With gasoline engines, however, we do not want to do that. In order to *control* the burning, we compress the mixture until it reaches a temperature near its ignition point. But we then introduce a spark to ignite the fuel. Thus the second event of the cycle is *compression*, and the third is *ignition* (Figure 2–18).

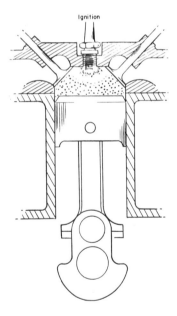

**Figure 2–18.** With the piston near top dead center, the spark plug ignites the compressed mixture.

## Power Stroke

Ignition, therefore, is the "middle" event in the five-event Otto cycle. It is the only event that does not require a separate stroke of the piston. Ignition occurs when the piston nears TDC on the compression stroke and is timed so that the maximum power from the burning gasoline is produced just after the piston starts down again.

The extreme heat from the burning gasoline causes the other gases in the fuel-air mixture to expand in a great surge of pressure. The downward pressure on a piston that is four inches in diameter often totals more than five tons! This is pressure enough to send it shooting down the cylinder with great force and to cause it to turn the crankshaft.

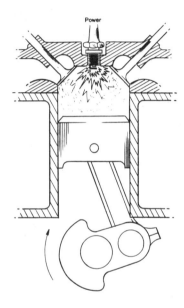

**Figure 2–19.** The extreme heat of combustion expands the trapped air and pushes the piston down with a great surge of energy.

## Exhaust Stroke

As the piston starts up again on its return stroke, the exhaust valve opens. By then, the 10,000 PSI pressure may have dropped as low as 70 PSI. But it is still several times greater than the pressure of the outside atmosphere. So, burnt gases rush out ahead of the upward-moving piston. Then the exhaust valve closes, the intake value opens, and the cycle starts over.

If the engine has only one cylinder, then only one stroke in four is a power stroke. This means that the crankshaft must "coast" through three more strokes before the cylinder fires again. It makes two complete revolutions for each power stroke. To provide for more continuous delivery of power, automotive engineers add additional cylinders. They time the ignition so that power strokes on different cylinders follow one another or even overlap to prevent the jerkiness that would otherwise be caused by these periodic power strokes. They also install a flywheel (Figure 2–20). As the crankshaft turns, the flywheel absorbs energy from each power stroke. Being heavy, the flywheel tends to keep spinning. So its kinetic energy helps to "smooth out" the rotation of the crankshaft.

Again, in the Otto-cycle engine, we have our four essentials of all heat engines. We have an engine. In the gasoline, we have potential energy that can be turned into heat. During ignition, only gasoline vapor and the oxygen in the air are involved in combustion. The other gases in the air mixture—almost four-fifths of the whole amount—are not active in the burning. It is these inactive gases that expand in the cylinder and become our working fluid. By means of compression, ignition, and controlled expansion, we can raise and lower the temperature of our working fluid as needed.

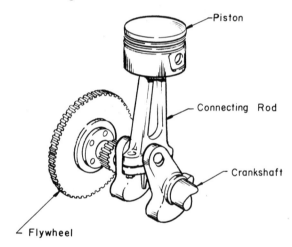

**Figure 2–20.**    The flywheel absorbs energy from each power output and releases it smoothly as kinetic energy. This tends to dampen the jerkiness that would otherwise be produced by the periodic power strokes.

## THERMAL EFFICIENCY

You now know that a heat engine is a machine that turns BTU's of heat into foot-pounds of mechanical energy. What, then, makes a *good* heat engine? Other things being equal, a good engine has high thermal efficiency. (*Thermal* means heat, as in *thermo*meter, or "heat measurer.")

If you have ever touched a hot engine, you know that all of the heat from the gasoline it burned was not being turned into mechanical power. If it were, the engine block and the exhaust manifold would not be so hot to the touch. The fact is that only a small part of the total amount of potential energy in automotive fuel ever reaches the wheels of a vehicle. Roughly a third of it is lost with the exhaust gases. Another third is lost to the radiator coolant and engine oil. Some 10% is lost in engine friction. Only about one-fifth to one-third is actually put to work (Figure 2–21).

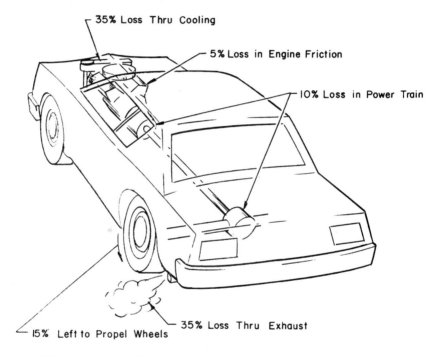

**Figure 2–21.** Only 15% of the potential energy in gasoline actually reaches the rear wheels.

It is obviously better to get as much power out of a gallon of fuel as possible. We can easily see how well an engine performs on this score. The exact number of BTU's in an amount of gasoline or Diesel fuel can be determined. The amount of work done by the engine as it burns that amount of fuel can be measured. Since one BTU equals 778 foot-pounds, the percentage of work output to energy input can be calculated. The higher the thermal efficiency, the "better" the engine. Measuring thermal efficiency gives us an extremely accurate way to compare the efficiency of different engines.

## REVIEW QUESTIONS

I. *Matching Questions*

1. Pick the correct definition from column B for each of the terms in column A.

| A. | B. |
|---|---|
| _____ 1. Foot-pound | 1. Molecules in motion when a solid turns into a gas. |
| _____ 2. Thermal Efficiency | 2. The capacity to do work. |
| _____ 3. Energy | 3. The amount of energy needed to lift one pound one foot. |
| _____ 4. Engine | 4. The amount of heat needed to raise one pound of water one degree Fahrenheit. |
| _____ 5. BTU | 5. A configuration of consecting forces supplying power to some kind of receptor. |
| _____ 6. Work | 6. A force acting upon an object and causing it to move. |
| | 7. The force exerted when a 200-pound man places all his weight on one foot. |
| | 8. A machine that turns some form of energy into mechanical work, usually in order to power another machine. |
| | 9. The percentage of potential heat energy in the fuel that actually reaches the wheels of the vehicle in the form of mechanical power. |
| | 10. British Term-Union radiator, designed to save heat energy. |

II. *Multiple-Choice Questions*

*Choose the one correct answer for each of the following:*

1. Liquids, gases and solids are

_____ A. Different states of matter

_____ B. Composed of different kinds of atoms

_____ C. Due to thermal efficiency

_____ D. Never used in EC engines

2. The molecules that make up all matter are constantly

_____ A. Changing into atoms

_____ B. Moving

_____ C. Electrifying surrounding particles

_____ D. Ionizing

3. Though energy cannot be created or destroyed, it *can* be

_____ A. Liquidated by exchange mechanisms

_____ B. Lost through aging and metal fatigue

_____ C. Added to metal by rust

_____ D. Changed from one form to another

4. Work output and heat energy could both be measured by the same unit because

_____ A. One BTU equals 538 foot-pounds

_____ B. Scientists did not realize at first the true nature of work.

_____ C. Both are units of energy

_____ D. None of the above.

III. *Questions of Recall and Application*

1. Choose from the list on page 42 the right label for each of the diagrams. Refer to the position of the valves and piston and explain how you know that you correctly labelled each diagram.

A.   Intake stroke
B.   Power stroke
C.   Compression stroke
D.   Ignition
E.   Exhaust

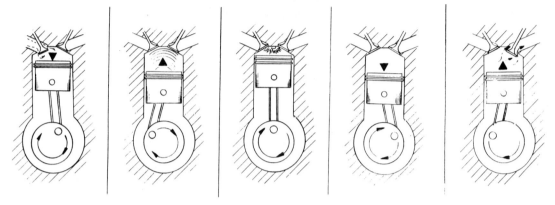

2. Which event of the Otto cycle does not take up its own piston stroke?

3. What are the four essentials of a heat engine? Refer to the diagrams for Question III-I, above and explain how they apply to an Otto-cycle gasoline engine.

4. Below is a diagram of a simple steam engine. Explain how it works and how it employs each of the four essentials of heat engines.

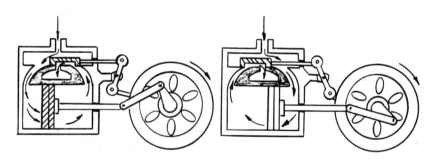

UNIT

# 3

# Alternatives to the Otto Cycle: What's Ahead?

As you learned in Unit 1, the four-stroke internal combustion, piston engine now in general use has been around a little over a hundred years. Since the early years of this century, it has consistently beaten its competitors in the marketplace. Today, however, an intensive search is under way for a replacement. Newspapers and trade journals bombard us constantly with stories of revolutionary new power plants. Almost all of them are considered by somebody to be "on the brink of a breakthrough" and certain to replace that dirty fuel-gobbler we know and love.

In this chapter, you will learn the background, the operating principles, and the state of development of most of these so-called "new, revolutionary" engines. You will see that, in most cases, they are neither new nor revolutionary. They are merely stages in the same painfully slow process of technological development that you have already traced in the history of the Otto-cycle engine. Still, they are worth knowing about. At present, nobody can know for sure that one of these alternatives will not win today's new technological race.

From this unit, you will get a general understanding of the functioning of each of these alternative power plants. You will also learn their advantages and disadvantages. Where possible, you will be told how the experts rate the chances of each contender against today's rapidly improving Otto-cycle engine.

The engine of tomorrow will make the best trade-off possible between two contradictory demands: Less pollution and better fuel economy.

**Figure 3–1.**   In little more than a hundred years, the Otto-cycle engine has thoroughly established itself. *Courtesy of Volvo of America.*

## POLLUTION

As more and more cars filled the roads, the automobile became an integral part of the American way of life. The private ownership of automobiles brought about great social changes in our nation during the first half of this century. The private car is now the backbone of our nation's transportation system. It has given us an individual mobility enjoyed by no other people. This independent transportation system has helped place our standard of living among the highest in the world.

**Figure 3–2.**   Widespread use of the automobile has literally transformed American society.

By 1950, however, an ugly problem began to be noticed: air pollution. Certain areas suffered atmospheric pollution caused by a combination of automotive and industrial emissions. Pollution reached levels that posed possible health hazards to those living and working in areas of high concentration. In 1957, the United States Public Health Service started a serious effort to determine the causes of air pollution and to define its relationship to the automobile.

The federally mandated Clean Air Acts of 1970 created the Environmental Protection Agency (EPA), empowered to formulate and enforce laws concerning sources of atmospheric emissions. Since 1968, all cars sold in the United States have had to pass ever-tightening emission specifications. Year by year, the standards became more difficult for the Otto engine to meet (Figure 3–3). By 1975, the manufacturers, through the addition of add-on devices, succeeded in reducing emissions levels to 97% less than pre-1961 engines. However, these reductions in pollution were not without compromise. Fuel economy plummeted so that, by the 1975 model year, fuel tank size for most cars had been increased by 20% or more to allow vehicle range between fuel stops to remain equal to pre-1975 levels (Figure 3–4).

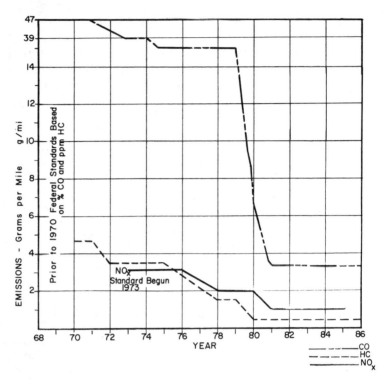

**Figure 3–3.** Year by year, federal anti-pollution laws are setting standards that are increasingly difficult for Otto-cycle engines to meet.

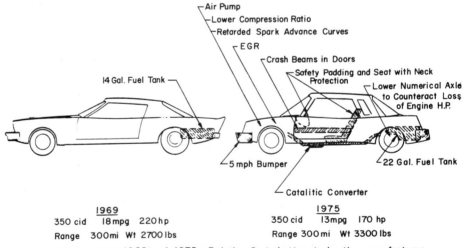

**1969**
350 cid   18 mpg   220 hp
Range   300 mi   Wt 2700 lbs

**1975**
350 cid   13 mpg   170 hp
Range   300 mi   Wt 3300 lbs

Between the years 1969 and 1975 Emission Control attempts by the manufacturers had increased fuel consumption by more than one third, lowered horse power by one third. Safety features required by federal law had increased vehicle weight by 20%.

**Figure 3–4.** Initial efforts to reduce levels of pollutants also decreased engine efficiency.

46

# THE ENERGY CRISIS AND THE PUSH
# FOR FUEL ECONOMY

For many years, Americans ignored the fact that fossil fuel resources are finite, that we can't grow more oil or coal. When we dig coal or pump oil from the earth, nothing replaces it. Sooner or later we will use it up.

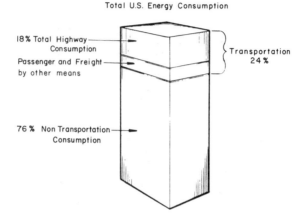

**Figure 3–5.** For too long, Americans ignored warnings that fossil fuel supplies are limited.

Until 1975, we had been buying more and more oil from the Middle East to supplement our increasing needs. Then the Arabs realized that, even though they were amassing great wealth from selling their petroleum, sooner or later their wells would run dry and their income stop. For these reasons, they reevaluated the worth of their oil and raised its price accordingly. This sudden price hike did much to bring on the energy crisis of the mid-1970's.

Because of the dangers of oil depletion, the federal government enacted the 1975 Energy and Conservation Act. In it, Congress set fuel economy standards for auto manufacturing through 1985. They also made the Department of Transportation responsible for formulating and evaluating present and future standards (Figure 3–6).

Today, the industry faces a two-fold dilemma. We are asked to produce engines with high fuel economy but with practically no emission of pollutants. Designing both qualities into one engine will require new approaches. Most likely, it will mean changes inside the engine, where the fuel is burned, in order to increase thermal efficiency.

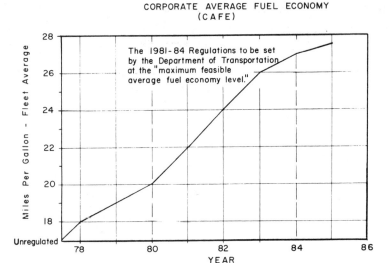

**Figure 3–6.** Department of Transportation average fleet standards to be met by U.S. auto manufacturers, 1978–1985.

## OBJECTIVES

When you have finished this chapter, you should be able to:

- Name the two objectives of today's new technological race and explain the reasons for each.

- Name and explain the working of two types of external combustion engines now under development (with the aid of appropriate diagrams).

- Demonstrate an understanding of five types of internal combustion engines, other than the four-stroke, gasoline-powered, spark-ignition engine.

- Demonstrate a general knowledge of the working principles of six types of internal combustion engines.

- Demonstrate a general understanding of three types of non-combustion power plants.

## PICTURING THE ALTERNATIVES

As you learned in Unit 2, almost all power plants that can be used for automotive purposes are varieties of the heat engine (Figure 3–7). You know, though, that one type of noncombustion (NC) automotive power plant does exist: the electric motor. And you know that both electric and steam power plants were once widely favored over Otto-cycle engines. In this unit, you will see that these old competitors are both back on the horizon again. Nobody can be sure yet whether they are gaining. But they are back in the race.

Along with them are several types of IC engines, each of which has certain distinct advantages over the traditional Otto engine. As the full meaning of the energy shortage becomes clear, the two-stroke engine will find application as a light, portable power source for motorized two wheelers, like mopeds, and in various recreational vehicles. The Diesel engine and the rotary, gasoline-powered engine will probably become more practical for automotive use. And, if a few remaining technical difficulties are solved, so may the gas turbine engine.

In the following pages, engines are grouped for discussion according to the breakdown shown in Figure 3–7. You will learn first about several varieties of IC power plants, starting with those most similar to the Otto-cycle engine. Then you will learn about two types of EC engines: One is our old friend, the steam engine. The other is an exciting new prospect which has yet to be adequately tested for automotive use: the Stirling-cycle engine. Finally, you will be asked to look again at the NC electric car. Indeed, you will learn about three different approaches now being tried in the renewed effort to make electric cars economically practical.

| | | Cooling and Radiation Loss | Friction Loss | Waste Heat Exhaust | Thermal Efficiency |
|---|---|---|---|---|---|
| Diesel |  | 20% | 5% | 40¢ | 35% |
| Gasoline Piston |  | 20% | 5% | 48¢ | 27% |
| Gas Turbine | 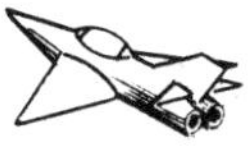 | 18% | 3% | 53¢ | 24% |
| Simple Steam Piston |  | 12% | 5% | 75¢ | 8% |

**Figure 3–7.** The Heat Energy Family.

# INTERNAL COMBUSTION ENGINES

When discussing IC engines so far in this book, we have focused on the Otto-cycle engine. That is natural and proper. Most automotive engines today are Otto-cycle engines. There are, however, several other types of IC engines. All of those discussed here as possible replacements for the Otto engine involve the same five events—intake, compression, ignition, power, and exhaust. As you know, the Otto engine performs these five events in four strokes. These four strokes are completed in two complete revolutions (720°) of the crankshaft. Ignition normally occurs just before TDC on the compression stroke (Figure 3–8).

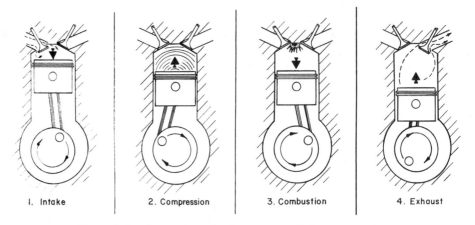

| 1. Intake | 2. Compression | 3. Combustion | 4. Exhaust |

**Figure 3–8.**    Remember the five events of the Otto cycle as you read in this chapter about alternatives to Otto-cycle engines.

## THE TWO-STROKE GASOLINE ENGINE

A second form of spark-ignition, gasoline-powered, piston engine is the two-stroke, or "two-cycle," engine. The two-stroke engine has the distinct advantage of providing one power stroke for each complete revolution (360°) of the crankshaft. This is possible because, in a two-stroke engine, the intake and compression strokes are combined as are the power and exhaust strokes. This means that the sparkplug fires every time the piston nears TDC.

Most small two-cycle engines do not use valves to control the incoming and outgoing gases. They depend instead on the movement of the piston to uncover holes ("ports") in the cylinder walls. This controls the admission of fresh fuel-air charges and the exhaust of spent combustion products (Figure 3–9).

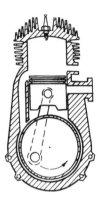

**Figure 3–9.** Instead of valves, two-stroke engines use piston travel to cover and uncover intake, transfer, and exhaust ports.

At the beginning of the cycle, the bottom edge of the upward-moving piston uncovers the intake port leading to the crankcase. At approximately the same time, it closes off the transfer port which leads to the crankcase by way of the transfer passage. This means that the upward-moving piston creates a partial vacuum in the crankcase. Outside atmospheric pressure, being higher, then forces more fuel mixture into the crankcase through the intake port (Figure 3–10). Meanwhile, the piston moves higher in the cylinder and covers the exhaust port. When that happens, the upward-moving piston begins to compress the fuel mixture in the cylinder.

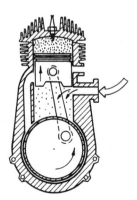

**Figure 3–10.** When the upward-moving piston creates a partial vacuum in the crankcase, more fuel mixture enters through the intake port.

As with the Otto engine, ignition occurs about the time the piston reaches TDC. Heat from the burning fuel causes a rush of power that is timed to peak just after the piston reaches TDC and starts down. As the piston approaches BDC on this power stroke, however, three things happen that do not occur in the Otto cycle. First, with the transfer port still covered, the downward-moving piston covers the intake port. This means that the dropping piston begins to compress the new fuel mixture in the crankcase (Figure 3–11). Meanwhile, the second occurrence has taken place. The piston has moved down enough to uncover the exhaust port and allow the hot exhaust gases to start escaping. A split second later, comes the third difference. The piston drops a little further and uncovers the transfer port. This allows the compressed fuel mixture trapped under the piston to surge out of the crankcase, through the transfer port, and into the cylinder (Figure 3–12).

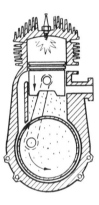

**Figure 3–11.** The dropping piston compresses the fuel mixture trapped in the crankcase.

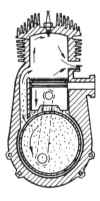

**Figure 3–12.** When the dropping piston uncovers the transfer port, compressed mixture surges out of the crankcase into the cylinder. Note that the incoming mixture helps force remaining gases out the exhaust port.

The new intake charge, rushing in under pressure, helps "push" remaining exhaust gases from the cylinder. (In shoptalk, this use of "cleanup" pressure is often called *scavenging.)* The piston, after reaching BDC and starting on its return stroke, covers first the transfer port and then the exhaust port. When it closes the transfer port, the fuel intake is shut off. When it closes the exhaust port, it begins to compress the fresh mixture trapped above the cylinder. Meanwhile, the crankcase inlet port is uncovered by the bottom of the piston. As new fuel enters, the cycle begins again.

## Advantages of Two-Stroke Engines

**More Power Strokes.**   Since every second stroke produces power, the crankshaft spends much less time coasting between power impulses. This, along with other advantages, gives it a very high power output for its weight.

**Fewer Moving Parts.**   Using ports instead of valves makes all the mechanical linkage needed to operate the valves of a four-cycle engine unnecessary. Other things being equal, the fewer the moving parts, the less wear and the fewer the maintenance problems.

**Less Lost Motion.**   The piston not only serves, instead of valves, to close the intake, transfer, and exhaust ports at the right times, but it also functions rather like a supercharger and an oil pump. It is piston movement that compresses the fuel mixture in the crankcase and moves it into the cylinder. Since the lubricant is commonly mixed into the fuel mixture, the piston is also its own oil pump because the piston is lubricating itself all the while. When we remember that the two-stroke engine gets one power stroke for every rotation of the crankshaft, we must be impressed with its elegance of design. Almost no motion is lost in it.

**Low Cost.**   All these advantages, taken together, give the two-cycle engine an economic advantage. It can be made cheaply, sold for a large variety of purposes, and operated at low cost.

But this, of course, is not the whole story. If it were, many automobiles would be using two-stroke power plants.

## Disadvantages of Two-Stroke Engines

**Higher Emissions.**   Because the lubricant is mixed with the fuel, some of it is burnt with the fuel and exhausted as smoke. Also, the use of a new charge of fuel mixture, under pressure, to scavenge exhaust gases has two bad side effects. First, it dilutes the fuel charge that stays in the cylinder, thus cutting down on fuel economy. Second, and more importantly, it allows some unburnt mixture to escape into the air. So the smoke from its burning lubricant and the emissions of unburnt fuel, combined with its "normal" exhaust, make the two-stroke engine a dirty power plant.

**Shorter Power Stroke.**    Although the power strokes are more frequent in the two-cycle engine, they do not last as long. Remember, the engine begins its exhaust cycle while the piston is moving down on the last part of the power cycle. Obviously, its effective power stroke, compared to that of a four-stroke engine, is much shorter. Figures 3–13 and 3–14 compare the length of the power cycle on two- and four-stroke engines. Notice that the power stroke on the Otto cycle lasts for half a crankshaft rotation, or 180°. But, as Figure 3–14 shows, on a two-stroke engine, the effective power stroke lasts for only about 120°.

**Shorter Time for Intake and Exhaust.**    In the four-cycle engine, the intake and exhaust cycles each take 180° of crankshaft rotation (Figure 3–14). However, in the two-stroke engine, the two events both take place on the same stroke. And both take proportionately less time. As Figure 3–14 shows, the exhaust cycle takes about 100° of crankshaft rotation and the intake cycle even less, about 90°. The shortness of this intake cycle is offset somewhat by the fact that the mixture is compressed in the crankcase. This causes it to rush into the cylinder faster when the transfer port opens. In practice, however, there is almost always some loss of efficiency and diminished fuel economy.

## Adaptations of Two-Stroke Engines

In order to overcome some or all of these disadvantages, manufacturers of modern two-stroke engines have introduced a number of adaptations.

### Number and placement of transfer ports

Instead of one transfer port, manufacturers commonly use five or more, spacing them, around the cylinder wall. This makes it easier to get a full charge of fuel mixture into the cylinder during that brief intake cycle. Often the transfer passages are turned upward near the ports, also. This sends the new fuel charge to the top of the cylinder and keeps loss through the exhaust port to a minimum.

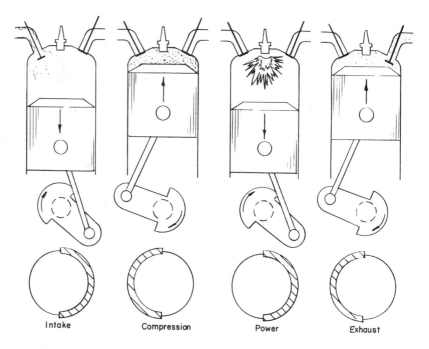

Intake     Compression     Power     Exhaust

**Figure 3–13.** Note that each stroke in the Otto cycle lasts for half a turn (180°) of the crankshaft.

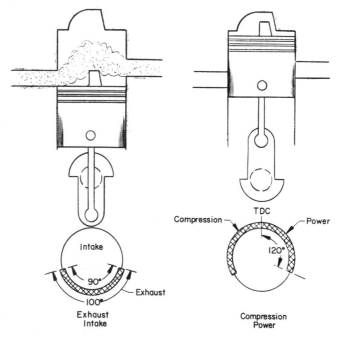

**Figure 3–14.** Instead of lasting for 180°, the *effective* power stroke on a two-stroke engine only lasts for about 120°.

**Figure 3–15.** Modern two-stroke engines may have five or more transfer ports, each placed exactly, to increase the size of intake charge.

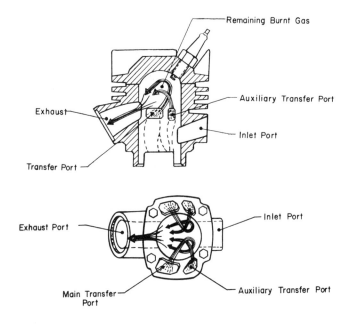

**Figure 3–16.** Upward-slanting transfer ports improve engine scavenging.

## Deflector-type piston heads

Another design feature, used by some manufacturers for cutting fuel loss through the exhaust port, is the deflector-type piston head. The deflector is simply a carefully designed "bump" on the piston. It serves to direct the incoming fuel mixture up towards the top of the cylinder and away from the exhaust port.

## Valves

Despite the economic advantages of eliminating conventional valves, manufacturers of two-stroke engines find that, in practice, the lack of valves causes difficulties. The precision castings necessary to produce engines with ports of exactly the right size and shape are expensive. And without valves it is difficult to adjust intake timing. Only by machining the cylinder ports or piston can the timing be altered. To overcome these difficulties, some manufacturers now use simple intake valves.

**Reed valves** are sometimes used to control the admission of fuel into the crankcase. The reed valve (Figure 3–17) uses crankcase pressure rather than piston position to control the entry of fuel and air. This valve works like a one-way door. It is blown open by the pressure of the outside atmosphere whenever crankcase pressure is low. And it is blown shut by crankcase pressure as soon as crankcase compression rises above outside atmospheric pressure.

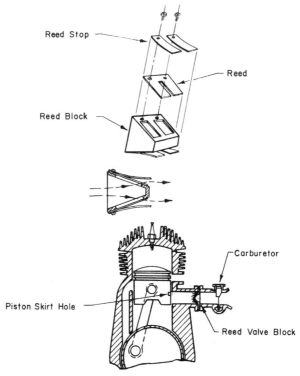

**Figure 3–17.** When the pressure inside the crankcase drops lower than the outside atmospheric pressure, this reed valve swings inward and permits a new intake charge. As the dropping piston increases crankcase pressure, the valve blows shut.

**Rotary valves** are another way of controlling crankcase charging on two-stroke engines. Instead of being opened and closed by the piston, the intake port on these engines is placed in the crankcase, well below the piston. The port is covered by a rotating disk that is mounted beside it on the crankcase housing (Figure 3–18). The disk has a hole in it at one point. It is rotated by linkage to the crankshaft, which opens and closes the intake port. When the hole in the disk lines up with the intake port, the port is open and the fuel mixture can enter. As the piston starts down, the crankshaft turns the disk and closes the port. The dropping piston compresses the mixture in the crankcase, as in other two-stroke engines.

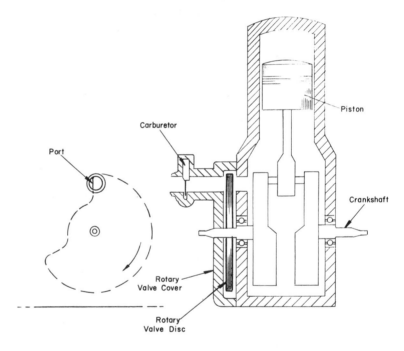

**Figure 3–18.** This rotary valve is turned by mechanical linkage to the crankshaft. When the hole in the valve lines up with the intake port, a new fuel charge can enter.

## The Future of Two-Stroke Engines

Because of problems with pollution and fuel economy, two-stroke engines are unlikely to be used widely as automotive power plants in the near future. Still, they are important to the automotive industry. They are widely used in recreational vehicles. In the U.S., as elsewhere in the world, motorcycles, motorbikes, and motor scooters may become more attractive to those who need cheap, dependable transportation as the price of gasoline rises. Meanwhile, the one undeniable fact about two-cycle engines is that there are a lot of them. Any mechanic who cares to service lawnmowers, chain saws, motor scooters, etc., can—in the right circumstances—find this a profitable sideline.

# THE DIESEL ENGINE

All the internal combustion engines discussed so far have been gasoline-powered spark ignition power plants. There is, however, another type of IC engine in widespread use—the Diesel. The major difference between Diesel- and gasoline-powered engines is in the method used to ignite the fuel.

On the intake stroke, instead of drawing a fuel-air mixture, as the gasoline engine does, the Diesel draws only fresh air. The Diesel then compresses its air charge much more than a gasoline engine compresses a fuel-air mixture. A gasoline engine typically compresses its mixture into a space one-eighth to one-twelfth of its normal atmospheric volume. But a Diesel may compress its charge of air into as little as one-twenty-first of its normal volume. Naturally, this greater compression causes the air charge to get hotter. Compression temperatures in Diesels often reach 1000° F (538° C) or more. Since Diesel fuel ignites at about 680° F (360° C), this is well above ignition temperature. At the end of the compression stroke, just before TDC, fuel is sprayed into the combustion chamber. The heat of the compressed air causes the fuel to ignite instantly, and as the flame spreads the power stroke begins.

The combustion process in the Diesel engine has two properties that give it advantages over the spark ignition engine. First, the pressure generated by Diesel combustion is more nearly constant. Instead of producing a sudden surge of energy, the expanding gases in Diesel combustion keep steady pressure on the piston during the power stroke. This provides a smoother, steadier source of power. With more force and less jerkiness, particularly at the lower end of the stroke, it can deliver a greater percentage of its power in usable form.

The second advantage of Diesel combustion comes from the fact that, on the intake cycle, the Diesel draws only fresh air. This abundance of air promotes more thorough burning of the fuel and reduces the emission of carbon monoxide.

Diesel engines can be either two-stroke or four-stroke power plants. Except for the differences in fuel injection and ignition, four-stroke Diesel engines operate in the same way as gasoline-powered Otto engines. Two-stroke Diesel engines, however, do not normally employ crankcase compression, as their gasoline-powered counter-parts do. Instead, two-stroke Diesels are equipped with superchargers.* Essentially, a supercharger is just a highly efficient air pump. In the two-stroke Diesel, it pumps pressurized air into the combustion chamber during the intake phase.

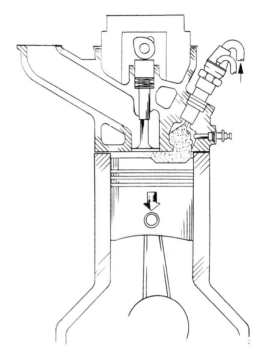

**Figure 3–19.** In a Diesel, no spark plug is necessary. The air in the cylinder is compressed until it is hotter than the ignition temperature of Diesel fuel. Then, when fuel is injected, it immediately ignites.

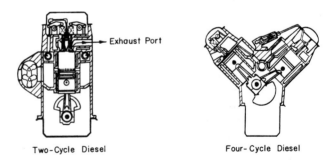

Two-Cycle Diesel                    Four-Cycle Diesel

**Figure 3–20.** Diesels can operate on either the two-stroke or the four-stroke cycle.

---

*Supercharger theory and applications will be explained fully in Section 3, Unit 7.

## Advantages of the Diesel Engine

**Fuel Economy.** "The Diesel," says one top research engineer, "offers the most immediate chance for significant fuel saving over the spark ignition engine."[1] The saving is possible because Diesel fuel contains more BTU's per pound than gasoline and burns in an engine which, typically, has a thermal efficiency of 30–35%. The saving can be realized immediately because the Diesel is so similar to the gasoline engine. This similarity suggests a second advantage.

**Established Technology.** Because the Diesel resembles the gasoline engine so closely in design and operation, manufacturers and service personnel can change over to Diesels easily. Much of the technology of the Otto engine applies also to the Diesel. Moreover, those aspects of Diesel technology which are distinctive are by no means new. The Diesel has already earned a reputation for reliability and economy in industrial applications. In Europe it has long been rather popular as a passenger car engine. All this experience is available to American manufacturers now beginning to market Diesels.

## 3 & 4 Cylinder Diesel Power

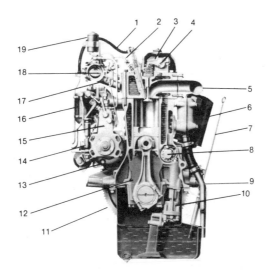

1. Thermostat Feed Line
2. Injector Fuel Line
3. Rocker
4. Rocker Shaft
5. Exhaust Manifold
6. Oil Filter
7. Oil Level Indicator
8. Camshaft
9. Oil Vapor Vent Pipe
10. Oil Pump
11. Flywheel
12. Crankshaft
13. Starter Motor
14. Fuel Pump
15. Injector Pump
16. Fuel Filter
17. Intake Manifold
18. Air Intake
19. Thermostart Reservoir

**Figure 3–21.** A great deal of technological experience is available to guide the manufacturer who decides to produce Diesel power plants for passenger cars. *Courtesy of Ford Industrial Division.*

[1]Robert S Rarey, "Advanced Automotive Powerplants," a paper presented to the University of Michigan management briefing seminar, Traverse City, Michigan, Aug. 11, 1978. Mr. Rarey is Chief Research Engineer, Power Plant Research, Chrysler Corporation.

**Interchangeability.** Diesels designed for automotive use can already come close to gasoline engines in size, weight, and cost. They readily fit into cars designed for gasoline engines. Some of the radically new engines would require extensive modifications in vehicular design. This is not true of the Diesel.

**Emissions.** Two of the three federally regulated pollutants present no problems for the Diesel. Diesel exhaust is relatively free of hydrocarbons and carbon monoxide, both of which are hard to control in gasoline engines.[2] However, two other pollutants, nitrogen oxides and particulates, may present problems for Diesel manufacturers. The Diesel can meet today's EPA standards for nitrogen oxide emissions. Experts also predict that automotive Diesels will be able to meet standards already scheduled to take effect. But if stricter laws are written, as some environmentalists hope, nitrogen oxide standards could be set too low for the Diesel to meet and remain competitive. As this is being written, the EPA is also establishing standards for particulate emissions. ("Particulates" is a technical name for what is commonly called soot.) Diesels exhaust considerably more particulates than gasoline engines. So, again, the economic fate of the Diesel engine may hinge on the levels set by future lawmakers. By present standards, the Diesel is comparatively clean.

## Disadvantages of the Diesel Engine

In addition to being limited in its ability to control nitrogen oxide and particulate emissions, the Diesel has a few other disadvantages.

**Performance.** Diesels seldom get the same power output as spark-ignition engines of equal displacement. The difference can be offset by adding a supercharger, but this adds disproportionately to the cost of the engine.

**Public Acceptance.** Despite its record of dependability, the Diesel's cost, noise, and odor still present problems. It remains to be seen how important these disadvantages will be to the car-buying public. To customers who consider them important, they will make Diesel power plants less attractive.

---

[2]The three pollutants now regulated by the federal government are hydrocarbons, carbon monoxide, and nitrogen oxides. These will all be discussed in Unit 4. Meanwhile it may help you to understand this unit if you simply think of hydrocarbons as unburned fuel and carbon monoxide as *partially* burned fuel. Nitrogen oxides are simply by-products of high-temperature combustion.

## The Future of the Diesel Engine

American manufacturers are now bringing out Diesel-powered cars in some quantity. It seems highly likely that the Diesel engine will become increasingly important in the immediate future. It can give better fuel economy now. It can meet all presently adopted clean-air standards. And its production requires little or no revolutionary technology. Whether the Diesel long remains a leader in today's economic sweepstakes is a matter of surmise. In large part, of course, it depends on the success of developers of the other power plants discussed below. And perhaps equally important will be the exact levels of emissions accepted by future clean-air laws. If those laws do not handicap Diesel engines too much, Diesel cars could be abundant by the turn of the century.

## THE ROTARY ENGINE

Though most IC engines use cylinders and pistons for their combustion chambers, other possibilities do exist. One of the more interesting and successful alternatives is the rotary combustion (RC) engine. Instead of a piston, the RC engine uses a three-sided part called a "rotor." The rotor is mounted off-center on a geared shaft. It turns eccentrically inside a rotor housing, which instead of being perfectly round is shaped a little like a figure-eight. The rotor is tightly sealed to the housing on its two sides. As it turns, its three tips are always tight against the figure-eight shaped wall of the housing. The space between each side of the rotor and the housing wall increases and decreases twice on each turn of the rotor. Thus, each of those three spaces can function as a separate combustion and expansion chamber.

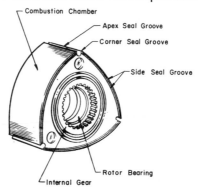

**Figure 3–22.**   Instead of a piston-type expander, the rotary engine uses a special three-sided part called a rotor.

# THE RC CYCLE

Figure 3–23 shows the operation in detail.

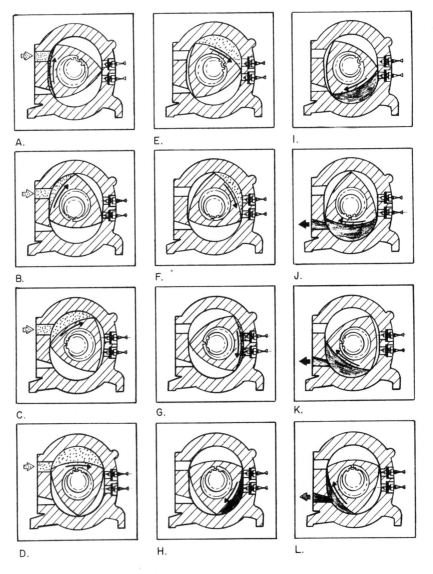

A.  B.  C.  D.  E.  F.  G.  H.  I.  J.  K.  L.

**Figure 3–23.**   The above diagrams trace the complete rotary cycle. For a detailed explanation, see pages 63–65.

# Intake

Frame A of Figure 3–23 shows that the rotor tip has just uncovered the intake port. Notice that the space between the rotor face and the housing wall is at its smallest. As the rotor turns, in frames B and C, this space enlarges and draws in the fuel charge. By frame D, the chamber has reached maximum size, and the rotor tip has begun to close off the intake port.

# Compression

In frame E, the rotor tip has passed the intake port completely. As the chamber volume shrinks, in frames F and G, the fuel mixture is compressed. To promote thorough burning, two spark ignitions occur in quick succession when the mixture is fully compressed, frame G.

# Power

Frames H and I show the rotor turning under the pressure of the expanding combustion gases.

# Exhaust

Frame J shows that the rotor has turned enough to uncover the exhaust port. As the rotor continues to turn, it serves as its own scavenger, frame K, and sweeps remaining gases out the exhaust port. Frame L shows the rotor just before it closes the exhaust port and moves on to a new intake cycle.

Hopes for the RC engine have fluctuated since its invention by Felix Wankel in 1957. In the mid-1970's, the rotary was hailed by some as a sure replacement for the Otto-cycle engine. Expectations for it were high. Some manufacturers designed cars for the easy installation of RC engines. With the fuel crisis, however, the rotary engine was forgotten almost overnight. When American manufacturers saw that fuel economy would soon be as important as emissions control, they returned their attention to piston engines. Now, however, it seems possible that the picture is changing again. The peculiar advantages of the so-called Wankel-cycle engine are so attractive that researchers are reluctant to give up on it.

## Advantages of RC Engines

**Fewer Moving Parts.** The rotor opens and closes intake and exhaust ports somewhat as the piston does in a conventional two-stroke engine. One advantage of this, as you learned from our earlier discussion of two-stroke engines, is that valves and valve train parts become unnecessary. A typical rotary, in fact, has about one-third fewer moving parts than a comparable Otto-cycle engine.

**Smooth Power Output.** Each side of the rotor, remember, creates a separate combustion chamber. Of course, each side passes the spark plugs once on each revolution of the rotor. So there are three power impulses for each rotor turn. The gear ratio on the power output shaft causes the shaft to turn three times for each rotor revolution. Therefore, the RC engine produces one power impulse for each complete turn of the power shaft. This makes it a smooth, steady source of power.

**Weight and Size.** Perhaps the biggest advantages of the rotary are its lighter weight and smaller size. A 100 hp Mazda RC, for instance, weighs only 290 pounds. The comparable piston engine by the same manufacturer is fourteen pounds heavier, six inches longer, eight inches wider, and four inches higher. Such savings in size and weight give the manufacturer important cost advantages.

## Disadvantages of RC Engines

**Durability.** As is usual in the early stages of a technological development, RC engines have not yet been made completely reliable. They have yet to achieve the rugged dependability of conventional gasoline and Diesel engines. The seals around the rotor housing have proven particularly likely to cause trouble. This difficulty, however, seems now to be almost overcome.

**Fuel Economy.** Being without valves, the RC engine, like the conventional two-stroke engine, loses so much unburnt fuel through the exhaust port that its fuel economy is greatly diminished. Efficiency is also lost because of the sealing problems just mentioned. And the fact that it is not yet possible to control the motion of the fuel charge in the combustion chamber is another limiting factor. There is no way to assure maximum combustion efficiency on every power stroke.

**Pollution.** Probably the biggest disadvantage of the RC engine is the amount of hydrocarbons and carbon monoxide in its exhaust. In comparison with other modern power plants, the rotary is a very dirty engine.

## The Future of the RC Engine

Most of the disadvantages listed above seem to be solvable. Research now under way suggests that better fuel delivery systems can significantly improve the rotary's fuel economy. Its sealing problems may soon be solved, too. The big question is whether RC exhaust can be cleaned up. If this can be done without cancelling out the unique advantages of the rotary power plant, then it certainly has a future. If not, its future—for automotive use—is limited. The RC engine now appears to be in the same stage of development that the piston engine was in about 1930. It will be interesting to see whether technology and economics work together to create conditions that will allow rotary engines to flourish in the 1980's.

## THE GAS TURBINE ENGINE

For almost forty years, American manufacturers have been steadily conducting research on a different type of rotary engine. Technically, the gas turbine engine is also a rotary power plant. It has no rotors to form revolving combustion chambers like those just described in the Wankel-cycle RC engine, but the direct output of gas turbine combustion is power with a rotary motion. In this sense, it is a rotary engine.

The gas turbine engine differs from other IC engines because it uses *continuous* combustion. Heat energy from continuous combustion is turned into mechanical power by a process called the Brayton cycle. The Brayton cycle includes the same events found in the Otto cycle. However, each event occurs continuously in the Brayton cycle, and each takes place in a section of the engine designed especially for it.

**Figure 3–24.** G.M. Detroit Diesel Allison Division's GT Series industrial gas turbine engine was developed for use in vehicles. *Courtesy of Detroit Diesel Allison Division, General Motors Corporation.*

## THE BRAYTON CYCLE

Figure 3–25 shows how each of the Otto-cycle events is localized in the gas turbine engine.

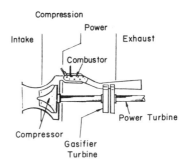

**Figure 3–25.**   In the gas turbine engine, air is drawn into the engine and compressed by the compression turbine. The compression forces it into the combustion chamber. Continuous combustion causes expanding gases to turn the power turbine on their way to the exhaust.

### Intake

Air is drawn into the engine by a specially designed compression turbine. A turbine is a propeller-like part with many blades or "paddles" on it. This compression turbine is designed to throw the incoming air outward, away from its center, with great force.

### Compression

The speed with which the incoming air is thrown outward compresses it into about one-fourth its normal volume. This is more than enough pressure to cause it to rush continuously into the combustion chamber.

### Power

Instead of periodic ignition sparks, the gas turbine relies on continuous, on-going combustion to generate its power. Compressed air is constantly being drawn in and fuel is being injected and burned. The heat from the combustion further expands the compressed air, causing it to burst through both the gasifier and power turbines with great force. The surge of expanding gases, of course, turns both turbines. Because the gasifier turbine is mounted on the same shaft as the compressor turbine, turning the gasifier also turns the compressor. So more fresh air is drawn in, and the process is maintained. Meanwhile, the escaping gas is also turning the power turbine, which is connected through gearing to the load.

## Exhaust

The simplest form of the gas turbine engine would then exhaust the spent gases out the tailpipe. However, a great deal of heat energy is wasted if this is done. By no means all of the heat in the expanding gases is turned into mechanical energy as the gases pass through the turbines. Automotive gas turbines, therefore, introduce into the exhaust stream a special device, called a *regenerator,* to improve thermal efficiency (Figure 3–26). The regenerator simply moves heat from the exhaust to the cool air being drawn into the combustion chamber. This preheats the intake charge and makes combustion more efficient. After passing through the regenerator, the cooled exhaust exits in the usual way, through the tailpipe.

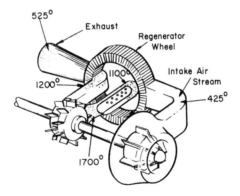

**Figure 3–26.** A regenerator is used to transfer "waste" heat from exhaust gases to the incoming air.

## Advantages of the Gas Turbine Engine

The gas turbine engine has not yet been tested commercially in the passenger car market, as have the Diesel and RC engines. But several manufacturers have invested a lot of time and money in their efforts to make it a practical automotive power plant. In 1964, Chrysler hand built fifty gas turbine cars. They loaned these experimental vehicles to 203 different people over two years. Over 1.1 million miles were put on the fifty cars. Much of the information in this chapter is based on the results of that experiment.

Chrysler has not been alone in its experimentation. Detroit Diesel Allison Division of General Motors and Ford's Industrial Engine Division both developed prototypes of gas turbine engines. These prototypes, however, were intended for industrial use, not for installation in passenger cars. They have since been installed in a variety of large vehicles. As a result of this experimentation, researchers know a good deal more about the strengths and weaknesses of the gas turbine engine.

**Figure 3-27.** In 1964, Chrysler hand-built fifty gas turbine cars. More than 200 people helped them road-test these vehicles over a two-year period. *Courtesy of Chrysler Corporation.*

**Figure 3-28.** This Greyhound bus is powered by a G.M. 404 gas turbine engine. *Courtesy of Detroit Diesel Allison Division, General Motors Corporation.*

**Figure 3–29.** Trucks powered by G.M.'s 404 gas turbine engine. *Courtesy of Detroit Diesel Allison Division, General Motors Corporation.*

**Fuel Economy.** The gas turbine engine can now come close to the Otto-cycle engine in overall fuel economy. Much greater efficiency will be possible if manufacturers can find reasonably cheap materials that can withstand the extreme heat of turbine combustion. Promising research is now under way to develop materials that are much more heat-resistant. If this research is successful, hotter combustion temperatures will make the gas turbine's fuel economy comparable to that of the Diesel.

**Emissions.** Gas turbine exhaust is naturally low in most pollutants. Until recently, there were difficulties with nitrous oxide emissions. However, experts now believe that the gas turbine can be made to meet future emissions standards without great cost or sacrifice in performance.

**Smooth Power Output.** Gas turbine power is continuous. It is completely free of vibrations that cause periodic ignition and back and forth cylinder travel. Those who tested Chrysler's gas turbine cars reported feeling as if the car was just "gliding" along.

**Adaptability.** The gas turbine can run on almost any liquid fuel. Chrysler reports that its recent model (Figure 3–30) performed well while burning pure Diesel fuel, denatured alcohol, unleaded gasoline, and several mixtures. What is more remarkable, no adjustments were necessary when fuels were changed. Of course, the gas turbines which are finally marketed may require some tuning when fuels are switched. But as the fuel shortage worsens, a power plant that converts easily will probably enjoy a competitive advantage.

**Dependability.** The gas turbine engine is a very simple machine. It has eighty percent fewer parts than a conventional gasoline engine. So there is little to go wrong. Test models have run the equivalent of 175,000 miles without needing major repair. The latest gas turbines are said to start instantly in cold weather. They require no warm-up period and almost no routine maintenance except for cleaning their air filters and, about every 25,000 miles, replacing their spark plugs.

**Figure 3–30.** Chrysler reports that its experimental gas turbine power plants run well on a wide variety of fuels. *Courtesy of Chrysler Corporation.*

## Disadvantages of the Gas Turbine Engine

**High Temperature Combustion.** The most important disadvantages of the gas turbine engine can be fairly well summarized in one word: heat. The gas turbine is only at its best when combustion temperature is above 2000° F (1094° C). Therefore, many parts of the gas turbine must be able to stand extreme heat. Unfortunately, however, the heat-resistant materials from which such parts can be made are rare and expensive. Recently developed alloys have already made it possible to raise combustion temperatures from 1500° (816° C) to 2000° F (1094° C). Chrysler is now working to produce ceramic turbine wheels. If they are successful, the temperature can be raised to 2500° F (1372° C), which would make the gas turbine a leader in fuel economy. Until such heat resistant materials become economical, however, the gas turbine engine is not likely to be commercially practical.

**High Cost Per Unit.** Expensive heat-resistant materials keep engine costs excessive. Assuming reasonable technological progress between now and 1985, gas turbine engines will still cost about one-third more than Otto-cycle power plants.

**New Technology Required.** Factories now manufacturing Otto-cycle engines could not be changed over to produce gas turbine power plants. Entirely new machinery would be necessary. With it, a new technology would have to be created. This adds both to the costs and the risks of any manufacturer who markets a gas turbine engine.

**Performance.** Until recently, noise, cold-weather starting, and inadequate engine braking frequently caused difficulty, but all the difficulties just named now seem to be solved. Still needing improvement are two other areas of turbine performance: fuel economy at low speeds and acceleration lag. The most recent models show improvement in low-speed fuel economy. However, it seems likely that some lag in acceleration will persist.

# EXTERNAL COMBUSTION ENGINES

Two kinds of EC engines are important enough to be discussed here. One, the Rankine cycle power plant, is really our old friend the steam engine. The other EC engine now on the scene is also an old-timer. In fact, the Stirling-cycle power plant is even older than the steam engine. You will see, however, that—despite its antiquity—the Stirling-cycle engine is by no means a has-been. Several experts predict that it is our most likely candidate for engines of the future. First, though, let us renew acquaintance with yesterday's favorite: the steam engine.

## THE RANKINE CYCLE ENGINE

If you remember our brief discussion of the steam engine, in Unit 2, you already know most of the essential facts about the Rankine cycle. Figure 3–31 diagrams the complete process. In the steam engine, combustion takes place continuously, outside the engine. Heat from the burning fuel is transferred to a separate closed system containing water. The water becomes a working fluid when it boils and turns into high pressure steam. All this takes place in burners outside the engine.

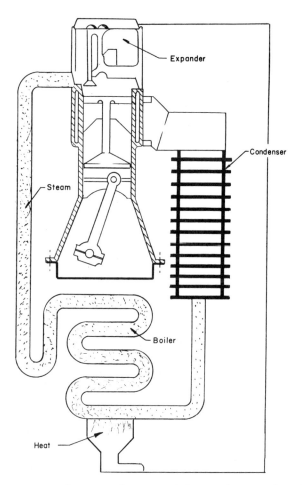

**Figure 3–31.** A schematic diagram of the Rankine cycle. Though a piston-type expander is usually used, the Rankine expander can be a turbine or rotor.

The pressurized steam is then piped into the engine where it is allowed to expand and perform work. The *expander* that is moved by the steam is usually a piston, but can also be a turbine or rotor.

Notice, though, that the Rankine cycle does not require any compression cycle. The process begins with water, which, in effect, is compressed steam. Keeping the water under pressure while it is boiling is all the "compression" needed. Notice also that, in the simple steam engine you studied in Unit 2, spent steam was exhausted after it moved the expander. This is not done in the complete Rankine cycle.

The "used" steam is not exhausted because spent steam, though somewhat cooler, is still hot. Because its heat energy would be wasted in exhaust, the Rankine cycle introduces a new component called a condenser. The condenser is a kind of radiator that absorbs much of the remaining heat when spent steam passes through it. This causes the steam to "condense," that is, to turn back into water. Then it can be returned to the heat exchanger and boiled again.

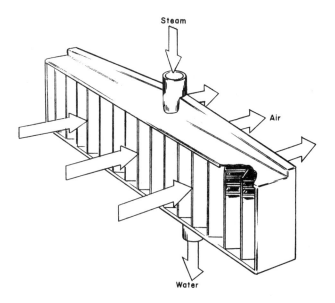

**Figure 3–32.** In the complete Rankine cycle, spent steam is not exhausted. Instead, a condenser is used to absorb the remaining heat and to convert the steam back into water.

## Advantages of the Rankine Cycle Engine

Many of the advantages that made the steam car popular in the gay nineties are even more important today. However, many of the specific disadvantages that caused it to lose out seventy years ago are also still with us. Though some of these disadvantages have now been overcome, some important ones persist.

**Clean Exhaust.** Since combustion takes place outside the engine, it can be carefully controlled. Steps can easily be taken to insure thorough burning of the fuel and, if necessary, removal of pollutants from the exhaust.

**Adaptability.** Because Rankine-cycle engines can burn virtually any fuel, they can use nonpolluting fuel. Experimental models have even been made to run from solar energy.

**Mechanical Efficiency.** Used with a piston-type expander, the Rankine-cycle engine can produce maximum torque at all engine speeds. Increasing power is simply a matter of letting more steam into the expander. This means that the vehicle's wheels can be connected directly to the crankshaft. Only a differential is needed and a transmission is unnecessary.

## Disadvantages of the Rankine Cycle Engine

**Thermal Efficiency.** The most important disadvantage of the Rankine-cycle power plant is its lack of thermal efficiency. A Rankine engine typically has a thermal efficiency of about 18–24%. This means that, whatever the fuel used, a *lot* of it must be consumed. The Rankine, therefore, makes up in fuel costs what it saves in other ways.

## Modern Adaptations

Various efforts have been made to improve the Rankine engine's thermal efficiency. Not all the ideas tried have proven equally practical. But, taken together, they do suggest that Rankine engines could conceivably someday power cars again. If so, however, it is doubtful that the Rankines which go back into production can still be properly called "steam engines."

**Different Working Fluids.** Experimenters have increased thermal efficiency by using working fluids other than steam. Recently Freon® type chemicals have been used. These boil at lower temperatures than water, so not as much heat is required to put them to work.

**Raising Combustion Temperature.** Another way to raise thermal efficiency is to increase combustion temperature. Hotter combustion insures more thorough burning so that the fuel gives up more of its potential energy. But as with the gas turbine engine, extreme heat makes severe demands on materials. New heat-resistant alloys or suitable nonmetalic materials must be created before Rankine heat exchangers become commercially practical. And special working fluids will have to be developed to function efficiently at such high temperatures.

## The Future of the Rankine Cycle Engine

At present, it seems doubtful that the advantages of the Rankine engine are great enough to justify the cost of developing the new materials necessary to make it competitive. The best current models are little more than engineering exercises. The picture could conceivably be changed by a major technological breakthrough. If commercial interest in Rankine-cycle engines is renewed, the designs that spark the revival are almost certain to use pistons for expanders. So any mechanic thoroughly grounded in Otto-cycle theory, if he is willing to keep up, can learn to service them.

## THE STIRLING CYCLE ENGINE

One of the most exciting alternatives to the Otto cycle is the Stirling cycle. As early as 1816, the Scotsman Robert Stirling began powering water pumps with his new invention. Within a few years, however, Stirling's engine was virtually abandoned in its infancy. Rapidly developing technology at that time made it possible for Rankine-cycle steam engines to beat out all competitors. Now that the pollution problem has become crucial, experts are looking at the Stirling-cycle engine with renewed interest.

**Figure 3–33.** This V-160 Stirling cycle power plant was produced by Stirling Power Systems, Ann Arbor, Michigan, to generate electrical power for recreational vehicles. *Courtesy of Stirling Power Systems Ltd.*

The Stirling engine is like the Rankine-cycle steam engine in two ways: (1) It uses continuous external combustion. (2) It uses the same working fluid over and over by recycling it within a closed system. Unlike the Rankine-cycle engine, however, the Stirling never allows its working fluid to turn into liquid. The Stirling piston is powered by varying the pressure of a gas, which is alternately heated and cooled within the sealed system. The gas generally used as the working fluid is hydrogen.

## THE STIRLING CYCLE

The most common type of Stirling engine moves the working fluid from place to place by means of a *displacer.* A displacer is a kind of second piston, above the power piston. It is connected mechanically to the power train through a hollow connecting rod on the power piston. You do not need to know the details of this hook-up in order to understand the basics of the Stirling cycle. However, if you are particularly interested, the schematic in Figure 3–34 will help you figure out the mechanics.

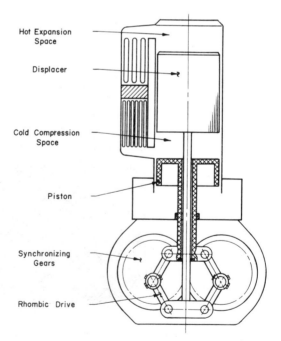

**Figure 3–34.** A Stirling engine has a rhombic drive connection and a hollow connecting rod on the power piston. This makes it possible for the displacer and the power piston to move at different rates and in different directions.

## Phase One

The Stirling cycle begins with the power piston at BDC and the displacer at TDC. This means that all the working fluid has been forced into the cold space between the two cylinders. This cooling of the working fluid lowers the pressure in the cold space and creates a partial vacuum.

## Phase Two

The power piston is, in effect, drawn up to TDC by the partial vacuum above it. As this happens, some of the working fluid is forced through the regenerator, heated, and released into the hot space above the displacer.

## Phase Three

The rapid expansion of the heated gas above the displacer drives it downward toward the cooler, lower-pressured gas below. As the displacer drops, it forces still more cold gas through the regenerator into the hot space.

## Phase Four

With almost of all the gas expanding in the hot space above the displacer, both displacer and piston are forced downward together. This "power stroke" lasts until the displacer begins to move upward. The mechanical linkage shown in Figure 3–34 causes the displacer to rise first, forcing the expanded gas back through the regenerator and into the cold space. When this is done, the engine has returned to stage one, and the cycle can begin again.

## Advantages of the Stirling Engine

One reason that the Stirling engine has again captured the imagination of automotive engineers is that, theoretically, it is nearly flawless. Its disadvantages seem less important when weighed against its unique advantages.

**Fuel Economy.** The Stirling engine has a higher theoretical efficiency than any other power plant discussed in this book. When perfected, its fuel economy should be at least 25-30 percent better than that of a comparable gasoline engine.

**Clean Exhaust.**   As with the Rankine-cycle engine, the Stirling's external combustion makes its fuel burning easy to control. Thus, it is easier to eliminate the incomplete combustion that produces much of the pollution in IC engines. The Stirling can meet all emissions standards now scheduled to take effect by January 1, 1986.

**Adaptability.**   Stirling engines can use a variety of combustible substances for fuel. In fact, models have even been constructed that run on solar energy. The Stirling's smooth, quiet operation also makes it suitable for a wide range of applications (Figure 3–35).

**Figure 3–35.**   A Stirling power plant installed in a motor home provides a quiet, clean source of energy. *Courtesy of Winnebago Industries, Inc.*

## Disadvantages of the Stirling Engine

**Weight and Cost.**   The most efficient versions of the Stirling engine today still require large quantities of stainless steel tubing, ceramic parts, and other expensive components. This makes them too heavy to be practical and too expensive to be feasible.

**Sealing Difficulties.**   Hydrogen is usually used for the working fluid in Stirling engines because it is so low on friction and so efficient at transferring heat. But hydrogen is extremely difficult to seal at high pressures and high temperatures. Leakage remains a major engineering problem.

    **Load Response.** To change loads, the average pressure of the hydrogen must be changed. Since the hydrogen works inside a sealed system, there is no simple way to adjust its pressure rapidly. This makes it difficult to produce the rapid power changes needed in an automotive power plant.

## The Future of the Stirling Engine

    Much research is now being done on Stirling engines, both in this country and abroad. The U.S. Department of Energy has sponsored work by Ford and Mechanical Technology, Inc., in the U.S. and by United Stirling in Sweden. The goal of this research is to advance the theoretical work far enough by 1985 to make large-scale commercial production practical. Further research, scheduled to start in 1984, will aim for an eventual 30-60% improvement in fuel economy. Meanwhile United Stirling plans to begin limited commercial production in 1982.

    The cost, the need for new types of high-pressure seals, and the heat-resistant materials required all combine to put the Stirling out of immediate reach. A marketable Stirling engine is most unlikely to be developed soon. But some experts are impressed with the efficiency, cleanliness, and adaptability of the Stirling. Of all the power plants now under study, they consider the Stirling most likely to survive the long-term competition. Other authorities are more dubious. Much depends on what happens elsewhere in the industry, of course. But it is conceivable that Stirling Engines could become commonplace in the 1990's.

# NONCOMBUSTION ENGINES

    The only noncombustion (NC) engine ever to power automobiles with any commercial success was the electric motor. And you know that, about seventy-five years ago, the gasoline engine decisively defeated the electric motor in commercial competition. Since then comparatively little research has been done to improve electric power plants. With today's emphasis on pollution control, however, experts are once again considering the possibilities of NC power plants.

Obviously, any electric power plant that "catches on" with the buying public must be better than those grandpa turned his back on two generations ago. All new engines today routinely exceed grandad's wildest dreams. So only a greatly improved electric car would have a chance at a comeback. Present efforts to improve electric-car performance are pursuing three different routes: (1) searching for more efficient batteries; (2) substituting fuel cells for conventional batteries; and (3) combining batteries with engines into hybrid systems.

## BATTERY POWERED VEHICLES

In an electric car the battery performs essentially the same function that the gas tank performs for a gasoline-powered vehicle. Both provide places to store potential energy, in chemical form, until it is converted into mechanical power by an engine. At first, it appears that battery-powered cars would cause less pollution because batteries do not use any of those fuels that produce our major pollutants. Actually, though, the use of batteries is not that advantageous.

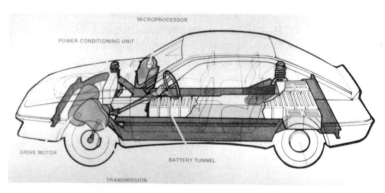

**Figure 3–36.** This car, delivered to the government in the spring of 1979, uses 18 lead-acid batteries to supply its 108-volt power system. *Courtesy of Chrysler Corporation.*

Electric car batteries must be charged frequently. This requires electricity from an external source. And 85% of our electric power is generated through combustion of hydrocarbon fuels. So instead of burning gasoline and Diesel fuel inside on-board IC engines, as we do now, electric car enthusiasts would have us burn other hydrocarbons—oil, natural gas, and coal—at generating plants. The pollution problem would not be solved. It would only be relocated.

Central power stations could be designed, in time, to burn other fuels. Meanwhile, they can be made to burn hydrocarbons as cleanly as possible. The advantages of centralized combustion, however, are still too slight and uncertain to offset the known disadvantages of electric cars.

No battery system presently available or foreseeable comes close to the energy storage efficiency of common gasoline. Today's best lead acid storage batteries cannot store more than 17 watt-hours of energy per pound. Almost no experts claim even to foresee batteries that will store more than 150 watt-hours per pound. By contrast, gasoline contains about 5900 watt-hours per pound. This means that, for the foreseeable future, the weight of its batteries will severely limit the performance of the electric car. The best that engineers have been able to do is to hold battery weight to about half the total weight of the vehicle.

# FUEL CELLS

In the late 1960's and early 1970's, there came a flurry of research on automotive fuel cells. Fuel cells, like batteries, convert chemical energy into electricity. They differ from batteries, however, because they must draw in fuels (usually hydrogen and oxygen) from the outside.

New interest in fuel cells was sparked when it became known that NASA used them as power sources for space vehicles. But this renewed interest in fuel cells, as possible on-board sources of automotive power, did not last long. Unless there is an unexpected breakthrough, no electric cars powered by on-board fuel cells are likely to be marketed.

This is not to say that fuel cells are completely out of the automotive picture. Researchers are working, under government sponsorship, to design huge fuel-cell power plants. Fuel cells produce virtually no pollutants. If they could be substituted for generators at central power plants, the use of electric cars would actually cut down on pollution. Such a development, obviously, would make the electric car a more interesting competitor.

## Advantages of Electric Cars

The future of the electric car is uncertain. But electric cars are beginning to recapture the interest of researchers and car buffs.

Electric cars are clean, quiet, dependable, and—for the owner, at least—pollution-free. Except for the cost of batteries, they are inexpensive to produce. They require little maintenance which can be performed economically without straining the capacity of established technology.

## Disadvantages of Electric Cars

All things considered, electric cars are costly and inefficient. Their performance and range are limited. They do not lend themselves to some of the conveniences modern car buyers take for granted. However, considerable research is under way to overcome these disadvantages. Therefore, a brief comment about each is necessary to give an accurate picture.

**Cost and Efficiency.**   Today's lead acid batteries are so heavy that they overburden the vehicle, in both weight and cost. It has been suggested that cost could be reduced if buyers leased their batteries instead of buying them. This would lower the buyer's initial cost, but it would do nothing to reduce the cost of operation. An expert recently compared the fuel costs of an experimental Chrysler electric to those of a conventional Dodge Omni. He found that fuel costs for the electric were almost 30% higher. Until better batteries are available, fuel costs for the electric car are likely to remain excessive.

**Range and Performance.**   At present, the most successful fleet tests report an average range of sixty-seven miles between battery charges. Models now under development are expected to attain a range of 146 miles at a constant speed of thirty-five miles per hour. Needless to say, today's electrics are unlikely to set any performance records. They also do not accelerate well, and they have trouble meeting federal safety standards.

**Convenience.**   All figures reported above assume that the entire output of the batteries is used to propel the vehicle. Auxiliary power sources would have to be developed for heating, air conditioning, and power steering.

## HYBRID POWER SYSTEMS

To overcome some of the disadvantages of battery-powered electric cars, engineers have designed combination, or "hybrid," power systems. The typical hybrid system consists of one main power source plus an auxiliary source. Either the main or the auxiliary power plant can be a battery. The other is usually an IC engine.

When the engine serves as the main source in a hybrid system, it is intentionally made too small to provide all the power needed. During operation, the engine constantly charges a battery. If the car accelerates or climbs a steep hill, energy from the battery provides the needed boost. The other option, a somewhat more likely design, uses the battery as the main power source. The engine, much smaller than in the previous example, runs only enough to keep the battery charged.

Theoretically, such hybrid systems have several advantages. They enable the engine to run constantly at its most efficient speed. Most pollution and wasted energy in IC engines come when changes in speed and load take the engine outside its optimum operating range. So there should be gains in both cleanliness and fuel economy. The auxiliary power source could also be used for heating, air conditioning, etc. But combining power sources adds complexity and increases cost. In practice, the greater complication often results in a loss in total energy.

## THE FUTURE OF ELECTRIC CARS

Despite all its disadvantages, the electric-powered vehicle may have a future. Unless major improvements are made in its range and performance, however, that future will not be on our highways and expressways. American manufacturers are now working, with government assistance, to develop models for urban, stop-and-go driving. Major telephone companies are already operating experimental fleets of battery-powered service vans. Chrysler and General Electric have just delivered an experimental, advanced state, four-passenger, electric sedan to the Department of Energy. It is said to have a maximum range of seventy-five miles and a top speed of fifty-five mph. This model—like one under development by General Motors—performs well enough to be considered for specialized use. If production and operating costs can be controlled, Americans may again be given the opportunity to own electric cars.

If so, it seems likely that the electric's chief appeal will be as a second car, used mostly for shopping and household errands. It could also find commercial use in cities as a taxicab, service vehicle, or short-run delivery truck.

**Figure 3–37.** Electric-powered vehicles may once again come to find limited use for urban and short-range driving. *Courtesy of GMC Truck Division, General Motors Corporation.*

## REVIEW QUESTIONS

1. Name the two major objectives of today's race to develop a better engine. Tell why each is important.

2. Consult the diagram below.

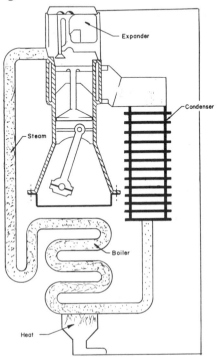

What is the name of the engine cycle represented? What working fluid is used? Why is there no compression stage? What is the function of the condenser?

3. Study the diagram below. Note the displacer, which gives this engine a kind of "double piston" design.

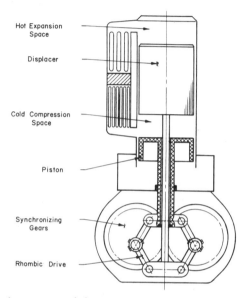

What is the name of this engine? Is it an IC or an EC engine? How can you tell? What is its working fluid? What is the function of the displacer? Explain in order the four phases of the cycle. Refer to pages 78–81 if you find it necessary to jog your memory.

4. Study the diagram below.

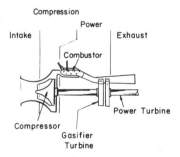

What is the name of this engine? What are the functions of the two turbines? How does the combustion process on this engine differ from those of other IC engines? What are some of the advantages of this engine? Refer to pages 68–69 to check your answers.

*Objective Questions*

1. Which of the following is NOT an advantage of the two-cycle IC engine?

_____ A.   Clean exhaust
_____ B.   More power strokes
_____ C.   Fewer moving parts
_____ D.   Low cost

2. For passenger car use, the biggest disadvantage of the Diesel engine is:

_____ A.   Its excessive fuel consumption
_____ B.   The new technology required by Diesels
_____ C.   Its lack of thermal efficiency
_____ D.   Its marginal performance

3. Why did the fuel crisis of 1974 bring development of the rotary engine to such an abrupt halt?

_____ A.   Rotary engines were so big and heavy that they wasted energy.
_____ B.   The rotary's jerky power output caused much energy to be lost in friction.
_____ C.   The rotary was high in both pollution and fuel consumption.
_____ D.   Rotary engines have so many moving parts that they are not economical.

4. The biggest obstacle to the development of an efficient gas turbine engine is that turbine engines

_____ A.   Are not designed especially to burn any one fuel
_____ B.   Run best only at extremely high combustion temperatures
_____ C.   Have a jerky power output with lots of bumps and vibrations
_____ D.   Produce too many pollutants in their exhaust

5. Which of the following pairs are *both* external combustion engines?

_____ A.   Diesel cycle and Rankine cycle engines
_____ B.   Stirling cycle and hybrid system power plants
_____ C.   Wankel cycle and fuel cell power plants
_____ D.   Rankine cycle and Stirling cycle engines

6. Which of the following is a continuous combustion engine?

    _____ A. Gas turbine
    _____ B. Diesel
    _____ C. Fuel cell
    _____ D. Rotary

7. Which of the following is NOT a heat engine?

    _____ A. The Brayton cycle engine
    _____ B. The electric motor
    _____ C. The Diesel
    _____ D. The air-cooled two-cycle engine

8. Which engine is most likely to use hydrogen for its working fluid?

    _____ A. Wankel
    _____ B. Diesel
    _____ C. Rankine
    _____ D. Stirling

9. Which engine would cause the least technological upheaval in the automotive industry if it replaced the Otto-cycle gasoline engine for passenger cars?

    _____ A. The Stirling
    _____ B. The Rankine
    _____ C. The Diesel
    _____ D. The Brayton

10. Deflector-type piston heads and reed valves are most likely to be used with:

    _____ A. Standard Otto-cycle gasoline engines
    _____ B. Two-cycle gasoline engines
    _____ C. Wankel cycle rotary engines
    _____ D. Special-use Brayton cycle engines

# UNIT

# 4

# DESIGN REQUIREMENTS FOR MODERN POWER PLANTS

To stay competitive in today's changing technology, it is not enough to know how engines are built. The mechanic who wants to stay up-to-date must be able to understand *why* each engine is built the way it is.

In this unit, you will learn to look at an engine from the viewpoint of an automotive engineer. Engineers try to design engines that meet a few very important requirements. Every engine marketed represents an effort to meet these same design requirements. After you learn why these requirements are important to manufacturers, you can train yourself to understand new engines by thinking of the goals of their designers.

**Figure 4–1.** A good mechanic trains himself to understand new engines by thinking of the goals of their designers.

A basic rule of machine design states that "form follows function." This is just a catchy way of saying that machines are built the way they are so that they can do their jobs. As you know, the job of almost any engine is to turn heat energy into mechanical energy. Obviously, the best engine is the one that converts energy in the "best way." In practice, it is the design requirements discussed in this unit that define the "best way."

## OBJECTIVES

When you have completed this chapter, you should be able to:

- Name six design requirements of modern automotive power plants and explain why each is important.
- Demonstrate, in answer to specific questions, the ability to apply your understanding of design requirements to new engines and new problems in automotive technology.
- Name five factors affecting engine cost.
- Distinguish recent design requirements from those that have long been considered important.

## DESIGN REQUIREMENTS

To be commercially practical, today's engine must have six characteristics. Two of them, "clean" exhaust and fuel efficiency, were not considered so important until recently. The importance of the other four design requirements, however, dates back to the beginning of the automotive industry. Manufacturers have always tried to produce engines that were (1) light-weight, (2) low-cost, (3) reliable, and (4) convenient.

All of these requirements are extremely important. Their relative importance changes as economic conditions change. For the foreseeable future, however, "clean" exhaust and fuel-efficiency are sure to be given special consideration. As is often the case in engine design, these two goals tend to exclude each other. So far, we have been able to produce very efficient power plants that pollute the air and gas-gobbling engines with clean exhaust. But nobody has been able to make the Otto-cycle engine succeed completely at meeting both requirements at once. Because these two requirements are intertwined, they will be discussed together. And because they are so important, they will be discussed first. Then we will consider the other design requirements.

**Figure 4–2.**   This mid-1950's D Jaguar race car is an excellent example of the principle that "form follows function." Its brutally powerful body is designed to cover the machinery that makes it move. Both outside and inside the car, functional design has a directness, an honesty, and a timely beauty that borders on art.

## CLEAN EXHAUST AND FUEL ECONOMY

Since 1968, the levels of pollutants allowed in the engine exhaust of all new cars sold in the U.S. have been strictly controlled. Government regulations have become increasingly severe and are scheduled to be lowered further, year by year, through 1985.

Though engine exhaust is the largest source of air pollution produced by cars, it is not the only one. From a car with no emissions controls, about 25% of the pollutants originate in the crankcase. Another 15% come from fuel tank and carburetor vents. Only about 60% of the car's damage to the atmosphere is done by engine exhaust. But environmentalists remind us that, if humanity is to survive, *all* pollution must be kept as low as possible. Therefore, it is essential to design engines with cleaner exhaust.

In Otto-cycle engines, there are only three ways to do this. The first is through better control of the fuel-air charge. This can be done by modifying the fuel and by making improvements in the manifold and carburetor. The second way is to control the combustion process so that the fuel burns more thoroughly and produces maximum power.

Third, is to remove pollutants from the exhaust after it has left the combustion chamber. Designers must keep all these possibilities in mind as they create new engines. Their job would be easier, however, if steps taken to remove one pollutant did not sometimes increase another.

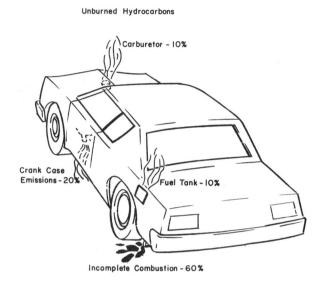

**Figure 4–3.**    Only about 60% of a car's total pollution comes from engine exhaust.

## Major Pollutants

The government's first stringent regulations were directed at carbon monoxide, hydrocarbons, and nitric oxides. More recently, legislation has been drafted to control admissible levels of particulates, or soot.

**Carbon Monoxide.** Carbon monoxide (CO) is a tasteless and odorless, but deadly, gas. It is produced when the fuel is not burned, or "oxidized," completely.

**Hydrocarbons.** Hydrocarbons are *unburned fuel*. When hydrocarbons are released into the air, however, the waste of energy is the least of the problems. Hydrocarbons combine with nitric oxides in the presence of sunlight to produce smog. Smog is an eye, throat, and lung irritant and a health hazard that increases the risk of lung disease and cancer.

**Nitrogen Oxides.**    Several oxides of nitrogen ($NO_x$) are produced when a fuel-air mixture is burned at high temperatures. Because high combustion temperature tends to *lower* emissions of hydrocarbons, engine designers are forced to compromise. They must accept some of each kind of pollutant. Otherwise, the very steps they took to get rid of one would raise another to dangerous levels.

**Figure 4–4.** Levels of carbon monoxide, hydrocarbons, and nitrous oxides are already controlled by law. Legislation may soon be passed to control the levels of particulate emissions.

**Particulates.**    Unlike the pollutants already mentioned, which are either gases or liquids, particulates are tiny bits, "particles," of solid matter. They are formed as by-products of the combustion process. Carbon soot forms when hydrocarbon fuel is broken down by combustion. Along with those carbon particles in the exhaust are microscopic fragments of metals. Some of these, like lead and bromides, come from additives in the fuels. Others are tiny pieces of the engine itself, which wears away during operation.

**Figure 4–5.** Particulate emissions, commonly called soot, differ from other major pollutants in that they are tiny bits of solid matter.

# Fuel Economy

You learned in Unit 2 that only a small part of the BTU's in the fuel are actually changed to mechanical power. Most of them are simply wasted. The waste is caused by two kinds of inefficiency: thermal and mechanical. A good engine keeps losses of both thermal and mechanical energy as low as possible.

**Thermal Losses.** Automotive engineers try to get maximum potential energy from the fuel into the working fluid. Only the heat that expands the fuel-air charge does work. Any potential that remains in unburnt fuel is lost. So is all the heat that is carried off by radiator coolant and motor oil.

**Mechanical Losses.** All engines lose some of the mechanical energy produced by fuel combustion. Friction between the internal parts of the engine consumes an average of 7-10% of the BTU's available in the fuel. Designers always try to keep these losses as low as possible.

Even the most efficient engines, however, lose almost two-thirds of the potential energy they draw from their fuel tanks. This fact is important to everyone in the automotive industry. It explains why the U.S. Secretary of Transportation recently challenged Detroit to "reinvent" the automobile engine. Secretary Brock Adams in effect asked manufacturers to make efficiency a primary design requirement.

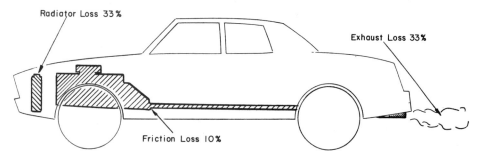

**Figure 4–6.** A good engine design keeps losses of both thermal and mechanical energy as low as possible.

# Light Weight

One way to increase fuel economy is to build a lighter engine that produces the same horsepower. This is a splendid accomplishment, when it can be done, for two reasons. First, one part of the engine's power output must always be used to move itself. The lighter engine uses less of its own output for self-propulsion. So this leaves more mechanical energy to drive the vehicle. The second advantage of a lighter engine is that it can fit into a lighter car. The less the strain on the suspension system, chassis, and frame, the lighter those parts can be. Consequently, the load on the engine can be lightened still more. For these two reasons, every pound that can be subtracted from an engine's weight shows up directly in improved performance. Some modern passenger cars can produce about one horsepower per pound of engine weight. Racing engines can get almost three horsepower per pound.

**Figure 4–7.**  Other things being equal, a lighter engine means a lighter car, and a lighter car is better.

## Low Cost

Other things being equal, the cheaper engine is the better. It was because of the price advantage that the gasoline engine beat out the steamer and the electric car in grandma's day. In the automotive industry, cost is determined by a combination of factors. We shall name only five.

**Materials.**  Engines made of common materials are usually cheaper than those that require exotic metals. The gas turbine engine is not yet competitive in part because the heat resistant materials needed for its turbines are still too expensive.

**Novelty.** In manufacturing, whatever is new costs money. Modest adaptations of established designs can be made at reasonable cost. But a completely new design requires an enormous investment. Totally new machines must be built to manufacture it. New tools must be manufactured to service it. New training manuals, technical material, etc. must be made available to specialists throughout the industry who will work with it. Conservative designs, on the other hand, can draw heavily on established technology. That is why Otto-cycle engines presently have big commercial advantages over gas turbines and Stirling engines.

**Figure 4–8.** Creating the necessary technology to produce a radically new type of engine costs vast sums of money. *Courtesy of Cross Company.*

**Demand.** Another important question is "How many?" If large numbers of an engine can be built and sold, then the per-unit cost is lower. Most of the "tool-up" costs remain the same, no matter how many are produced. So the first few models are the most expensive. For the same reason, the longer a manufacturer can keep selling copies of a design, the more profitable it becomes for him.

**Size.**   Larger engines require more materials and larger cars to carry them. And making cars larger requires still more materials. Since materials cost money, size obviously adds to the cost.

**Useful Life.**   Engines that are similar in performance may differ greatly in their durability. If low cost is the primary consideration, an engineer may be willing to use cast rather than forged metal for crucial parts. This will enable him to lower the cost of the car a few dollars. However, that engine may not stand as much hard use as the customer expects.

If, on the other hand, the manufacturer wants to assure his customer of long and satisfactory performance, he will use the more expensive parts and raise the price accordingly.

## Reliability

Because of the intense competition in the automotive industry, reliability is an extremely important design requirement. Few consumer products are expected to perform so consistently under all kinds of conditions and treatment. So manufacturers are forced to design into each engine a considerable margin for error. They know that many purchasers are going to abuse their vehicles and skimp on maintenance. They also know that such mistreatment is usually caused by ignorance. These customers seldom understand the serious consequences of their own neglect. So they are quick to blame the manufacturer when a long suffering engine finally gives out. For this reason, good business practice requires manufacturers to design engines that can "take it."

Figure 4–9.

Three-quarters of a century ago, grandpa bragged when his car did not break down on a trip, but today's customer takes dependable service for granted. He is inconvenienced and irritated whenever his car must be repaired. Therefore, any undependable engine, any power plant that requires more maintenance than ordinary, is soon driven off the market.

# Convenience

Critics of the automotive industry have often faulted manufacturers for not being responsive enough to the needs of society. They refer not only to the need for pollution control and fuel economy but also to other "good" things that car manufacturers could do for the public. Some safety proponents, for example, have suggested that many lives would be saved if cars were built so that only the driver's seat faced forward. The case of the backward seats provides a good example of the importance of convenience as a design requirement.

Suppose you were an executive in, say, the United States Motor Corporation. How eager would you be to make your company the *first* to bring out a car with rear-facing seats? Many customers might look upon them as a newfangled inconvenience. No matter how sound the idea is, in theory, all advantages of a development are lost unless people buy the cars that use it. Car manufacturers, therefore, are reluctant to introduce changes that might detract from customer convenience. The customer who doesn't like backward seats might walk down the street and find himself attracted to a competitor's car—without those bothersome seats.

No doubt, progress is slowed because manufacturers are too hesitant, but the competition is great and the possibility of loss is real. So manufacturers must *always* make customer convenience an important design requirement. And convenience is just as important in power plants as it is everywhere else.

A smelly or noisy engine will lose customers. An engine that requires special skill from the driver will not interest the hundreds of bad drivers, who also buy cars. Even a superior engine probably will not sell well unless it can be depended upon to start. Despite the energy crisis, Americans expect tomorrow's engine to be at least as convenient as today's. Manufacturers, of course, must develop cleaner and more efficient engines. But they can never forget that customer convenience is also an important design requirement.

## REVIEW QUESTIONS

*Objective Questions*

Clean exhaust
Fuel economy
Light weight
Low cost
Reliability
Efficiency
Convenience

1. Which two design requirements, in the above list, were not considered very important until recently?

_____ A.   Convenience and fuel economy
_____ B.   Clean exhaust and reliability
_____ C.   Light weight and low cost
_____ D.   Clean exhaust and fuel economy

2. Study the following list: (1) materials (2) demand (3) size (4) useful life. Which design requirement are all these factors logically connected to?

_____ A.   Low cost
_____ B.   Clean exhaust
_____ C.   Convenience
_____ D.   Reliability

3. After reading this unit, Ivan the Inventor decided to abandon his hope of selling his new engine design to a major auto company. Earlier, he had proven that his engine had a thermal efficiency of 55%. Which of the following *most accurately* describes why he decided to give up?

_____ A.   He realized that his engine could never be made to operate conveniently enough.
_____ B.   He saw that his engine could never get its exhaust clean enough to meet federal regulations.
_____ C.   He found that the platinum parts he had designed into his engine would make it too expensive.
_____ D.   Any or all of the above could be correct, but with the information given there is no way to know for sure.

4. Re-read question three again. Notice the thermal efficiency of Ivan's engine. Which of the following should NOT have caused him to lose faith in his invention?

_____ A. He saw that his engine could never be made small enough for automotive use.

_____ B. He realized that his engine could never compete on fuel economy.

_____ C. His engine was too heavy to be practical.

_____ D. His engine would last so long that dealer's service departments would lose money.

5. Other things being equal, a manufacturer would rather that next year's engine be:

_____ A. As different from this year's engine as possible.

_____ B. As efficient as a Rankine cycle steam engine.

_____ C. As similar to this year's engine as possible.

_____ D. Both A and B but not C.

## Questions of Recall and Application

1. The design requirements discussed in this chapter are those that are important for mass-produced passenger cars. Suppose you were designing a racing engine. Which design requirements would be even more important than they are in passenger car engines? Which ones would be less important? Why? Name some design requirements not mentioned in this chapter which would be important in a racing engine.

2. How would the relative importance of the design requirements change if, instead of a car engine, you were designing a power plant for a farm tractor?

3. Some of the power plants you studied in Unit 3 have been used successfully in trucks and buses but not in cars. Why might this be? Are the design requirements of truck engines the same as or different from those of car engines? Explain.

# ENGINE CONSTRUCTION

# 5

# The Cylinder Block

Although we have concentrated on "background," you now know a lot that will help you solve practical problems in the shop. You have a general understanding of Otto-cycle theory. You know how various heat engines work. And you know the requirements that engineers work to meet when they design engines. You can—and should—use what you already know to help you understand *why* engines are constructed as they are. Now we are ready to study engine construction, beginning with the cylinder block.

## PURPOSE AND IMPORTANCE OF THE BLOCK

The cylinder block is the foundation of the engine—all other parts are attached to it (Figure 5–1). Its most important function is to provide a strong, unmovable mounting for the crankshaft and cylinders (Figure 5–2). The purpose of the crankshaft is to change the up-and-down motion of pistons inside those cylinders into rotary motion. For the engine to run properly, however, the moving parts must keep their exact alignments and design distances. The job of the block is, quite simply, to keep things straight inside the engine.

That job, however, is not as easy to do as it sounds. The engine block is constantly beset by rapid and extreme changes in its operational environment. Its average metal temperature on a cold morning will shoot from 0° F (−18° C) to 225° F (107° C) in minutes. Internal pressures from lubricants and coolants can exceed 100 pounds per

**Figure 5–1.** The block is the foundation of the modern automotive engine. *Courtesy of Pontiac Division, General Motors Corporation.*

**Figure 5–2.** The most important function of the block is to provide strong, rigid support for the crankshaft and cylinders. *Courtesy of Buick Division, General Motors Corporation.*

square inch (psi), and those from combustion gases top 2000 psi. Stresses on the block caused by piston and crankshaft movement can be measured in tons! To design a block that will keep every part in position despite these contending forces is no trivial accomplishment. Yet the block, on the average, has a longer service life than any other part of a modern engine.

## OBJECTIVES

When you have completed this chapter you should be able to:

- State the design function of the engine block and explain its importance.
- Name the engine block configurations shown in various photographs and drawings.
- Demonstrate, by answering specific questions, a basic knowledge of foundry and die-casting processes.
- Explain, when given specific examples, why a particular engine design was used for a given vehicle.

## IMPORTANT FACTS ABOUT ENGINE BLOCKS

Blocks for modern liquid-cooled engines are cast as single units. The cylinders, cooling jackets and crankshaft bearing supports are all built into one large metal part. Cylinders, usually, are simply large holes in the block that guide the pistons. Cooling jackets are open passages around the cylinders. Coolant traveling through these passages absorbs heat, carries it to the radiator, and releases it into the air. Crankshaft bearing mounts are molded onto the block at specially designed bulkheads. These bulkheads are ribbed in order to reinforce the block and properly distribute the forces from the crankshaft.

At the top of the block is a flat, machined surface called the block *deck*. The cylinder head is bolted to the block at this point. As you will see later, the head serves to seal the cylinder at the top just as the piston seals it at the bottom. Downward combustion pressure is transferred immediately from the piston to the crankshaft. So each combustion stroke, in effect, tries to blow the cylinder head off the top and the crankshaft off the bottom. Heavy bolts are placed at special reinforced locations in the block to offset these forces. These head bolts carry the load through reinforced areas within the block to the main bearing bulkheads. Likewise, the bolts which fasten the main bearing caps direct the forces of the crankshaft through special bolt bosses to these reinforced areas of the block. Thus, the crankshaft is fastened securely beneath the cylinders.

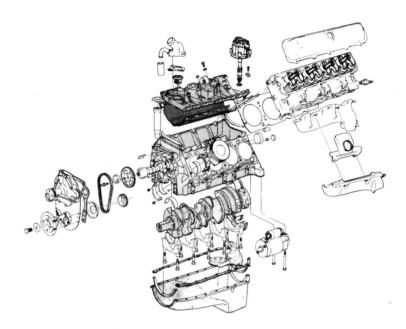

**Figure 5–3.**     These are the major parts of the engine block. *Courtesy of Oldsmobile Division, General Motors Corporation.*

## HOW BLOCKS ARE MANUFACTURED

The mechanic who has a general knowledge of foundry techniques has a real advantage. There is no better way for him to understand the "why's" behind the rules of good shop practice. Knowing how a block was built is a good way to understand what a mechanic should and should not do to it. Although more and more engine blocks are made of aluminum, the traditional practice is to cast the block in grey iron. So we will discuss first the manufacture of cast iron blocks.

The process begins with a container called a *core box*. Inside the core box is a liner shaped to match the *exterior* surfaces of the engine block. It is this core box that will serve as the container in which the block is cast. First, however, something must be done to make sure that openings are left inside the block for cylinders, water passages, etc. For this, manufacturers use special oil-sand cores.

Made of compressed sand and dampened with oil to keep them solid, these cores, or molds, are assembled inside the core box. They must be supported at some points from outside, and these supports leave "core holes" in the block. We will have more to say about core holes later, but first let us follow the casting cores inside that core box. After the lid goes on, a special alloy of molten iron is poured into the spaces between the cores and the liner. This iron, of course, forms the block. As the cast iron cools and sets, it breaks up the sand core. The cooled block is then taken out of the core box and shaken energetically to break up the remaining sand clods. Finally, the sand is poured out, and the block is sent to the machining line.

END CORE
CRANKCASE CORES
BARREL SLAB CORE
BARREL SLAB &
WATER JACKET CORE
ASSEMBLY
UPPER WATER JACKET CORE
LOWER WATER
JACKET CORE
FUEL PUMP
OPENING
CORE
OIL PUMP
MOUNTING
CORE
LOWER BORE CORE
END CORE
(FORMS FRONT OF FRONT OF
LEFT BLOCK AND REAR OF
RIGHT BLOCK)

**Figure 5–4.** To be sure that openings are left inside the block for cylinders, water passages, etc., manufacturers use special oil-sand cores. *Courtesy of Chrysler Corporation.*

On the machining line, special attention is given to the cylinder decks and to the rails where the oil pan and lifter cover fit. Cylinders are bored and honed. Oil passages and threaded openings are drilled. Those that require threading are tapped, and the main bearing mounts are bored. Two of these operations are especially important to the mechanic.

**Figure 5–5.** This automatic engine block machine can "broach" various block deck surfaces at speeds up to 165 feet per minute, while removing .187" (4.75mm) of material in a single cut. *Courtesy of Cincinnati Milacron.*

**Figure 5–6.** Automatic equipment for finishing modern engine blocks will broach, bore, drill, tap, and prepare the block for assembly. *Courtesy of Cross Manufacturing Company.*

## Oil Passages

The first is the drilling of the oil passages that carry lubricating oil to moving parts within the block. Most oil passages are drilled, starting from outside and cutting inward. When passages must make turns, intersecting holes are drilled (Figure 5–7). At times manufacturers may be forced to drill extra passages in order to route the oil properly. In such cases, they use special plugs to close off some passages and direct the oil where they want it. You will find three types of plugs used for this purpose. The first is a small, soft-metal plug which is simply wedged or snapped into place. These are similar to the core plugs (the so-called "freeze-out" plugs) discussed below. But sometimes, instead of using these, manufacturers simply thread the end of the passage and install a threaded pipe plug. The third method of plugging passages is used only with aluminum blocks. It consists, simply, of a steel ball, pressed securely in place. You can expect to encounter all three kinds of plugs, from time to time. So you should be aware of their purpose.

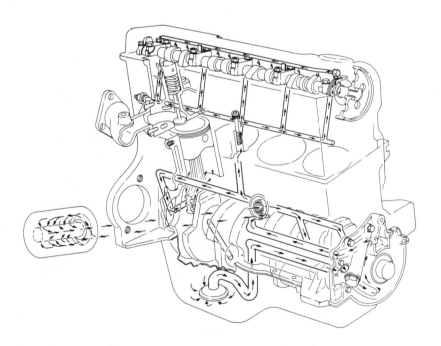

**Figure 5–7.** In the engine's block, intersecting holes are drilled to carry oil around turns to all the moving parts within the block. *Courtesy of American Motors Corporation.*

**Figure 5–8.**   Three types of plugs are used to close off some oil passages so that the oil is directed properly: (a) cup-type plug, (b) threaded plug, (c) pressed-in steel ball.

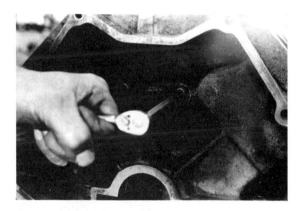

**Figure 5–9.**   The threaded type oil plug is easiest to remove and replace, but the mechanic will encounter all three types from time to time.

## Main Bearing Bores

Another machining-line operation that has special meaning for the mechanic is machining the main bearing bores. Though main bearing caps are cast separately from the block, they are machined and bolted in place before the final boring operation. These holes are machined to a very fine tolerance. To keep this precision, the cap must always remain just where it was when these holes were bored. This is why you will be told often that you must replace main bearing caps exactly as you find them. The mechanic must never interchange caps or reverse their ends.

## Core Holes

Earlier, we mentioned the core holes, left by the supports which fastened the sand-oil cores in place. Cast-iron blocks may have a number of such holes along the sides and in the ends. They lead through the outside wall into the coolant passages and are normally sealed with soft steel plugs. Mechanics often call these "freeze-out" plugs. A widespread myth says that, if the coolant freezes, the plugs will give way before the block is damaged. That may sometimes happen, but a good mechanic knows blind luck when he sees it. The real purpose of those holes, he knows, is to support the sand-oil cores during manufacture. Similar, though usually smaller, core holes appear in the deck. These, however, are blocked off by the head and gasket so only the freeze-out plugs are visible from outside.

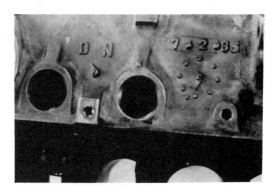

**Figure 5–10.** The so-called "freeze-out plugs," which are visible from outside, are actually core holes.

There are two common styles of freeze-out plugs. One is cup-shaped, with edges that taper like those of a pan. The cupped plug is driven into the machined core hole (Figure 5–11). This causes the tapered sides to wedge it tightly in place.

The second type of plug is dish-shaped. It only fits core holes that have been especially cut to form a "ledge" in the wall of the opening (Figure 5–12). The plug is placed over the hole with the "bottom" of the dish pointed out. Then it is struck with a special tool to make it turn "inside out." This forces the outside edges of the plug firmly against the walls and gives a good seal.

**Figure 5–11.** Installed, a cup-type plug looks like this.

**Figure 5–12.** This dish-shaped plug only fits core holes that have been especially cut to form a "ledge" in the wall of the opening.

## Aluminum Blocks

Until a few years ago, aluminum blocks were cast in foundries using procedures similar to those used in producing iron blocks. But the properties of aluminum were not well understood. So some traditional foundry methods, not suited to aluminum casting, continued to be used. This caused production problems and difficulties with quality control. During that period, the higher cost of aluminum also made its use in large displacement V–8 engines uneconomical. But with the perfection of aluminum die-casting in recent years, all this began to change. It now seems likely that more and more engine blocks will be die-cast of aluminum.

Die-casting is performed completely by machine. These complex machines force molten aluminum into precision steel molds, or dies. In a few minutes, the aluminum alloy cools, and the dies automatically move away from the cast piece. That block is then ejected from the machine, more hot aluminum is pumped in, and the machine begins casting another block. Despite the huge investment in these casting machines and the higher cost of aluminum, die-casting has several advantages. Blocks are produced much more quickly. Less skilled labor is needed, especially since the softer aluminum is easier to machine. And of course, the lighter weight of aluminum permits savings elsewhere in the car.

## MAJOR CONSIDERATIONS IN BLOCK DESIGN

### Choice of Material

The automotive engineer thinks very carefully about whether to use a block of aluminum or cast iron. He must choose the metal that is best for his design. But he cannot think only of the theoretical properties of the metals themselves. He must also consider the limitations of foundry technology. These limitations are especially important when he decides upon the shape of his block and the metal thicknesses needed in it.

### Thickness

Thickness gives strength to the block. Exact control of thickness is necessary, both to withstand load-caused stresses and to allow proper heat exchange between components. On the other hand, no part of the block should be thicker than necessary, for extra thickness means extra weight. Thus, blocks are thick only at key points: accessory mounting pads, strengthening ribs, and similar reinforced areas.

Such niceties of design are possible because modern foundries have virtually eliminated movement of the sand core during casting. This allows engineers to use very thin walls inside the block. Until about thirty years ago they could not do this because the slightest core movement during casting weakened thin walls. These advances in casting technology made the modern, lightweight V–8 engine possible. Inside the blocks of those V–8's, which dominated the industry from the 1940's into the 1970's, were intricate patterns of thin-walled passages. Only when the technology was developed to produce these thin walls could engineers make full use of the V–8 design. For reasons such as this, metal thickness is a major consideration whenever an engineer sets out to design a block.

**Figure 5–13.** Note the key points where the block is thickened by accessory mounting pads, strengthening ribs, etc.

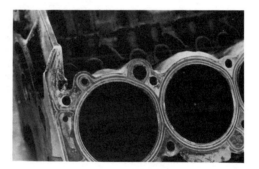

**Figure 5–14.** Only when the technology was developed to produce these thin internal walls could engineers make full use of the V-8 design.

## Shape

Another important consideration is shape. The placement of the cylinders and of all the moving parts affects the shape of the block. But the engineer is not completely free to arrange things as he wishes—his engine must fit into certain, specific cars. So the size and shape of their engine compartments may also limit his choices. To see how all these considerations work together, let us follow engineer Paul Sand through the beginning of his latest design job at United Motors. Both

Paul and his company are imaginary, but the kind of thinking he does in this example goes on all the time in Detroit.

Paul has just been asked to design the engine for United's new Consumer's Special. He knows that the Special is to be a front-engine, rear-wheel drive vehicle that weighs about 2500 pounds. It must carry five people and give reasonably good performance.

You probably already know that engines are sized according to their cubic inch displacement (cid). (You will learn in Unit 10 exactly what cid is and how to calculate it.) For now, just understand that Paul immediately begins thinking of the best displacement for the new engine. He figures that the Special requires an engine of around 150 cubic inches (2458 cc) to give the required performance and economy. Experience tells him that it is usually cheaper and more efficient to distribute his 150 cid among four cylinders.

**Figure 5–15.** Like all engine compartments, the compartment of a Dodge-Plymouth Horizon will only hold an engine of a specific size and shape. The engineer must consider the size of the compartment when designing his engine. *Courtesy of Chrysler Corporation.*

Paul also knows that it is generally best to plan an engine from the inside out. So he starts thinking about how he wants to arrange those four cylinders. The three basic patterns of cylinder placement are (1) in-line, (2) opposed, and (3) "V".

His simplest choice would be to build an *in-line* engine, placing the cylinders in a row, one after another. But in-line engines are long and tall. A 150 cid in-line power plant would not fit into the Consumer

Special's streamlined engine compartment. Another choice would be an *opposed* design. In an opposed engine, Paul would divide his cylinders into two pairs and place them on opposite sides of the crankshaft (Figure 5–16). This would make the engine shorter and flatter, but it would be too wide to fit between the front wheels. As a third choice, Paul could combine the in-line and opposing patterns. Instead of placing cylinders on opposite sides of the crankshaft, he could just slant them away from each other. This so-called "V" pattern produces a power plant that is lower and shorter than an in-line engine of the same size. Yet it is narrower than a comparable opposed engine.

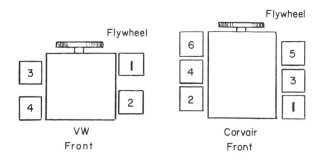

**Figure 5–16.** In an opposed engine, cylinders are divided into two pairs and placed on opposite sides of the crankshaft.

**Figure 5–17.** Arranging the cylinders in two pairs and placing them on opposite sides of the crankshaft make the engine shorter and flatter. *Courtesy of Volkswagen of America, Inc.*

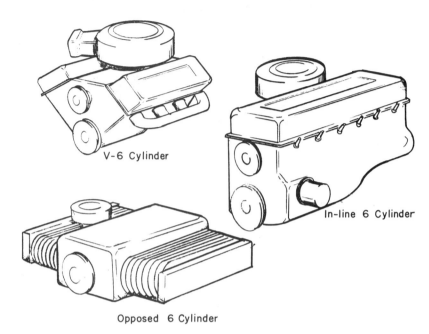

V-6 Cylinder

In-line 6 Cylinder

Opposed 6 Cylinder

**Figure 5–18.**   This V-8 engine is shorter and lower than an in-line engine, but it is still narrower than an opposed engine.

How could Paul be so sure that he should use a four-cylinder engine? The decision really is not as simple in practice as we have made it sound. If there were the slightest doubt, Paul would check out all possibilities before he made up his mind. But his judgement in this case was in keeping with standard trade practice. Generally, engines smaller than 150 cubic inches are built with four cylinders. Engines in the 150–250 cubic inch (2500–4097cc) range have six cylinders. And those larger than 250 cubic inches (4097cc) have eight.

Notice that we did not mention three, five, or seven-cylinder engines. Until recently, only even numbers of cylinders were used because it was easier to keep the crankshaft in balance with an even number of power impulses. But exceptions are now on the market. The three-cylinder Daihatsu Charade and the five-cylinder Audi (Figure 5–19) are two gasoline-powered exceptions. And Mercedes Benz has brought out a five-cylinder Diesel-powered passenger car (Figure 5–20). Since these "odd-numbered" engines seem to be performing well more of them may appear in the future.

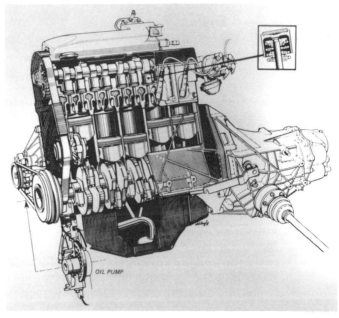

**Figure 5–19.** The Audi engine has five cylinders and is one of the few engines on the market with an odd number of cylinders. *Courtesy of Porsche-Audi, Volkswagen of America, Inc.*

**Figure 5–20.** This Mercedes-Benz is powered by a five-cylinder Diesel engine. *Courtesy of Mercedes-Benz of North America.*

## Block Designs for V–8 Engines

If Paul had been asked to design an engine for a very heavy car, he almost certainly would have chosen a V–8 block. Before World War II, however, this would not have been the case because large passenger car engines then were almost always "straight eights," that is in-line eight-cylinder power plants.

Straight eights were popular for a number of reasons. They ran smoothly, performed well, and produced maximum power at slow speeds. But the straight eight block is too long and tall for modern cars.

As soon as improved casting technology made possible the mass production of V–8 blocks, they began to dominate the large-car market. Besides being shorter and flatter, V–8 blocks are also lighter and stronger. And the V–8 engine has a number of operational advantages.

The V–8 block generally allows the engineer greater flexibility in designing the cylinder head and valve layout. Since V–8 blocks are "squarer" and more rigid, they can withstand heavier crankshaft loadings and higher speeds. These advantages translate into more power and greater fuel economy.

## Crankshaft Support

An important thing to know about any block is where and how it supports the crankshaft. Two patterns are in common use. One is the deep skirt or Y design. In this design, the center line of the crankshaft is completely "inside" the block (Figure 5–21). Notice in Figure 5–21 that the bottom of the block extends well below the crankcase bearing mounts. Surrounding the crankshaft with cast metal in this way provides maximum strength and rigidity. The part of the casting that extends down around the crankshaft is the so-called skirt. Deep skirted engines, being stronger and heavier, usually run quieter and last longer. They are widely used in trucks, heavy equipment, and large passenger cars.

Unfortunately, however, they are also bigger, heavier, and more expensive. To offset these disadvantages, manufacturers sometimes do away with the skirts and go to an *underslung* crankshaft and a V block (Figure 5–22). Notice that, in this design, the center line of the crankshaft is very close to the bottom rail of the block. In a sense, the crankshaft hangs beneath the block by its main bearing caps. Although they are lighter and cheaper, V blocks do sacrifice some strength.

**Figure 5–21.** In the deep skirt block design, the center line of the crankshaft is completely "inside" the block.

**Figure 5–22.** Manufacturers use an underslung crankshaft block to offset the disadvantages of the skirts.

# Cylinders

In cast-iron engines, the common practice is to cast the cylinder wall right into the block. To produce the finished cylinder, the manufacturer simply machines the cast-iron walls of the cylinder.

Other methods of cylinder construction are also used. The two most common are the so-called wet-sleeve and dry-sleeve designs. Dry sleeves are used in many aluminum blocks and in heavy duty commercial engines. The sleeve is an alloy steel liner that is simply pressed into the cylinder hole that was cast into the block.

Wet sleeves are most likely to be found in tractors, trucks, and heavy equipment. They are also popular among some European car manufacturers. They are called wet sleeves because they come in direct contact with the engine coolant. Wet sleeves usually slide into special holes bored in the bottom of the block. Rubber "0" rings are used to seal the sleeve to the block at the bottom of the hole, and the head gasket prevents leakage at the top. This keeps the coolant from leaking into the crankcase or the combustion chambers.

Another kind of cylinder that the mechanic sees occasionally is the one used in early Chevrolet Vega engines. Blocks for these engines were die-cast of a special silicon-aluminum alloy, but did not use dry sleeves. Instead, a special etching process was used to remove the aluminum from the cylinder walls. This process exposed the silicon and, in effect, created a hard silicon lining. Chevrolet, however, soon redesigned those blocks to use cast-iron sleeves.

**Figure 5–23.**   Another kind of cylinder that the mechanic sees occasionally is the one used in early Chevrolet Vega engines. In this process, the metal is etched away from the special silicon aluminum alloy which formed the block. This leaves the cylinders lined with silicon.

## Skirted and Skirtless Cylinders

Cylinders in most deep block designs are *skirtless*. Notice in Figure 5–24 that the bottom edge of the cylinder is completely surrounded by the cast iron block. This design gives the cylinder wall excellent support and maximum exposure to the coolant. In blocks with underslung crankshafts, however, cylinder walls may be *skirted*. It is important to understand the difference between a skirted *block* and a block with *skirted cylinders*.

**Figure 5–24.** Cylinders in most deep-block designs are skirtless.

The "skirt" on a block, as you learned above, serves to enclose the crankshaft and add rigidity to the block. Skirted cylinders, on the other hand, more often appear on blocks that are not skirted. They simply extend their cylinder walls down into the crankcase (Figure 5–25). This provides additional guidance to the piston, so that—on the downstroke—it can drop almost to the bottom of the block. A big advantage of skirted cylinders is that they enable the engineer to reduce the height of his engine without reducing its displacement. Their disadvantages, obviously, are the sacrifice of strength and the fact that the coolant never comes in direct contact with the cylinder skirts.

**Figure 5–25.** Skirted cylinders more often appear on blocks that are *not* skirted. They simply extend their cylinder walls down into the crankcase.

## Cylinder Numbering

Because the mechanic must have a foolproof way of referring to a specific cylinder on a specific engine, manufacturers number the cylinders on their engines. Though some numbering practices have become customary, variations are so common that they often cause trouble. Whenever the slightest doubt exists, the smart mechanic will check the service manual to learn the numbering system.

American manufacturers consistently number the cylinders from front to rear. In applying this rule to a traverse-mounted engine, just remember that the accessory end is always the "front." The number one cylinder is at that end. It is important to remember, however, that some foreign manufacturers begin numbering at the rear, or flywheel, end of the motor. Cylinders on V–8 engines are most commonly numbered in the order in which their connecting rods attach to the crankshaft.

In opposed engines, the sequence varies from manufacturer to manufacturer. Numbering may start at the flywheel end, go down one side of the block and back up the other. That is the sequence used by Volkswagen, but other manufacturers use other systems. The best rule, whatever the engine, is to check the manual. That Is even better advice for working with opposed engines.

Figure 5–26 shows the more common numbering systems used by American manufacturers.

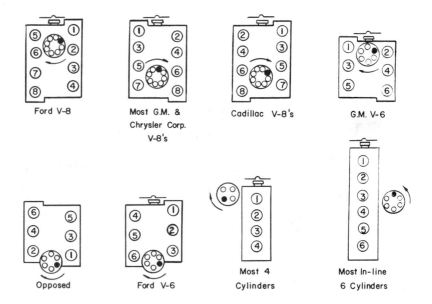

**Figure 5–26.** Manufacturers number the cylinders on their engines as a foolproof way of referring to a specific cylinder on a specific engine.

# REVIEW QUESTIONS

*Objective Questions*

1. Joe says: "Most steel engine blocks are sand cast."

   Jim says: "Most aluminum blocks are die cast."

   Who is correct?

   _____ A.  Joe only
   _____ B.  Jim only
   _____ C.  Both are correct
   _____ D.  Both are wrong

2. Why is a V–8 block better suited for use in modern passenger cars than a "straight 8" block?

   _____ A.  It is not as tall
   _____ B.  It is not as long
   _____ C.  Neither A nor B are correct reasons.
   _____ D.  Both A and B are correct reasons.

3. Which block design most commonly uses skirted cylinders?

   _____ A.  Skirtless V–block
   _____ B.  Skirted Y–block
   _____ C.  In-line blocks of six or more cylinders
   _____ D.  Both A and B above, but not C

4. Which block design is most likely to produce problems of over-heating in the bottom portion of the cylinders?

   _____ A.  Skirted Y–block
   _____ B.  Skirtless V–block
   _____ C.  In-line block
   _____ D.  Opposed block

5. Mutt says that it usually costs more to manufacture an engine with wet sleeves than a comparable engine with dry sleeves.

   Jeff says that wet-sleeve type blocks are found on many foreign cars.

   Who is correct?

   _____ A.  Mutt only
   _____ B.  Jeff only
   _____ C.  Neither Mutt nor Jeff
   _____ D.  Both Mutt and Jeff

6. Paul says that engines smaller than 150 cid (2458 cc) usually have six cylinders.

Peter says that engines larger than 250 cid (4097 cc) usually have eight cylinders.

Who is right?

_____ A.  Paul only
_____ B.  Peter only
_____ C.  Both Paul and Peter
_____ D.  Neither Paul nor Peter

7. Ted says that aluminum blocks are cheaper than cast iron.

Tim says that less skilled labor is needed to manufacture die-cast aluminum blocks than cast-iron blocks.

Tony says that building engines with aluminum blocks makes it possible to save money elsewhere in the car.

Who is correct?

_____ A.  Ted only
_____ B.  Tim only
_____ C.  Tony only
_____ D.  All the above

8. The most important function of the engine block is:

_____ A.  To support the head assembly
_____ B.  To give weight and stability to the car
_____ C.  To hold the engine properly in the engine compartment
_____ D.  To provide a strong, unmovable mounting for the crankshaft and cylinders.

Following are four pictures of different kinds of engine blocks. In the space provided place the letter designation of the picture that shows

9. An opposed engine design_____

10. A skirted Y–block_____

11. A skirtless V–block_____

12. An in-line block_____

(a)                               (b)

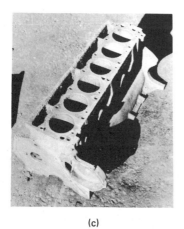

(c)                               (d)

## Questions of Recall and Application

1.  Explain fully the advantages and disadvantages of both die-cast and sand-cast blocks.

2.  Why were V–8 engines not widely used until after World War II?

3.  Describe the most common cylinder numbering systems for

    A.  In-line engines
    B.  V–8 engines

4. Choose any car to which you have access. As a special "head exercise," explain to your own satisfaction why the engineer chose that particular engine design for that car. Could any other designs have worked as well in that chassis? What would be their effects on the following?

   A.  Overall weight
   B.  Weight distribution
   C.  Fuel economy
   D.  Handling and power
   E.  Ease of maintenance
   F.  Cost

5. Using the following photograph as a guide, see if you can name from memory the parts of the block.

UNIT

# 6

# The Crankshaft, Bearings, and Lubricant System

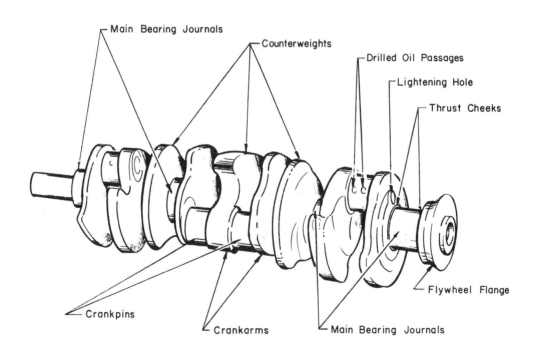

The main function of the block, as you learned in Unit 5, is to provide solid support for the crankshaft. And the purpose of the crankshaft is to convert the up-and-down motion produced by the pistons into rotary motion. The mechanics of this conversion are essentially the same as those used in pedaling a bicycle (Figure 6–1). Every schoolboy knows that the up-and-down motion of his legs causes the bicycle pedals to go *around*. And since those pedals are attached to the chain sprocket, that new *rotary* motion is carried by the chain to the rear wheel.

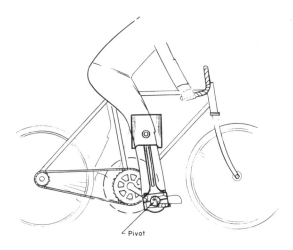

Pivot

**Figure 6–1.** The function of the crankshaft is to solve a familiar problem in mechanics: It converts up-and-down, or "reciprocal," motion into rotary motion.

Figure 6–2 compares the mechanical components of the bicycle with those of the engine crankshaft. Note that the pedals of the bicycle rotate around the main shaft or "axle" of the sprocket. The comparable center of rotation for the crankshaft is the center line of the main bearing journals. Main bearing journals are the sections of the crankshaft where it is fastened to the block (Figure 6–3). With these sections held securely in place by the main bearings, the crankshaft rotates in place. Since the sections between the bearings are offset, like cranks, they are sometimes called *crank pins* or *crank throws*. (Their more technical name is *connecting rod journals*.) It is at these crank pins that the crankshaft is linked to the piston by *connecting rods* (Figure 6–4). As the pistons move up and down like the legs of a cyclist, the connecting rod journals revolve, just as bicycle pedals do. So in both cases energy which goes in as up-and-down, or "*reciprocal,*" motion is turned immediately into circular motion.

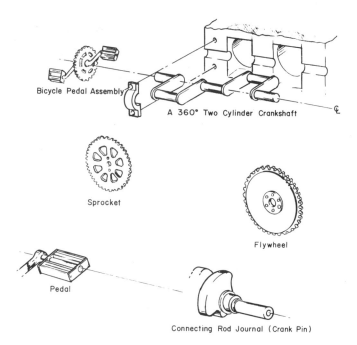

Bicycle Pedal Assembly

A 360° Two Cylinder Crankshaft

Sprocket

Flywheel

Pedal

Connecting Rod Journal (Crank Pin)

**Figure 6–2.** Each functioning part of the crankshaft matches a similar part of the bicycle pedal assembly.

**Figure 6–3.** The main bearing journals are held securely to the block by the main bearings. This permits the crankshaft to rotate in place but keeps vibration to a minimum.

**Figure 6-4.** The pistons are attached to the crankpins by means of connecting rods.

The functional similarity of the crankshaft and the bicycle pedal assembly has been stressed for a reason. It should suggest, correctly, that common sense will take you a long way towards understanding this extremely important part of the engine. But it should not mislead you into believing that crankshaft operation is a simple subject. Compared to the pressure exerted by a cyclist, the forces that propel the crankshaft are enormous. Every horsepower that reaches the rear wheels must pass through it. So the shape, balance, and construction of the crankshaft must meet extremely exacting standards to ensure efficient engine operation.

## OBJECTIVES

When you have completed this chapter, you should be able to:

- Identify the important parts of the crankshaft by using their proper technical names and explain the function of each.

- Demonstrate, by answering specific questions, an understanding of how each of the following contributes to correct crankshaft operation:

Balance
Firing order
Cylinder angle
Stroke
Lubrication

- Explain the advantages and disadvantages of both forging and casting, as techniques for use in the manufacture of crankshafts for automotive engines.
- Demonstrate, by answering specific questions, a knowledge of the properties needed in material used to make crankshaft bearings.
- Demonstrate, by answering specific questions, a basic knowledge of bearing function and design, including familiarity with the following:

  Common types of bearings
  Bearing crush
  Oil grooves
  Oil holes
  Bearing location methods

- Demonstrate, by answering specific questions, a general knowledge of the design and function of the engine lubricating system.
- Explain which bearing materials are and are not suitable for each specific automotive application.
- Apply the knowledge gained from this and preceding chapters to go beyond what you have been taught and correctly answer questions that pose problems for you to think through for yourself.

## CRANKSHAFT DESIGN AND CONSTRUCTION

To carry its tremendous loads, the crankshaft must be carefully designed and made of materials that are equal to the task.

## Construction

Almost all automotive crankshafts today are manufactured in one of two ways: casting or forging. We shall discuss first the older method, forging.

**Forging.**  There are two methods of forging. In the first, a red hot chunk of steel, called a *billet,* is hammered into approximate shape by a special machine known as a drop forge. The machine then drops the still-hot billet into a special die and continues to pound it until it takes the shape of the die. By sending it through a series of dies, the manufacturer shapes the billet more and more like a finished crankshaft. Finally it emerges as what is called a crankshaft *blank*. The blank is then machined into a finished crankshaft.

In the method just explained, the forging of the crankshaft puts crank throws correctly in place from the outset. The second method differs only in that the crank throws are all forged on the same plane as the main bearing journals. Thus, at this stage in its manufacture the crankshaft blank could lie flat on a bench. All its bends are in two dimensions. Then, in an additional step, the still-hot casting is twisted, in order to "wind" all the crank pins to their proper angles (Figure 6–5). Afterwards, the blank is heat-treated and machined to complete the crankshaft.

**Figure 6–5.**   The presence of forging lines shows that this crankshaft was forged in a single plane and then twisted. The twisting serves to "wind" connecting rod journals into position.

The advantage of forged crankshafts is strength; the disadvantage is cost. The strength is due, in part, to the greater density of the steel used in forging. But the forging process also leaves the grain in the steel running parallel to the major lines of force that will act on the crankshaft. So both factors combine to make forged crankshafts extremely rugged (Figure 6–6). For this reason, they are preferred for performance and heavy duty engines. Because of the greater cost of forging, however, many automobile crankshafts are not forged but cast.

**Figure 6–6.** Because of the density of the material used in them and the direction of the grain in the steel, forged crankshafts are much stronger. For this reason, they are preferred for performance and heavy duty applications.

**Casting.** Improvements in foundry technology make it possible for crankshafts to be cast to exact standards of shape and weight. Cast crankshafts can be made of ductile cast iron, which is much cheaper than the 1045–4340 steel required in forging. Precision casting also means that cast crankshaft blanks require very little machining. This, too, reduces cost.

In addition to the loss in strength, cast cranks also have the disadvantage of being slightly bigger. Because they are made of lighter iron, the counterweights, which help to keep the crankshaft in balance, must be bigger.

# Design

To do its job properly, the crankshaft must turn smoothly in place. The slightest bumpiness or irregularity at high speeds will cause energy to be lost and produce needless stress on the bearings, connecting rods, and block. So the crankshaft must be designed to maximize balance and minimize vibration.

# Forces to be Balanced

We can better understand why balance is so important if we think for a moment about the forces acting on the crankshaft. These forces are of two kinds.

**Static Forces.** A handy way to remember the effect of static forces is to associate the word *static* with the word *status*. Just remember that static forces tend always to *keep* the crankshaft in its present *status*. If the crankshaft is at rest, the static forces tend to keep it at rest. An outside force must use energy to start it moving. But once it turns over, the static forces tend to keep it moving. If the crankshaft is properly designed, the static forces tend to keep every part spinning in exactly the same pattern of rotation. It must then be stopped by outside forces.

**Dynamic Forces.**    These other forces, which act on the crankshaft from outside, are called dynamic forces. Whereas, static forces tend to keep the crankshaft in its present state, dynamic forces tend to change things. Some of them, like the frictional drag of the main bearings, are undesirable side effects of imperfect "cures."

Others, like the power strokes of the connecting rods are central to the function of the crankshaft (Figure 6–7). Every power stroke tends to speed up the crankshaft so that it can continue doing its job. So neither dynamic forces nor static forces are all good nor all bad. They are just factors that engineers and mechanics deal with. But where crankshafts are concerned, they are very important factors.

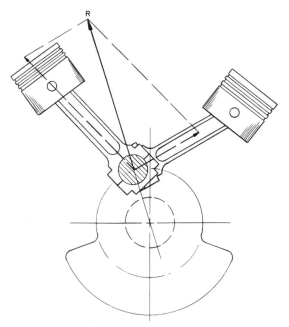

**Figure 6–7.** When all the forces acting on the crankshaft are combined in engine operation, their combined effect tends to "lift" the crankshaft in the direction of the arrow.

Dynamic forces are important because every substance—even steel—has some "give." Even a forged crankshaft flexes and bends under pressure. And whatever bends the crankshaft is moving it out of the circle of its intended rotation. If this *deflection* is great enough, it upsets the balance of the static forces and causes wobbling and vibration. Too much deflection will lead, in time, to metal fatigue, breakage, and catastrophic damage to the engine (Figure 6–8). It is important, therefore, that crankshafts be designed to balance both static and dynamic forces.

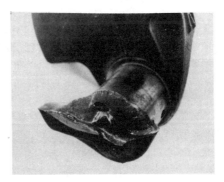

**Figure 6–8.** This crankshaft probably operated thousands of miles before its partial fracture gave way completely. The flexing of normal operation had polished the outer edges of both parts to a high finish by the time the crankshaft failed.

## Static Balance

If you have ever driven on a tire that was badly out of balance, you no doubt remember how the constant hammering of the heavier side on the pavement made the whole car shake. That illustrates the importance of static balance. Anything that causes uneven rotational forces produces much the same effect in the crankshaft. The most important factor in keeping static forces in balance is the crankshaft's shape. This is particularly evident in the size and placement of the crank throws and the use of counterweights.

### Size and placement of crank throws

To maintain static balance, the connecting rod journals are spaced evenly around the axis of the crankshaft. Moreover, the offset of each of these crank throws is exactly one-half the piston stroke. Extreme accuracy is necessary in most crankshaft dimensions for a number of reasons. But the simple fact that bigger journals are heavier makes it obvious that inequalities in the size of crank throws will tend to create static imbalance.

**Counterweights.** In practice, however, engineers must consider more than the weight distribution of the crankshaft itself. The bottom part of the connecting rod rotates with the crank pin. So engineers add to the crankshaft, at carefully calculated points, heavy sections called *counterweights* (Figure 6–9). These counterweights are always heavy enough to balance the centrifugal force produced by the rotating parts. Usually they are made a little heavier. On most engines, the additional weight also helps reduce vibration due to the up-and-down pounding of the connecting rods. The forces from this up-and-down piston movement, of course, are not static but dynamic. Thus, on most engines, counterweights contribute to both static and dynamic balance.

**Figure 6–9.** Counterweights are added to the crankshaft to balance the centrifugal force produced by moving parts. On most cars, additional weight is added to compensate for part of the reciprocating forces as well.

**Calculating the Placement of Crank Throws.** It takes a good command of physics and mathematics to calculate exactly the forces acting on a crankshaft. But it is a simple matter to figure how crank throws should be spaced. The goal, remember, is to place them evenly around the axis of the crankshaft.

Our basic Otto-cycle theory reminds us that all pistons must complete all four strokes in two turns of the crankshaft. Since there are 360° in a circle, two turns of the crankshaft equals 2 × 360° or 720° of rotation. To find the angles between crank throws, we simply divide the degrees of rotation (720°) by the number of cylinders. It works like this:

| Degrees of Rotation | | Number of Cylinders | | Angle Between Crank Throws |
|:---:|:---:|:---:|:---:|:---:|
| 720° | ÷ | 4 | = | 180° |
| 720° | ÷ | 6 | = | 120° |
| 720° | ÷ | 8 | = | 90° |

Figure 6–10 shows at least one example of a crankshaft built according to each calculation.

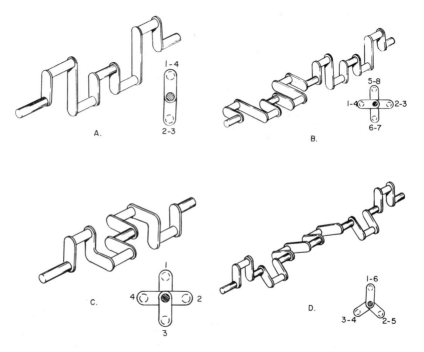

**Figure 6–10.** Crank throws must be placed exactly to maintain crankshaft balance and provide for even firing order. Here are some common patterns.

## Dynamic Balance

The same factors often influence both static and dynamic balance. We mentioned that this was true of crankshaft counterweights. In this section, you will see that it is also true of some other factors we have already discussed. Usually, though, when we speak of dynamic balance, we have something different in mind. We are thinking of design features like cylinder placement and firing order or of engine parts like the flywheel and vibration dampener.

Now that you know how to calculate the best positions for the crank throws, let us consider an aspect of static balance that is closely related to crank pin placement.

**Firing Order.**    The order in which the pistons transmit power impulses to the crankshaft is important to keeping it in balance. To understand this better, let us suppose that we ignored firing order. What would happen if we took a six-cylinder in-line engine and fired the cylinders in order, from front to rear (1–2–3–4–5–6)?

Let us assume, for simplicity, that the crankshaft was already turning at a moderate speed and that the static forces were in balance. The power impulse from number one cylinder is, of course, a powerful dynamic force. It slams downward on the connecting rod journal with a load of more than two tons. So it tends to "jerk" the crankshaft into a faster rotation. But remember that this force acts most strongly on the very front of the crankshaft. The rest of the crankshaft, being in static balance, tends to maintain the old speed. It wants to lag behind the powered end. If we now fire number two cylinder, also at the front end of the crankshaft, this only makes the problem worse. By the time we have fired all cylinders in this order, the crankshaft will be twisted somewhat like a rubber band. And the static forces will be in discord. The harder the crankshaft tries to unwind, the more vibrations there are.

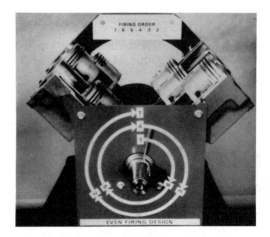

**Figure 6–11.**  Buick's new even-firing V-6 provides a good example of how modern technology continues to develop solutions for engineering problems that have long been considered "impossible." *Courtesy of Buick Division, General Motors Corporation.*

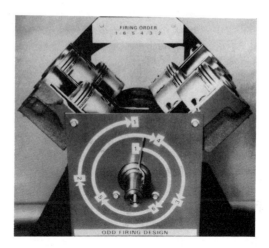

**Figure 6–12.** Until 1977, the V-6 engine was handicapped by an uneven firing order. This required excessively heavy counterweights on the crankshaft and an extra-heavy flywheel. *Courtesy of Buick Division, General Motors Corporation.*

To prevent this twisting effect, firing order is carefully controlled. Firing is timed so that the power impulse always tends to "boost" the lagging section of the crankshaft. Actually, most six-cylinder, in-line engines fire either 1–5–3–6–2–4 or 1–4–2–6–3–5. Notice that both orders spread out the power impulses along the crankshaft.

**Cylinder Angle.** With any engine design except the in-line or the opposed arrangement, we must also consider the problem of cylinder angle. Obviously, firing order and cylinder angle must be considered together in the design, for instance, of a V–type engine. And it happens that we can figure the proper angle with the same formula we use to calculate the angles for crankshaft throws. All we do is take the number of degrees in two revolutions (720°) and divide by the number of cylinders.

| Degrees in Two Crankshaft Revolutions | | Number of Cylinders | | Desired Angle Between Cylinders |
|---|---|---|---|---|
| 720° | ÷ | 6 | = | 120° or 60°* |
| 720° | ÷ | 8 | = | 90° |
| 720° | ÷ | 12 | = | 60° or 120°* |

*After using this formula to calculate cylinder angles for V–type engines, we always have two options. Obviously we can slant our cylinders at the angle indicated by the number we get from our division. Our second option is to subtract the resulting number from 180° and use the remainder. Thus V–6's and V–12's will both deliver balanced power impulses with cylinders that are either 120° or 60° apart.

Not all V–type engines are designed according to this formula, but the exceptions require special measures to ensure balance. Buick's 1975 V–6 provides a good example. Like earlier V–6's manufactured by General Motors, this engine had a 90° V–block. Also, like them, it contained a crankshaft with three crank throws spaced 120° apart. Of course, this combination produced uneven firing impulses. Though special steps were taken to compensate for them, Buick, in 1977, introduced a redesigned crankshaft that provided an even firing order. The new-type crankshaft has six connecting rod journals instead of three.

The even distribution of firing impulses improved crankshaft balance and reduced vibration so much that twenty pounds of weight could be removed from the flywheel.

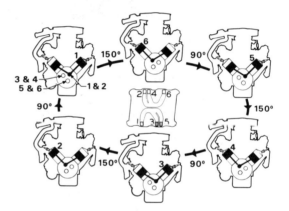

**Figure 6–13.** Uneven firing order required in production V-6 engine prior to Buick's development of its new split-throw crankshaft. *Courtesy of Buick Division, General Motors Corporation.*

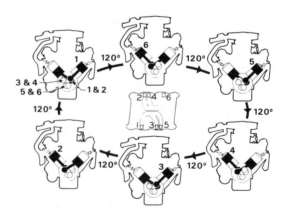

**Figure 6–14.** The Split-throw crankshaft made possible an even firing order in the 90° V-6 engine. It replaced the older crankshaft shown in Figure 6–13. *Courtesy of Buick Division, General Motors Corporation.*

**Figure 6–15.** By using the split-throw crankshaft, Buick was able to get an even, 120° firing sequence in the V-6. *Courtesy of Buick Division, General Motors Corporation.*

**Flywheel.** The purpose of the flywheel, as you learned in Unit 3, is to absorb kinetic energy from the power strokes and smooth out the rotation of the crankshaft. In effect, it converts a dynamic force into a static force. Its weight causes it to resist changes in crankshaft speed. So the flywheel is an important factor in dynamic balance.

**Figure 6–16.** The purpose of the flywheel is to absorb kinetic energy from the power strokes and thus to ''smooth out'' the rotation of the crankshaft.

**Vibration Dampener.** Many crankshaft designs also include a smaller flywheel at the accessory end. The primary purpose of this *vibration dampener* (sometimes called a *dynamic balancer* or *harmonic balancer*) is to assist in the control of torsional vibration. But it may double as a source of power for such belt-driven accessories as the alternator, water pump, etc.

The vibration dampener consists of a weighted outer ring bonded to an inner hub by a layer of rubber (Figure 6–17). As the firing impulses tend to "wind up" the crankshaft, the static forces in the outer ring tend to keep an even speed. This drag flexes the rubber and smoothes out the differences in speed. The flexing rubber absorbs the small amounts of energy involved in the crankshaft "winding" and releases it into the air as heat.

**Figure 6–17.** The layer of rubber in the vibration dampener enables it to compensate somewhat for the crankshaft's tendency to "wind up" during operation.

# ENGINE BEARINGS

All engines have some moving and some stationary parts. Where moving parts come into contact with stationary parts, bearings are often necessary. A bearing has two functions: It supports the moving part and reduces friction.

## Bearing Function No. 1: Support

In the case of the crankshaft, "support" means more than "holding up" this very heavy part. To support the crankshaft, the bearings must also withstand the hundreds of pounds of force that hammer each connecting rod journal 250 or more times a minute. And the support must be complete. A "give" of only .002 of an inch (.05mm) is enough to upset the dynamic balance of the crankshaft and perhaps ruin the engine.

## Bearing Function No. 2: Reduction of Friction

Imagine that some shade-tree mechanic somewhere tried to build an engine without main bearings. Perhaps he looked at that mirror-smooth finish on the crankshaft journals and was impressed. He may have reasoned that if he could machine the mounts on the block to a matching smoothness he could do away with these bothersome bearings. What is going to happen when he tries out this idea? Why won't it work?

**What Causes Friction?** If he could only look at one of these polished metal surfaces through a microscope, he would know immediately (Figure 6–18). Viewed close up, even the smoothest surface looks like a vast expanse of mountains, knolls, hills, and valleys. Figure 6–19 shows what happens when two of these smooth surfaces come into contact. Notice that only the "peaks" of the "mountains" actually touch. But if we apply a heavy load to one surface, as in Figure 6–20, tremendous pressure focuses on those tiny points of actual contact. This pressure generates heat, actually welding these tiny contact points together. If one of the surfaces is moving, the welds are immediately broken. But the mountaintops saw against each other, causing resistance and generating heat. This breaks off some of the mountaintops and creates loose metal "boulders" which roll around and cut away even more metal (Figure 6–21).

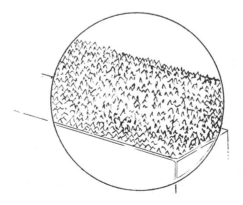

**Figure 6–18.** Even a polished metal surface appears as rough as a moonscape when viewed under a microscope.

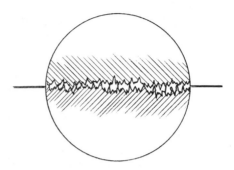

**Figure 6–19.** When two "smooth" metal surfaces slide against each other, there is always enough roughness to cause friction.

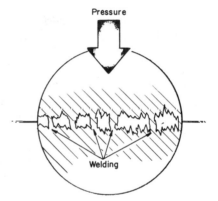

**Figure 6–20.** If metal parts contact each other under heavy load, the pressure will generate enough heat to "weld" their microscopic "mountaintops" together.

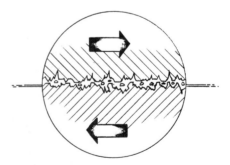

**Figure 6–21.** If the welded parts slide against each other, the motion breaks the welds, and chunks of the mountaintops will begin rolling around, causing more heat and further wear.

This magnified view illustrated what happens whenever two metal surfaces rub each other hard enough to cause friction. An important point about friction is that contact between *similar* materials creates more friction than contact between different materials. You can see why this is true by glancing at Figure 6–22. Notice that the "mountains" on similar materials are about the same size. They interlock quite well, and when one surface moves, something has to give. But surfaces on dissimilar materials don't fit together as well so they take a smaller "bite" off each other.

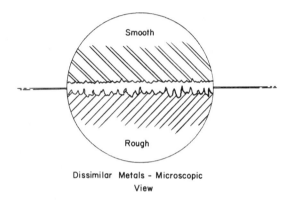

Dissimilar Metals - Microscopic
View

**Figure 6–22.** When dissimilar materials contact each other, their surfaces take less of a bite out of each other. This explains why bearings reduce friction.

To reduce friction between moving parts, therefore, automotive engineers often insert a dissimilar substance between them. For this purpose, the two most commonly used substances are lubricants and bearings.

## Characteristics of Bearing Materials

Because the parts protected by bearings are often crucially important, the bearings must be made of suitable materials. A good bearing material has at least seven characteristics.

**1. Fatigue Strength.**    Fatigue strength is the number of hours at a specific pressure the bearing operates before deteriorating. For the bearing to provide the necessary support to a moving part while withstanding heavy loads, it must have great fatigue strength.

**2. Conformability.** A material that is fluid enough or flexible enough to adjust its own shape to the space around it is said to have conformability. It is important for main bearings and connecting rod bearings to be conformable. This enables them to take up some of the "slack" when the crankshaft or connecting rod wears, warps, or bends.

**3. Embedability.** The two most common causes of bearing failure are insufficient lubrication and excessive dirt. Engineers try to reduce damage due to dirt by making bearings of soft materials. These soft materials are said to have high embedability. That is, they yield to dirt particles and trap them. This prevents the damage that those particles would otherwise do to the more expensive machined parts.

**4. Surface Action.** Though bearings are normally used in combination with lubrication, they must be able to function "dry" for short periods. During start-up and under heavy load conditions, for instance, the crankshaft turns with little or no lubrication. At such times the bearing's own surface action is the crankshaft's only protection from friction wear.

**5. Resistance to Corrosion.** During engine operation, combustion by-products interact with each other and with the lubricating oil to produce various acids. Because acids tend to corrode metal, and corroded metal soon deteriorates, it is important that bearings be made of material that resists this corrosion.

**6. Temperature Strength.** Many substances that meet the other requirements for bearings start to soften or melt at high temperatures. A molten bearing would obviously be unable to carry the necessary loads. For this reason, a good bearing material must be able to maintain its strength at high temperatures.

**7. Thermal Conductivity.** Inside the combustion chamber, heat is the mechanic's friend. There, it expands the working fluid and produces power. But the heat energy that is lost through friction is worse than a waste. It is a destructive force that must be disposed of. Otherwise, it will break down the lubricating oil, further increase friction, and eventually cause the moving parts to "seize," or weld together. Thermal conductivity is the bearing's ability to absorb heat and carry it quickly to the bearing housing. This makes it possible for the metal back on the bearing to release the heat to the coolant or the oil. A bearing that conducts heat well runs cooler and lasts longer.

## Commonly Used Bearing Materials

No single metal has all seven of the characteristics we would like in a bearing. So most bearings combine two or three metals into precision inserts which fit into machined bores in the block, connecting rod, or other housing. Two-metal, or *bi-metal*, bearings may consist of a steel backing coated on the "inside" with a soft bearing material (Figure 6–23). A three-metal, or *tri-metal*, bearing might begin with a similar steel backing, but bonded onto it are two different layers, each consisting of a different soft metal (Figure 6–24).

**Figure 6–23.** Bimetal bearings usually consist of a steel backing coated on the inside with a soft bearing material. *Courtesy of TRW Corporation.*

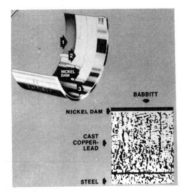

**Figure 6–24.** Trimetal bearings usually have two layers of different bearing materials bonded to a steel backing. *Courtesy of TRW Corporation.*

**Babbitt.** The most common of these soft metals is called babbitt, which is itself an alloy, or mixture, of four metals. Babbitt contains 83% lead, 15% antimony, 1% tin, and 1% arsenic. The conformability, embedability, and surface action of babbitt are superb. But being made mostly of lead, it has rather low temperature strength. Its melting point is around 475°F (245°C).

**Copper-Lead Alloy.** Improved temperature strength results when a copper-lead alloy is bonded to a steel backing at high temperatures. Copper-lead bearings also have superior fatigue strength. However, they corrode easier and have less satisfactory surface action.

**Aluminum.** Well-suited for modern automobile bearings, aluminum can be alloyed with various other metals for various applications. For certain uses, aluminum bearings are cast in a single unit, with no backing. More commonly, aluminum is combined with steel backing to produce bi- or tri-metal bearings. Aluminum equals or excels other bearing materials on every point but cost. To reduce cost, manufacturers sometimes make only the bottom half of a main bearing of aluminum. This gains the advantages of aluminum at the point of greatest loading. But it allows them to save by using a cheaper material for the top half of the same bearing.

## Bearing Designs

Many different types of bearings are in use. But for automotive power plants the multi-layered precision insert design mentioned earlier is by far the most common. These inserts are manufactured to such exacting specifications that no machining or hand fitting is necessary.

**The Full-Circle Bearing.** Precision insert bearings are found in two varieties: (1) the one-piece or "full circle" bearing and (2) the two-piece, "split" bearing design (Figure 6–25). The full circle design is used where it is possible to slip the rotating shaft through the bearing. Many camshaft bearings are of the full-circle type.

**The Split Bearing.** Where the bearing must be assembled around the shaft, the split bearing is used. Most main bearings and connecting rod bearings are split bearings.

The *bearing housing,* for split bearings, consists of a *saddle* and its accompanying *cap.* The saddle is the fixture that is built into the bulk of the part. In a main bearing, the saddle, or bearing mount, is supported by cross-webs in the block. On a connecting rod, it is the part built into the bottom of the rod. The cap is the detachable half-circle that is removed when bearings are installed. This process is used for the most common type of split bearing, known as the *straight shell* design.

**Figure 6–25.** Full-circle bearings (left) are used where it is possible to slip the rotating shaft through the bearing during installation. Where this is not possible, split bearing designs (right) are used.

Another important kind of split bearing is the *flanged shell* or "thrust" bearing. The thrust bearing is built like a straight shell bearing except that its sides have "lips" that bend towards the backing at right angles. This lip extends past the housing and crowds the nearest crank throw (Figure 6–26). A special machined surface on the crank throw, called a "thrust cheek," stays in contact with the thrust bearing. In this way, it acts as a shim to control front-to-rear play in the crankshaft.

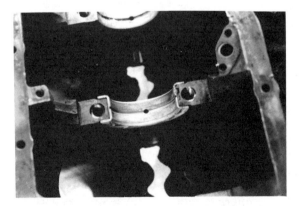

**Figure 6–26.** This flanged shell bearing, or thrust bearing, has a lip that extends past the bearing housing. This lip crowds against a machined thrust cheek on the nearest crank throw and prevents front-to-rear motion in the crankshaft.

Connecting rod bearings and most main bearings are of the straight shell type. But it is common for an engine to have one flanged shell bearing. This thrust bearing is usually located on the journal nearest the flywheel or in the middle of the crankshaft. In some cases, special thrust washers, or "spacers," are used instead of thrust bearings to keep the crankshaft in position.

## Bearing Spread

Bearing inserts are usually flatter and shallower than their housings (Figure 6–27). This flatness, called *bearing spread,* is designed into the bearing for two reasons. For one thing, it means that the bearing will have to be snapped into its housing. This slight forcing ensures the tight fit necessary for proper functioning. Second, bearing spread also makes installation easier. When the bearing is snapped into place, it remains in position even when the open side of the cap or saddle must be turned downward.

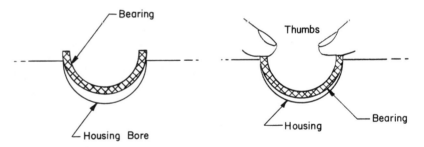

**Figure 6–27.** Bearings are usually made flatter and shallower than their housings. Snapping them into place ensures a good tight fit and makes it easier to keep them in place during installation.

## Bearing Crush

To assure that the back of the bearing fits perfectly against its housing, bearings are intentionally made longer than their housings (Figure 6–28). This extra length is called *bearing crush.* It is measured to a fine tolerance and may be as small as .001 inch (.0254mm). When the matching ends of the bearing press against each other during assembly, they force themselves properly into the housing. Without this uniform contact between bearing and housing, the bearing would not provide proper support and would be unable to get rid of heat fast enough.

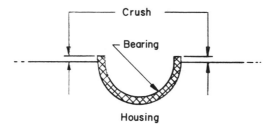

**Figure 6–28.** To assure that bearings fit firmly against the back of the housing, they are made slightly longer than their housings. This extra length, or "crush," presses against the other half and forces the bearing against its housing.

## Bearing Locating Devices

Bearing crush causes the back of the bearing to press so tightly against the housing that it is unlikely to spin in place. As an additional precaution and as a means of making sure that the bearing does not slide sideways, special *locating devices* are used. The two most common locating devices in automotive power plants are the locating lug and the locating dowel.

**Locating Lug.** The locating lug is a small off-set area on the end of the bearing (Figure 6–29). This creates an extended "lip" which fits into a matching groove in the housing.

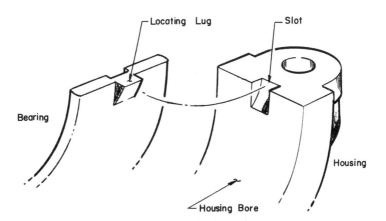

**Figure 6–29.** The locating lug on the bearing fits into a matching groove on the housing. This prevents the bearing from spinning inside the housing or from slipping sideways.

**Locating Dowel.**   Instead of lugs on the bearings, some engines have dowels pressed into the bearing's housing. This *locating dowel* is actually nothing more than a round pin that extends through a matching hole in the bearing and locks it securely in place (Figure 6–30).

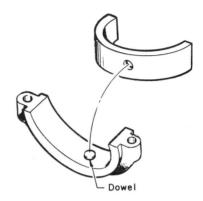

Dowel

**Figure 6–30.**   On some engines, dowels are used instead of lugs as bearing locating devices. Their purpose, of course, is the same.

## Oil Clearance

For a bearing to function properly, a constant supply of oil must flow between it and the part it protects. Space must be provided between the bearing and the shaft for this oil. The *oil clearance*, or *bearing clearance*, is the result of careful engineering. It varies from engine to engine but is seldom less than .0005 inch (.0027mm) or more than .0025 inch (.0635mm).

**Oil Grooves.**   Under heavy loads, the bearing clearance may not always be able to deliver enough oil where it is needed. Some bearings, therefore, have special grooves to channel additional oil to those locations (Figure 6–31). Sometimes, these grooves are an integral part of the engine's lubrication system. In main bearings, for instance, they usually feed oil to passages inside the rotating crankshaft. From there, the oil moves along the shaft to openings in the crank pins, where it serves to lubricate the connecting rod bearings.

Unless they are necessary for such secondary supply functions, however, engineers now try to avoid using oil grooves. Removing material to make the grooves reduces the load-bearing surface and places the rest of the bearing under a heavier load. This has been found to reduce service life.

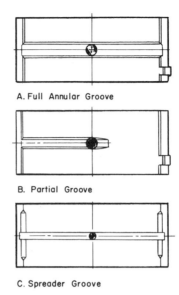

A. Full Annular Groove

B. Partial Groove

C. Spreader Groove

**Figure 6–31.** Some bearings have special oil grooves to ensure that adequate oil is delivered when high speeds or heavy loads reduce oil clearance to a minimum.

**Oil Holes.** Main bearings and all other bearings that receive lubrication through their housings must have holes in them. These holes line up with the oil passages. If oil is also fed into the rotating shaft, the oil hole usually connects to the necessary oil groove. The groove then serves as a little reservoir which assures a constant supply of pressurized oil to the shaft (Figure 6–32).

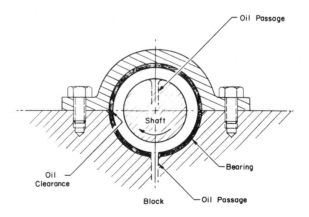

**Figure 6–32.** Bearings which receive oil through their housings must have special oil holes which line up with their oil delivery passages.

## Important Design Functions of Bearings

From what has been said about bearings, it should be clear that they perform several very important functions. They:

- Provide support to moving parts under heavy loads.
- Absorb wear that would otherwise occur to more expensive parts.
- Facilitate maintenance, in that they can be replaced more easily and more cheaply than the parts they protect.
- Maintain lubrication and reduce friction.

# ENGINE LUBRICATION SYSTEM

We said earlier that two substances are often placed between moving parts to reduce friction. The first is bearing material and the second is lubrication. You have just learned how bearings work. Now let us examine the function of a lubricant.

## How Lubrication Works

Remember those mountains and valleys we saw when we looked through a microscope at a polished metal surface? Remember how they grab onto each other and produce friction when two metal surfaces rub together? The bearing, being made of a different metal, reduces friction somewhat. But what happens when we put a layer of oil between the bearing and the rotating shaft?

As Figure 6–33 shows, the molecules of oil nearest to the metal tend to cling to it. This fills up the valleys and, if the parts are properly lubricated, also sandwiches a film of oil between opposing mountaintops. The molecules in the oil between mountaintops are free to roll and slide about. This reduces friction dramatically. The entire process resembles what happens when you put rollers under a heavy refrigerator. When that is done, a housewife who could not even tip it before can move it easily. Oil molecules serve as "rollers" between moving metal parts.

To keep things in perspective, however, we should remember the actual dimensions of the substances we are describing. The layer of oil that supports the shaft inside a bearing, for instance, is only about .0001 inch (.00245mm) thick. So the oil film in which all that molecular action takes place is not as thick as a grain of talcum powder!

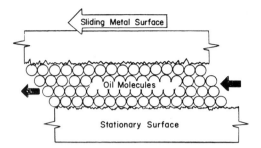

**Figure 6–33.** During lubrication, molecules of oil separate metal surfaces and serve as "rollers" between the moving parts.

## Lubrication of Rotating Shafts

Lubricating a shaft that rotates inside a fixed bearing introduces some additional factors. The lubricating action inside main bearings, for instance, does not operate as consistently and uniformly as the explanation above would suggest. In this case, a change in any one of three factors will affect lubrication. These three factors are (1) speed, (2) load, and (3) oil supply. To see these variables at work, let us look at what happens inside a main bearing when you start your car.

Figure 6–34 shows the position of the crankshaft before you touch the starter. Notice that the weight of the crankshaft rests directly on the bottom of the bearing. All the oil clearance is spaced around the sides and top. So those metal mountains on the crankshaft surface, which you saw in Figure 6–18, have a good bite on the bearing. When you start your car, therefore, the crankshaft, in trying to turn clockwise, will first climb the right side of the bearing (Figure 6–35). This explains why a very large percentage of all bearing wear takes place during the first few seconds of engine operation.

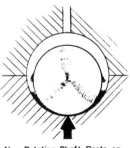

Non Rotating Shaft Rests on Bearing

**Figure 6–34.** When the crankshaft is at rest, its weight causes it to settle against the bottom of the bearing. This crowds all the lubricant into the top and sides of the oil clearance. When the crankshaft turns, friction will produce momentary wear on the bottom of the bearing.

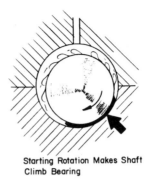

Starting Rotation Makes Shaft
Climb Bearing

**Figure 6–35.** As the crankshaft starts to turn clockwise, the friction at the bottom causes it to "climb" the right side of the bearing.

As soon as the oil pressure builds up and the speed of the crankshaft begins pulling oil under it, hydrodynamic lubrication begins (Figure 6–36). Note that at this point the shaft is literally riding a tiny wave of oil inside the bearing. At normal speeds and loads, it balances itself on that wave a little bit like a person on a surfboard. And like the surfer, it repositions itself on its wave to adjust for reasonable changes in speed, load, or oil pressure.

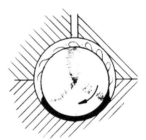

Effect of Oil Wedge Under
Load Keeps Shaft and
Bearing Separated

**Figure 6–36.** As soon as the oil pressure builds up, the crankshaft begins pulling oil under itself. Afterwards, during normal operation, the crankshaft is always surrounded by oil.

But extreme changes can make a complete adjustment impossible or even cause a "wipe out." What most commonly happens is that an extremely high speed under heavy load causes the supportive wave of oil to get too thin. This allows the crankshaft to drop low enough inside the bearing for those mountaintops to begin dragging. The resulting friction causes rapid wear and builds up heat. In time, the bearing will deteriorate and fail.

A more extreme change, such as the sudden loss of oil pressure, is even worse. In this case, the supporting wave of oil is completely lost and the crankshaft skids on the bearing, building up more and more heat. This soon melts the bearing material, which then tends to stick to the cooler crankshaft. By this time, bearing material is being ripped out in chunks, the shaft has lost its support, and the steel backing may well be spinning inside the housing. Both the block and the crankshaft are being severely hammered, and catastrophic damage is only seconds away.

It should be clear from the preceding examples that good lubrication is essential to proper engine operation. To provide lubrication to their bearings and other moving parts, all modern automotive engines use *full pressure lubrication systems*. All the parts of this system work together to deliver a regulated supply of pressurized oil to all lubrication points (Figure 6–37).

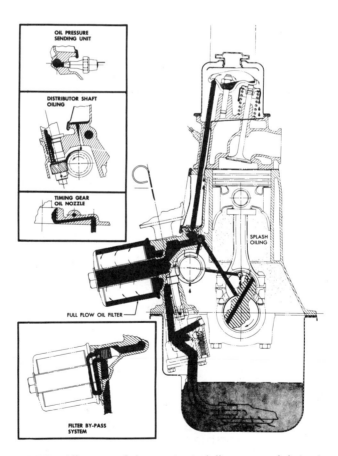

**Figure 6–37.** All parts of the engine's full pressure lubrication system work together to deliver a regulated supply of pressurized oil to all lubrication points. *Courtesy of Oldsmobile Division, General Motors Corporation.*

## Oil Pump

The heart of a full pressure lubrication system is the oil pump (Figure 6–38). This is always a positive displacement pump that is driven—either directly or indirectly—by the camshaft. A *positive displacement pump* differs from the centrifugal type pump used to pump water in the cooling system. Centrifugal pumps work like turbines. The faster they turn, the more they pump in each rotation. For an oil pump, however, we need a different kind of action. We want the volume pumped to be the same for each rotation of the pumping mechanism, regardless of speed. By using a positive displacement pump, we are able to build up the pressure needed for adequate lubrication. And we also ensure that, run at low speeds, the engine is properly oiled. In the engine, this pump picks up oil from the engine sump, or oil pan.

**Figure 6–38.** The positive displacement oil pump is the heart of the engine's full pressure lubrication system. *Courtesy of Sealed Power Corporation.*

## Primary Filtering Device

Before the oil is drawn into the pump, it passes first through a wire mesh screen (Figure 6–39). This screen, located at the oil intake in the sump, is called a *primary filtering device*. It protects the pump from large pieces of dirt and chunks of solidified oil by-products, which would cause damage or excessive wear.

**Figure 6–39.** The primary filtering device protects the oil pump from large pieces of dirt and sludge.

## Oil Galleys

Within the block, oil is delivered by drilled openings called *galleys* or *headers*. The oil pump delivers pressurized oil to a main oil galley. (See Figure 6–37.) The main oil galley then feeds the oil to the main bearings and to all other bearings and moving parts.

## Oil Pressure Relief Valve

To regulate oil pressure, an oil pressure relief valve controls the flow to the main oil galley. The valve is operated by a spring. This spring is preset to give way when the pressure of the oil pumped to the main galley rises too high. Collapse of the spring opens a direct route from the oil supply line to the overflow return line. Thus enough oil is detoured back to the sump to reduce pressure to the specified level. This ensures the maintenance of design pressure throughout the engine. It also provides a means of adjusting for wear throughout the service life of the engine. As bearing clearances enlarge with wear, for instance, more oil is required to maintain the specified pressure. In this case, the oil pressure relief valve returns less to the sump and provides the needed pressure.

## Oil Filter

Most systems are also supplied with an oil filter to remove minute bits of dirt, particles of bearing materials, and other contaminants (Figure 6–40). We will look more closely at the components of the lubrication system in Unit 13. Meanwhile, this general introduction will be useful background information for you. It will help in numerous ways as we study the other internal parts of the engine.

**Figure 6–40.** Most engine lubrication systems include an oil filter to remove minute bits of dirt and contaminants.

## REVIEW QUESTIONS

*Objective Questions*

1. Using the following diagram, determine the two possible firing orders of this four-cylinder in-line engine. Assume that the number one piston has just fired.

_____ A.   1, 3, 4, 2 and 1, 2, 4, 3
_____ B.   1, 2, 4, 3 and 1, 4, 3, 2
_____ C.   1, 2, 3, 4 and 1, 4, 3, 2
_____ D.   1, 3, 4, 2 and 1, 4, 3, 2

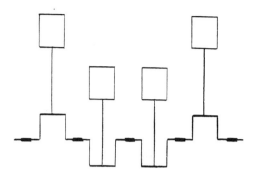

2. What would the most efficient cylinder angle be for a V–12 engine?

_____ A. 90°
_____ B. 150°
_____ C. 30°
_____ D. 60°

3. Pete says that contact between two different materials creates less friction than contact between two pieces of the same material.

Paul says that Pete is right and that this is why bearings are used.

Putnam says that Pete is right and that is why lubrication is used.

Who is right?

_____ A. All three
_____ B. Pete and Paul
_____ C. Pete and Putnam
_____ D. None of them

4. Stroke is equal to

_____ A. 720° of revolution
_____ B. Twice the connecting rod journal offset
_____ C. Half the connecting rod journal offset
_____ D. None of the above

5. The function of the vibration dampener or dynamic balancer is

_____ A. To prevent crankshaft windup
_____ B. To keep the consectors in static balance
_____ C. To dampen fringe impulse vibration
_____ D. To increase harmonics

6. Match the numbered parts with their proper names:

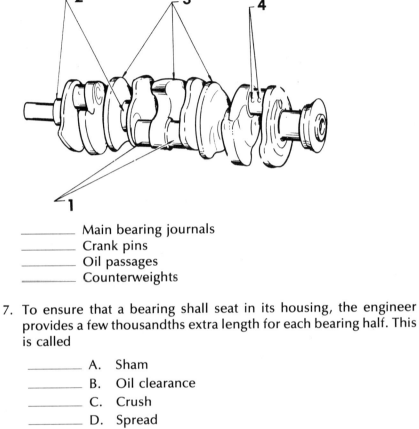

_____ Main bearing journals
_____ Crank pins
_____ Oil passages
_____ Counterweights

7. To ensure that a bearing shall seat in its housing, the engineer provides a few thousandths extra length for each bearing half. This is called

_____ A. Sham
_____ B. Oil clearance
_____ C. Crush
_____ D. Spread

8. The oil pressure relief valve

_____ A. Opens when a predetermined pressure is reached.
_____ B. Maintains oil pressure as bearings wear.
_____ C. Is controlled by spring pressure.
_____ D. All of the above.
_____ E. None of the above.

9. Babbitt is an alloy consisting mostly of

_____ A. Lead
_____ B. Copper
_____ C. Aluminum
_____ D. Iron

10. The type of lubrication system used on most modern engines is called

    _____ A. Splash

    _____ B. By-pass

    _____ C. Dry sump

    _____ D. Full pressure

11. The oil pump in a modern automobile engine is:

    _____ A. A centrifugal pump.

    _____ B. Powered directly or indirectly by the camshaft.

    _____ C. A positive displacement pump.

    _____ D. Both B and C but not A.

    _____ E. Both A and B but not C.

## Questions of Recall and Application

1. Using what you have learned about bearings in Unit 6, explain why babbitt bearings would be unsuitable for racing applications. What type of bearing alloy would be best for that purpose? Why?

2. Ask your instructor for samples of a forged crankshaft and a cast crankshaft. If possible try to get samples of both kinds from Chevrolet V–8 engines. Can you identify which is which? How can you tell? How many different clues can you find? Which one is heavier? Why?

3. Why do you think the radius of crankshaft journals is tapered to "bleend" the journal into the crank "cheek?" Why is this fillet area not machined square?

4. It is often necessary to subtract small amounts of metal late in the manufacture of a crankshaft to bring it to perfect balance. Can you tell how this was done with your crankshaft? (Hint: Look for holes and pads that have no specific design function.)

5. Explain why the counterbalance weights on a cast crankshaft must be larger than on a comparable forged crankshaft. Why, in light of what you learned in previous chapters, is this a disadvantage?

6. Explain why bearings are made so soft.

# Pistons, Rings, and Connecting Rods

By now, you know exactly what we mean when we say that the block is the foundation of the engine. And you know how the crankshaft converts reciprocating motion into rotary motion. But how does the energy generated in combustion reach the crankshaft? To understand this, you must first understand the design and mechanics of the piston assembly.

## THE PISTON ASSEMBLY: AN OVERVIEW

The piston assembly is the major working assembly of any internal combustion engine. Its major parts are the piston, the rings, the piston pin, and the connecting rod (Figures 7–1 and 7–2).

**Figure 7–1.** The piston assembly is the major working assembly in any internal combustion engine.

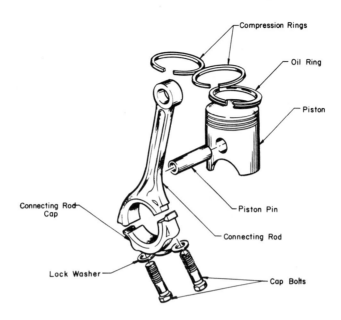

**Figure 7–2.** The piston assembly comprises the piston, the piston pin, the rings, and the connecting rod.

## The Piston and Rings

Figure 7–3 shows a detailed view of a typical piston and labels its most important parts. You should learn the proper names for these parts now. They are used throughout the rest of this book and by mechanics in everyday shop talk.

**Piston Head.**    The top surface of the piston is called its head. Piston heads are not always flat. Some curve upward into the combustion chamber. Some are "caved-in," and others are shaped irregularly. The function of the piston head, of course, is to supply the movable wall necessary to make the cylinder serve as an expander.

**Land.**    The area around the outside diameter of the piston, between the head and the first ring groove is called a *land*. The areas between ring grooves are also called lands. Lands hold the rings in position. The lowest ring groove marks the bottom of the land area of the piston.

**Compression Ring Grooves.**    The upper two grooves are for *compression* rings. The function of compression rings is to seal the piston

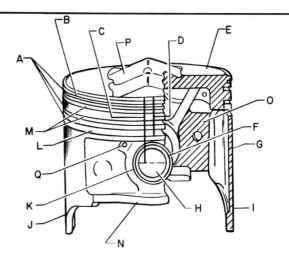

## PISTON NOMENCLATURE

The following nomenclature has been developed in over half-a-century of usage within the industry. The majority of these terms have been adopted and approved by the Society of Automotive Engineers.

### A  LAND

That part of the piston above the top ring or between ring grooves. The lands confine and support the piston rings in their grooves.

### B  HEAT DAM

A narrow groove cut in the top land of some pistons to reduce heat flow to the top ring groove. This groove fills with carbon during engine operation and reduces heat flow to the top ring.

### C  COMPRESSION DISTANCE (OR HEIGHT)

The distance from the center of the pin hole to the top of the piston.

### D  RING BELT

That area between the top of the piston and the pin hold where grooves are machined for the installation of piston rings.

### E  PISTON HEAD

The top piston surface against which the combustion gases exert pressure. The piston head may be flat, concave, convex or of irregular shape.

### F  PISTON PINS (WRIST PINS OR GUDGEON PINS)

Connections between the upper end of the connecting rod and the piston. Pins may be held in one of three ways:

    A. Anchored in the piston with the bushing in the upper end of the connecting rod oscillating on the pin.

    B. Clamped in the rod with the pin oscillating in the piston.

    C. Full floating in both connecting rod and piston with lock rings or other devices preventing the pin from contacting the cylinder wall.

**Figure 7–3.**   The beginning mechanic should learn the names for the important parts of the piston. They are needed in everyday shoptalk. *Courtesy of Perfect Circle Division of the Dana Corporation.*

## G   SKIRT

That part of the piston located between the first ring groove above the pin hole, and the bottom (open end) of the piston. The skirt forms a bearing area in contact with the cylinder wall.

## H   PIN HOLE

An opening through the piston skirt to carry the piston pin.

## I   MAJOR THRUST FACE

That portion of the piston skirt which carries the greatest thrust load. This is on the right side when viewing the engine from the flywheel end with the crankshaft rotating counterclockwise.

## J   MINOR THRUST FACE

That portion of the piston skirt which is opposite the major thrust face.

## K   PISTON PIN BUSHING

A bushing fitted between piston pin and piston pil hole to obtain a better bearing material. Used particularly with iron pistons.

## L   OIL RING GROOVE

A groove cut into the piston around its circumference, at the bottom of the ring belt or at the lower end of piston skirt. Oil ring grooves are usually wider than compression ring grooves and generally have holes or slots through the bottom of the groove for oil drainage to the interior of the piston.

## M   COMPRESSION RING GROOVE

A groove cut into the piston around its circumference, in the upper part of the ring belt. The depth of groove varies depending on piston size and types of rings used.

## N   BALANCE PADS

Extra aluminum generally cast on or below the wrist pin bosses. This material is machined off as necessary to "balance" the piston to a specified weight.

## O   STRUTS

Stamped, sheet steel reinforcements cast into the piston between the thrust faces on the inside of the wrist pin bosses. Their function is control expansion.

## P   VALVE RELIEF

A cast or machined depression in the head of the piston. This assures clearance between the piston and valve when the piston is at the top of its stroke and the valve is open.

## Q   OIL HOLES TO PINS

Holes drilled from the outside or bottom of the wrist pin bosses to the inside of the pin hole, which permits the entrance of oil for lubrication between the wrist pin and the wrist pin bosses.

Figure 7–3 (continued)

tightly in the cylinder. This prevents combustion gases from escaping around the piston, which would waste energy, reduce performance, increase oil consumption, and possibly cause damage to the bearings.

**Oil Ring Groove.** The lowest and, usually, the widest groove is for the oil control ring (Figure 7–4). Inside this groove, there are usually holes on slots leading to the inside of the piston. Excess oil is scraped off the cylinder wall by the oil control ring and forced through these holes. Inside the piston, it may be put to further use or allowed to drop back into the engine sump.

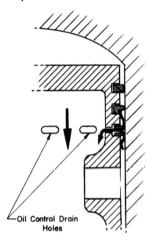

Oil Control Drain
Holes

**Figure 7–4.** The oil control ring scrapes excess oil from the cylinder wall and forces it through special drainback holes to the inside of the piston. There it may be put to further use or allowed to drain back into the engine sump.

**Skirt.** The lower part of the piston, beneath the oil ring groove, is called the *skirt*. Its function is to hold the piston straight inside the cylinder.

## The Connecting Rod

The piston is connected to the crankshaft by a strong, rigid *connecting rod*. Seen in cross-section, this rod is shaped like the letter "I" (Figure 7–5). It is carefully engineered for strength and lightness. At its bottom end, as you learned in Unit 6, it houses the connecting rod bearing and attaches to a connecting rod journal on the crankshaft. Mechanics usually refer to this end of the rod simply as the "big end," to distinguish it from the "little end," which fastens to the piston.

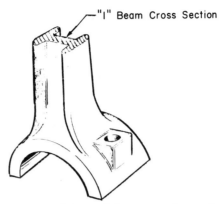

—"I" Beam Cross Section

**Figure 7–5.**   A cross-sectional view of the connecting rod shows that it is shaped like a capital "I."

## The Piston Pin

Running through a special *pin bore* in the skirt of the piston is a hollow shaft called a *piston pin* or *wrist pin*. Inside the hollow skirt of the piston, this wrist pin also runs through a bore in the little end of the connecting rod. In this way, the piston is securely attached to the connecting rod.

These, then, are the parts you will learn about in this unit. When you know more of their design, manufacture, and function, your understanding of modern engines will be much more thorough. And your potential as a mechanic will be much greater.

## OBJECTIVES

When you have finished this unit, you should be able to:

- Distinguish between forged and cast connecting rods.
- Demonstrate, by answering appropriate questions, a knowledge of the most important design features of connecting rods.
- Identify the various kinds of pistons and name and explain their most important design features.
- Choose the best kind of piston and piston rings for the conditions under which various engines operate.

# A CLOSER LOOK AT PISTONS

The mechanical linkage in the piston assembly appears, at first glance, to be absurdly simple. Small boys apparently design more complex hook-ups to steer soapbox cars. So it is easy to forget the decades of painstaking research that have brought this part of our technology to its present level of perfection.

## Characteristics of a Good Piston

Despite the simple appearance of a modern piston, its every feature is the product of careful thought and research. A good mechanic should know and respect the demands that must be met if an automotive piston is to give satisfactory service.

**Heat Resistance.** The piston head and upper cylinder walls are exposed to the hottest temperatures in the engine. With each ignition, combustion temperature may flare to more than 3,000° F (1650.2° C). The piston head and rings reach a normal operating temperature of 400°–600° F (204.6°–315.8° C). Meanwhile, the piston skirt, just a couple of inches away, may stay a fairly constant 200° F (93.4° C). The piston must withstand both extreme temperatures and extreme *difference* in temperatures (Figure 7–6).

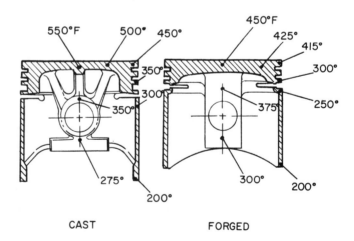

CAST                    FORGED

**Figure 7–6.** The piston must withstand both extreme temperatures and extreme differences in temperatures.

**Strength.**    The entire piston assembly must be strong enough to withstand extremely high combustion pressures in addition to other loads developed inside the engine. Combustion pressures alone commonly exceed 1000 pounds per square inch (6,815 kpa). In an engine with a 4-inch (101.6mm) cylinder diameter, this means that the compression load carried to the connecting rod by the piston at every power stroke exceeds 12,000 pounds (5460 kg).

**Light Weight.**    To understand why pistons and connecting rods must be light, we should recall some concepts learned in earlier units. In Unit 2, you learned that all moving objects have a kind of energy called *kinetic energy*. Later, in Unit 6, you learned that one group of forces acting on the crankshaft were called *static* forces. Static forces, we said then, tend always to keep things in the same status. If an object is moving, static forces tend to keep it moving. If it is at rest, they tend to keep it at rest. Both of these concepts, kinetic energy and static forces, are closely related to a third and very important concept that we need now to learn. This new concept is called *inertia*.

Inertia is the *tendency of an object to resist a change in its state of rest or motion*. We can think of inertia as the *source* of those static forces we already know about. A ball bearing lies still on a workbench because of inertia. If you push it with your finger, you impart to it enough kinetic energy to overcome its inertia. Then its inertia tends to keep it rolling. And you must again use kinetic energy to stop it with your finger. Remember that inertia always *opposes* any *change* in the status of an object. The heavier an object, the greater its inertia. A heavy bearing is both harder to start and harder to stop than a light one—it has greater inertia.

All this is important because it helps us understand the advantages of lightness in pistons and connecting rods. When that 12,000 pounds (82,740 kpa) of combustion pressure surges against the piston head, it literally shoots the piston down the cylinder. After the piston starts downward, however, the combustion pressure is not the only force acting on it. At these high speeds, it also gets a huge boost from its own inertia. And, of course, the heavier the piston assembly, the greater its inertial loading.

There is an important difference, however, between combustion forces and inertial forces. As the piston shoots downward, it transmits virtually all the combustion forces to the crankshaft. But the inertial forces that build up on the down stroke add nothing to the power output. They must simply be overcome at the bottom of the stroke. There, the piston slows to a stop and, exactly at BDC, reverses its direction. At that moment, its inertial forces drop to zero. Of course they immediately build again as the piston starts upward. But every stroke must begin and end with the inertial forces at zero. To neutralize them in this way requires energy. And energy that is used for this purpose will never reach the rear wheels; thus, unnecessary inertial forces actually diminish power output.

These inertial loadings are important factors in engine operation. Even with an "average" V–8 engine cruising at 55 mph and 2500 rpm, inertial loadings are around 3000 pounds. To keep this fact in perspective, you might remember that 3000 pounds comes close to matching the weight of the car.

The two most important causes of inertial loadings are the speed of crankshaft rotation and the weight of the piston assembly. Because considerable speed is necessary in automobile engines, the best way to reduce inertial loadings is to reduce the weight of the entire piston assembly. A good place to start is with the piston.

**Tightness.**   In addition to being strong, heat resistant and lightweight, the piston should fit reasonably tightly in the cylinder. It cannot fit tightly enough to contain the compression gases. That is the function of the rings. Between the piston and the cylinder wall, there must be room enough for the piston to expand with combustion heat. Even after expansion, the piston should not crowd out the supporting film of lubricating oil or produce excess friction. But it should fit closely enough to keep properly aligned in the cylinder. This approximation to the size of the cylinder reduces "play" and assists in the control of oil used to lubricate the cylinders.

## Piston Manufacture

The material which offers the best combination of the features desired in a piston is aluminum. So pistons for modern passenger car engines are either cast or forged from aluminum alloys. These alloys are both strong and light. Their lightness keeps inertial forces to a minimum, and their strength enables them to carry the necessary loads. Aluminum is also an excellent conductor of heat. It quickly carries excess combustion heat away from the piston head and releases it to the cylinder walls and lubricating oil.

## Thrust Faces

As the crankshaft rotates, it causes the connecting rod to swing back and forth beneath the piston. This tends to "sling" the piston outward against the sides of the cylinder walls. These centrifugal forces tend to thrust the piston back and forth at right angles to the crankshaft. The two sides of the piston that are positioned at right angles to the crankshaft, therefore, are called *thrust faces* (Figure 7–7). Engineers and mechanics distinguish between the two thrust faces.

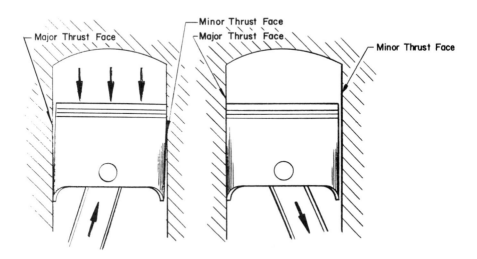

**Figure 7–7.** The centrifugal force of the connecting rod causes the piston to ride the minor thrust cylinder wall on the combustion stroke and the major thrust wall on the power stroke.

**Major Thrust Face.** The side of the piston that is "slung" against the cylinder wall on the down stroke is called the major thrust face. A mechanic viewing an American engine from the flywheel end can usually assume that the major thrust sides of the pistons are on his right.

**Minor Thrust Face.** On the compression stroke, the piston tends to ride the left wall of the cylinder. That side of the piston, therefore, is called the minor thrust face.

**Piston Pin Offset.** The lower end of the connecting rod crosses the crankshaft centerline just as the piston reaches TDC on the compression stroke. This tends to throw the major thrust face of the piston against the cylinder wall with considerable force. To reduce this piston "slap," the piston pin is not positioned exactly in the center of the piston (Figure 7–8). It is offset slightly towards the major thrust face, making the compression forces greater on the bigger side of the piston head. This imbalance "tips" the piston so that the bottom of the cylinder is already in contact with the major thrust face before the power stroke begins. Then, instead of slapping, the piston "wipes" against the major thrust side of the cylinder. This offset sacrifices some power, but it reduces noise and increases engine life. However, in race cars, where power is more important than noise and durability, piston pins may be offset on the *minor* thrust side.

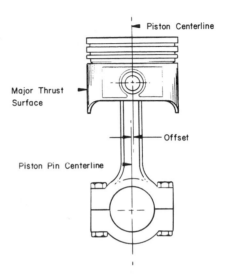

**Figure 7–8.** The piston pin is offset slightly in the piston so that more compression forces will press on the larger side. This causes the piston to tip slightly in the cylinder.

## Piston Markings

Because wristpins are offset, it is extremely important that pistons not be reversed in the cylinders. Manufacturers commonly mark piston heads to indicate how they should be positioned. The mark may be a notch, an arrow, or even a letter "F," signifying the side that goes toward the front of the engine (Figure 7–9). Some foreign manufacturers, however, mark pistons on the side that faces rearward. Whenever there is the slightest doubt, the mechanic should check the specifications for the engine he is working on.

Any relevant information about its size and weight is also marked on the head of the piston. If it is of standard size, that will usually be indicated by "std." If not, its actual size over standard will be given. Normally oversized replacement pistons will be marked ".010," ".020," ".030," ".040," or ".060" to indicate the amount over standard. Instead of decimals, however, these sizes may be indicated by whole numbers: 10, 20, 30, 40, and 60. Likewise, a code letter will sometimes indicate the piston's weight. Replacement pistons must always match these specifications exactly.

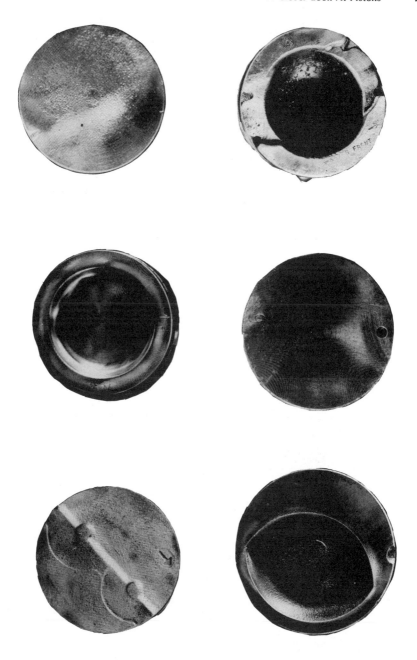

**Figure 7–9.** Manufacturers use different means of marking pistons to show how they should be positioned. It is extremely important that they not be swapped or reversed.

# Piston Design

To appreciate the careful thought that has gone into the design of the automotive piston, you have only to examine it carefully.

**Cam Grinding.** If you measure a piston skirt, you will find that it is not round, but oval-shaped. The diameter is always greatest if you measure from one thrust face to the other (Figure 7–10). This means that, when the engine is cold, the cylinder wall clearance is greater on the "front" and "rear" sides of the piston. When engine operation heats up the pistons, they expand into these clearances. This keeps clearance on the two thrust faces reasonably constant regardless of engine temperature. Consequently there is better piston alignment, reduced wear, and less noise.

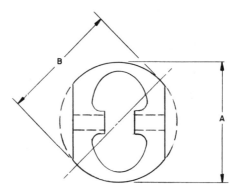

Dia. A - Dia. B = Cam Piston Skirt

**Figure 7–10.** Pistons are not perfectly round but cam ground. Their diameter is greatest when measured from one thrust face to the other.

**Head Size.** Measurement also reveals that the diameter of the piston head is smaller than the skirt. The reason for this is that the head is made thicker and heavier to withstand the high combustion pressures. It contains more material and is exposed to higher temperatures. Both factors cause it to expand more during engine operation. Therefore, it is made smaller to allow adequate clearance after expansion.

**Skirt Taper.** Skirts are made larger at the bottom than at the top. The upper part of the skirt, near the rings, runs much hotter and expands more. Tapering the skirt allows for this difference.

# Types of Piston Skirts

Piston designs are varied to match them to the requirements of specific engines. The type of skirt chosen is one example of such an adaptation.

**Slipper Skirts.** On modern short-stroke engines, the skirt may extend to its full length only on the two thrust surfaces. The U-shaped openings on its front and rear sides allow the crankshaft counterweights to clear when the piston is at BDC (Figure 7–11). The longer skirts on the thrust faces still maintain piston alignment. And the metal omitted to provide for crankshaft clearance makes the piston lighter. Pistons designed in this way are said to have *slipper skirts*.

**Figure 7–11.** Slipper skirts are used to clear the crankshaft counterweights in short-stroke engines.

**Full-Skirted Pistons.** The older piston design, in which skirts extend their full length all around the piston, is called a *full-skirted* or *trunk* piston. It is still used in many heavy duty truck and commercial vehicle engines (Figure 7–12).

**Figure 7–12.** Full-skirted pistons are still used in long-stroke engines, where crankshaft clearance is not a problem.

## Methods of Controlling Expansion

Several methods are used to cause pistons to expand into the desired clearances and to prevent expansion that would interfere with proper operation. Among the most common are slotted skirts, steel struts, and heat dams.

**Slotted Skirts.**  Many full-skirted pistons have slotted skirts (Figure 7–13). This permits them to operate with minimum clearance and still allows for thermal expansion.

**Figure 7–13.**  Slotted skirts permit the piston to expand when hot and still maintain piston clearance. The hole at the end of the slot ensures that the slot will not cause a crack to extend into the land area.

**Steel Struts.**   To control the direction and amount of expansion in slipper skirted pistons, steel struts are often used (Figure 7–14). These struts are cast into the piston on the inside of the wristpin bosses.

**Figure 7–14.**   The steel strut controls the direction and amount of expansion as the temperature increases.

**Heat Dams.**    On some pistons, a narrow groove is cut around the top land, between the piston head and the top ring groove. During engine operation, this groove fills with carbon. The carbon acts as an insulator and restricts the transfer of heat to the ring area.

## Surface Finish

Some piston surfaces have special finishes to reduce friction. Two types of finishes—machined grooves and tin plating—are in common use.

**Machined Grooves.**    The skirts on some pistons are grooved with tiny, horizontal rings designed to trap oil and improve lubrication. These shallow grooves are precision machined to about .0005 inch (.0127mm). Oil flowing vertically down the piston tends to follow the contour of the grooves and spread over the piston surface. This ensures adequate lubrication even when the engine is under heavy load.

**Tin Plating.**    Some aluminum pistons have tin-plated skirts. Because tin is not as vulnerable to friction damage as aluminum, a .0005 inch (.0127mm) coating of tin greatly reduces scoring.

## DESIGN AND FUNCTION OF PISTON RINGS

The demands on the piston rings in early automobiles were, by today's standards, not great. When typical compression ratios were around 5:1, engines ran cooler, with less pressure on the rings, and no need for oil pumps. The rotating crankshaft simply churned in the oil sump and splashed enough oil to lubricate the bearings and cylinder walls. Excess lubrication was no problem; so oil control rings were not necessary. Simple cast-iron compression rings were used. Much bigger and heavier than today's rings, these were, for a long time, ¼ inch (6.35mm) thick.

## Modern Ring Design

Modern engines have higher compression ratios, higher coolant and oil temperatures, and faster crankshaft rotations. These developments have greatly increased the demands made on piston rings. So various improvements have been introduced to meet these demands. Among them are the invention and perfection of the oil control ring, the development of better ring materials, and the creation of better ring designs.

**Oil Control Rings.**    Higher compression ratios brought greater bearing loads, which, in turn, made pressure lubrication necessary. With pressure lubrication and faster crankshaft rotation, too much oil is sometimes sprayed on the cylinder walls. To prevent excess oil consumption, special oil control rings have been developed to remove this oil. There are various designs for these oil control rings. But since their invention in the 1920's, virtually all oil control rings have had two important design characteristics (Figure 7–15).

**Figure 7–15.**    Since their invention in the 1920's, virtually all oil control rings have had two important design features: narrow ring faces and drainback holes. *Courtesy of Perfect Circle Division of the Dana Corporation.*

*Narrow ring faces* have provided high cylinder wall pressure by concentrating all the forces in a small area. This keeps excess oil from getting past the rings. To hold these narrow faces against the cylinder wall, special rings are commonly placed behind them in the ring groove. These special rings, designed to provide additional spring tension, are called *expanders.*

*Holes, slits, or other openings* in the ring have been matched with holes leading from the oil control groove to the inside of the piston. The oil scraped off the cylinder walls can then be forced through these holes into the hollow piston skirt. From there, it drops back into the oil pan.

In modern engines, oil-control rings may be either of the one-piece or the multipiece design. The one-piece ring is usually made of cast iron. Though its basic design has not changed since the 1920's, its details have been improved. Its narrower faces give it better pressure against the cylinder. Wider slots provide better return drainage. The corners of those slots are now rounded, since this has been found to reduce the buildup of sludge.

The more recent multipiece design for oil control rings uses several specialized components. Typically, it has two extremely thin rings that actually contact the cylinder. One of these *rails* lies flat against each side of the oil groove. A *spacer* holds them in place and allows clearance for oil return (Figure 7–16). Behind them, an expander presses them firmly against the cylinder wall. The expander and spacer are often manufactured as a unit. At least one manufacturer coats spacers with teflon to prevent clogging. Multipiece oil rings provide better cylinder wall conformity at high speeds and, being lighter, reduce inertial loadings.

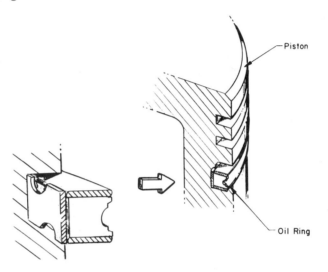

**Figure 7–16.** Modern multi-piece oil control rings consist of two *rails*, which lie flat against the sides of the ring groove and a *space expander*, which holds them in place. Sometimes a separate expander is used.

## Ring Materials

To lengthen service life, under today's harsher operating conditions, manufacturers have developed special materials to enable rings to resist abrasion and scuffing. Abrasion is wear caused when particles of dirt, oil, or foreign matter get caught between moving metal parts. Scuffing is wear caused by friction between the metal parts themselves. Materials that resist one kind of wear quite well are often vulnerable to the other. Though the rails of multipiece oil control rings are made of steel, compression rings are usually cast of special iron alloys. Then, to improve performance, they are coated or plated. Different coating materials are used for different requirements.

**Anti-scuff coatings** are used on compression rings to help them retain oil and to reduce scuffing during the break-in period. These coatings are usually iron oxide, but phosphates are also used. Some manufacturers plate their rings with a thin .0002–.0004 inch (.005–.01mm) layer of tin. Where additional scuff resistance is needed, as in racing and in other heavily loaded engines, molybdenum rings are common (Figure 7–17). On many molybdenum rings, the face is grooved to .004–.008 inch (.01–.02mm), and liquid molybdenum is sprayed into this groove. So above and below the molybdenum center of the ring face are "shelves" of strong cast iron.

**Anti-abrasion plating** is also used, especially where the engine's operating environment is expected to be dusty. Farm vehicles, cars driven regularly on gravel roads, and heavy duty construction equipment should usually be equipped with rings of this type. The facing of these rings is plated with chromium. In extremely dusty conditions, chrome-plated rings last up to five times as long as plain cast-iron rings (Figure 7–18). The rails in most oil control rings are also chrome-plated.

Some rings, instead of being cast iron, are made of ductile iron. The strength and hardness of ductile iron better withstands the demands made on racing and heavy duty engines. One manufacturer, who has produced ductile iron rings since 1959, boasts that not one of his rings has ever broken. Entire pistons have melted in use, but left their ductile rings intact. Of course, ductile iron rings may also be plated or coated with any of the materials described.

## Compression Ring Design

The top compression ring is exposed to the severest operating conditions because the hot compression gases act directly on it. A molybdenum ring is often used here, even if the lower compression ring is chrome-plated. Pistons on trucks and heavy duty vehicles may have a steel or iron insert cast into the piston crown. The top groove is machined in this insert so that the strength material can support the compression ring better.

Two kinds of forces are used to hold compression rings against the cylinder wall. First, there must be enough *mechanical* force to hold the ring in place during the intake stroke. Unless an expander is used, the ring itself must have enough spring to provide this mechanical force. A second kind of force is used on the power stroke. As Figure 7–19 shows, compression rings are designed to allow combustion gases to spill over their top sides and get in behind them. The gases, under extremely high pressure, then push the ring tightly against the

**Figure 7–17.** Molybdenum facings provide added scuff resistance in high temperature applications.

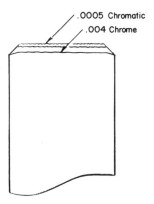

**Figure 7–18.** Chrome-faced rings are superior in their ability to withstand abrasive wear. This makes them ideal for use in dusty environments.

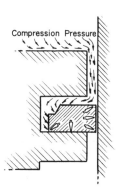

**Figure 7–19.** Combustion gases are allowed to spill over the top of the compression ring and get in behind it. The pressure of the gases then pushes the ring tightly against the bottom of the ring groove and outward against the cylinder walls. So the gases are contained by their own force.

bottom of the ring groove and outward against the cylinder walls. In effect, therefore, the compression ring uses the force in the expanding gases themselves to prevent their escape.

Viewed in cross section, most modern rings are not rectangular. Often, they have tapered faces (Figure 7–20), or they may have material cut out of one edge (Figure 7–21). Both are means of doing the same thing. They reduce the area of contact between the ring and the cylinder wall. This concentrates the force into what is called a *line contact* and provides a better seal. It is easy to see how the taper accomplishes this, since only the long side extends far enough to reach the cylinder.

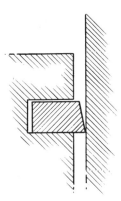

**Figure 7–20.** Tapering the face of a compression ring allows only one thin line of contact with the cylinder wall. This *line contact* concentrates all the force into a small area and gives a better seal.

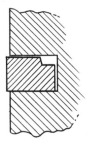

**Figure 7–21.** Cutting material out of the corner of a compression ring—whether by *chamfering* or *counterboring*—causes the ring to twist in its groove. This produces a line contact seal.

Cutting material out of one edge also produces a line contact seal. Whether we simply cut off one corner to get a *chamfered* ring or cut a little "step" called a *counterbore,* the effect is the same. The ring then tends to twist in its groove. This twist will produce a line contact seal at one edge of the ring. To assist in oil control, the lower compression ring is often counterbored on its lower outside edge. This causes it to curl upward when the piston is on the downstroke. The seal at the bottom edge then wipes any remaining excess oil back towards the oil control ring. Rings designed to do this are commonly called *scraper rings* (Figure 7–22).

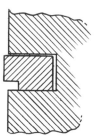

**Figure 7–22.**   If the lower compression ring is counterbored on its lower outside corner, it will curl upward on the downstroke. This forms a line contact seal on the lower edge and tends to wipe excess oil back towards the oil control ring. Such rings are called *scraper* rings.

## Choosing Piston Rings

Numerous factors are involved in deciding on the best ring for any specific application. However, the beginning mechanic can generally rely on the following guidelines:

- *On engines with slightly scored cylinder walls that have not been fully reconditioned,* use plain cast-iron rings. They will seat better and conform better to imperfect cylinder walls.
- *In new or rebored cylinders* consider chrome rings, especially if the engine will be used in a dusty environment.
- *When cylinders are in especially good condition,* consider molybdenum rings. Moly rings are particularly good when the engine will be subjected to heavy loads or high operating temperatures. But unless the cylinder walls are in excellent condition, they will not give good service.

The most important guideline, however, is always to read the manufacturer's instructions packaged with each set of rings. Most manufacturers produce different kinds of rings for use under different circumstances in the same engine model. Neither the manufacturer nor the customer is well served if a mechanic fails to choose the best rings for anticipated operating conditions.

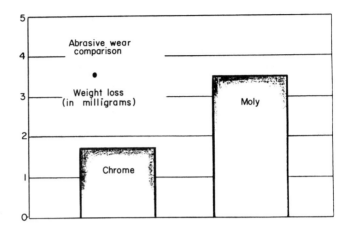

**Figure 7–23.** When used in the same operating conditions, molybdenum-faced rings show almost twice as much abrasive wear as chrome-faced rings.

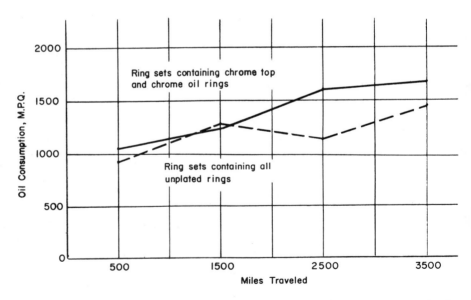

**Figure 7–24.** The superiority of chrome-plated rings is apparent in the higher mileage-per-quart shown by the solid line.

# PISTON PINS

The pins that attach the piston to the connecting rod are usually made from case-hardened steel tubes. This hollow design provides the necessary strength without adding excess weight. To assure a proper fit in the piston and rod, the pin is precision finished on its outside surface.

## Methods of Attachment

Four different methods of attaching connecting rods to pistons are in reasonably common use. The names used here indicate the means used to secure the rod to the piston *pin*.

**Press Fit.** The most common method, in passenger car engines, is to press fit the wrist pin into the connecting rod bore. This prevents the pin from turning in the rod. The ends of the pin fit into specially honed holes in the aluminum piston. The sides of these holes provide bearing surfaces and permit the pin to oscillate as the crankshaft turns.

**Full Floating.** A different method leaves the wristpin free to rotate in both the connecting rod and the piston. In this free-floating design, a bronze bushing in the connecting rod serves as a bearing and reduces friction. Since the pin is loose enough to slide sideways in the piston bosses, measures must be taken to limit this movement. Otherwise the pin could work its way into contact with the cylinder walls. Two methods are used to prevent this: snap rings and spacer plugs. When snap rings are used, they are clipped into special grooves in the ends of the piston pin bore. This confines the pin to the area between the retaining rings. When spacers are used, they are plugged into the hollow ends of the wristpin. Teflon or soft aluminum "buttons" are left extending from the ends of the pin. If the spacer slides too close to the cylinder wall, the smooth button acts as a bearing surface and prevents scuffing.

**Locking Bolt.** Sometimes a locking bolt or set screw is screwed through one of the piston bosses into the piston pin (Figure 7–25). This prevents pin rotation. A bronze bushing is then installed in the small end of the connecting rod. This precision bushing has enough clearance to allow the rod to oscillate on the stationary pin.

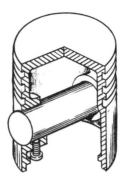

Piston Pin Lock Bolt

**Figure 7-25.** Sometimes the wrist pin is secured to the piston by a locking bolt or set screw. The bolt is screwed through the piston pin boss into the piston pin. The pin is then left free to turn in the connecting rod.

**Bolted Clamp.** The small ends of some connecting rods act as "pinch-type" clamps (Figure 7-26). The wristpin simply slides through the clamp during assembly. When bolted in place by their locking bolts, these clamps fit tightly on the piston pin, but the pin is left free to turn in the piston. When this design is used, the piston bosses may or may not have bronze bushings.

**Figure 7-26.** Some rods have pinch-type clamps made into their small ends. The wrist pin slides through the clamp. When tightened, the clamp secures the piston pin. In this method, the pin is allowed to turn freely in the piston pin bosses.

## Methods of Lubricating Piston Pins

Lubricating oil may be delivered to the wristpins in a number of ways. Three commonly used methods are:

**Pressurized Lubrication from Crankshaft.** When the piston pin is supported by a bushing in the connecting rod, an oil passage may be drilled the length of the rod. This allows the pressurized oil in the connecting rod bearing to flow upward and lubricate the piston pin bushing (Figure 7–27).

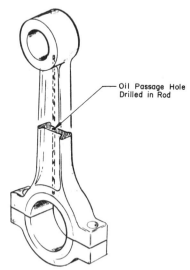

Oil Passage Hole
Drilled in Rod

**Figure 7–27.** Oil passages in some rods deliver pressurized oil from the connecting rod bearing to the bushing in the piston pin end of the rod.

**Splash Lubrication Through Hole in Rod.** Another method is simply to drill a hole from the little end of the connecting rod through to the pin bore (Figure 7–28). Oil splashing into this hole then flows down and lubricates the piston pin.

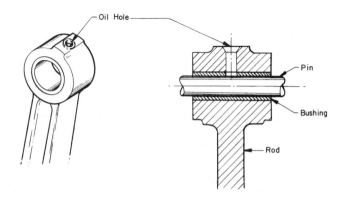

Oil Hole

Pin

Bushing

Rod

**Figure 7–28.** An oil hole is sometimes drilled in the small end of the connecting rod. Oil splashing into this hole can then drain downward and lubricate the piston pin.

**Drainback of Oil from Oil-Control Rings.** Where the pin moves freely in the piston, lubrication is often provided by the oil control ring. Oil forced to the inside of the piston is simply allowed to drain onto the wristpin. Sometimes holes are drilled through the piston pin bosses to provide a better path to the piston pin (Figure 7–29).

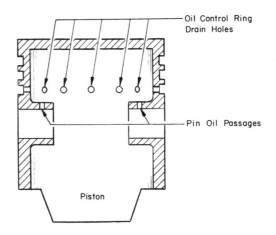

**Figure 7–29.** On some pistons, oil holes in the top of the piston pin bosses divert some of the drainback from the oil control rings and use it to lubricate the piston pins.

Not all engines use visible passages or holes to deliver oil to their piston pins. Many are designed so that the pins are properly lubricated by the splashing of the crankshaft.

## CONNECTING RODS

Strength and lightness are the two most important requirements for a connecting rod. Weight is important because of the rod's complex pattern of motion. It rotates *and* moves up and down, both at the same time—and at very high speeds. This means that the connecting rod itself is responsible for much of the total inertial loading produced by the piston assembly. So a slight reduction in the weight of the rod can make for a big reduction in inertial loadings. This is the big advantage of the rod's I-shaped cross section. It gives maximum strength for minimum weight.

Strength is particularly important because, in the connecting rod, enormous forces are concentrated in a tiny area. All the combustion loading *plus* all the inertial loading must be carried in one slender rod. When concentrated in the rod, the combustion forces alone can easily exceed 15,000 pounds per *square inch*.

Nor do all these forces stress the rod in the same way. Compression forces, obviously, press *down* on the rod. They tend to squash it endwise. But inertial forces are greatest at TDC and BDC, when the rod must start the motionless piston moving in the opposite direction. The inertial tensions at this point tend to stretch the rod (Figure 7–30). And these forces, too, are enormous. On many engines at 6000 rpm, inertial loads on the rod will exceed 11,000 pounds psi.

**Figure 7–30.** The effects of extreme inertial loadings can be seen in this connecting rod. It was literally stretched out of shape by inertial forces during high-speed operation.

## Types of Connecting Rods

Most automotive connecting rods are either forged or cast of steel. You learned in Unit 6 that forged parts are generally stronger, heavier, and more expensive than cast parts. In the case of connecting rods, however, the forged part is actually lighter. The reason is that it takes less forged metal to give the required strength. Therefore, there is an overall saving in weight. But forged connecting rods, like forged crankshafts, are more expensive. So some car manufacturers take advantage of the newer foundry techniques and cut costs by using rods of cast steel.

Two other types of connecting rods are sometimes found in racing engines and similar performance vehicles. The first is the forged aluminum rod, which is also used in aircraft engines. Forged aluminum gives the necessary strength but, being lighter, it also makes great reductions in inertial loadings at high speeds (Figure 7–31).

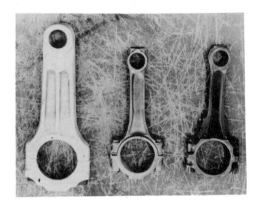

**Figure 7–31.** Being smaller, forged steel connecting rods are actually lighter than cast-steel rods. But forged aluminum rods, being even lighter, have the smallest inertial loadings at high speed.

A second and newer type of performance rod is molded in plastic. One process uses a composite mixture of epoxy plastic, carbon, and boron fibers. This is said to produce a rod that is not only lighter than aluminum but also stronger than steel. It is possible that this and similar manufacturing processes, first developed in the aerospace industry, will find greater use in automotive technology.

## Rod Manufacture

A mechanic who knows a little about how connecting rods are manufactured has a real advantage. He can then understand the logic behind many of the important warnings he reads in the service manuals. The method used to create the housing for the connecting rod bearing is particularly important.

**Cast Rods.**    Connecting rods are cast in one piece. Next the "bolt holes" are drilled, which are later used to attach the bearing cap to the big end. The hole is then bored to create the bearing housing. A final cut separates the bearing cap from the end of the rod.

**Forged Rods.**    Caps and rods are forged separately. The bolt holes are then drilled and their mating surfaces machined. Next the cap is bolted in place and the hole bored for the bearing.

Whichever method is used, notice that the connecting rod and bearing cap are manufactured as a unit. As with main bearing caps, it is extremely important that these never be swapped around or reversed.

## Connecting Rods and Crankshaft Balance

The weight of all major parts in piston assemblies is extremely critical to crankshaft balance. Manufacturers carefully match connecting rods and pistons when they are attached to the crankshaft. And the position of these parts must remain the same throughout the life of the vehicle. The mechanic must never interchange connecting rods nor pistons. When a piston or connecting rod must be replaced, it must be of the same weight as the old part.

Connecting rods are built with extra metal at points called *balancing bosses* (Figure 7–32). These bosses may be located on the bearing cap, the beam, or the little end. Metal is machined from these bosses to bring the rod within weight and balance specifications.

**Figure 7–32.** Balancing bosses are placed at different places on different connecting rods. The rod can be brought within weight and balance specifications by machining metal from these bosses.

## How Rods Lubricate Cylinder Walls

In many engines, connecting rods perform the secondary function of lubricating the cylinder walls. For this purpose, a small oil passage is drilled through to the bearing housing in the big end of the rod. This "spit hole" is positioned so that it will line up periodically with the oil passage in the crankshaft (Figure 7–33). When that happens, the pressurized oil momentarily squirts through the hole in the rod onto the cylinder wall. On V–8 engines this spit hole usually opens when the piston is near BDC and is designed to squirt oil into the matching cylinder in the opposite bank. On in-line engines, the spit hole opens when the piston nears TDC. In this case, the spit hole is always aimed at the major thrust wall of the cylinder.

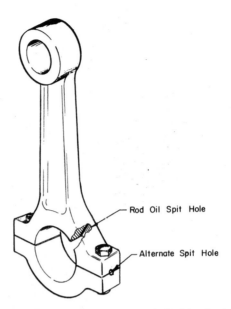

Rod Oil Spit Hole

Alternate Spit Hole

**Figure 7–33.** A spit hole is sometimes drilled in the big end of the connecting rod to provide lubrication to the cylinder walls. Periodically, the spit hole lines up with the oil passage in the main bearing. This allows a squirt of pressurized oil to shoot out the hole onto the cylinder.

## REVIEW QUESTIONS

*Objective Questions*

1. Which type of connecting rod is strongest?

_____ A.  Cast iron

_____ B.  Forged steel

_____ C.  Cast aluminum

_____ D.  Both A and C

2. The purpose of the squirt hole in a connecting rod is to:

_____ A.  Help lubricate the cylinder walls.

_____ B.  Bleed off excess rod braking oil.

_____ C.  Prevent "air locks" in the oil passages.

_____ D.  Allow oil to flow up the connecting rod passage to the wristpin.

3. Most connecting rods are shaped according to which design?

_____ A.  Truss type
_____ B.  Main beam
_____ C.  "I" beam
_____ D.  None of the above

4. Slipper type pistons are commonly found

_____ A.  In racing engines.
_____ B.  In heavy duty Diesel applications.
_____ C.  Only in older passenger cars.
_____ D.  In most modern passenger cars.

5. Aluminum pistons are cam ground to

_____ A.  Make them lighter.
_____ B.  Give them a smooth finish.
_____ C.  Clear ring lands.
_____ D.  Allow for expansion.

6. Which of the following statements about pistons is true?

_____ A.  Head shape affects compression ratio.
_____ B.  Struts help control expansion.
_____ C.  Piston heads may be indented to clear valves.
_____ D.  All of the above.

7. Which ring groove has holes drilled through to the inside of the piston?

_____ A.  Top ring groove
_____ B.  Second ring groove
_____ C.  Third ring groove
_____ D.  All three of the grooves

8. What is the purpose of the holes discussed in Question 7?

_____ A.  To relieve pressure behind the ring.
_____ B.  To direct pressure to the ring.
_____ C.  To allow oil to drain through.
_____ D.  To make the piston lighter.

*Answer TRUE or FALSE*

_____ 1. It is important that connecting rod bearing caps not be reversed nor swapped around.

_____ 2. Entire pistons and rods can be interchanged from one cylinder to another without adverse effects.

_____ 3. Pistons may use two compression rings.

_____ 4. Wristpins (piston pins) are usually hollow.

_____ 5. Pistons having press fit pins use circlip type retainers.

_____ 6. Aluminum pistons may be tin-plated.

_____ 7. Balancing bosses are always located on the rod cap.

_____ 8. Molybdenum rings prevent scuffing.

_____ 9. Wider rings seal better than narrow rings.

*Match Each Entry in the Left Column With Its Correct Description in the Right Column*

_____ 1. Strut

_____ 2. Heat dam

_____ 3. Inertial loads

_____ 4. Compression loads

_____ 5. Full floating pin

_____ 6. Offset pin

_____ 7. "F" mark

_____ 8. Third ring

_____ 9. Expander

_____10. Teflon oil control ring

A. Helps control piston expansion

B. Keeps high temperatures away from top ring

C. Tends to stretch rods

D. Tends to bend rods

E. Bushing in rod small end

F. Equalizes thrust force

G. Indicates front of piston

H. Controls oil flow

I. Increases ring pressure

J. Prevents clogging

K. Resists abrasion

L. Reduces friction

*Questions of Recall and Application*

1. What are some good guidelines to follow in choosing which type of rings to install in a particular vehicle?

2. From memory, try to sketch a connecting rod and label its most important parts. When finished, check your work by comparing your sketch with the pictures in this unit.

3. Ask your instructor to supply you with several types of pistons to examine. Practice classifying them and naming their design features, drawing on the information you have learned from this unit.

UNIT

# 8

# Cylinder Head and Combustion Chamber

From all that has been said so far, it would be natural to assume that the head assembly is relatively unimportant. We have barely mentioned it in our discussion and have shown it in drawings and photos just lying on top of the block. But the cylinder head is much more than a lid for the cylinders. No part is more important than the head assembly in determining engine efficiency (Figure 8–1).

**Figure 8–1.**   No part is more important in determining engine efficiency than the cylinder head assembly. *Courtesy of Chrysler Corporation.*

In Unit 3 we said that the keys to better fuel economy and lower emissions would probably be found inside the combustion chamber, where the fuel is burned. It is the head that forms the combustion chamber. In this unit and the one following, you will learn two important ways in which the head assembly contributes to engine efficiency.

You will learn that the essential alternation of intake and exhaust strokes in the Otto cycle means that engines, like people, must breathe in order to function. They must take in air on the intake stroke and let out air on the exhaust stroke. And you will see that engines, like people, can breathe either slightly or deeply. It will soon become clear that the way an engine breaths helps determine its efficiency and power output. Suddenly, the parts that assist in breathing take on new importance. The valves that admit and expel the air, the parts that open and close those valves, and the passages that carry air to and from them all become crucial. And most of them in most engines are located in the cylinder head. So one very important way in which the head assembly contributes to power output is by determining breathing efficiency.

A second way is by controlling the combustion process. Obviously, the more thoroughly the fuel is burned, the more power can be produced. And the better the combustion heat is controlled, the less waste and wear there is. Since it is in the head that combustion takes place, it is in the design of the head that ways must be found to control combustion.

Much of what we know today about the control of combustion is due to the work of the Englishman, Harry Ricardo. Ricardo devoted his life to the scientific study of engine combustion. His discoveries, which were great enough to win him knighthood in his own day, are still being put to use. Today's new stratified charge systems, for instance, use design features that Ricardo first envisioned in 1922. Sir Harry is credited with saying first something that has since become a truism among engineers: *The most important single factor in developing power in an engine is the shape of the combustion chamber.* The shape of the combustion chamber, like the efficiency of engine breathing, is determined by the design of the cylinder head.

## OBJECTIVES

When you have completed this unit, you will be able to:

- Explain how engine breathing considerations might affect the design of the cylinder head.
- Name two combustion chamber shapes and explain the advantages of each.

- Name three basic engine designs and demonstrate a knowledge of the advantages and disadvantages of each.
- Explain the function of a camshaft and tell why its location is an important factor in the design of the cylinder head.
- Name two modern variations on the basic I-head design and demonstrate a knowledge of the advantages and disadvantages of each.
- Name the two materials most commonly used in the manufacture of cylinder heads and know the advantages and disadvantages of each.

## Cylinder head construction

Figure 8–2 shows a modern cast-iron cylinder head. An in-line engine uses only one such head. A V–type or opposed engine requires one for each bank of cylinders. Usually, the heads on V–type or opposed engines are interchangeable.

**Figure 8–2.** Most cylinder heads for large liquid-cooled engines are cast of iron alloys. Iron is cheaper than aluminum and usually serves well enough for production model passenger cars. But the young woman's cast aluminum Buick V–8 head weighs only 18 pounds. The young man is holding an identical head cast in grey iron. It weighs 47 pounds. Though aluminum heads add about $50 to the cost of this V–8, they reduce its weight by 58 pounds.

Cylinder head production generally uses the same foundry techniques and materials used in the manufacture of blocks. Most cylinder heads for liquid-cooled engines are cast of iron alloys. Iron is cheaper than aluminum and serves well enough for production model passenger cars. However, aluminum heads have occasionally been used on passenger car engines. In the 1960's, Oldsmobile built an aluminum alloy V–8 engine. Buick marketed a 300 cid (4916cc) V–8 with aluminum heads on a cast-iron block. Chrysler first built its so-called "slant six" engine with a die-cast aluminum alloy block and heads. In air-cooled engines, where superior heat transfer qualities are needed, aluminum is still widely used, but it remains too expensive for extensive use in liquid-cooled power plants.

A cast-iron head, is much less expensive because it is nearly completed when it comes from the mold. The combustion chamber, the oil passages, the coolant passages, and the valve ports, guides, and seats are all cast in place (Figure 8–3). As the table in Figure 8–4 shows, only six machining operations are needed to complete a cast-iron block.

Aluminum blocks are far from finished when they are cast. Additional components must be installed (Figure 8–5), and many more machining operations are necessary (Figure 8–6).

**Figure 8–3.** Cast-iron cylinder heads require less machine work to prepare them for use. The combustion chamber, the oil passages, the coolant passages, and the valve ports, guides, and seats are all cast in place. *Courtesy of Cincinnati Milacron.*

1. Broaching the block to head surface and the manifold surfaces.
2. Drilling and tapping holes for manifold attachments, valve gear, spark plugs, etc.
3. Finishing oil and coolant passages.
4. Drilling headbolt holes.
5. Drilling and reaming valve guides.
6. Finishing valve seats.

**Figure 8–4.** Table of machine operations for cast-iron heads.

**Figure 8–5.** Because aluminum is so soft, steel parts must be installed in aluminum heads to prevent excessive wear. These parts are unnecessary in cast-iron heads.

1. Mill head to block surface.
2. Mill all gasket and cover surfaces.
3. Drill and tap all holes for manifold, valve gear, spark plugs Etc.
4. Install steel inserts for guide pins and dowels required to center various attachments.
5. Drill oil passages and oil return holes.
6. Drill and tape various oil and water passage plugs.
7. Drill ream and precision fit bronze or cast–iron valve guides.
8. Spot face and install steel valve spring seats.
9. Counter bore and flycut valve seat recesses and install steel valve seats.
10. Finish valve seats.

**Figure 8–6.** This table lists machining operations required to finish aluminum cylinder head castings.

# CYLINDER HEAD DESIGN

Three things determine the design of an engine cylinder head. The first is the method of cooling to be used. The second is the shape desired in the combustion chamber. And the third is the mechanism by which the valves will be opened and closed.

## Method of Cooling

Temperatures inside the combustion chamber may easily reach 5000° F (2762° C), but aluminum alloys melt at about 1100° F (593° C), and cast-iron alloys melt at about 2000° F (1094° C). Obviously, a method must be provided for quickly getting rid of the excess heat. Otherwise, the engine will almost immediately destroy itself. In practice, the cylinder walls and major head castings should not exceed 500° F (260° C). It is difficult to design a power plant that can run hotter than that and still keep acceptable design clearances when it is cool. And since engine oil begins to break down at 250°–300° F (120°–149° C), it is extremely difficult to lubricate any engine part that has more than doubled that temperature. The only alternative is to carry 25–35% of that heat energy away from the combustion chamber before it harms the engine.

**Liquid Cooling.** Most modern automotive engines use a liquid coolant to conduct this heat to the outside air. They can do this because their cylinders and combustion chambers resemble, in one way, the living room of your home. If you have ever seen a house under construction, you know that, between the 2″ × 4″ studs that support those interior walls, there are hollow spaces. The engine also has hollow spaces, called *water jackets*, surrounding its high-temperature areas (Figure 8–7).

Instead of cold air, however, these water jackets are filled with liquid coolant, usually a mixture of water and glycol base alcohol. As this coolant is pumped past the high temperature areas, it absorbs the excess heat and carries it to the radiator. There, the heat is released into the air.

It is important to realize that coolant circulation is no hit or miss affair. The design of the coolant passages and the flow of coolant are both critical to efficient operation. Since different areas of the engine are exposed to different temperatures, the volume, speed and direction of coolant flow must be closely controlled—too much cooling of one area can cause as much trouble as insufficient cooling of another (Figure 8–8).

**Figure 8–7.**   Water passages surround the combustion chamber to provide space for coolant flow. *Courtesy of Pontiac Division, General Motors Corporation.*

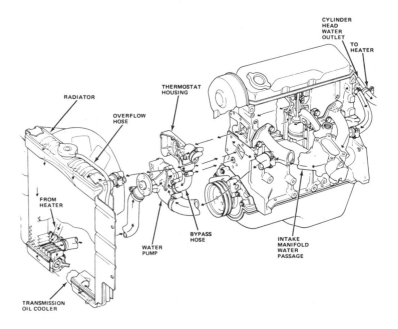

**Figure 8–8.**   An exploded view of a water-cooled engine and the components of its cooling system. *Courtesy of American Motors Corporation.*

**Air Cooling.**   Air is used instead of water as a coolant in the second method. This method is more often in engines for motorcycles and recreational vehicles than for passenger cars. Instead of a water jacket, air-cooled engines are equipped with cooling fins. These fins are cast as part of the head and cylinder block. Their size and placement is carefully planned (Figure 8–9). They must provide enough surface area to allow the transfer of excess engine heat to the outside air. Motorcycle engines usually depend on the vehicle's movement to force air through the cooling fins. But passenger cars often use blowers and special ducts, or *shrouds,* to control the direction and speed of air flow. This provides better temperature control.

**Figure 8–9.**   On an air-cooled engine, the size and placement of the cooling fins are as carefully planned as the coolant passages in the head of a liquid-cooled engine.

## Combustion Chamber Design

There are two combustion chamber designs in common use: wedge-shaped and hemispheric.*

**The Wedge-Shaped Design.**   This design increases combustion efficiency by creating turbulence among the burning gases (Figure 8–10). *Turbulence* means nothing more than rapid movement, or stirring. You know what happens if you rapidly stir a cup of hot coffee. It quickly cools down. The same process operates in the combustion chamber to prevent unburned gases from igniting until the proper time. Turbulence keeps the hotter gases blowing from the center of the chamber past the chamber walls. There, like the swirling coffee in your cup, they give up their heat to the outside walls. This prevents accidental ignitions caused by "hot spots" elsewhere in the chamber and causes

---

*Commonly used combustion chamber designs will be discussed in Units 11 and 12, when we consider engine breathing and combustion in more detail.

faster and more complete burning. We can think of turbulence as fanning the flame and, at the same time, blowing unburned fuel towards it.

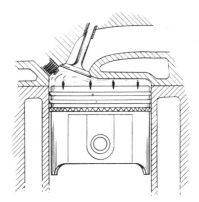

**Figure 8–10.** The wedge-shaped combustion chamber is particularly good at creating turbulence.

Because wedge-shaped chambers are very effective in producing turbulence and because they are simple and inexpensive, they are widely used in passenger cars. They require little or no machining and present the design engineer with no serious problems of valve layout (Figure 8–11).

**Figure 8–11.** Valve layout is seldom a problem when a wedge-shaped combustion chamber is used.

**Hemispheric Design.**   "Hemi-heads" or hemispheric combustion chambers are used only when manufacturing cost is not as important as power. The word *hemisphere* can be broken into two parts: *hemi,* meaning "half" and *sphere,* meaning "ball." A hemispheric combustion chamber, therefore, is one that is shaped like a half ball. A true hemi-head does not create much turbulence, but it does allow more desirable valve sizes and better spark plug placement (Figure 8–12). The big disadvantage of the hemispheric chamber is that it requires much more machining after casting, which makes it expensive to produce (Figure 8–13).

**Figure 8–12.** Though hemispheric combustion chambers do not create much turbulence, they permit larger valves and better spark replacement. The big advantage of hemispheric combustion chambers is their breathing efficiency.

**Figure 8–13.** As can be seen in the hemispheric chamber of this head from a Lotus racing machine, the combustion chambers of a "hemi-head" must be highly machined. This increases costs but makes a dramatic difference in performance.

In practice, modern power plants almost never use either the wedge-shaped or the hemispheric combustion chamber in its "pure" form. We must remember that there is more to the combustion chamber than a simple opening cast in the head. The top of the piston makes up one whole side of it. And the valves, cylinder wall, spark plug, and even the edge of the head gasket are part of it. They often introduce irregularities into its shape. The engineer may not always be happy with the influence of those irregularities on efficiency, but he recognizes their necessity. So he weighs one demand against another, places every component carefully, and strikes the best compromise he can. As often as not, this leads him to some combination of the wedge and hemispheric shape since he would like to combine the best features of both. That would give the more efficient combustion at the lower manufacturing cost (Figure 8–14).

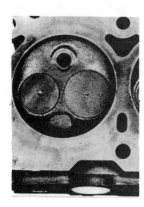

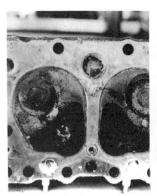

**Figure 8–14.** As often as not, the mechanic finds neither a true wedge shape nor a true hemispherical combustion chamber. The two patterns have been merged in any number of compromise designs.

# Valve Operating Mechanism

The third important consideration in the design of the cylinder head is the mechanism that opens and closes the valves. All modern automotive engines drive the valve opening mechanisms with power from the crankshaft. This power, however, cannot be carried directly from the crankshaft to the valves. The crankshaft revolves twice for each time a given valve is supposed to open. So any movement produced by the crankshaft must be slowed by exactly half before it is transmitted to the valves. The timing of the valves, of course, is crucial. So the part that gears down the speed of the crankshaft to the proper speed for valve operation is among the most important parts of the engine. This is the job of the camshaft.

**The Camshaft.** The camshaft not only opens the valves, but also controls exactly how long they remain open. The means by which it does this is what gives it its name. A *cam,* in mechanics, is simply a smooth bump or projection, offset on one side of a wheel (Figure 8–15). Any round shaft is just an extremely thick wheel; therefore, the length of the camshaft allows room for a separate cam to operate each valve (Figure 8–16).

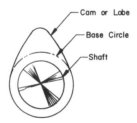

**Figure 8–15.** A *cam,* in mechanics, is simply a bump or lobe offset on one side of a wheel or shaft.

**Figure 8–16.** As the camshaft turns, each cam acts like a separate lever and opens its valve at the correct time.

All of the cams extend straight out from the center line of the shaft. That is, they do not lean towards either end of the shaft. In order to achieve proper valve timing, the cams are offset at different angles around the camshaft. As the camshaft turns, each cam acts like a separate lever and opens its valve at the correct time. The exact means by which power from the camshaft reaches the valves varies with engine design.

All camshafts are designed to turn at exactly one-half the speed of the crankshaft. This is done by using gears or sprockets of exactly the right sizes. A gear at the end of some camshafts meshes directly with a gear on the accessory end of the crankshaft. Where the camshaft must be mounted further away from the crankshaft, either a chain or a cogged belt may be used to drive a sprocket on the camshaft.

We shall learn more about camshaft operation and construction in Unit 9. It should be clear, however, that an extremely important factor in any valve operation mechanism is the location of the camshaft. The camshaft itself is not necessarily mounted in the head, but its location is always a major consideration when the head is being designed. Within certain limits, the placement of the camshaft determines the size and location of the valves.

## CAMSHAFT PLACEMENT AND HEAD DESIGN

There are three basic designs for the cylinder heads of automotive engines: the L-head, the F-head, and the I-head. The letters are not abbreviations for longer names but reminders of the shape of each of those capital letters, which provide rough diagrams of the position of the valves in relation to the cylinders in each design. Not all of these designs are used in automobile engines today. But an understanding of each is necessary to appreciate fully the factors that enter into the design of the cylinder head.

### The L-Head

In an in-line engine with an L-head design, the camshaft is usually located to one side and slightly above the crankshaft. In V–type engines, it is directly above the crankshaft. In either case, the valves are placed beside the cylinder, in the block (Figure 8–17). You can easily see why this design is also called a "flat head." Since the entire valve mechanism is in the block, the head does not have to provide room for that assembly. For this reason, the head, as a whole, can be thinner and flatter. However, you may have some trouble finding the L that gives this design its name, unless you look for an *upside down* L (Figure 8–18).

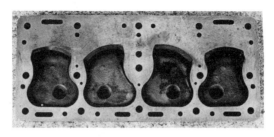

**Figure 8–17.** In the L-head design, the valves are placed in the block, alongside the cylinders.

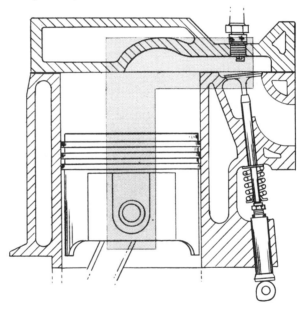

**Figure 8–18.** Once you know to look for an *upside-down* "L," it is easy to see why the flathead design is also called an L-head.

At one time, the L-head design was the most common of all. But it has not been used in passenger cars for over twenty years. A limited number of multi-cylinder flatheads are still used for industrial and farm machinery. Even for these specialized uses, however, I-head designs are replacing the L-head. The last common application of the flathead seems to be in the single-cylinder lawn mower engine (Figure 8–19).

**Figure 8–19.** About the last common application of the flathead design is found in the engines used for lawn mowers.

## Advantages

No engine design can possibly come to dominate the automotive industry as the L-head did prior to World War II unless it has certain advantages. The L-head has several:

**Economy** is probably its biggest advantage. Casting an L-head is a rather simple matter. Only the combustion chamber and the cooling method require attention—coolant passages for water-cooled engines and cooling fins for those that are air-cooled. Machining operations are limited to dressing the head-to-block mating surfaces and drilling the holes for the head bolts.

**Lightness** is a second big advantage of the L-head. It can be lighter for two reasons. First, less mechanical linkage is needed to drive the valves, since the entire mechanism is located in the block. This saves the weight of the larger reciprocating parts that are necessary when the valve operating mechanism is in the head. Second, because the L-head can be flatter and smaller, it can be made with less material. Other things being equal, therefore, an L-head built with today's technology might well show a considerable reduction in overall engine weight.

**Smaller size** is another important advantage of the L-head. Being flatter, it can fit into a smaller engine compartment, which reduces the weight and cost of the entire car.

## *Disadvantages*

Despite the advantages just named, however, the L-head design has been phased out. Why? The most important reasons, perhaps, are the disadvantages inherent in the flathead design.

**The large combustion chamber** in the flathead is the source of several difficulties. Yet there is no way to do away with it. Placing the valves in the block makes a large combustion chamber necessary, for the valves must open upward, into the combustion chamber itself. The roof of the combustion chamber must be high enough to allow the valves to open fully. Unlike other head designs, the L-head cannot rely on piston travel to supply some of this clearance.

Therefore, L-type heads cannot produce the high compression ratios needed for peak thermal efficiency in modern automobiles. So one reason that the larger combustion chamber limits engine efficiency is that it lowers the achievable compression ratio. Another is that, in a larger chamber, it is difficult to control combustion. It becomes difficult to place the spark so that the fuel mixture will burn efficiently throughout the chamber.

**The small valves** which must be used in order to fit them into the block are another disadvantage. Full efficiency requires that the engine be able to breathe freely. It should draw in enough fuel mixture on each intake stroke to produce a full surge of power after ignition. But engines breathe hundreds of times faster than humans. For this reason, engine efficiency is greatly affected by any obstruction that hinders the free intake and expulsion of air. When valves are made small enough to fit into the block, they are also small enough to interfere with free breathing.

**The twists and turns** necessary to get the fuel-air mixture into the combustion chamber also restrict breathing in an L-head engine. Because less mixture can be drawn in on each intake stroke, the L-head produces less power for any given size engine.

# The F-Head

Early efforts to overcome the breathing difficulties and the limitations on the compression ratio of the L-head led to the F-head design (Figure 8–20). Notice that the designers of the F-head placed the intake valve in the head and introduced a rocker arm assembly to operate it off the camshaft. However, they did not move the camshaft. The exhaust valves, still located in the block, were operated in exactly the same way.

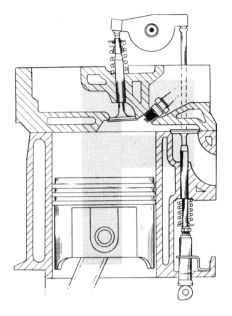

**Figure 8–20.**   Placing the intake valve in the head and leaving the exhaust valve in the block produced the so-called F-head design.

## Advantages

The F-head engine does have two advantages, although it fails to make the best of either of them.

**Improved breathing** results from putting the intake valve in the head. This makes it possible to use a larger valve and a much straighter intake port.

**A higher compression ratio** is also possible in the F-head design. When the intake valve is removed from the block, the offset portion of the combustion chamber can be narrowed considerably. Since the piston stroke remains the same, this reduction in the size of the combustion chamber has the effect of raising the compression ratio.

## Disadvantages

Though use of overhead intake valves made the disadvantages of the F-head less severe, it did not get rid of them. The improvements it made in breathing and compression, while real, were not great. It retained the disadvantages of the flathead, and added one more.

**The more complicated mechanism** necessary to open overhead valves added reciprocating weight to the engine and complicated the design of the head. All the problems with inertial loadings which were mentioned in our discussion of the piston assembly also exist in the up-and-down motion of the rocker assembly.

In a word, then, the F-head combined the disadvantages of the flathead and the disadvantages of an overhead valve design. Yet it did not fully realize the advantages of either. Perhaps this explains why the last F-head engine disappeared from the American market in the late 1960's.

## The I-Head or OHV Head

Virtually all cars now manufactured use some variety of the I-head or "overhead valve" design. I-head engines went all the way in the direction hinted at by the F-head design. In the I-head design, both intake and exhaust valves are located in the head, over the pistons (Figure 8–21).

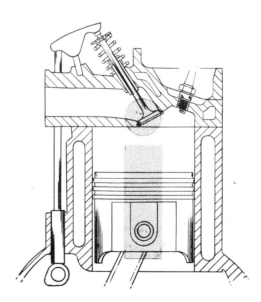

**Figure 8–21.** With both valves positioned above the cylinders, we have an I-head design. Almost all modern American production cars use some variety of the I-head design.

## Advantages

With all the valves in the head, the engineer has much more freedom in deciding on the shape of the combustion chamber. He can also use any of a variety of ways to operate the valves. By capitalizing on this flexibility, designers have given the I-head two important advantages.

**Improved breathing** is a natural consequence of the greater freedom in valve placement and the shorter, straighter air flow that comes with overhead valves.

**Figure 8–22.** The shorter, straighter air flow characteristic of an I-head can be seen in this cutaway view of the intake port in an Oldsmobile head.

**Easier repair** is a second advantage. Simply removing the head gives the mechanic access to almost all the parts that are likely to need servicing.

## Disadvantages

Although the overhead valve design is not without its disadvantages, these are not serious enough to prevail over the advantages just noted. Otherwise, the I-head would not have beaten out its competitors so completely. But the disadvantages are real, and as a mechanic, you should be familiar with them. Such knowledge helps when you encounter difficult problems in diagnosis. It also provides a basis for understanding the changes still being made to improve overhead valve designs.

**More operating parts** produce both maintenance and operational problems. The more parts there are, the more likely it is that one of them will wear or malfunction. And since most of the additional parts are reciprocating parts, there are even more problems with inertia in I-head engines than in F-heads. At high speed, inertial loadings cause an operational problem known as *valve float*.

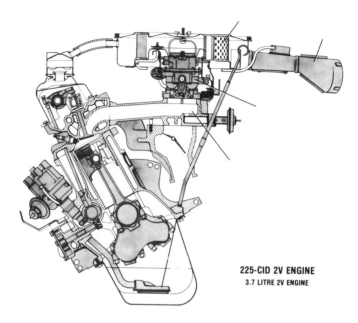

**225-CID 2V ENGINE**
3.7 LITRE 2V ENGINE

**Figure 8–23.** The additional parts needed to operate the overhead valves of an I-head engine can be clearly seen in this cross-sectional view. *Courtesy of Chrysler Corporation.*

To understand valve float, you should first recall the explanation in Unit 8 of how the piston assembly behaves at the end of a stroke. To reverse directions, the piston must first slow to a complete stop, then build its speed again for the return stroke. In the I-head engine, each reciprocating part in the overhead valve assembly goes through the same delaying process with each change of direction. And those momentary hesitations sometimes cause difficulties because the camshaft, which is supposed to control the duration of the valve's opening, does not pause. It rotates steadily. At low speeds, those valve train hesitations cause little difficulty. You will see in the next unit that, except when pushed open by the camshaft, overhead valves are kept closed by special valve springs. Normally, the strength of these springs is great enough to force the valve train to "catch up" to the camshaft soon after the valve's momentary pause. But at high speeds, the inertial forces are much greater. The valve may then be hurled open with such force that, after reversing its direction, it takes far too long to close. This, of course, invites catastrophic damage. If one of those floating valves happens to strike the piston or the other valve, the engine may well be ruined. Valve float, of course, is a particular problem for I-head engines.

**Figure 8–24.**  If a floating valve happens to strike the piston or the other valve, catastrophic damage will result. In this case, the valve stem broke into three pieces, and the valve head wedged in the head of the piston. As often as not, such a mishap will ruin an engine.

**Cost** is also greater for engines with overhead valves. The number of parts and the complexity of the overhead valve assembly both make I-head engines more expensive to manufacture.

One way to overcome some of these disadvantages in the I-head design is to move the camshaft. We can keep the basic I-head design and put the camshaft above the cylinders with the valves. This variation of the basic I-head design is commonly called the "overhead cam" engine.

# Overhead Camshafts

Two kinds of overhead cam designs are in fairly widespread use. Whichever method is used, simply putting the camshaft over the cylinders produces several important advantages.

## *Advantages of the single overhead camshaft (SOHC)*

If the only thing we do to the camshaft is to mount it on the head, we have gone to a single overhead cam (SOHC) design. There are three immediate advantages to this.

**The simpler valve mechanism** requires fewer parts and less maintenance. The reciprocating parts have less total weight; so there is less likelihood of a problem with valve float.

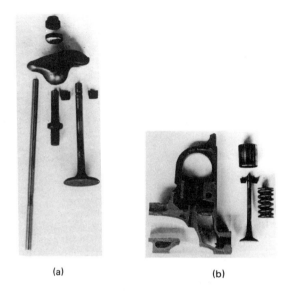

(a)                    (b)

**Figure 8-25.** Photo A shows the valve train parts used in a standard I-head engine. Photo B shows the parts needed when an overhead camshaft is used. The savings in weight reduces inertial forces so that valve float is no longer an important problem

**The greater freedom in the placement of valves** and air passages allows the engineer to make considerable improvements in engine breathing.

**Higher compression ratios** are possible because, with the valves located over the cylinders, the combustion chamber can be much smaller. Also, the engineer does not have to be so dependent on the requirements of the valve opening mechanism in placing the valves. This greater flexibility allows him to shape the chamber to achieve more efficient burning.

## *Disadvantages of the single overhead camshaft*

**Cost** is the SOHC's big disadvantage. To provide a mounting for the camshaft and valve train, the head of a SOHC engine must be more complex. In manufacturing, complexity costs money.

**Engine height** is another disadvantage of SOHC engines. Placing so much of the valve mechanism on top of the head produces a taller power plant, which requires a larger engine compartment.

**Figure 8-26.** Though mechanically simpler, a design using an overhead camshaft requires a taller engine.

It is possible to intensify the advantages of the SOHC design without adding much to its disadvantages. To do this, we simply install a second camshaft in each head. Then we can use one camshaft to operate the intake valves and the other to open the exhaust valves. This gives us a double overhead cam (DOHC) design (Figure 8-14).

## Advantages of the double overhead camshaft (DOHC)

Using two camshafts provides an additional method of controlling engine performance. It also makes it possible to capitalize on the advantages of the SOHC design.

**Control of valve time is easier** when separate camshafts are used for intake and exhaust valves. It sometimes helps to be able to change the timing of one valve without affecting the other. This can only be done when the valves are driven by separate camshafts. The DOHC design gives the mechanic this additional way of controlling engine performance.

**Figure 8-27.** Using two overhead camshafts in a DOHC design makes it possible to adjust the timing of either the intake or exhaust valves without affecting the other.

A **further reduction in the weight and complexity of the valve train design** results when two camshafts are used. The rocker arms used on most SOHC engines are no longer needed because the valves can operate directly off the cams. This eliminates most of the reciprocating weight and, with it, the problem of valve float.

**Still better breathing** results from the DOHC arrangement. With no rocker assembly to get in his way, the designer has even more freedom in placing valves and air passages. He can make sure that there are no unnecessary restrictions on free breathing. In practice, DOHC engines almost always have hemispherical combustion chambers. This means that the spark can be placed for maximum combustion efficiency. With all these advantages, the DOHC engine is capable of a higher level of performance than any other variety of I-head engine.

Its most important disadvantages are its cost and the special steps needed to achieve proper timing.

# VALVE PORTS

The passages cast into the head leading to the intake and exhaust valve openings are called *ports*. These ports help determine breathing efficiency. They should be as large in diameter as possible, as straight as possible, and free of obstructions. Sometimes, however, ports must be angled or reduced in size to allow space for oil and coolant passages or for parts of the valve operating mechanism (Figure 8–28).

**Figure 8–28.** Ports must sometimes be angled around other parts of the engine. Notice how this intake port snakes behind the opening for the push rod.

## Siamesed Ports

Some head designs, most often those on in-line engines, run both intake and exhaust ports in from the same side of the head. When this is done, engineers sometimes save space by arranging for like valves on side-by-side cylinders to share the same port. One intake port will supply fuel mixture through the intake valves of both cylinders and one exhaust port will carry off the gases from both exhaust valves. Ports designed to serve two cylinders in this way are called *siamesed ports* (Figure 8–29).

**Figure 8–29.** When intake and exhaust ports enter from the same side of the engine, designers sometimes save space by planning for like valves on side-by-side cylinders to share the same port. Ports which connect with two cylinders in this way are said to be *siamesed*.

## The Cross-Flow Head

When intake and exhaust valves are located on opposite sides, the design used is known as a *cross-flow head* (Figure 8–30). This design often allows for straighter ports and improved breathing. One striking example, which also serves to emphasize all that we have said about the importance of head design, is Pontiac's four-cylinder, 151 cid engine. Until 1979, this engine used a conventional in-line cylinder head with intake and exhaust valves on the same side. But with its 1979 models, Pontiac went to a crossflow design (Figure 8–31). The better breathing and more accurate fuel distribution that resulted from this change greatly improved the engine's performance. The overall result was significantly better horsepower and torque from an engine that was thirty-five pounds lighter and got about 10% better gas mileage.

**Figure 8–30.** When intake and exhaust valves are located on opposite sides of the chamber, the head is said to follow a *cross-flow* design.

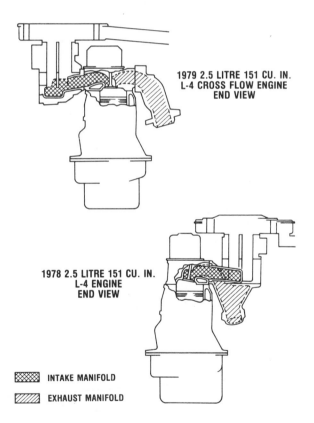

**Figure 8–31.** In 1979, Pontiac substituted this cross-flow head for the conventional in-line head formerly used on its four-cylinder, 151 cid (2500 cc) engine. This produced better breathing and more accurate fuel distribution. Consequently, the engine's overall performance was improved dramatically. *Courtesy of Pontiac Division, General Motors Corporation.*

## REVIEW QUESTIONS

*Objective Questions*

1. On V–8 engines

    _____ A. Left and right side cylinder heads are interchangeable
    _____ B. Left and right heads are not interchangeable
    _____ C. Intake and exhaust ports are on the same side of the head
    _____ D. None of the above

2. Mechanic "A" says the head gasket seals the block and head surfaces.

    Mechanic "B" says the head gasket controls and directs coolant flow in a liquid-cooled engine.

    Who is correct?

    _____ A. Mechanic "A"
    _____ B. Mechanic "B"
    _____ C. Both are correct
    _____ D. Both are wrong

3. Aluminum heads normally

    _____ A. Use replaceable valve guides and seats
    _____ B. Use integral valve guides and seats
    _____ C. Are cheaper than cast iron
    _____ D. Are used on heavy duty engines

4. DOHC engines commonly use a _____ combustion chamber.

    _____ A. Hemispherical
    _____ B. Polyspherical
    _____ C. Wedge
    _____ D. None of the above

5. In air-cooled engines, _____ are used to direct the cooling air to the desired parts of the engine.

    _____ A. Head gaskets
    _____ B. Heat dams
    _____ C. Turning vanes
    _____ D. Shrouds

6. The flathead design is correctly called an

_____ A. L-head
_____ B. F-head
_____ C. I-head
_____ D. OHC head

7. Mechanic "A" says that siamesed ports can "breathe" best. Mechanic "B" says cross-flow heads restrict engine breathing. Who is correct?

_____ A. Mechanic "A" only
_____ B. Mechanic "B" only
_____ C. Both A and B are correct
_____ D. Neither A nor B is correct

8. The F-head design is

_____ A. Used mostly in racing and other high performance designs
_____ B. Obsolete
_____ C. The cheapest design
_____ D. The best "breather"

9. Cylinder head temperatures on air cooled engines normally do not exceed

_____ A. 2800°F
_____ B. 1200°F
_____ C. 500°F
_____ D. 100°C

10. The cylinder head is

_____ A. Of little importance to engine efficiency
_____ B. The cheapest part of the engine to build
_____ C. Just a lid for the cylinder
_____ D. The most important single assembly in determining the efficiency of the internal combustion piston engine

## Questions of Recall and Application

1. How does the choice of head design affect the engine's lubrication system?

2.  List three advantages of aluminum alloy heads.

3.  List three advantages of cast-iron heads.

4.  How might the method of engine cooling affect the choice of cylinder head materials?

5.  Why might die-cast cylinder heads be different to design and produce?

6.  Name two combustion chamber shapes.

7.  How would engine head design improve performance?

8.  What advantages might a DOHC head have over a push rod activated OHV head?

9.  List the advantages of a cross-flow design for an OHV head over a conventional head.

---

### THINGS TO DO AND THINK ABOUT

1.  Visit a wrecking yard or local mechanic. Ask permission to examine some used cylinder heads of different kinds. Notice the various port designs and valve layouts. Why are they made the way they are? How does the valve layout affect the port shape?

2.  Obtain a discarded cylinder head and make it into a cutaway model for your instructor.

3.  Look at an engine head gasket. Notice how it covers and restricts the coolant flow between the head and block. What might occur if it were installed backward or upside down?

4.  Using as a model and guide the cutaway cylinder you made, how could you improve engine breathing by redesigning the head? How would this change the rest of the engine?

# UNIT

# 9

# Valves and Valve Trains

You learned in Unit 8 that the cylinder head is much more important than earlier discussions could indicate. One reason the cylinder head is so important is that—in modern engines—it houses the valves. And the valves are the very heart of the engine (Figure 9–1).

**Figure 9–1.** One reason the cylinder head is so important is that—in modern engines—it houses the valves. *Courtesy of Chrysler Corporation.*

The housewife who drives her four-cylinder Pinto down the expressway at fifty miles per hour is not likely to think once of the valves in her car's engine. But each of those eight valves must open and close 1500 times a minute to keep her gliding along at that speed. Each must open exactly on time every time, cycle after cycle. Beyond that, the four exhaust valves must resist 1100° heat and the 1500 pound pressure they receive with each combustion stroke for years. Modern valves often give up to 100,000 miles of trouble-free operation. They are the results of impressive accomplishments in automotive engineering. The housewife may be able to take them for granted, but the mechanic cannot.

The basic functions of the valves, put into words, sound absurdly simple. All the valve has to do is let the fuel mixture in, seal the combustion chamber tightly, and let the spent gases out. But to get this job done reliably and dependably in the hostile environment of the combustion chamber is not simple. It took engineers most of the first half of this century to learn how to do it well.

So a lot of thought has gone into those valves in that housewife's car and into the mechanism that opens and closes them. The mechanism in her engine, of course, provides only one of several possible ways of controlling valves in automotive power plants. The well-trained mechanic should be familiar with all the commonly used valve operating mechanisms. "Valve jobs" are perhaps the most common of the major engine service operations. So hardly a day goes by when the mechanic does not need to use in the shop the information contained in this unit.

---

## OBJECTIVES

When you have completed this unit you will be able to:

- Draw a rough sketch of an automotive valve and label its more important design features.
- Name the materials used in valve manufacture, tell how each material is used, and explain its advantages and disadvantages.
- Identify, in appropriate diagrams and photographs, the parts in at least three different types of valve trains and explain the operation of each.
- Demonstrate, by answering specific questions, a knowledge of the advantages and disadvantages of at least three different valve operating systems.

- Explain, when asked about a specific head design, how the positioning of the valves in the combustion chamber was influenced by the designer's choice of valve operating mechanism and vice versa.

# THE POPPET VALVE

You know from our mention of reed valves and rotary valves in Unit 3 that different kinds of valves have been used in internal combustion engines. But for automotive applications, the dozens of other valve designs tried over the past 100 years have definitely lost out to the poppet valve (Figure 9–2). Experiments with other valve designs go on, but they are, today, merely engineering exercises. It was a poppet valve which controlled the breathing on Henry Ford's first gas buggy (Figure 9–3). And for the foreseeable future anyway, the poppet-type valve will continue to be *the* valve for automotive engines.

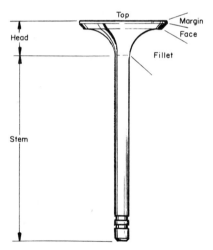

**Figure 9–2.** You will need to know the name and purpose of the features of the poppet valve.

However, the valves you will work with as a mechanic exceed anything Ford could have dreamed of at the turn of the century. The poppet type valves of eighty years ago were so unreliable that cylinder heads were designed to allow for "instant" valve jobs. Special valve access plugs in the head made it possible to remove the valves without disassembling the engine. A few minutes under a roadside shade tree were all that great granddad needed to install a new set of valves. Those old-fashioned valves only lasted for a few thousand miles. So granddad probably spent more time alongside the road than he cared to. Can you imagine his reaction if someone had told him that, in just a few decades, it would be commonplace for a valve to open and close 200 million times without failing?

**Figure 9–3.** A poppet valve controlled the breathing on Henry Ford's first gas buggy. *Courtesy of the Motor Vehicle Manufacturers' Association of the United States of America.*

## Design Features of the Poppet Valve

There is no better way to begin a study of engine valve trains than by getting to know the poppet valve. To read the shop manuals and specifications that you will consult daily, you will need to know the nature and purpose of each of its features. Figures 9–2 and 9–4 label the most important ones. Notice that the flat, circular surface is properly called the valve *head.* The head faces the inside of the combustion chamber. The long rod-like shank attached to the back side of the valve head is the *stem.* The stem fits into a precision opening, the valve *guide,* positioned in the engine cylinder head (Figure 9–4). The valve stem must fit tightly into the valve guide to prevent oil leakage. For this reason, auto manufacturers specify exactly the amount of stem clearance permissible in the valve guide.

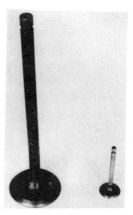

**Figure 9–4.** For automotive applications, other valve designs have lost out to the poppet valve. For the foreseeable future, anyway, the poppet-type valve will be *the* valve in automotive engines.

Note in Figure 9–2 that the valve head has a certain "thickness" before its edge angles sharply towards the valve stem. That thickness is the valve's *margin;* the angled surface is its *face*. Both are extremely important when a mechanic is deciding whether to reuse a valve. Do not confuse the valve "face" with the valve "seat", which is its proper mating surface (Figure 9–4). The valve face is the key part of the valve, located on the "underside" of the *valve* head. The valve seat is the matching angled surface, located in the *cylinder head*.

Notice in Figure 9–4 the spring positioned around the upper end of the valve stem. The retainer that holds this spring in place is locked into place by a set of *keepers* or *spring retaining keys*. These keys (mechanics are more likely to call them "keepers") fit into one or more *keeper grooves* near the end of the valve stem (Figure 9–5). Notice also the *chamfer*, the angled ring that slightly "sharpens" the stem tip. This chamfer serves to counteract the natural tendency of the metal to spread, as it is repeatedly hammered by the rocker arm.

**Figure 9–5.** The retainer around the upper end of the valve stem is held in place by a set of "keepers" or retaining keys.

Study Figures 9–2 and 9–4 until you know the correct names of the parts of the valve. You will need to remember them, in order to read the rest of this unit with understanding. Beyond that, they are terms you will use frequently throughout your career as an automotive mechanic.

## Valve Train Design

The unit consisting of the valves, the camshaft, and all the linkage used to connect them is called the *valve train.* In designing the valve train, the engineer is always working towards three goals: (1) breathing efficiency; (2) durability; and (3) cost efficiency. As always, he is forced into tradeoffs in his effort to match his engine to its design requirements.

There are no foolproof formulas to guide his decisions in planning a valve layout, but there are some basic rules that a mechanic should know.

1. *The diameter of the intake valve should be a little less than half the diameter of the cylinder bore.* The intake valve should be rather large in order to let in as much fuel mixture as possible. Normal atmosphere pressure, remember, is the only thing pushing the intake charge into the chamber.

2. *The exhaust valve should be about 85% as large as the intake valve.* The exhaust gases, being under pressure, will rush out through a smaller opening so the exhaust valve does not have to be as large as the intake valve.

3. *The amount of valve lift should equal about 25% of its head diameter. Lift* is the technical name for the distance a valve is raised off its seat when it is fully open (Figure 9–6).

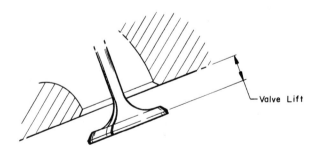

**Figure 9–6.** *Lift* is the technical name for the distance a valve is raised off its seat when it is fully open.

# Types of Poppet Valves

The poppet valves in common use today come in three different shapes: the *flathead,* the *tulip head,* and the *SAE standard head.*

**The Flathead.**  The most common design in today's automotive engines is the flathead valve (Figure 9–7). The flathead valve is strengthened by a very large fillet area, where the stem joins the head. This extra strength helps it maintain proper head and stem alignment despite the high temperature beating it takes during operation.

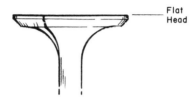

**Figure 9–7.**  The most common design in today's automotive engine is the flathead valve.

**The Tulip head.**  Dish-shaped valve heads are often found in modern high-performance engines (Figure 9–8). The so-called *tulip head* design has several advantages. The hollowed center makes it lighter, but the thickness around the outside edge and the large fillet area give it strength. The fillet surface, being very smooth, produces an additional advantage. As the gases blow over its curved surface, they form an air-flow pattern known as a *venturi.* (You will learn about venturis when you study carburetion.) The effect of a venturi is to increase air speed and lower its pressure. In other words, the highly polished fillet on the tulip head valve creates a strong suction. This, in turn, increases the engine's breathing efficiency by a good margin. This is just one example of how subtle changes in the valve, the valve seat, or the port can make dramatic differences in performance.

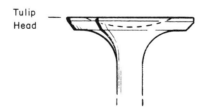

**Figure 9–8.**  In modern high-performance engines, dish-shaped valve heads, called *tulip heads,* are found. These valve heads have several advantages.

**The SAE Valve Head.**   A third type of poppet valve has a head that is slightly convex, or dome-shaped. This SAE design makes the head thickest in the center to increase its strength there (Figure 9–9). The underside of the head, however, blends into the stem without much of a fillet radius.

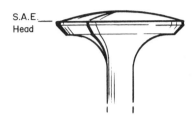

**Figure 9–9.**   The SAE design makes the head thickest in the center to increase its strength there.

Engineers disagree about the theoretical desirability of keeping the valve head well supported and rigid. Some experts feel that the valve head should be allowed to flex during operation so that it could conform better to irregularities in the valve seat. In practice, however, valves designed to flex in this way do not usually last as long as less flexible valves. (Figure 9–10.)

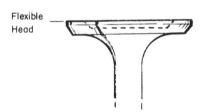

**Figure 9–10.**   Despite their theoretical superiority, flexible valves, such as this one, do not usually last long.

## Valve Construction

Exhaust valves, as we have noted, are exposed to much more punishment than intake valves. They must keep their strength and resist warping and corrosion at extremely high temperatures. For this reason, they are usually forged of special steel alloys. Typically, such an alloy will combine chromium and nickel with small amounts of carbon, manganese, silicone, and molybdenum.

Since intake valves are exposed to less stress, they can be made of cheaper materials. Every new intake charge absorbs heat from the preceding combustion stroke as it blows over the intake valve on its way in. In practice, the temperature of the intake valves in most engines seldom exceeds 800° F (420° C). Most intake valves, therefore, are made of mild steel as this material costs less and performs satisfactorily.

## Other Valve Materials

Some exhaust valves are forged of stainless (austenitic) steel. It has more impact strength and better resistance to corrosion at high temperatures. But it also costs more, has less scuff resistance, and expands more when it is hot. In fact, thermal expansion may be as much as 40% greater with stainless steel valves. This makes it much harder to maintain proper clearances at all temperatures.

**Bi-Metal and Tri-Metal Valves.**   To adapt the valve parts better to their different operating conditions, some valves are made of more than one metal. The different metals are welded together so that the finished valve combines the advantages of all of them. It is most important that the head resists corrosion and withstands heat. The face must resist warpage and bending even though it gets extremely hot while slamming shut, say, 1500 times a minute. But materials with excellent heat resistance tend to have little resistance to friction. This presents a difficulty because the valve stem must slide up and down in the valve guide, with minimum lubrication, millions of times.

Manufacturers, therefore, often cast the head of high-temperature steel alloy and weld it to a stem made from an alloy that resists wear better in sliding applications (Figure 9–11). To further reduce wear and galling inside the valve guide, that part of the valve stem is often plated with chromium.

**Figure 9–11.**   Manufacturers often cast the valve head of high-temperature steel alloy and weld it to a stem made from an alloy known to resist wear better in sliding applications. In this valve, a similar weld between the scuff-resistant stem and the hardened rocker arm contact area can be seen.

**Aluminized Valves.**   Where high-temperature corrosion is a special problem, aluminized valves may be used instead of expensive stainless steel alloys. Aluminized valves are manufactured by spraying a hot plasma of ionized aluminum onto the valve head and fillet. Such coatings have been found to double the service life of standard steel valves in high-corrosion environments.

**Sodium-Cooled Valves.**   A valve stem that demands special attention is found on the sodium-cooled valve. Remember that in normal operation a valve may be literally red hot. For it to function properly, it must pass this heat rapidly to cooler parts of the engine, which in turn transfer it to the liquid radiator coolant. To help cool the valves in many heavy duty engines, valve stems are made hollow and partially filled wih sodium (Figure 9–12). Sodium is a metal that melts at 208° F. When the engine is operating and the valve is moving up and down, the sodium turns into liquid and sloshes up and down inside the stem. First, it is thrown towards the sizzling head of the valve where it absorbs part of the heat. Then, as the valve reverses its movement, the sodium is hurled into the cooler stem where it gives up heat. (The stem then transfers the heat to the engine head through the valve guide.) This circulation may reduce valve temperature by as much as 200° F. Lower operating temperature, of course, means longer valve life.

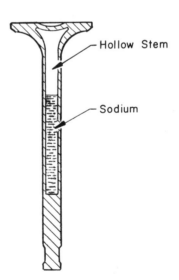

**Figure 9–12.**   To help cool the valves in many heavy duty engines, valve stems are made hollow and are partially filled with sodium. Special precautions are necessary when working with sodium-cooled valves.

Sodium-cooled valves are rarely used in production model passenger cars for two reasons. First, the large stem diameter required to house the sodium requires a much stronger valve train. Second, the additional materials and complex process required to manufacture sodium-cooled valves make them very expensive.

> **CAUTION:** Sodium can be very dangerous material. It causes severe burns if it gets on the skin. Dropped into water, it bursts into flame. Tightly sealed inside the valve stem, sodium is safe enough, but a sodium-cooled valve with a cracked or broken stem is potentially dangerous. Discarded sodium valves should be disposed of in accordance with governmental regulations. Though they are not always marked, sodium valves can usually be recognized by the thickness of their stems.

# BASIC VALVE ASSEMBLY AND RELATED PARTS

There is no accepted label for that portion of the valve train shown in Figure 9–2. But it seems logical to consider all the components below the rocker arm as one unit. Although not all engines have rocker arms, the assembly of parts beneath the rocker arm is basically the same in all modern automotive engines. So for the purposes of discussion, we shall call this portion of the valve train the *basic valve assembly*. It consists of the valve, valve guide, valve spring, valve seat, spring retainer, keepers and (on some engines) the valve rotator.

## Valve Guides

Two kinds of valve guides are in general use today.

### Integral valve guides

In many engines using cast iron cylinder heads, the valve guide is just an accurately drilled hole in the cylinder head (Figure 9–13). This type is called an *integral valve guide*.

**Figure 9–13.** In many engines using cast-iron cylinder heads, the valve guide is just an accurately drilled hole in the cylinder head called an *integral valve guide.* In other engines, replaceable valve guides are used.

## Replaceable valve guides

Where serviceability is an important consideration, or where the metal in the valve stem is not compatible with that in the head, *replaceable guides* are used. Replaceable guides of cast iron, bronze, or some similar alloy are frequently found in aluminum heads. These replaceable valve guides are, in effect, precision-finished tubes, intentionally made slightly larger than the holes they fit into. Machinists install them in the head by a special process known as interference press fitting. The interference press fit then holds the guide securely in place.

## Functions of the valve guide

The valve guide performs three functions. First, it provides a bearing surface on which the valve stem can slide. Second, it carries heat from the valve stem to the engine's cooling system. Third, it centers the valve head exactly in its seat. If the valve head is not properly centered, serious problems soon develop.

When the alignment is bad enough to prevent a gas tight seal, the pressurized combustion gases escape through the opening at tremendous speeds. At high temperatures, this quickly destroys both the valve and its seat. Sometimes an off-center valve is close enough to proper alignment to let the valve head flex and seal. In this case, the valve guide is sure to wear rapidly (Figure 9–13a). And the valve head may actually break off and cause catastrophic damage (Figure 9–14).

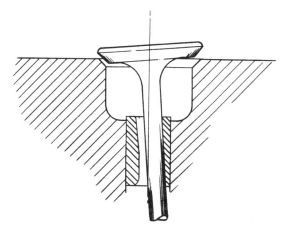

**Figure 9–13a.** An improperly seated valve will wear the guide quickly.

**Figure 9–14.** An off-center valve guide could cause the valve head to break off and cause catastrophic damage.

## Normal wear patterns for valve guides

Even when valves are perfectly centered, their stems do not push evenly against all sides of the valve guide. The rocker arms tend to exert a sideways thrust on the valve stem. In time, this causes both ends of the valve guide to wear in a funnel-shaped or bell-mouthed pattern (Figure 9–15). To reduce this wear, most valve guides are designed so that their length is about seven times as great as their inside diameter. Such a ratio does not prevent bellmouthing, but does minimize it.

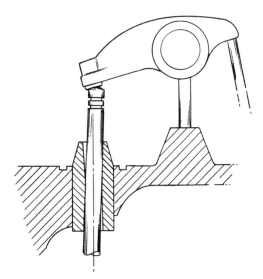

**Figure 9–15.**   Rocker arms tend to exert a sideways thrust on the valve stems. In time, this causes both ends of the valve guide to wear in a funnel-shaped or bell-mouthed pattern.

# Valve Seats

Even a perfect valve cannot provide a gas tight seal unless its mating seat is in good shape. Three methods are used to provide this seat.

### Integral seats

In many cast iron heads, the valve seats are simply machined into the casting. These *integral seats* are not normally used in aluminum heads or in applications where wear and corrosion resistance are especially important. In those situations, the head is more likely to be equipped with *seat inserts.*

### Seat inserts

A seat insert is a ring-shaped piece of metal made to be press fitted into a precision recess in the cylinder head (Figure 9–16). Like the replaceable valve guide, the seat insert is usually made a few thousandths of an inch larger than the hole it fits into. When it is installed, the resulting interference fit secures it in place and improves heat transfer. When integral seats are damaged beyond service limits, seat inserts are sometimes installed as a means of repair.

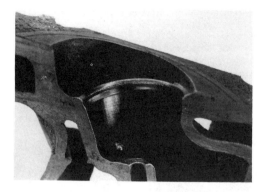 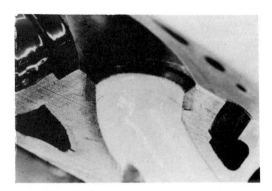

**Figure 9–16.** A seat insert is simply a ring-shaped piece of metal made to be press-fitted into a precision recess in the cylinder head.

## Induction hardened seats

A recently developed process for reducing wear and corrosion on internal valve seats is *induction hardening*. It became common a few years after the move towards unleaded gasoline as it minimizes the effects of unleaded fuels. To produce an induction hardened seat, a special induction coil is placed over the valve seat area. A high-frequency electric current is then passed through the coil to set up a magnetic field. The magnetic field heats the iron around the valve seat to a preset temperature. When the seat is hot enough, the induction coil is removed and the seat is *quenched,* to cool it rapidly under controlled conditions. This way, the hardness of the valve seat can be exactly controlled.

## Operating problems with valve seats

The extreme temperatures and pressures of the combustion chamber keep the valve seat under almost constant stress. These stresses can warp the head or distort the valve seats so that the guide is no longer centered properly in the seat. This leads to the spacing and wear problems already mentioned; therefore, designers try to keep both mechanical and thermal stresses to an absolute minimum.

Designers try to minimize the head warpage by carefully positioning the head bolts and specifying the exact torque to which they should be tightened. And, as we saw in Unit 8, they plan the cooling system carefully to keep thermal distortion to a minimum (Figure 9–17). Where seat inserts are used, the engineer or mechanic must take their higher operating temperature into account. Since they normally run about

150° F (66° C) hotter than integral seats, some seat inserts require special heat resistant valves.

**Figure 9–17.** The cooling system is carefully planned to keep thermal distortion to a minimum.

## Valve face and seat dimensions

The angle of the valve face and its matching seat is very important. The two surfaces are not always cut at *exactly* the same angle, but where a difference does exist, it is very slight. So for the moment, we will assume that the valve face and seat are angled alike. Experience has shown that automotive engine valves usually give better service if the face angles are either 30° or 45° (Figure 9–18).

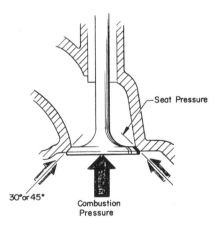

**Figure 9–18.** The two best seat angles are 30° and 45°.

The 45° angle is particularly good for getting a tight seal. The 30° angle allows better gas flow between valve and seat when the valve first starts to open. This helps in breathing, but 30° valves do not seal very well.

For these reasons, 30° angles are used only on intake valves, and are not used unless air flow is important and the likelihood of particles catching on the valve face is low.

**Seat width.**   The actual width of the valve seat and its area of contact with the valve face are both important. Specified seat widths differ from engine to engine, but they are seldom narrower than .040 inch (1 mm) or wider than .090 inch (2 mm). If specifications are unavailable and a mechanic has no choice except to guess, $^1/_{16}$ inch or .060 inch (1.5 mm) is a good average. Note in Figure 9–19 that the area above the seat is usually ground at a 30° angle and that the throat area below the seat is cut to 60°. There are three reasons that seat width must be measured so precisely.

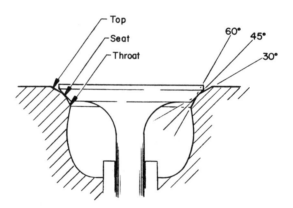

**Figure 9–19.**   The area above the seat is usually ground at a 15° or a 30° angle. The throat area below the seat is normally cut to 60°.

**1. The sealing pressures** from the valve spring and the gases inside the chamber must be neither too great nor too slight. If the face is too wide, the pressure from the gases will not be concentrated enough to give a good seal. But too narrow a face concentrates all the force in too small an area. This can soon deform both the valve face and seat.

**2. Cleaning action** results from contact pressures that are great enough to squeeze any particles which happen to get trapped between the valve face and head. A particle which was not soon knocked loose and blown off could, of course, cause serious problems. The valve would not seal; so the engine would lose compression; and the valve would soon burn (Figure 9–20).

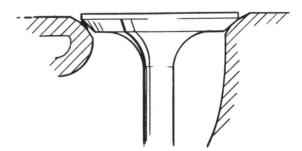

**Figure 9–20.**   A particle trapped between the valve face and seat could cause serious problems. The valve would not seal; so the engine would lose compression, and the valve would soon burn.

**3. Heat transfer** is another function of the valve seat that can only be performed properly by a seat of the correct width. The seat carries away about three-fourths of the heat from the valve face. Though the seat cannot be so wide that it causes sealing problems, it must be wide enough to allow for the necessary heat transfer.

### Interference angle

Some manufacturers specify that the angles of the valve seat and valve face should differ by a small amount. This difference, called the *interference angle,* may be as little as one-fourth of a degree or as much as one degree. The interference angle provides a line contact seal, by concentrating pressure around the outside edge of the valve. This allows better spacing during break-in. But the interference angle is quickly worn away in operation. It usually disappears after 100 miles or so (Figure 9–21).

## Valve Springs

The function of the valve spring is to close the valve as soon as the camshaft permits it to close. It must be strong enough to move not only the valve, but all the valve train parts as well (Figure 9–22). Valve float can occur if inertia in the valve train causes slack to develop between

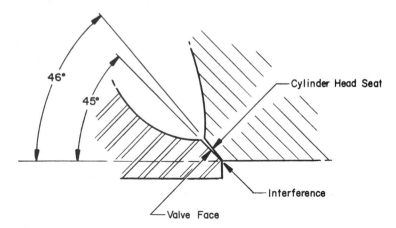

**Figure 9–21.**  The interference angle helps during break-in. But it is quickly worn away in operation, disappearing after 100 miles or so.

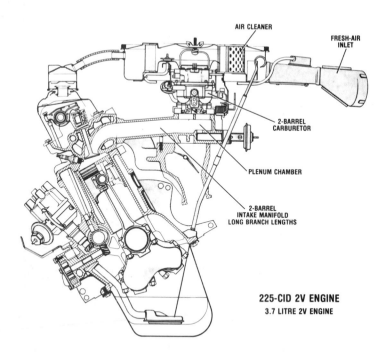

**Figure 9–22.**  The valve spring must be strong enough to move not only the valve but all of the valve train parts as well. *Courtesy of Chrysler Corporation.*

components. The valve spring must have enough strength to prevent that, but it cannot be too strong. That would put too much pressure on the valves' seats and cause rapid wear or deformation. This is an excellent reminder of the importance of lightness in valve train components. When those parts are lighter, the valve springs can do an adequate job without putting too much pressure on the valve seats.

Almost all automotive engines use coil-type valve springs. Some efforts have been made to create linkages that would enable the camshaft to pull the valve shut after opening it. These *desmodromic* valve systems, however, have met with little success in passenger cars. Some modern motorcycles successfully use hairpin type springs and others use torsion bars to close their valves.

Some coil-type valve springs are wound unevenly, with their lower coils tighter and closer than their upper coils. These are called *variable-rate* springs.

## Harmonics

The rapid compression and relaxation of the valve springs tends to set up vibrations that interfere with its proper function. These vibrations, called *harmonics,* can cause the spring to lose tension during part of its cycle or—in extreme cases—to break. To dampen these harmonic vibrations, some valve springs are equipped with flat inner springs designed to rub against the valve spring itself. Other designs use a closely wound inner spring which dampens vibrations when it is compressed enough to bring its coils into contact with each other. To increase the overall spring tension, some valve springs are made up of two coil springs. The springs are usually coiled in opposite directions to help reduce harmonics (Figure 9–23).

**Figure 9–23.** Some valve springs are made up of two coil springs, the purpose of the second spring being to increase overall valve spring tension. In this design, the springs are usually coiled in opposite directions in order to reduce harmonics.

## Spring Retainers and Keepers

Most keepers have a split cone design. They are usually machined from high quality steel and heat-treated to give them maximum strength and hardness. Retainers are either forged or machined from high quality steel except where weight is a major factor. When lightness is important, they are made from heat-treated aluminum alloys or titanium, which is lighter than aluminum but 30% stronger.

## Valve Rotators

When leaded gasoline is used, valve life is longer and sealing is better if the valve is made to rotate on its seat. This rotation has several advantages. The rotary action provides added cleaning action by helping to dust off any particles that get trapped between the valve face and seat. It ensures proper valve stem lubrication by spreading oil evenly inside the valve guide. Because it constantly changes the parts of the valve that are in contact with any hot spots in the valve guide or seat, it also allows the valve to operate with a uniform face temperature. Rotation also evens out the wear on the valve tip caused by the rocker arm and reduces the build-up of deposits on the stem.

### Methods of ensuring rotation

Three methods are used to ensure adequate valve rotation.

**Release-Type Valve Assembly.** The oldest method uses a release-type basic valve assembly. In engines using this method, the retainer has designed into it a section shaped like an upside down cup (Figure 9–24). The tip of the valve stem does not quite reach the inside bottom of this cup. Therefore, when the rocker arm pushes on the outside "bottom" of the cup, it depresses the spring slightly before the valve begins to open. This releases the tension on the valve and allows the spring vibrations to "bounce" it into rotation. Few modern automotive engines still depend on release-type valve assemblies.

**Positive Valve Rotators.** A special device called a *positive valve rotator* is often either built into the retainer or placed beneath the valve spring to act as its seat. There are various designs for these rotators. Some use ball bearings and springs (Figure 9–25). Others combine a coil spring with a flat Bellville-type spring (Figure 9–26).

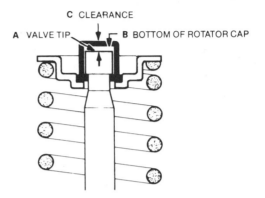

**Figure 9–24.** In engines with a release-type basic valve assembly, the retainer has designed into it a section shaped like an upside down cup. Acting on this "cup," the rocker arm releases spring tension on the valve and allows spring vibrations to bounce it into rotation. *Courtesy of the Dana Corporation.*

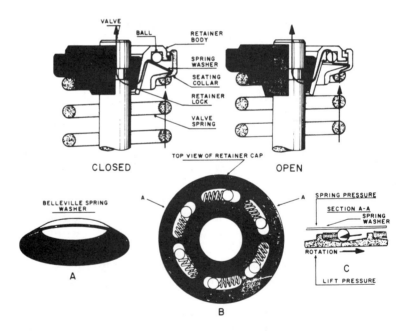

**Figure 9–25.** A special device called a positive valve rotator is often either built into the retainer or placed beneath the valve spring to act as its seat. Some use ball bearings and springs in their design. *Courtesy of the Dana Corporation.*

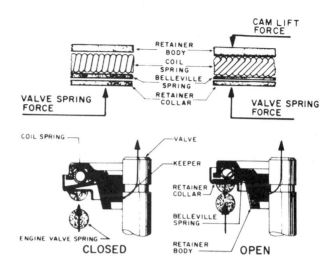

**Figure 9–26.** Some rotators combine a coil spring with a flat bellville-type spring. *Courtesy of the Dana Corporation.*

The mechanic should always read the manufacturer's directions to learn exactly how a given valve rotator is supposed to work. Generally, all these positive valve rotators convert reciprocating motion into rotary motion. They take a tiny fraction of the reciprocating motion in the valve train and use it to nudge the valve into constant rotation.

Fewer engines are equipped with positive valve rotators since American manufacturers began designing passenger car engines to burn unleaded fuel. Without the lubricating effect of the lead additive, valves turned by positive rotators are particularly susceptible to scuffing.

**Offset Rocker Arm Contact.**   Some manufacturers design rocker arms so that they do not wipe against the exact center of the valve tip. By slightly offsetting the point of rocker arm contact, a slight twisting motion is generated that tends to rotate the valve.

## VALVE TRAIN AND CAMSHAFT

To follow the remaining discussions in this book, you will need to know the definitions of four important technical terms.

**1. Duration.** The length of time that a valve is open is called *duration*. But mechanics and engineers do not measure duration in units of time, like minutes or seconds. The actual time that the valve remains open varies with engine speed. So in mechanics, duration is always measured in degrees of crankshaft rotation. This measure does not vary with speed. In our simplified explanation of the Otto-cycle in Unit 2, we said that each of the four strokes took one-half (180°) a crankshaft rotation. In practice, it works much better, however, if the duration of the intake valve is a good deal longer than 180°. Intake duration for a high performance passenger car may easily be as much as 290° (Figure 9–27).

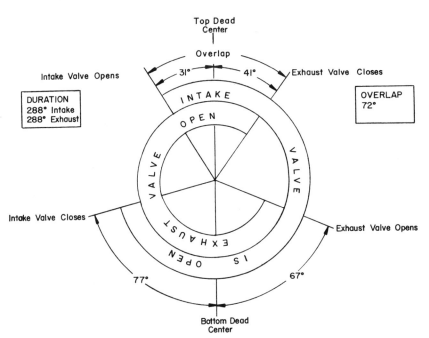

**Figure 9–27.** Intake duration should be a good deal longer than 180°. Intake duration for a high performance passenger car may easily be as much as 290°.

**2. Overlap.** To lengthen intake duration, it is necessary that, for a short period, the intake and the exhaust valves both be open at the same time. This *overlap* period begins as the piston nears TDC on the exhaust stroke and ends by the time the piston has a good start downward on its intake stroke. You will see in Unit 11 how much valve overlap can contribute to engine breathing.

**3. Lift.**  As you know, *lift* refers to the distance a valve raises above its seat when it is fully open. Lift is normally measured at the valve seat in thousandths of an inch. But sometimes it is measured at the cam lobe. Depending on the type of valve train used, this may or may not equal a measurement taken at the valve seat. If rocker arms are used, their mechanical advantage must be used as a multiplier in order to calculate the actual lift at the seat (Figure 9–28).

**Figure 9–28.**  Depending on the type of valve train used, lift may or may not equal a measurement taken at the valve seat.

**4. Cam Contour.**  The shape of the cam controls when and how fast the valve opens and closes. It also determines how far it opens and how long it stays open. So *cam contour* has more effect on the engine's breathing efficiency than any other component in the valve train. Figure 9–29 gives the accepted trade terms for identifying different areas of the cam lobe.

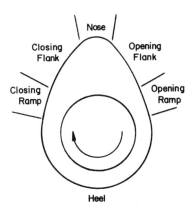

**Figure 9–29.**  Cam contour has more effect on the engine's breathing efficiency than any other component in the valve train.

## Camshaft Construction

Most passenger car camshafts are cast from hardenable grey iron or steel alloys. Some camshafts, intended for heavy duty or racing engines are machined from solid steel. Camshafts are normally made in one piece, with any necessary accessory gears being cast as integral parts of them. They are case hardened to make them resist wear better, and this hardening makes them very brittle. Dropping a camshaft will normally break it.

## Valve Operating Mechanisms

In Unit 8, you were given a general understanding of the valve layout in each of the common head designs. Now, however, it is time for a closer look. When you finish this chapter you should have a fairly detailed understanding of each common type of valve train. So as you read about each design, be sure that you find the answers to these three questions: (1) Where is the camshaft located in that design? (2) What exactly is it that turns the camshaft? (3) How exactly is the power from the camshaft carried to the valve?

### L-head valve trains

In the flathead design, as you know, the camshaft is located in the block above and to one side of the crankshaft. It is usually driven from the crankshaft by meshing gears at the accessory end. Sometimes, however, sprockets are used instead of gears. In this case, they are connected by a chain (Figure 9–30).

**Figure 9–30.** Sometimes sprockets are used instead of gears to drive the camshaft from the crankshaft.

Since L-head valve trains consist of nothing more than the basic valve assembly, their operation is direct and simple. As the camshaft turns, its lobes operate *lifters* or *tappets,* fitted into special holes in the block directly above each cam lobe. As the lifter follows the cam contour it converts the rotary movement of the cam, at just the right time, into up-and-down motion. The upper end of the lifter acts directly on the tip of the valve stem, so the cam lobes must supply the total valve lift. To give their cams the extra height needed, camshafts in L-head engines must be larger and heavier than those in I-head power plants.

The lifters in L-head engines are almost always *solid lifters.* They are simply hollow cast-iron tubes which are closed at the camshaft end. The other end is threaded and fitted with a special bolt and locking device (Figure 9–31). This provides a method of adjustment so that excessive clearance between the lifter and the valve stem can be removed.

**Figure 9–31.** One end of solid lifters is threaded and provided with a special bolt and locking device. This provides a method of adjustment so that excessive clearance between the lifter and the valve stem can be removed. *Courtesy of Sealed Power Corporation.*

## The basic I-head valve train

In the basic I-head design, the camshaft is located and driven just as it is in the L-head. But with its overhead valves, two more parts must be added to the valve train. They are the *push rod* and the *rocker arm* (Figure 9–32).

The push rods rest on the lifters and extend through special holes in the block to press against the bottom of the rocker arm at one of its ends. The rocker arm is simply a precision designed seesaw. Its function is to turn the upward motion of the push rod into downward motion which can depress the spring and open the valve. In some engines, rocker arms also provide a means of adjusting valve train clearances.

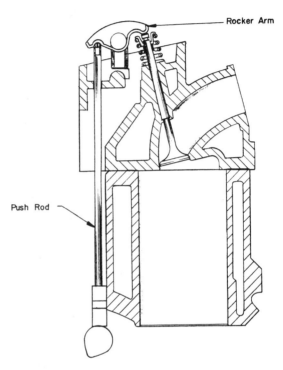

**Figure 9–32.** With overhead valves, two more parts must be added to the valve train: (a) the push rod, and (b) the rocker arm.

**Rocker Arm Ratio.** Most rocker arms are designed with a mechanical advantage so that they increase valve lift. That is, they make the valve open downward further than the camshaft pushes upward. To understand how this works, think of a seesaw. Do you remember what you did when you wanted to seesaw with another youngster who was much bigger than you? The usual solution was to move the teeter board off center and give the shorter end to the bigger kid. Younger boys are glad to do that because they know that whoever is on the long end gets a longer ride (Figure 9–33).

The camshaft, like the big boy, has ample power to operate the rocker arm from the short end. So it too is placed off center. This makes the valve end move downward further than the camshaft end moves up, so the camshaft lobe can be smaller, and the whole camshaft can be made smaller and lighter (Figure 9–34). The exact amount of this mechanical advantage is called *rocker arm ratio.* On most passenger cars, the rocker arm ratio is between 1.5:1 and 1.7:1. Seldom does it exceed 2:1.

A.                                                                                            B.

**Figure 9–33.** The camshaft, like the big boy on the seesaw, has ample power to operate the rocker arm from the short end. So it, too, is placed off center.

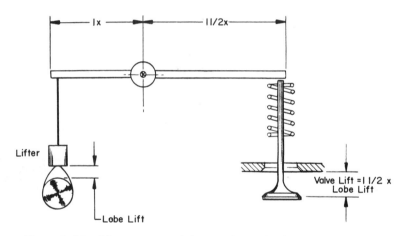

**Figure 9–34.** The amount of the mechanical advantage is called *rocker arm ratio.*

## Kinds of Rocker Arms

Rocker arms are made in a variety of ways and from a variety of materials (Figure 9–35). Forged, cast, and stamped rocker arms are all in common use. Forged steel rocker arms are the strongest, cast iron the cheapest. Stamped steel is probably lighter than either and stronger than aluminum, which is also used.

**Figure 9–35.** Rocker arms are made in a variety of ways and from a variety of materials.

Rocker arms are supported and attached to the cylinder head at their pivot points. All the rocker arms may be mounted on one rocker arm shaft. Or each rocker arm may be mounted separately on its own stud.

**Shaft-Supported Rocker Arms.** In this method the shaft that secures the rocker arms is itself supported by cast-iron pedestals (Figure 9–36). These pedestals may be cast either as integral parts of the head or bolted to it. A precision ground tubular shaft is used and is normally heat treated.

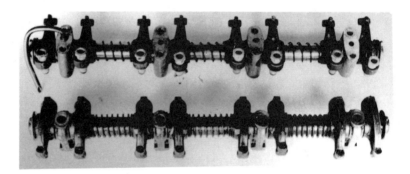

**Figure 9–36.** The shaft securing the rocker arms is itself supported by cast-iron pedestals.

Oil is pressured into the shaft through special passages on hollow bolts in the mounting pedestals. The ends of the shaft are capped, so all the oil is forced to the rocker arms through holes in the bottom of the shaft. Lubricating at the bottom of the shaft places the oil at the point of greatest wear. Both the valve spring and the push rod press *upward* on the ends of the rocker arm.

Rocker arms mounted on tubular shafts may be either cast or stamped. When cast-iron rocker arms are used, the rocker arm bores are often fit with replaceable bronze or brass bushings (Figure 9–37).

**Figure 9–37.** It is common practice, when cast-iron rocker arms are used, to fit the rocker arm bores with replaceable bronze or brass bushings.

**Stud-Mounted Rocker Arms.** When individual studs are used, they are topped by ball-shaped pivots which fit into sockets made into the rocker arms. The rocker arms themselves may either be cast or stamped. Sockets are also provided to seat the push rods (Figure 9–38). Where a clearance adjustment is provided, it is usually a retaining nut above the ball pivot. Turning this nut raises or lowers the ball and, with it, the rocker arm.

**Figure 9–38.** Rocker arms may either be cast or stamped.

Holes in the push rod sockets allow oil to be pumped up through the hollow push rods into the oil passages in the rocker arms. The shape of the rocker arm socket enables it to trap oil and keep the ball pivot lubricated. Less often, hollow support studs are used to feed oil to the ball pivots (Figure 9–39).

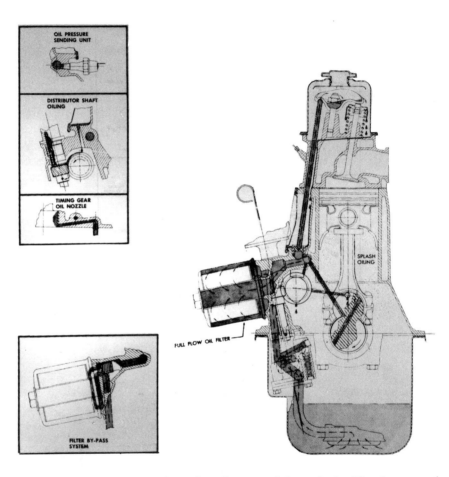

**Figure 9–39.** Notice how the oil pumped through the lifter is pumped up through the hollow push rod onto the topside of the rocker arm. *Courtesy of Chevrolet Motor Division, General Motors Corporation.*

## Hydraulic Lifters

The lifters used on most modern engines are hydraulic. Hydraulic lifters provide automatic lash adjustment and reduce the valve tappet noise which is frequently a nuisance with solid lifters. *Valve lash* is a label used to refer to the sum of all the clearances between parts of the valve train. Some lash is necessary so that the valve mechanism will still close the valves tightly after operating heat expands its parts. As with solid lifters, one is allotted to each valve. So a modern V–8 has sixteen.

Figure 9–40 shows a cutaway view of an installed hydraulic lifter. Like a solid lifter, it sits in a special guiding hole in the block and rides on the cam lobe. The difference is that the hydraulic lifter automatically adjusts valve lash during operation and maintains zero clearance.

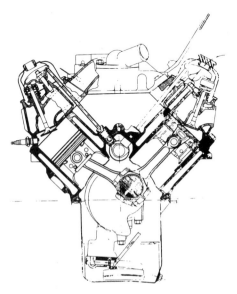

**Figure 9–40.** Like a solid lifter, a hydraulic lifter sits in a special lifter bore in the block and rides on the cam lobe. *Courtesy of Chevrolet Motor Division, General Motors Corporation.*

**Advantages of Hydraulic Valve Lifters.** The hydraulic lifter offers six specific advantages:

1. It eliminates the need for periodic adjustments of valve clearance.

2. It quiets valve train operation by a wide margin.

3. It reduces pounding on the valve seat and thus contributes to longer valve life.

4. It compensates automatically for changes in the engine's operating temperature.

5. It compensates automatically for normal wear in valve train components.

6. In some engines it also provides positive lubrication to the overhead parts of the valve train.

**Lifter Construction.** Most hydraulic lifters consist of the nine parts shown in the exploded views provided by Figure 9–41. Named in order starting at the top, these parts are:

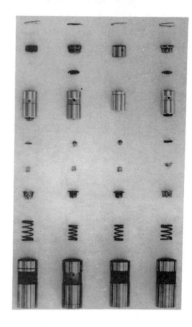

**Figure 9–41.** Most hydraulic lifters consist of the nine parts shown here. *Courtesy of the Dana Corporation.*

1.   Circlip-type plunger retainer
2.   Push rod seat
3.   Metering disk (used only on lifters which supply oil through their push rods to lubricate the overhead parts of the valve train).
4.   Plunger
5.   Check ball
6.   Check ball spring
7.   Ball and check spring retainer
8.   Plunger spring
9.   Follower, or body

These parts are shown assembled in Figure 9–42.

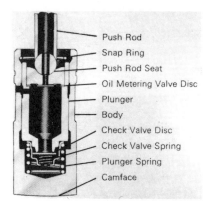

- Push Rod
- Snap Ring
- Push Rod Seat
- Oil Metering Valve Disc
- Plunger
- Body
- Check Valve Disc
- Check Valve Spring
- Plunger Spring
- Camface

**Figure 9–42.** An assembled hydraulic lifter looks like this. *Courtesy of Sealed Power Corporation.*

**Lifter Operation.** In operation, all the hollows in the lifter are filled with oil. Some oil is trapped in the body of the lifter beneath the plunger. This oil supports the plunger when pressure on the valve train is at a maximum. When the pressure lessens, the plunger spring expands to keep the valve train free of lash. A small amount of oil moves upward around the plunger and back down through the check ball valve to compensate for these changing forces.

Figure 9–43 shows a hydraulic lifter in position, with the valve closed. The lifter is riding on the base circle of the cam, and inside the lifter, the plunger spring is pushing the plunger upward to eliminate any lash.

As the cam nose moves under the lifter (Figure 9–44), the pressure of the collapsed valve spring tries to force the plunger downward in the body of the plunger. At this point, the oil trapped beneath the plunger supports it. However, the lifter is designed to let a small amount of trapped oil squish past the plunger.

After the lobe has passed under the lifter the engine valve closes and the valve spring is relaxed (Figure 9–45). In the lifter, the plunger spring expands to keep lash from developing in the valve train. As this happens, oil inside the hollow plunger is allowed to pass through the check valve and refill the space in the bottom. So the cycle starts again.

If the lifter is designed to supply oil to the rocker arm assembly, that function is performed as shown in Figure 9–46. Oil is supplied to the inside of the plunger through special holes in the plunger and body of the lifter. The oil is then forced through a metering hole, through an opening in the push rod seat, and up the hollow push rod to the rocker arm.

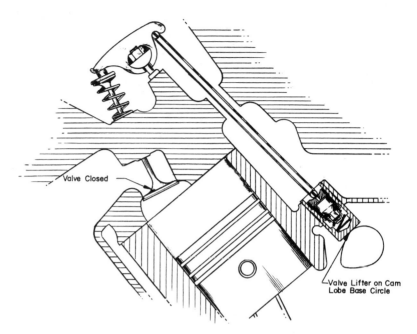

**Figure 9–43.** A hydraulic lifter in position, with the valve closed.

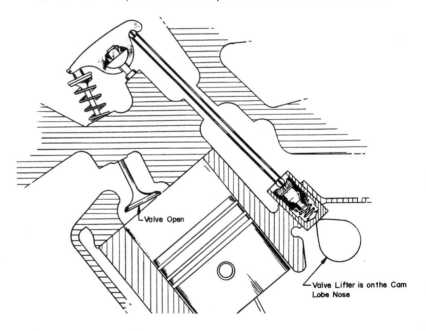

**Figure 9–44.** Here the cam nose moves under the lifter while the pressure of the collapsed valve spring tries to force the plunger downward in the body of the lifter.

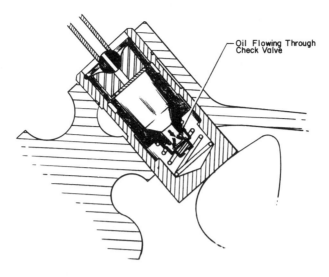

Oil Flowing Through
Check Valve

**Figure 9–45.** After the lobe has passed under the lifter, the engine valve closes, and the valve spring is relaxed.

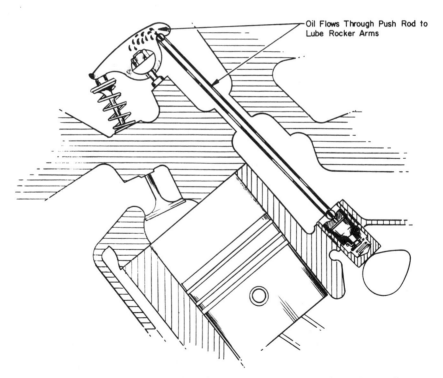

Oil Flows Through Push Rod to
Lube Rocker Arms

**Figure 9–46.** If the lifter is designed to supply oil to the rocker arm assembly, that function is performed like this.

**Cam-to-Lifter Contact.**    The relation of the bottom, or *face,* of the lifter to the cam surface is very important. Though the lifter face looks flat, it is not. It is rounded to about a .002 inch crown in the center. Moreover, the appearance of the cam lobe is equally deceptive. The nose of the cam is not squared across from one side to the other as it seems to the naked eye. Actually one side of the lobe is about .007 inch higher than the other. The rounded face of the lifter lets it contact the cam lobe just slightly off center (Figure 9–47).

This is desirable for two reasons. First, it prevents excessive wear on the long side of the cam, which—if the lifter were flat on the bottom—would be subjected to high loading. Second, the eccentric wiping by the cam rotates the lifter in its bore and thus ensures an even wear pattern on both lifter and cam. Here, as elsewhere, such small details make big differences. Loads on the lifter and camshaft can easily reach 100,000 psi during normal operation. Therefore, steps taken to improve the efficiency of valve train operation pay big dividends in longer service life and less maintenance.

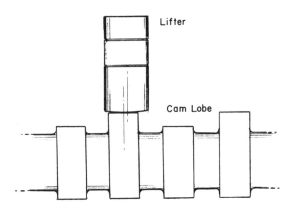

**Figure 9–47.**   The rounded face of the lifter enables it to contact the cam lobe just slightly off center.

## Valve Stem Seals

A problem that exists in any overhead valve engine is oil leakage between the valve stem and guide. Steps must be taken to control oil leakage in any variety of the I-head engine design (Figure 9–48). In many I-head engines, seepage past the valve stems is the major cause of excess oil consumption. It causes three problems that design engineers would like to prevent:

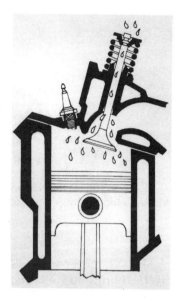

**Figure 9–48.** Steps must be taken to control oil leakage in any variety of the I-head engine designs. *Courtesy of the Dana Corporation.*

**1. High Emissions of Hydrocarbons.** When the leakage is bad enough, it causes smoking as well as emissions of noxious gases. Such "smokers" are illegal in some states and a first rate nuisance anywhere.

**2. Carbon Deposits in the Combustion Chamber.** Carbon build-up in the combustion chamber increases the effective compression ratio of the cylinder. It then becomes necessary to use high octane fuel to prevent ping and detonation (Figure 9–49).

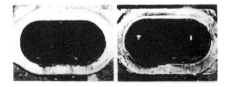

**Figure 9–49.** When carbon builds up in the combustion chamber, it becomes necessary to use high octane fuel to prevent ping and detonation. *Courtesy of the Dana Corporation.*

**3. Carbon Deposits on the Valve Stem.** When carbon builds up on the valve stem, its free action inside the guide is impeded. This interferes with breathing and lowers engine efficiency (Figure 9–50).

**Figure 9–50.** When carbon builds up on the valve stem, its free action inside the guide is impeded. *Courtesy of the Dana Corporation.*

**Methods of Control.** Since it is essential that overhead valve trains be lubricated well, there is always a generous supply of oil in the area of the valve guide. Several factors combine to draw a portion of that oil into the combustion chamber. Gravity, normal atmospheric pressure, cylinder vacuum, and a venturi created by exhaust gases rushing past the guide—all play a part in causing this kind of oil consumption (Figure 9–51).

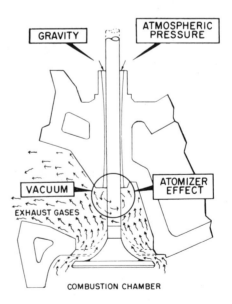

**Figure 9–51.** Gravity, normal atmospheric pressure, cylinder vacuum, and a venturi created by exhaust gases rushing past the guide—all play a part in causing oil consumption. *Courtesy of the Dana Corporation.*

Besides keeping stem-to-guide clearances to very fine tolerances, manufacturers use two other means of reducing oil leakage. Some install metal shields, called *deflectors,* above the valve spring. In some cases, this deflector may be designed into the valve spring retainer. When this is done, an "0" ring is fitted into a machined groove in the valve stem, just under the valve keepers. The outside of the "0" ring seals against the inside edge of the spring retainer and stops oil from flowing down the stem (Figure 9–52).

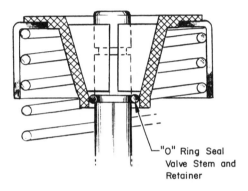

"0" Ring Seal
Valve Stem and
Retainer

**Figure 9–52.** In some types of deflectors, the outside of the "O" ring seals against the inside edge of the spring retainer and stops oil from flowing down the stem.

Another common type of deflector is the *umbrella seal* (Figure 9–53). This is simply a rubber cup with a hole in its bottom just large enough for the valve stem. It is installed "upside down" over the tip of the valve stem. This forms a kind of umbrella inside the valve spring which deflects excess oil away from the valve guide.

A second way of diverting oil away from the guides is through the use of *positive valve guide seals* (Figure 9–54). These seals work like backwards piston rings—instead of expanding, they contract. Their design allows them to meter enough oil for stem lubrication, but they stop the flow of air and oil because their inner sealing surfaces wipe excess oil off the valve stem before it can reach the guides.

Perfect Circle Division of Dana Corporation has developed a positive valve seal that uses a teflon insert to seal around the stem (Figure 9–55). For this purpose, a teflon surface has several distinct advantages over a standard rubber sealing surface. First, teflon is chemically inert, so it does not decompose or interact with lubricants or combustion by-products. Second, it has a higher temperature tolerance. It resists heat and stays flexible over a very wide range of temperatures. Also, teflon's extremely low coefficient of friction makes it virtually self-lubricating.

Teflon-type positive guide seals are manufactured in several designs (Figure 9–56). In the design that uses a teflon insert inside a rubber seal, the rubber, with the help of a spring steel retainer, seals around the outside of the guide. The teflon, of course, seals the stem. This design provides flexibility for the teflon if guide wear causes the valve to wobble. The manufacturer claims that this seal successfully controls oil loss in guides with as much as .006 inch clearance. In engines with valve springs that are very small in diameter, smaller all-teflon seals are used.

**Figure 9–53.** A common type of deflector is the umbrella seal, a rubber cup with a hole in its bottom just large enough for the valve stem.

**Figure 9–54.** A second way of diverting oil away from the guides is through the use of positive valve guide seals. *Courtesy of Perfect Circle Division of the Dana Corporation.*

**Figure 9–55.** A positive valve seal utilizing a teflon insert to seal around the stem has been developed. *Courtesy of Perfect Circle Division of the Dana Corporation.*

**Figure 9–56.** Teflon-type positive guide seals are manufactured in several designs. *Courtesy of Perfect Circle Division of the Dana Corporation.*

Many car manufacturers now install these Perfect Circle valve seals as original equipment. Others use positive valve guide seals of their own, which are more or less similar in design. Tests have shown that these seals dramatically reduce oil consumption through worn guides (Figure 9–57).

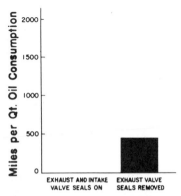

**Figure 9–57.** Tests have shown that positive guide seals dramatically reduce oil consumption through worn guides. *Courtesy of Perfect Circle Division of the Dana Corporation.*

Positive valve guide seals can be installed in almost any engine built in the last twenty-five years. Sometimes, no modification is necessary on the outside of the guide. In other engines, a simple machining operation by the mechanic adapts the guide for the installation. Detailed instructions for this procedure are included in most shop manuals.

## OVERHEAD CAMSHAFT DESIGNS

An almost infinite variety of subtle design differences have been introduced in the manufacture of overhead camshaft engines since the mid 1950's. It is beyond the scope of this book to describe them all. The overview presented here, however, will give you a sound foundation on which to base the detailed knowledge that comes only from experience in the shop.

## SOHC Valve Trains

Most SOHC valve trains can be classified into three basic designs:

### The cam-in-head design

The so-called cam-in-head design uses rocker arms that are operated by a camshaft mounted low in the head (Figure 9–58). The most obvious feature of this design is the fact that the camshaft operates the rocker arms from the *bottom,* pressing upward on them, much as push rods do in a simple I-head design. Placing the camshaft beneath the rocker arms in this way has the advantage of reducing slightly the height of the engine. In this design, the valves may or may not be arranged in a cross-flow pattern.

Normally, cast rocker arms are used. They are usually shaft-mounted and equipped with adjustment screws. An alternate design by Opel uses stamped steel rocker arms with built-in hydraulic lifters. Another interesting modification is found on some BMW rocker arms (Figure 9–59). These have rollers on their valve ends to reduce friction and wear on the guide.

### SOHC designs using rocker arms

More common than the cam-in-head design is the rocker arm variation of the SOHC engine. In this design, the camshaft is mounted on pedes-

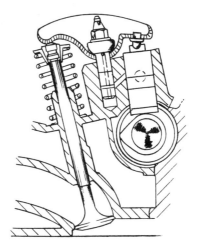

**Figure 9–58.** The so-called cam-in-head design uses rocker arms which are operated by a camshaft mounted low in the head.

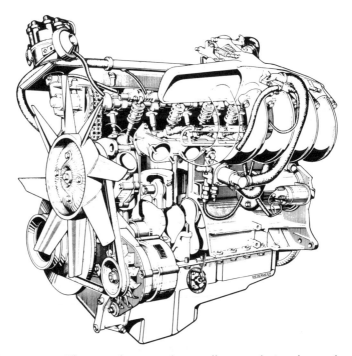

**Figure 9–59.** These rocker arms have rollers on their valve ends to reduce friction and minimize wear on the guide. *Courtesy of BMW of North America.*

tals at the very top of the engine. The cams press *downward* on the rocker arms which are beneath the camshaft (Figure 9–60). The common practice is to place the pivot point at one end of the rocker arm and the valve at the other. The cam lobe is then placed so that it will push down on the middle.

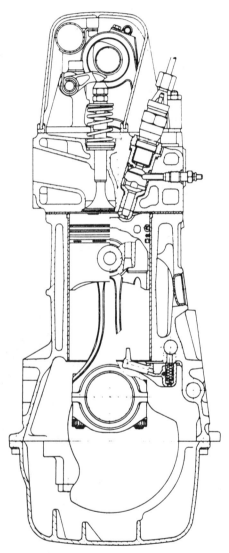

**Figure 9–60.** In SOHC designs using rocker arms, the camshaft is mounted on pedestals at the very top of the engine. The cams press downward on the rocker arms which are beneath the camshaft. *Courtesy of Mercedes-Benz of North America.*

In this design, the pivot ends of the rocker arms may be supported in either of three ways. They may be shaft-mounted (Figure 9–60), mounted on adjustable ball studs (Figure 9–61), or supported by self-adjusting hydraulic lifters (Figure 9–62).

**Figure 9–61.** Pivot ends of the rocker arms may be mounted on adjustable ball studs.

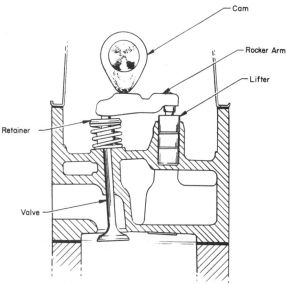

**Figure 9–62.** Pivot ends may be supported by self-adjusting hydraulic lifters.

This engine is taller than one built in the cam-in-head type. But it offers the designer greater freedom in choosing the shape of the combustion chamber and the location of the valves.

## SOHC designs without rocker arms

The last variation of the SOHC design dispenses with rocker arms altogether. It operates the valves directly off the camshaft. In this design, the engineer does not have much choice about placing his valves. They must be directly under the camshaft. Most engines of this design use cup-shaped tappets. The mouth of the cup fits over the basic valve assembly and into a specially bored opening in the head (Figure 9–63).

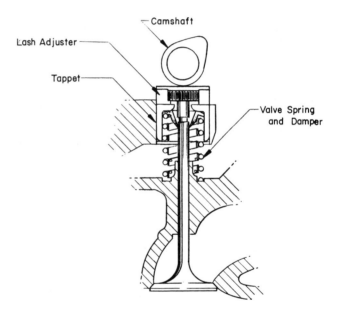

**Figure 9–63.** This variation of the SOHC design dispenses with rocker arms altogether.

Two methods are used to adjust valve clearance on this kind of SOHC engine. The most common method is to insert *spacers* or shims between the valve stem tip and the inside top surface of the tappet. This normally requires removal of the camshaft and tappets, which is a tedious and time-consuming operation. However, it does not need doing often, for there is relatively little wear on this kind of valve train. In its Rabbit series, Volkswagen introduced a design feature that greatly simplifies this adjustment (Figure 9–64). They designed a place to insert spacers at the top of their cam followers. Using their special tools, it is possible to adjust clearance without removing the camshaft.

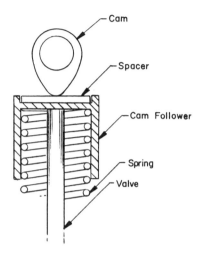

**Figure 9–64.** Volkswagen introduced in its Rabbit series a design feature which greatly simplifies the adjustment of valve clearance.

A different method of adjustment was developed for Chevrolet's 140 cid Vega engine. The tappet on the Vega is also cup-shaped. But it has built into it a special adjustment setting which can be operated with an Allen wrench. An Allen-headed screw has one side ground flat to form a tapered "ramp" (Figure 9–65). The screw is threaded through the tappet at a 5° angle, but the tapered ramp on the screw is square to the axis or the tappet. This means that the flat side of the screw and the top of the follower are in even contact. Therefore, the clearance between them is minimal and the wear is evenly distributed. The mechanic makes an adjustment in one-turn increments, with each turn changing clearance by .003 inch (Figure 9–66).

## DOHC Valve Trains

In most DOHC engines, the cam activates the valves directly, without the assistance of rocker arms. They usually use cup-type cam followers with shim-type adjustments similar to those just discussed in SOHC engines

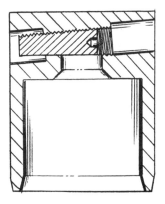

**Figure 9–65.** On Chevrolet's 140 cid Vega engine, the tappet contains an adjustment mechanism which can be operated with an Allen wrench. The flat-sided screw is threaded through the tappet at a 5° angle. But the tapered "ramp" on the flat side of the screw is perpendicular to the axis of the tappet.

**Figure 9–66.** The mechanic makes an adjustment in one-turn increments, with each turn changing clearance by .003″.

## CAMSHAFT DRIVE SYSTEMS

The mechanism that connects the camshaft to the crankshaft is of crucial importance to accurate timing. A number of ways are used to drive automobile camshafts. Generally, the decision about which method to use in a given engine is influenced by the location of the camshaft and the levels of noise, accuracy, and cost considered acceptable.

# Gear-Driven Systems

Gear driven camshafts on L-head and OHV engines normally consist of only two gears (Figure 9–67). A smaller steel gear on the crankshaft meshes with a large fiber or aluminum gear attached to the camshaft. Fiber or soft aluminum is used to reduce noise, and *helical* teeth are used on the gears for the same reason. Helical teeth are angled so that they do not run straight across the face of the gear (Figure 9–68).

**Figure 9–67.** Gear-driven camshafts on L-head and OHV engines normally use only two gears.

**Figure 9–68.** Helical teeth are angled so that they do not run straight across the face of the gear. This reduces noise.

For alignment, the shaft opening in each gear is slotted, to create what mechanics call a *key way*. There is a similar key way in each shaft. A matching piece called a *key,* is fitted into the key way on the shaft. This key extends above the circumference of the shaft enough to fill the key way in the gear. The key way in the gear is then aligned with the extended key, and the gear is locked into place on the shaft (Figure 9–69). Special marks, called *timing marks,* on each gear make it possible for the mechanic to ensure the proper relationship of camshaft to crankshaft during assembly.

## Chain-Driven Systems

When a timing chain drives the camshaft, it runs off a small sprocket on the crankshaft. This sprocket is usually keyed on the crankshaft in the manner just described for gears. But the larger sprocket, on the camshaft, is indexed to the cam with pins or bolts.

On plain I-head (OHV) engines, a special chain is used to connect the two sprockets. Called *silent chain,* it operates much more quietly than the bicycle-type roller chain formerly used. In some engines, noise and vibration are further dampened by a nylon coating on the cam sprocket teeth.

There is one important difference between gear-driven and chain-driven camshafts which the beginning mechanic should note and remember. When motion is transmitted from one gear to another, the direction of rotation is reversed. So a two-gear system for driving the camshaft turns it in a direction opposite that of the crankshaft. No such reversals take place in chain and sprocket systems.

Because silent chain systems usually use only short lengths of chain between sprockets, no special tensioning drivers are needed to keep slack out of the chain.

## Chain Drives for OHC Engines

Silent chain is not normally used on OHC engines for two reasons. First, silent chain has so much stretch that it is unsuitable for use in such long lengths. Second, the timing chain on OHC engines is often used to drive the oil pump and distributor, as well as to turn as many as four different camshafts. It is desirable for the chain to be flexible in both directions so that it can snake around all those sprockets.

The chain that is used on OHC engines is of a double-roller type. Because of the long lengths used, some type of automatic tensioning device is normally designed into this kind of cam drive system (Figure 9–70).

## Valve Timing Marks
### 1949-57 CARS

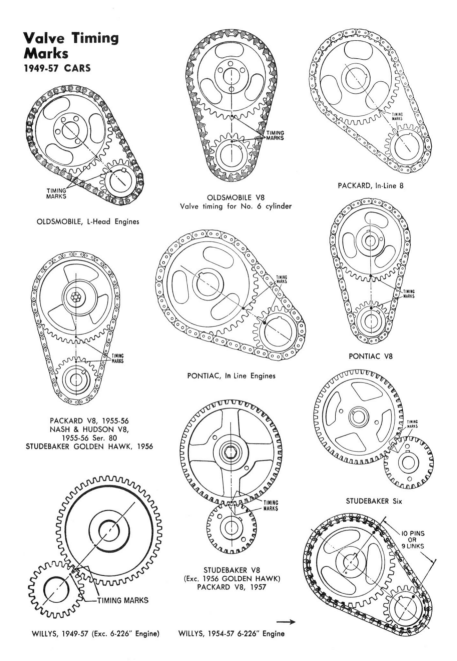

OLDSMOBILE, L-Head Engines

OLDSMOBILE V8
Valve timing for No. 6 cylinder

PACKARD, In-Line 8

PACKARD V8, 1955-56
NASH & HUDSON V8,
1955-56 Ser. 80
STUDEBAKER GOLDEN HAWK, 1956

PONTIAC, In Line Engines

PONTIAC V8

STUDEBAKER Six

STUDEBAKER V8
(Exc. 1956 GOLDEN HAWK)
PACKARD V8, 1957

WILLYS, 1949-57 (Exc. 6-226" Engine)

WILLYS, 1954-57 6-226" Engine

10 PINS
OR
9 LINKS

**Figure 9–69.** Timing marks on each gear make it possible for the mechanic to ensure proper relationship of camshaft to crankshaft during assembly. *Courtesy of McQuay-Norris Manufacturing Corporation.*

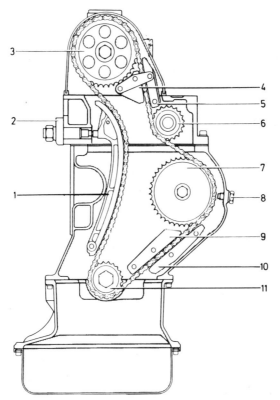

| | |
|---|---|
| 1 | Tensioning rail |
| 2 | Chain tensioner |
| 3 | Camshaft gear |
| 4 | Inner slide rail |
| 5 | Outer slide rail |
| 6 | Guide wheel |
| 7 | Intermediate sprocket (injection timer) |
| 8 | Chain locking screw |
| 9 | Inner slide rail |
| 10 | Outer slide rail |
| 11 | Crankshaft gear |

**Figure 9–70.** Because of the long lengths required in the timing chains of engines with overhead camshafts, some type of automatic tensioning device is usually used. *Courtesy of Mercedes-Benz of North America.*

## Cogged Timing Belts

A cheaper and quieter way of driving overhead camshafts was developed in Europe in the 1950's. It was refined and introduced in the United States in the late 1960's, by Pontiac. Since then it has come into widespread use. Instead of chain, this method uses a belt of oil-resistant synthetic rubber molded over a stranded steel or nylon cord. Teeth molded into the rubber on the inside of the belt engage the teeth of the sprockets and maintain the proper timing (Figure 9–71).

These cogged timing belts have virtually no stretch and require no lubrication. So the oil-tight housings and special lubrication methods required on chain-driven systems are not necessary. In recent years, the flexible timing belt has made inexpensive, small displacement

OHC engines possible and practical. No doubt many of the people driving cars with OHC engines today would not have been able to afford them had it not been for this one invention.

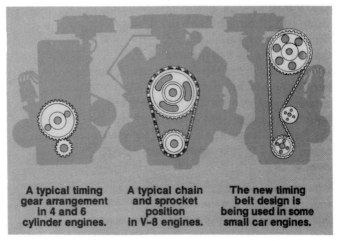

**Figure 9-71.** When a timing chain is used to drive the camshaft, it runs off a small sprocket on the crankshaft. *Courtesy of TRW Corporation.*

## REVIEW QUESTIONS

*Objective Questions*

1. Oscar says, "Exhaust valves are usually forged of steel alloys." Oswald says, "Exhaust valves are usually about 85% of the size of intake valves."

   Who is right?

   _____ A. Oscar only
   _____ B. Oswald only
   _____ C. Both
   _____ D. Neither

2. Three common types of poppet valve are:

   _____ A. Reed, SAE, and tulip head
   _____ B. Flathead, SAE head, and tulip head
   _____ C. Rotary, tulip head and flathead
   _____ D. Rotary, reed, and flathead

3. A disadvantage of austenitic (stainless) steel exhaust valves is

_____ A.  The 40% greater thermal expansion of stainless steel.
_____ B.  Their poorer scuff resistance in the valve guide.
_____ C.  Both A and B.
_____ D.  Neither A nor B.

4. Frank says, "Aluminized valves are designed to resist corrosion at high temperatures."

Fritz says, "Sodium-cooled valves are normally used only on heavy duty engines."

Who is correct?

_____ A.  Frank
_____ B.  Fritz
_____ C.  Both
_____ D.  Neither

5. Which type of valve requires special safety precautions?

_____ A.  Sodium cooled
_____ B.  Austenitic steel
_____ C.  Aluminized
_____ D.  Mild steel intake valves

6. Pete says, "The valve guide is used to insulate the cylinder head and lessen wear on it."

Paul says, "The valve guide is used to carry heat away from the valve stem and to center the valve head in its seat."

Who is correct?

_____ A.  Pete only
_____ B.  Paul only
_____ C.  Both
_____ D.  Neither

7. The bell-mouthed wear pattern is normal in

_____ A.  Push rods in OHV engines.
_____ B.  Valve guides in DOHC engines.
_____ C.  Cam followers in SOHC engines.
_____ D.  Valve guides for valves operated by rocker arms.

8. Joe says, "Excess oil leakage occurs only through intake valves."

   Jim says, "Excess oil leakage occurs through both intake and exhaust valves."

   Who is correct?

   _____ A.   Joe only
   _____ B.   Jim only
   _____ C.   Neither Joe nor Jim
   _____ D.   Andy Granitelli

9. Which type of engine design is least likely to use rocker arms?

   _____ A.   L-head
   _____ B.   F-head
   _____ C.   I-head
   _____ D.   SOHC

10. Tom says, "The diameter of the intake valve is normally a little less than half the diameter of the cylinder bore."

    Ted says, "The diameter of the exhaust valve is normally a little less than half the diameter of the intake valve."

    Who is right?

    _____ A.   Tom only
    _____ B.   Ted only
    _____ C.   Both Tom and Ted
    _____ D.   Neither Tom nor Ted

11. The camshaft and crankshaft are most likely to rotate in opposite directions when the camshaft is driven by

    _____ A.   Silent chain
    _____ B.   Double-link roller chain
    _____ C.   Cogged belt
    _____ D.   Gears

12. Richard says, "Push rods are not found on I-head engines."

    Roger says, "Rocker arms are not normally found on DOHC engines."

    Who is correct?

_____ A.   Richard

_____ B.   Roger

_____ C.   Both Richard and Roger

_____ D.   Neither Richard nor Roger

13. Which design gives the design engineer the *greatest* amount of freedom in deciding where to place his valves?

_____ A.   SOHC engine without rocker arms

_____ B.   Cam-in-head type engine

_____ C.   F-head engine

_____ D.   DOHC engine

14. Joe says, "*Interference angle* is the term used to refer to a slight difference between the angle of the valve face and the angle of its matching face."

John says, "The interference angle, in practice, is usually lost by the time the engine has been in service for 100 miles or so."

Who is correct?

_____ A.   Joe only

_____ B.   John only

_____ C.   Both Joe and John

_____ D.   Neither Joe nor John

15. *Duration* is measured in

_____ A.   Hours

_____ B.   Degrees

_____ C.   Rods

_____ D.   Cubic centimeters

16. Keith says, "*Solid* valve lifters are actually hollow."
Kevin says, "Hydraulic lifters create valve lash."
Who is correct?

_____ A.   Keith only

_____ B.   Kevin only

_____ C.   Both Keith and Kevin

_____ D.   Neither Keith nor Kevin

17. The face of a hydraulic valve lifter is

   _____ A.  Dish-shaped
   _____ B.  Moon-shaped
   _____ C.  Pointed
   _____ D.  Dome-shaped

18. Basil says, "Umbrella type deflectors are used to prevent the leakage of oil through the valve guides."

   Bob says, "Positive valve guide seals are used to prevent the leakage of oil through the valve guides."

   Who is correct?

   _____ A.  Basil only
   _____ B.  Bob only
   _____ C.  Both Basil and Bob
   _____ D.  Neither Basil nor Bob

19. The period of time when the intake and exhaust valves are both open at the same time is called

   _____ A.  Duplication
   _____ B.  Duration
   _____ C.  Contour
   _____ D.  Overlap

20. Sam says, "Positive valve rotators are either built into the valve retainer or placed under the valve spring in order to cause the valve to rotate on its seat."

   Steve says, "Positive valve rotators are the only means available for causing valves to rotate during operation."

   Who is right?

   _____ A.  Sam only
   _____ B.  Steve only
   _____ C.  Both Sam and Steve
   _____ D.  Neither Sam nor Steve

# ENGINE OPERATION

# 10

# Basic Engine Math and Measurements

By now, you have a fairly sound knowledge of the basic physics applicable to the operation of engines of various kinds. But just knowing about engines, energy, work, heat BTU's, foot-pounds, and thermal efficiency is not enough. If you are serious about working with engines, you must be able to measure the effects of your work. Whether you are rebuilding engines or simply making adjustments to improve their performance, you must be able to do a few simple calculations. Otherwise, you really cannot do your work well.

A truism in auto racing says, "Don't change anything unless you understand what that change will cause and why; and only make changes you can measure." Thousands of dollars are wasted by amateurs "doing what Joe did." In automotive technology, *how much* is usually as important as *what*.

## OBJECTIVES

When you have finished this unit, you should be able to do the following:

1. Define these terms:

   (a) bore
   (b) stroke
   (c) displacement
   (d) compression ratios
   (e) horsepower

1. indicated horsepower
2. brake horsepower
3. SAE horsepower

(f) engine efficiency

1. mechanical efficiency
2. volumetric efficiency
3. thermal efficiency

2. Calculate on a "live" engine:

(a) cylinder displacement of a standard engine, one that has been bored, and one that has been stroked
(b) volumetric efficiency
(c) brake horsepower
(d) mechanical efficiency
(e) piston head

---

## DETERMINING ENGINE DISPLACEMENT

It is common practice to indicate engine size in terms of *displacement*. The displacement of a single cylinder is the total space taken up as the piston moves from BDC to TDC. Multiplying this volume times the number of cylinders gives the total engine displacement. To make it easier to understand the arithmetic, we will compute, as examples, some common engine displacements. All we need to know, for this computation, are three measurements: (1) cylinder bore diameter, (2) stroke, and (3) number of cylinders.

*Cylinder bore diameter* is simply the distance across the cylinder at its widest point. This diameter is necessary because the first step in computing displacement is to calculate the *area* of the piston head, and to do that we begin with the cylinder bore diameter (Figure 10–2). The top of the piston head is, of course, a circle. So to compute its area, we use the formula for the area of a circle that we were taught in school.

FORMULA: $\pi R^2$ = area of piston head or bore

Where $\pi$ = 3.1416
And R = radius of bore

In case you have forgotten, the symbol $\pi$, pronounced "pie," always equals 3.1416 when rounded to four decimal places. And the *radius*, by definition, is simply one-half the diameter.

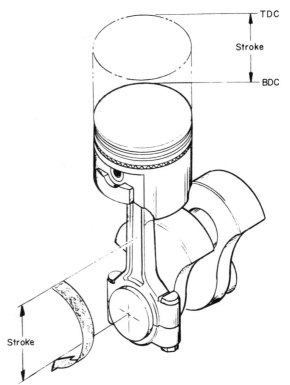

**Figure 10–1.** Displacement is the total space covered by the movement of the piston head from BDC to TDC. It is measured in cubic inches or cubic centimeters and is commonly used to indicate engine size.

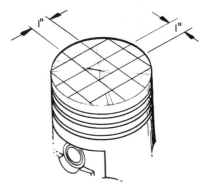

**Figure 10–2.** The surface area of the top of the piston (including the top side of the compression chamber) is the dimension used in calculating displacement. It is, of course, the same as the cylinder bore diameter.

So to compute the area of the piston head on a Ford 351 engine, we begin with the fact that its bore diameter is four inches. Since the radius is half the diameter, the radius in this case equals 4″ ÷ 2″. Therefore, our calculation proceeds like this:

FORMULA: $\pi R^2$ = area of piston head or bore

Substitution: 3.1416 × 2² =
Solution:      3.1416 × 4 = 12.566 square inches of area for one cylinder. (For our purposes we will be accurate enough, if we round off to one decimal place, e.g., 12.6)

Our next step in figuring an engine's total displacement is to calculate the displacement volume of a single cylinder. For this, we take the area just calculated and multiply it by the engine's *stroke*. Stroke is the distance traveled by the top of the piston in one full movement from BDC to TDC. So the formula for finding the displacement of one cylinder is:

FORMULA: BA × S  = displacement of one cylinder

Where BA = bore area
And S  = stroke

The Ford 351 has a stroke of 3.5″, or 3½″. Therefore, we apply our formula like this:

FORMULA: BA × S = displacement of one cylinder

Substitution: 12.6 sq. in. × 3.5 in. =
Solution: 12.6 sq. in. × 3.5 in.    = 44.1 cu. in., the displacement of one cylinder

All that now remains, to get the total displacement of the engine, is to combine the displacements of all the cylinders. Since each piston displaces the same volume, this is a simple task. We just multiply the displacement of one cylinder times the number of cylinders in the engine. In the case of the Ford 351, which is an eight-cylinder engine, this works out in a surprising way.

FORMULA (in words):
area × stroke × number of cylinders = Total Displacement

FORMULA (in symbols):
$\pi R^2$ × S × N = Total Displacement

Substitution and Solution:

44.1 cu. in. × 8 = 352.8 cu. in.

Interestingly enough, the engine Ford marketed as its "351 cid" actually has a displacement of 352.8 cu. in. Possibly they were influenced by the fact that they had formerly sold an engine designated as a 352. Perhaps they did not want to create confusion by giving two engines the same displacement designation. At any rate, it is not uncommon for manufacturers to allow themselves slight inaccuracies in naming engines. The Chevy 327, for instance, actually has a displacement of only 326.72 cu. in.

Before we begin running through some practical applications, study the complete formula once more to be sure that you understand every part of it. If you ever need to refresh your memory, this is probably the version you will want to look up:

FORMULA: $\pi R^2 \times S \times N$ = Total Displacement Volume

Where $\pi$ = 3.1416
  R = Bore Radius (half the bore diameter)
  S = Stroke
  N = Number of cylinders

As you see, a change in any one of the three displacement variables—bore, stroke, number of cylinders—will alter the engine's total displacement.

Suppose wear in the cylinders of our Ford 351 engine made it necessary to bore the cylinder .040″ oversize. Can you calculate the engine's new displacement? Using the formula you just learned, and knowing that our 351 cid engine has been bored oversize. 040″, we simply add the additional .040″ to the standard bore diameter and use the same formula. Our new diameter is 4.040″ for each cylinder. So the new radius is 2.020″. We first square the radius:

2.020 × 2.020 = 4.0804

*Remember: the diameter is not the same mathematical expression as the radius squared.* A common mistake is to double the radius instead of multiplying it by itself. Correctly computed, the new displacement is:

FORMULA: $\pi \times R^2$ = bore area

Substitution: $3.1416 \times 2.020^2$ =
Solution: 3.1416 × 4.0804 = 12.8189 = 12.82 sq. in. per cylinder

Now we have the new area of the bore: 12.82 sq. in., approximately. Since the stroke remains the same 3.5", we multiply the area by the stroke:

FORMULA: BA × S = displacement of one cylinder

Substitution and Solution: 12.82 × 3.5 = 44.87 cubic inches

The displacement of our bored cylinder is now 44.87 cubic inches. To find the total engine displacement, we multiply this single cylinder displacement by the total number of cylinders:

44.87 × 8 = 358.96

So our engine is now almost 359 cubic inches. Boring the cylinders only .040" oversized increased the total displacement by 6.6 inches. This is a good example of how, in automotive technology, little changes can make big differences. That is why these formulas are useful. They enable you to take the guesswork out of your trade.

Now suppose you were to change crankshafts in this engine, so that your new crankshaft provided a ¼" longer stroke. Instead of the stock stroke of 3.5" or 3½", that would give us a 3.75" stroke. If we multiply our .040" overbore by our new stroke, we get:

FORMULA: $\pi R^2$ × S × N = Total Engine Displacement

Substitution: 12.82 sq. in. × 3.75 in. × 8 =
Solution: 12.82 sq. in. × 3.75 in. × 8 = 384.6 cu. in.

Those "slight modifications" have now added over 31 cubic inches to the engine's displacement.

# COMPRESSION RATIO

In Unit 2, when we discussed the Otto cycle, we talked briefly about the compression stroke. We said that as the piston moves upward during the compression stroke, it squeezes the trapped fuel/air mixture. We said that the tighter we squeeze the mixture, the higher the temperature rises. And the higher the mixture temperature, the more easily the mixture ignites. If we raise the temperature too high, the mixture may ignite before we want it to. In that case, peak pressure from combustion will act on the piston before the crankshaft is in the proper position to put that pressure to work. So we need a way of *measuring* compression.

The measure used to indicate the amount the engine compresses each intake charge is known as the *compression ratio*. This ratio expresses a comparison between the volume into which the charge is squeezed when the piston is at TDC, and the total volume of the cylinder with the piston at BDC (Figure 10–3). The area in which the charge is compressed is, of course, the combustion chamber. The space inside the combustion chamber is also called the *clearance volume*.

We can express compression ratio as:

$$\text{C.R.} = \frac{\text{total volume in a cylinder above the piston at BDC}}{\text{total volume in a cylinder above the piston at TDC}}$$

or, more technically,

$$\text{C.R.} = \frac{\text{piston displacement + clearance volume}}{\text{clearance volume}}$$

Remember that enlarging the cylinder displacement will increase the compression ratio. If we over-bore the cylinder and keep the clearance volume the same, we are compressing a larger volume of fuel into the clearance volume. Thus, we are increasing the compression ratio.

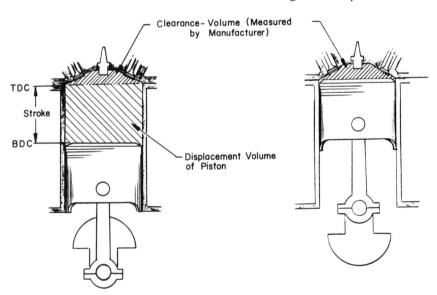

**Figure 10–3.** The compression ratio expresses a comparison between the volume allowed the fuel mixture when the piston is at BDC and that allowed with the piston at TDC.

The ratio in most modern engines is between 8:1 and 9:1. (This measurement is expressed orally as "eight to one", etc.) Figure 10–4 shows diagrammatically the two measures involved in the computation of the compression ratio.

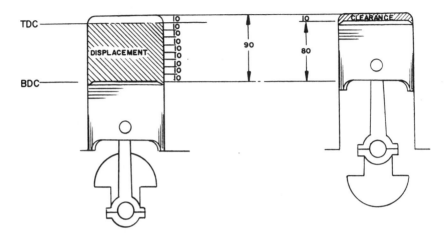

**Figure 10–4.**   To calculate an engine's compression ratio, simply add its clearance volume to its displacement volume and divide by the clearance volume. This allows the clearance volume to stand as 1 in ratio to the figure that results from the division.

The maximum compression ratio usable in an engine is controlled by a number of factors:

1.   The ignition temperature of the fuel;
2.   The temperature of the intake air;
3.   The density (weight) of the intake air; and
4.   The shape of the combustion chamber.

In turn, the compression ratio of an engine affects its performance in a variety of ways. Specifically, it:

1.   Increases the pressure developed in combustion and therefore the power developed by the engine;
2.   Causes the flame to burn faster;
3.   Raises the charge temperature closer to its ignition temperature; and
4.   Raises the temperature developed in the combustion chamber.

## AVERAGE PISTON SPEED

Few mechanics ever need to be concerned with average piston speed except as an approximate measure of engine durability or life. In your father's youth, when engines had long strokes and small bores, piston speed was an important consideration. Today, it is not so important, but you should still learn to compute it. It sometimes gives you a handy way to gauge the length of time an engine you are working on will last.

Computing average piston speed is a process of determining how far each piston moves in the cylinder in one minute.[1] The factors that enter into the calculation are the length of the stroke and the number of revolutions per minute or rpm. Stroke length must be multiplied by two (S × 2) because the piston moves from top to bottom and back to the top each time the crankshaft revolves once. If the stroke is given in inches, a factor of twelve is used to convert inches per minute to feet per minute.

The formula for piston speed is:

$$\frac{S \times 2 \times rpm}{12} = \text{piston speed in feet per minute}$$

Where $S$ = stroke reported in *inches*

As an example, let's compute the piston speed for our Ford 351. The engine has a stroke of 3.5 inches. Its maximum is 5500 rpm. We could calculate it like this:

FORMULA: S × 2 × rpm

Substitution and Solution: $\dfrac{3.5 \times 2 \times 5500}{12} = 3{,}208$ feet per minute piston speed

At 5500 rpm, then, each piston in our 351 travels well over half a mile per minute.

## MEASURES OF ENGINE POWER

In Unit 2 we discussed some of the basic physical factors affecting engine power. Let's review these factors and see how they can be used to measure engine performance.

---

[1]Some authorities call this dimension of engine performance by the simpler term *piston speed*. We prefer to call it *average piston speed* because the speed of the piston varies with its position in the cylinder. It moves fastest through the middle of the stroke. (See Figure 11–6.)

## Physical Factors Affecting Engine Power

*Torque* is the precise mathematical expression for leverage or rotating force around a pivot point (Figure 10–5).

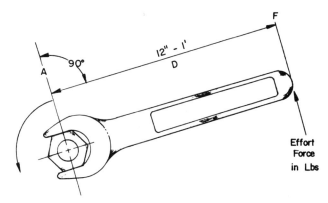

**Figure 10–5.** A twisting or rotating force is called *torque*. Torque is measured in pounds inch or pounds foot; the force of a one-pound weight acting on a lever one foot from a pivot point equals one pound foot.

The force, F, on the wrench produces leverage on the nut at point A. The amount of leverage, L, is expressed as torque.

FORMULA: F × L = Torque at A

Where F = Force
and L = Length of Lever

Substitution: 10 lbs. × 12 in. =
Solution: 10 lbs. × 12 in. = 120 lbs. in. or 10 lbs. ft.

(Note: The force must act 90° to the length of line A-B).
*Work* describes the energy used in moving some object.
We can express work mathematically as:

FORMULA: Work = Force × Distance

Symbolically: W = F × D

As you know, the work performed by the high-pressure gases pushing one piston through one power stroke is not all used to turn the rear wheels. In a multi-cylinder engine, part of this work is used moving the other cylinders through their intake, compression, and exhaust strokes. Figure 10–6 shows in graph-like form the pressure within the cylinder and the work performed by the gases. Only in the darkened area, though, is there enough pressure to perform work. This diagram is for a naturally aspirated (non-supercharged) engine. You will see, in Unit 14, that four stroke supercharged engines do some positive work on the intake stroke. This is true because their intake charges enter at a higher than atmospheric pressure.

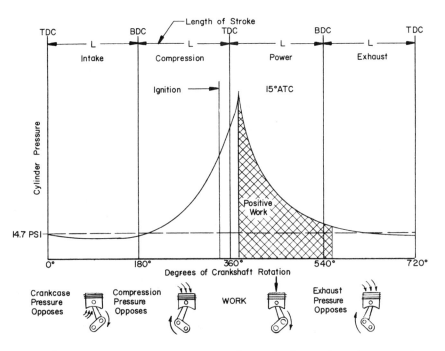

**Figure 10–6.** In an IC engine, work is only done when the expander is moved by combustion forces. This is the shaded area in the above graph showing the cylinder pressure in a normally aspirated gasoline engine.

## Horsepower

Power is the measure of how much work is done in a given period of time. Since work equals force times distance (or F × D), to compute power, all we do is calculate the amount of work done and divide by a unit of time.

$$\text{Power} = \frac{\text{Force} \times \text{Distance}}{\text{Time}} = \frac{F \times D}{T}$$

In mechanics, work is commonly measured in horsepower.

**Definition:** A *horsepower* is the amount of work necessary to lift 33,000 pounds one foot in one minute.

To compute horsepower, therefore, we adapt the formula for power, in this way:

FORMULA: $\dfrac{\text{Force (in pounds)} \times \text{Distance (in feet)}}{\text{Time (in number of minutes)} \times 33{,}000} = \text{Horsepower}$

or, in more abstract symbols,

$\dfrac{F \times D}{T \times 33{,}000} = \text{Horsepower}$

Where F = Force in pounds
D = Distance in feet
T = Time in minutes

# Brake Horsepower (BHP)

The torque of a rotating shaft can be measured by a simple device called the *prony brake*. The prony brake was the forerunner of the modern *dynamometer* now commonly used in well-equipped shops. In the prony brake, a torque load (or drag) acts as a brake and slows the engine down. So we call the horsepower developed at the drive shaft, *brake horsepower* or BHP.

**How to find the work done in one revolution.** The diagram in Figure 10–7 shows how the force, F, on the scales is caused by the drag of the shaft, S, twisting the lever arm R. Since motion of the engine and brake is relative, the force, F, may be considered as moving around the dotted line. The work of *one* revolution is:

Force × Distance of one Revolution = Work done in one revolution

Since we are measuring rotary movement, the *distance* of one revolution makes up one complete circle. So to compute that distance, we need to recall the formula for computing the circumference of a circle:

Circumference = $2 \times \pi \times R$ or $2\pi R$

When this is substituted into the above formula, we get this formula:

F × $2\pi R$ = Work done in one revolution
Where F = Force
R = Radius

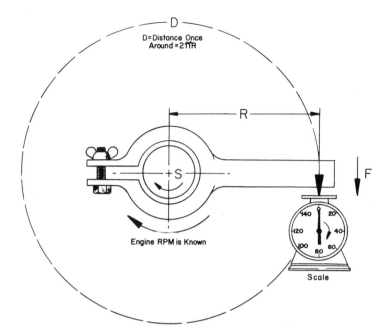

**Figure 10–7.**    Brake horsepower is measured with a device called a prony brake. Applied to the drive shaft, the prony brake places a torque load on the engine. The twisting of the lever arm (R) can then be recorded on the scale.

To convert this into terms of horsepower, we must find the total work done in one minute. Since we know the amount of work done in one revolution, we only need to know how many times the shaft goes around in one minute. This is *rpm*. With this information, we can calculate BHP using this formula:

$$\text{FORMULA:} \quad \frac{F \times 2\pi r \times rpm}{33{,}000} = \text{Brake Horsepower}$$

Where  F  = Force in pounds
R  = Radius
rpm  = revolutions per minute

or

$$\frac{\text{Torque} \times 2\pi \times rpm}{33{,}000} = \text{Brake Horsepower}$$

Since every application of the formula involves both $2\pi$ and 33,000, we can combine these two terms into a constant. This enables us to simplify the formula into a form that is usually more convenient:

$$\frac{\text{Torque in pounds foot} \times \text{rpm}}{5252} = \text{Brake Horsepower}$$

Where: 5252 is a constant derived from $\dfrac{2\pi}{33,000}$

# DYNAMOMETER

Modern versions of the prony brake called dynamometers find everyday use in shops as diagnostic tools in testing engine performance (Figure 10–8). The *chassis dynamometer* allows the mechanic not only to measure the engine's power output at the wheels but also makes it possible for him to simulate various road loads and driving conditions in the shop.

**Figure 10–8.** Instead of simple prony brakes, modern shops use dynamometers as diagnostic tools to test engine performance. *Courtesy of Clayton Manufacturing Company.*

An *engine dynamometer* (Figure 10–9) is used for experimental testing and development of various engine designs. There are two types of dynamometers in common use: the *hydraulic absorption dynamometer* and the *electric dynamometer*. In the hydraulic absorption system, the engine rotates a turbine with numerous blades. The turbine is encased in a housing which is filled with a fluid, usually water. As the turbine rotates in the fluid, a load is placed on the engine. Fluid can be added or removed to increase or decrease the load. The other part of the housing is connected like the prony brake through an arm to a scale. As the housing tries to rotate with the turbine, it applies force to the scale. Because we know the length of the arm, the force in pounds (measured by the scale), and the rpm of the engine, we can calculate horsepower.

**Figure 10–9.** Engine dynamometers like this are used in the experimental testing and development of various engine designs.

The electric dynamometer works differently. A large generator is connected to the engine crankshaft. The output of the generator is measured in watts of electrical energy. Since 746 watts of electrical energy equal one horsepower, we can read the engine's power.

## Measured Horsepower vs. Road Horsepower

A significant amount of the horsepower produced by an engine is required just to keep it turning. The sliding and rotating parts, the valve train, and all the drive accessories consume *friction horsepower.* Sometimes the published horsepower ratings of a given engine are unrealistic because they do not allow sufficiently for friction horsepower.

For example, until a few years ago, it was common practice for manufacturers to give horsepower ratings of, say, 375 HP for a 327 cu. in. engine. But if horsepower was measured on a chassis dynamometer, you might be lucky to obtain 175 *road HP* at the rear wheels. The reason for this large difference was this: When the manufacturers ran an engine on a dynamometer, they had no alternator connected (1–5 HP drag), no water pump hooked up (5–10 HP drag with fan), no exhaust system connected (10–25 HP drag), and no air cleaner working (0–5 HP drag). Nor, were they using stock ignition timing and carburetion. The drive train parts, air conditioning, and power steering (10–25% drag) were also disconnected.

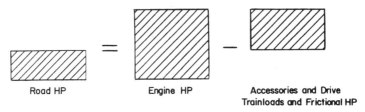

Road HP     Engine HP     Accessories and Drive
Trainloads and Frictional HP

**Figure 10-10.** The horsepower that counts, at least to the consumer, is road horsepower. Because so much power is used to drive accessories and is lost in friction, road horsepower may be less than half the total power output of the engine.

## Volumetric Efficiency

A measure of an engine's performance in filling its cylinders with air for the combustion process is called *volumetric efficiency*. As volumetric efficiency increases, the power developed by the engine increases in direct proportion.

If each cylinder on the intake stroke could take its full displacement volume of *dry air* at *standard temperature and pressure*, the engine's volumetric efficiency would be 100%. (By "dry", we mean simply free of water vapor.) Since the *weight* of this volume of dry air at standard conditions is constant for a specific temperature, the weight of air becomes the basis for volumetric efficiency. The following formula shows you how to express volumetric efficiency:

$$\text{vol. eff.} = \frac{\text{lbs. of standard air in one intake stroke}}{\text{lbs. of standard air per cylinder displacement}}$$

If an eight-cylinder engine's total displacement is 305 cid (5000 cc), then the displacement of one cylinder would be 38.125 cid (625 cc). If this engine was achieving 100% volumetric efficiency, then this cylinder would be filled with exactly 38.125 cu. in. (625 cc) of air. Since we want to measure volumetric efficiency with the engine running, we must keep in mind that we are not only talking about filling this volume in eight cylinders but also of doing so two, three, or even five *thousand* times per minute. Remember, the crankshaft must turn twice to complete one cycle of four strokes. So at 200 rpm one cylinder completes 100 intake strokes. Yet large amounts of air pass through an engine, especially when it is "revving." At 10,000 rpm, it might be taking about 1,525,000 cu. in. per minute. Because such large numbers are hard to work with, volumetric efficiency is commonly measured in cubic feet, not cubic inches, per minute. The abbreviation for cubic feet per minute is *cfm*.

## Calculating Volumetric Efficiency

Let us calculate how many cubic feet of air our engine should draw in on one revolution. To find out, we simply convert the engine's displacement, which is reported in cubic inches, into cubic feet. Since there are 1728 cubic inches in a cubic foot, all we do is divide by 1728:

FORMULA:    $\dfrac{\text{displacement in cu. in.}}{1728 \text{ cu. in.}}$ = cubic feet in one revolution

EXAMPLE:    $\dfrac{305 \text{ cu in.}}{1728 \text{ cu. in.}}$ = .1765 cu. ft.

On each revolution, our 305 cid engine displaces .1765 cubic feet of air.

Now let's figure the volume that flows through the same engine at its maximum rpm of 6,000. We just multiply .1765 cubic feet by 6000 rpm and divide the result by two. (Remember, there is only one intake stroke for every two revolutions).

FORMULA (in words):

$$\dfrac{\text{Displacement in cubic feet} \times \text{Revolutions per minute}}{2} = \text{cubic feet per minute}$$

FORMULA (in symbols):

$$\dfrac{D \times rpm}{2} = cfm$$

Where D = Displacement in cubic feet
rpm = revolutions per minute
cfm = cubic feet per minute

Substitution and Solution:    $\dfrac{.1765 \times 6000}{2}$ = 529.5 cubic feet per minute

So 529.5 cfm would be the ideal flow rate for our engine.

If we actually measure the actual volume of air entering the engine, we would very likely find the flow rate to be about 450 cfm. Knowing this, we could find the percent volumetric efficiency in this fashion:

FORMULA (in words):

$$\dfrac{\text{flow rate cfm actual}}{\text{flow rate cfm ideal}} = \% \text{ volumetric efficiency (vol. eff.)}$$

85% vol. eff. would be considered outstanding for a normal passenger car.

## Thermal Efficiency

The measurement of the total percentage of potential energy in the fuel which is transformed into actual brake horsepower is called *thermal efficiency*. When we talk about brake horsepower (BHP) for our calculation, we are talking in terms of *brake thermal efficiency*.

FORMULA (in words):

$$\text{Brake Thermal Efficiency} = \frac{\text{BHP (measured as output/hr.)} \times 100\%}{\text{Fuel energy (measured in BTU's) input/hr.}}$$

One horsepower equals approximately 2544 BTU's per hour. Gasoline has approximately 18,500 BTU per lb., and pump gas weighs about 6 lbs. per gallon. Using these units, an engine's thermal efficiency can be calculated by the following method:

$$\text{Thermal Efficiency} = \frac{\text{BHP} \times 2544 \text{ BTU}}{18,500 \text{ BTU} \times \text{lbs. of gasoline per hr.}}$$

As an example, let's figure the thermal efficiency of a turbo-charged SAAB 900 which developes 29 HP at 65 mph and uses 2 gallons of fuel per hour. The mileage per gallon is easy to figure. We can use the above formula like so:

$$\frac{\text{BHP } 29 \times 2544}{18,500 \times 12^*} = 33.2\%$$

*(2 × 6 lbs. per gallon)

Something must be wrong, because we know that most gasoline engines have a thermal efficiency of approximately 25%. However, we said our SAAB was a turbo-charged engine. We will learn in Unit 11 how turbo-charging an engine increases its thermal efficiency.

The brake thermal efficiency of most gasoline piston engines is between 25–30%.

To calculate *fuel efficiency*, we must again use some math:

Remember:   automotive pump gas has about 18,500 BTU/lb.
one BTU = 778 ft. lbs. of energy
pump gas weighs about 6 lbs. per gallon

The HP energy available when one *gal.* of gasoline is burned in *one* hour is

$$6 \text{ lbs.} \times 18,500 \text{ BTU} \times 778 \text{ ft. lbs.}$$

$$33,000 \text{ ft. lbs. per min.} = 1 \text{ HP}$$

$$60 \text{ min.} = 1 \text{ hr.}$$

$$\frac{6 \times 18,500 \times 778}{33,000 \times 60} \qquad \frac{HP}{1 \text{ gal. gas hr.}} \quad \text{or} \quad \frac{43.6 \text{ HP}}{\text{per gal. hr.}}$$

Only 25–30% of the potential heat energy in the fuel is converted to useful work (BHP). The rest is lost in varying amounts (depending on the engine design) as shown by the diagram. This holds true for the average *naturally aspirated engine;* a turbo-charged engine wastes less heat energy.

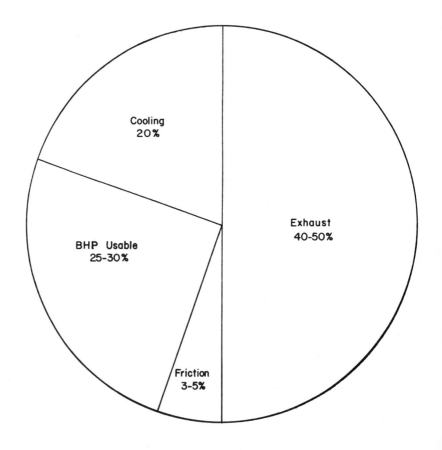

**Figure 10–11.** Where the energy goes.

## REVIEW QUESTIONS

*Objective Questions*

1. In order to calculate piston displacement, you must know:

    _____ A. Bore and stroke
    _____ B. Radius rod length
    _____ C. Clearance volume/cylinder diameter
    _____ D. Valve lift and CR

2. The total space above a piston at TDC is called:

    _____ A. Piston displacement
    _____ B. Clearance volume
    _____ C. Compression ratio
    _____ D. Valve lift clearance

3. What percentage of heat energy that enters the Otto engine is actually put to "work"?

    _____ A. 25–30%
    _____ B. 3–5%
    _____ C. 20%
    _____ D. 40%

4. BHP is:

    _____ A. Measured on an electric dynamometer
    _____ B. The power delivered to the rear wheels
    _____ C. Used for license fees only
    _____ D. Bore × stroke × CR

5. If the piston displacement of one cylinder is 48 cid and the engine has four cylinders, what is its total cylinder displacement?

    _____ A. 192 ci + the clearance volume
    _____ B. 192 × 25 ÷ T
    _____ C. 192 cid
    _____ D. 384 ci

6. The rate at which work is performed is called

    _____ A. Torque
    _____ B. HP
    _____ C. MEP
    _____ D. RPM

7. Joe says piston speed indicates how long an engine will last.
   John claims piston speed relates to the compression developed in the cylinder.

   Who is correct?

   _____ A.  Joe
   _____ B.  John
   _____ C.  Joe and John
   _____ D.  Neither one

8. Alex says reducing the clearance volume will increase the compression ratio.

   Aaron says increasing the bore diameter can increase the compression ratio.

   Who is correct?

   _____ A.  Alex
   _____ B.  Aaron
   _____ C.  Both men
   _____ D.  Neither one

9. Thermal efficiency relates to

   _____ A.  Mileage
   _____ B.  $\dfrac{\text{HP out}}{\text{BTU in}} \times 100\%$
   _____ C.  Economy
   _____ D.  All of the above
   _____ E.  None of the above

10. Valve life on most OHV engines is a product of:

    _____ A.  Base circle D-Lobe height × Rocker ratio-valve lash
    _____ B.  Valve lash + lobe height − Base circle × $\pi$
    _____ C.  Valve height × Rocker ratio-lash
    _____ D.  None of the above

*Questions of Recall and Application*

Calculate the Displacement for the Following Engine Dimensions

| Bore | Stroke v | Number of Cylinders |
|------|----------|---------------------|
| 4.36″ | 3.85″ | 8 |
| 4.00″ | 4.00″ | 8 |
| 4.36″ | 3.59″ | 8 |
| 4.00″ | 3.18″ | 6 |
| 4.32″ | 3.75″ | 8 |
| 3.40″ | 4.125″ | 6 |
| 3.40″ | 4.125″ | 6 |
| 3.875″ | 3.25″ | 4 |
| 3.875″ | 3.53″ | 6 |
| 4.00″ | 3.00″ | 8 |

1. Use your shop manual to look up the following engine strokes. Then, calculate the piston speed.
   A. A 6 cylinder 250 cid Chevy turning 3800 rpm
   B. A 302 cid Ford turning 5800 rpm
   C. A 1969 Dodge 440 with 3-2 barrels developing maximum brake horsepower
   D. A 225 cid Mopar slant 6 at 4000 rpm
   E. A Mustang 2800 cc V-6 turning 600 rpm

2. An eight-cylinder engine with a 4.36″ bore is bored .040″ oversize. What is its new bore?

3. The above engine had a stroke of 3.59. What was its original total displacement?

4. Calculate its new total displacement.

5. It had a compression ratio of 11-1. What was its clearance volume?

6. What is its new compression ratio (after boring)?

7. An engine has a combustion chamber size of 100 cubic centimeters and uses flat top pistons and the bore of 4.00″ and stroke of 3.25″. What is the compression ratio?

8. *Thermal efficiency.* You have a car that burns three gallons of fuel per hour at 55 mph. It has a thermal efficiency of 25%. How many HP is it developing at 55 mph?

9. What is the thermal efficiency of a car that develops 20 HP at 55 mph and uses only 2 gallons of fuel per hour?

# Engine Breathing and Volumetric Efficiency

*Courtesy of Schwitzer Division, Wallace-Murray Corp.*

Our physics teacher used to ask us, "How are you doing?" "How are you bearing up under all that weight?"

"What weight?" we asked.

"Why, the 1100 pounds of air you're holding up!" It was his way of being sure that we never forgot the true meaning of the term *normal atmospheric pressure*. At sea level, normal atmospheric pressure is 14.7 pounds psi. That teacher was gently urging us to think about this fact. Because atmospheric pressure is so important to the breathing efficiency of an engine, we now challenge you to do the same.

A good way to begin thinking about atmospheric pressure is to visualize the atmosphere as an ocean of air. Like any other ocean, it is more or less level on its upper surface. But the ocean floor is made up of mountains and valleys as well as plains (Figure 11–1). The depth of this atmospheric ocean varies greatly from one place to another on the earth's surface. If you've ever heard a motorcycle engine gasping and laboring in rarefied mountain air, you already know that differences in these depths can be important to the mechanic.

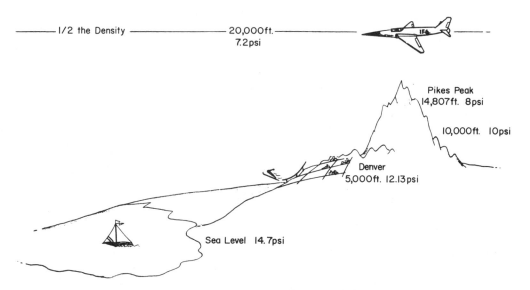

**Figure 11–1.** A good way to begin thinking about atmospheric pressure is to visualize the atmosphere as an ocean of air, with the floor of the ocean made up of our hills and valleys.

To see how this importance comes about, let us consider just one square inch of the earth's surface. If we suppose that square inch to be on a beach somewhere at sea level, our explanation is simplified. For directly above that square inch of beach, extending upward for approximately 100 miles, is an inch-square column of air (Figure 11–2). As you know, air—like all matter—is made up of atoms and molecules. In air, those molecules are spaced far apart, so air is very light. But it does have weight. In fact, that entire 100 mile-high column of air above our square inch of beach weighs 14.7 pounds. That is the meaning of the term *normal atmospheric pressure.*

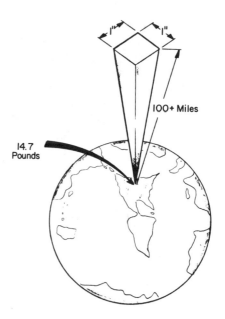

**Figure 11–2.** Above a square inch of beach, extending upward for approximately 100 miles, is an inch-square column of air weighing 14.7 pounds. That weight is normal atmospheric pressure.

The physics teacher's point then, was simple. Almost everybody has as much as seventy-eight square inches of surface area on the top of his head and shoulders. And seventy-eight times 14.7 pounds equals 1146.6 pounds of air, pressing down on each person walking along our beach. To us, that half ton of air is no burden at all. In fact, we miss it when we find ourselves atop a tall mountain with less air above us.

In this unit, you will see that the pressure, weight, and density of air are variables of great importance to an engine's breathing efficiency. You will find that these and other variables are controlled by engineers and mechanics in a number of ways. And you will learn that in the breathing of most engines, normal atmospheric pressure plays a crucially important role.

## OBJECTIVES

When you have completed this unit you should be able to:

- List and explain at least five factors that increase an engine's volumetric efficiency.
- List and explain at least five factors that decrease an engine's volumetric efficiency.
- Explain the effect of supercharging on each of the following:

  volumetric efficiency
  charge density
  engine torque
  thermal efficiency

- Demonstrate by answering specific questions an ability to apply the principles of engine breathing discussed in this unit to typical problems involving various engine designs.

## VOLUMETRIC EFFICIENCY

Calculating volumetric efficiency is the best way to measure an engine's breathing success. If every intake stroke could completely fill every cylinder with dry air at standard temperature, the volumetric efficiency of an engine would be 100%. You will learn later in this unit that it is actually possible for volumetric efficiency to exceed 100%. But this almost never happens when normal atmospheric pressure is used to push the intake charge into the engine. Unless special steps are taken, the amount of air actually drawn into the engine is less than the theoretical maximum. The figure you get when you calculate the volumetric efficiency of an engine tells you how much less.

### Air Density

You may remember that the formula for calculating volumetric efficiency specified dry air at "standard temperature." Depending on whose system of measurement is used, standard temperature is defined as either 59° F (15° C) or 72° F (22° C). The important point to notice is that temperature and moisture are both important factors in determining volumetric efficiency. High temperatures and high humidity both lower the density of the air being used.

**Air Density and Combustion.**   The energy released in combustion is directly proportional to the weight of the fuel and air brought together in the combustion chamber. Weight is actually a better indicator of combustion efficiency than volume because weight takes account of density. It tells us not only how much "room" those air molecules are spread through but also how thinly they are dispersed. That is important because it is the actual number of molecules involved in the combustion process which determines energy output.

Only a fraction of those air molecules are actually used in combustion. The scientific name for burning is *oxidation*. Combustion depends on *oxygen*. Automotive combustion is merely the process by which atoms and molecules of fuel combine with atoms and molecules of oxygen. The other gases in the air are important only because the combustion heat expands them and they become our working fluid. Oxygen itself is the key to the combustion process.

Yet air is only 21% oxygen. The remainder includes 75% nitrogen, .05% carbon dioxide and 1.5% other gases and chemicals (Figure 11–3). Thus, we must consider the density as well as the volume of the air used in combustion. Only then can we accurately estimate the number of oxygen molecules available.

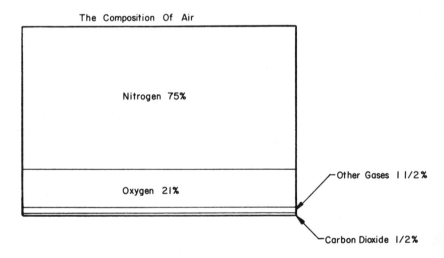

**Figure 11–3.**   Air is only 21% oxygen.

**Factors Affecting Air Density.**   Normally, anything that lowers the density of the air outside an engine will lower the engine's volumetric efficiency. We have already named several factors.

*Altitude and barometric pressure* were mentioned in our example of the motorcycle laboring over a mountain. There is less air above a mountain top than above our beach. So the atmospheric pressure is less and the air molecules are not squeezed together as tightly. The difference is great enough that neither people nor engines can breathe at altitudes much higher than 15,000 feet unless special measures are taken. So altitude is one important factor which affects air density (Figure 11–4).

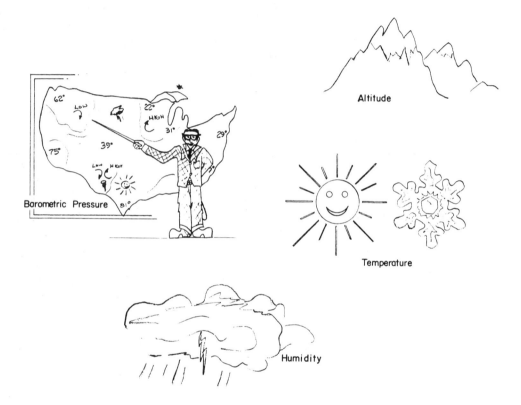

**Figure 11–4.** Among the factors affecting air density are altitude, weather, heat, and moisture.

Another is weather. You have no doubt seen TV weathermen map out high and low pressure areas during their forecasts. So you know that, even at sea level, the atmospheric pressure is not always exactly 14.7 pounds per square inch. It changes with the weather. These weather-caused changes in barometric pressure also affect air density.

*Air temperature and relative humidity* were mentioned in the formula for calculating volumetric efficiency. The reason that the formula specifies dry air at standard temperature, we said, is that these things affect air density. Of course, air density lowers as the temperature increases. So adding heat causes the molecules in any substance to space themselves further apart.

The influence of moisture on air density may not be as obvious. But water vapor weighs only about five-eighths as much as dry air, so its density is less. Therefore, as the percentage of moisture increases, air density decreases. In practice, of course, the most common cause of changes in moisture content, or humidity, is the weather. But relative humidity, though related to barometer pressure and temperature, is different. It is well to remember the distinction between these three weather-caused influences on air density.

## NORMALLY ASPIRATED ENGINES

A more scientific name for engine breathing is *aspiration*. Engines that rely on normal atmospheric pressure to fill their cylinders with air are said to be "normally aspirated." Their breathing system works much like yours. You open your lungs, and atmospheric pressure pushes air in through your nose and mouth. When the dropping piston enlarges a cylinder and the intake valve is open, a similar thing happens. The engine "inhales" through its intake ports. To understand the engine's breathing cycle, however, it is best to begin by considering a cylinder that has just fired.

### The Exhaust Stroke

Engine breathing occurs so rapidly that it is pointless to try to measure it precisely in conventional hours, minutes, and seconds. A V–8 engine racing at 7000 rpm draws 28,000 "breaths" per minute and "exhales" an equal number of times. We cannot measure those events with a stopwatch, and doing so would not tell us very much, anyway. The actual time that passes during any event is not as important as time in relation to other events taking place inside the engine. For that kind of measurement, as you know, we measure time in crankshaft rotations. And when we want to speak precisely about rotations of less than a full turn, we report the number of degrees of rotation.

A full rotation totals 360°, since there are 360° in a circle. Because each cylinder only fires once in two crankshaft rotations, the full Otto cycle takes 720°. It is *not* true, however, that each of the four strokes actually takes 180°, as we assumed earlier. We can see this easily if we follow our ignited cylinder completely through its power and exhaust strokes.

**Exhaust Valve Opens About 60° BBDC.** By the time the piston has moved two-thirds of the way down the cylinder, most of its power surge has passed. There is little more useful work to be gotten from the combustion gases after that. Nothing is lost if the exhaust valve opens while the piston is still moving down on its power stroke. A typical engine, therefore, might be designed so that the valve begins to open about 60° before bottom dead center (BBDC).

This has the advantage of giving the exhaust gases a head start on their way out. At that point, pressure in the combustion chamber—though dramatically less than it was a fraction of a second earlier—is still much higher than that of the outside atmosphere. So the exhaust gases start rushing out as soon as the exhaust valve opens. Meanwhile, the piston continues downward, reverses direction, and starts up again on the exhaust stroke. At this point, inertia becomes a major factor.

In Unit 8 we explained how inertial forces cause the piston's speed to vary inside the cylinder. Each stroke, we said, begins and ends with the piston motionless at dead center. At that point, the mechanical forces acting through the connecting rod are exactly balanced by the inertial forces from the piston's previous stroke. Inertia, we said then, is the tendency in matter to resist a change in its state of motion. When you punch a ball bearing with your finger, the bearing continues to roll across your bench after your finger has stopped tracking it. Once your finger starts it moving, the bearing's own inertia tends to keep it in motion.

Exhaust gases are much lighter than the bearing, but they also have inertia. And the accelerating piston "punches" them thousands of times harder than you could hit your bearing. In fact, it sends them pouring out the exhaust valve so fast that their inertia continues to carry them away after the piston starts down again. On some engines, therefore, the exhaust valve may not close until 30° after top dead center (ATDC) on the intake stroke. Common practice would close it about 12-15° ATDC, but even this earlier closing allows an exhaust duration of about 255° (Figure 11–5).

**Intake Valve Opens About 15° BTDC.** By the time the piston is slowing to a stop at the end of its exhaust stroke, inertial forces in the escaping combustion gases are at their peak. So those gases are creating a strong suction as they rush out of the combustion chamber. To take advantage of this suction, the intake valve opens about 15° BTDC. This period when both valves are open is called valve overlap. Its purpose is to enable the incoming fuel-air mixture to gain speed before the intake stroke actually starts. The suction caused by the escaping exhaust gases causes speed to build rapidly in the incoming fuel charge so their inertial forces can be at their peak throughout the entire intake stroke. A small amount of fuel charge may be lost through the exhaust valve. But this is not totally without advantage because it ensures adequate scavenging and helps to cool the sizzling exhaust valve.

By the time the piston passes BDC and begins its compression stroke, the incoming charge is surging in. It has so much inertia that the fuel mixture continues to crowd in, even though the piston is moving upward. Only when the piston is about 60° ABDC does the intake valve close. So the duration of intake, on a typical engine, might well be about 255° also. And the effective compression stroke does not start until about 60° ABDC; therefore, it lasts for only about 120°.

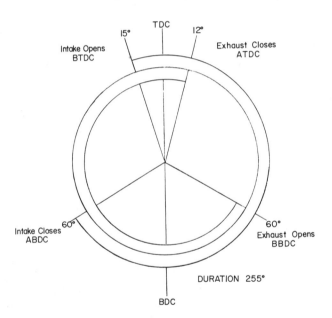

**Figure 11–5.** Because of valve overlap, the duration of the exhaust cycle is often 255° or more.

You will see in the next unit that the combustion process is well under way by the end of this compression stroke. But now, let us use your newly acquired knowledge of these details of the Otto cycle to look at some of the ways they affect the breathing of normally aspirated engines.

## Piston Speed and Volumetric Efficiency

The variation in piston speed caused by inertial forces is shown graphically in Figure 11–6. Notice how much less the piston travels for a given amount of crankshaft rotation when it is near the end of a stroke. As the crankshaft rotates 90°, from point one to point two, the piston only moves through the darkened area A. But as the crankshaft turns its next 90°, from point two to point three, the piston moves the entire distance B. Notice that the period of slowest travel comes precisely at the point where valve overlap takes place. This explains why the breathing cycle just described is best suited for an engine that will be operated at moderately high speeds.

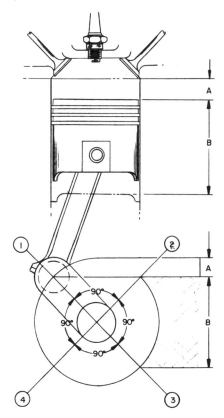

**Figure 11–6.** The piston takes much less time for a given amount of crankshaft rotation when it is near the end of a stroke. (A) is the distance the piston travels for 90° of rotation near the top of its stroke. (B) is the distance it travels in the bore on the next 90° of crankshaft rotation.

At low speeds, there is no need for much valve overlap. The incoming charge fills the chamber almost as fast as the piston enlarges it. Outside atmospheric pressure, remember, is a more or less constant 14.7 psi. When the engine turns slowly, each valve is open longer, in actual clock time. Thus, there is plenty of time for normal atmospheric pressure to fill the cylinder with fuel mixture. In fact, if there is much overlap, some of the exhaust gases will back up through the intake valve and dilute the incoming charge. (This is why racing engines do not idle well.) And a good deal of the fresh charge will escape unburned out the exhaust valve.

It is only when the engine speeds up that valve overlap begins to pay off. As soon as piston speed reaches the point where the intake charge lags behind the dropping piston, it becomes advantageous to keep the intake valve open longer. Speed, therefore, is an important determiner of volumetric efficiency. A camshaft designed for the long duration and overlap requirements of a performance car will not produce good breathing at low speeds. And one that reduces the overlap enough to get maximum efficiency at low speeds will choke the engine at high rpm.

## Ports and Engine Breathing

Since atmospheric pressure is more or less constant, only a limited volume of air can enter through a hole of a given size. Let us think of the intake port as such a hole. The intake manifold simply extends that hole up to the carburetor (Figure 11–7). The amount of air flowing in will be affected by two things: (1) the difference between the pressure inside the cylinder and that in the outside atmosphere and (2) the size of the openings at the valve and throttle. If we kept both the valve and throttle open all the way, more air could pass through. And if we scaled the whole system to a bigger diameter, still more could pass through.

Thus, it would seem that, in the intake system at least, bigger is better. But that is only partly true. More air *can* come through a bigger pipe, but whether it does or not is determined largely by the inertial forces in the air stream. A large diameter system does not actually restrict breathing, but neither does it put inertial forces to work in favor of better aspiration.

**Velocity.** The easiest way to build velocity is to *reduce* the diameter of the pipe. When you partially block the end of a water hose with your thumb, pressure builds up in the hose and forces water through the smaller opening with much greater velocity. The same principle is at work in the intake system.

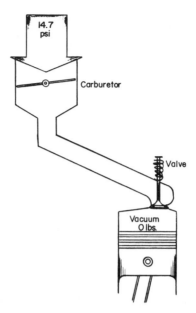

**Figure 11-7.** Only a limited volume of air can enter through a hole of a given size. Thinking of the intake port as such a hole, we can see that the intake manifold simply extends that hole into the carburetor.

It is important that velocity be kept reasonably high for two reasons. The first, and most obvious, reason is that a high-velocity intake charge will rush in faster and fill the cylinder more completely. In short, velocity improves volumetric efficiency (Figure 11–8). Second, velocity tends to prevent fuel drop out. When the air flow is too slow, fuel droplets tend to collect on the intake manifold and port (Figure 11–9). If this happens, uneven fuel charges may soon start reaching the different cylinders. And that decreases both thermal and volumetric efficiency.

The physics involved are like those of a dust storm. High velocity winds can easily carry so much sand in the air that a person must wear goggles to see and carry a filter to breathe through. But as soon as the wind slows, the sand settles. Since we do not want our vaporized fuel to settle, we must keep our intake air flow at a fairly high velocity.

**Bends and Turns.** The path from the carburetor to the intake valve is not merely one long hole. Engineers try to keep both intake and exhaust tubing as straight as possible. But as you learned in Unit 8, some bends and turns are always necessary.

When an air stream is forced to turn sharply, the air behaves exactly like any other matter would. It tends to resist the change of

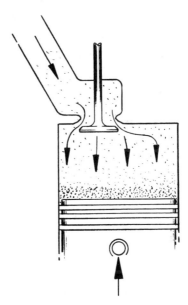

**Figure 11–8.**    A high-velocity intake charge will rush in faster and fill the cylinder more completely. In short, velocity improves volumetric efficiency.

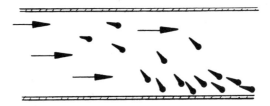

**Figure 11–9.**    Velocity tends to prevent fuel drop out. When the air flow is too slow, fuel droplets tend to collect on the intake manifold and port.

direction. That causes it to crowd the downstream side of the pipe at the bend and creates a low-pressure area just beyond the bend (Figure 11–10). This turbulence, in effect, reduces the diameter of the flow through the turn. In many engines, the intake charge must pass through a series of sharp turns to reach the combustion chamber. There will be a pressure change and a corresponding drop in velocity and volume at each turn.

**Other Obstructions.**    Any other obstructions that produce turbulence in the air stream also reduce breathing efficiency. In the intake port, the valve and valve guide often create such obstructions. Cavities provided for push rods, head bolts, and cooling passages produce other necessary limitations on port design.

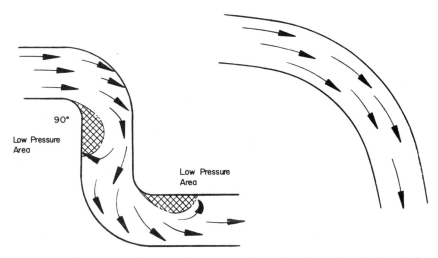

**Figure 11–10.** When an air stream is forced to turn sharply, the air behaves exactly like any other matter would: The air stream tends to resist the change of direction. Notice that this creates a low pressure area just beyond the bend.

# Combustion Chamber Design and Breathing Efficiency

For engine breathing, each combustion chamber layout presents its own advantages and disadvantages.

**Hemispherical combustion chambers,** for instance, have the advantage of their valve placement. With valves just across that dome-shaped chamber from each other, they are almost perfectly placed to maximize scavenging and breathing efficiency (Figure 11–11). But during that critical valve overlap period, both valves and the head of the piston are in the combustion chamber at the same time. Unless the timing is exactly right one of those valves can slam into the other or into the piston, instantly turning a beautiful engine into a catastrophe. Mechanically, it takes very little to cause such a nightmare. Just a 3° advancement of the intake cam on Alfa Romeo's DOHC design, for instance, is enough to horrify any car lover.

**I-head designs,** usually have the advantage of parallel valves (Figure 11–12). So the valves are unlikely to collide with each other, but their valve lift and duration are limited. Recklessness with the timing or lift can easily bring a valve into catastrophic contact with the piston (Figure 11–13).

**Figure 11–11.**    With valves just across that dome-shaped chamber from each other, they are well placed to maximize scavenging and breathing efficiency.

**Figure 11–12.**    I-head designs usually have the advantage of parallel valves, so the valves are unlikely to collide with each other.

**Figure 11–13.**    Recklessness with the timing or lift can easily bring a valve into catastrophic contact with the piston.

# INTAKE AND EXHAUST TUNING

It is possible for engineers to control engine breathing so precisely that for a very narrow rpm and torque range they can exceed 100% volumetric efficiency. To do this, they concentrate on the air flow to and from the engine. They carefully plan the lengths and diameters of both intake and exhaust manifolds, to coordinate them perfectly with the timing of the valves and the firing order of the cylinders. Two different approaches are used in tuning intake and exhaust systems.

## Acoustical Tuning

Acoustically tuned systems look and function much like the tubes of a pipe organ. This approach is most commonly used to tune exhaust systems. It depends for its effectiveness on a sound wave generated inside the exhaust pipe. The hot exhaust gases blow out of the cylinder into the exhaust pipe at 20-100 psi. As they do so they literally "whistle" a sound wave into being. That wave travels down the exhaust pipe at about seventeen hundred feet per second. When it bursts out the tailpipe it no longer has the exhaust pipe for a resonance chamber. So its acoustical character is instantly changed. This sudden change in wave quality, starts an "echo" wave traveling back up the exhaust pipe.

If no special steps were taken, this echo would simply run back and forth until it died out. But the object of acoustical tuning is to have that echo wave reach one of the exhaust valves just before the end of its exhaust stroke. If it does, it will create a low pressure area in the exhaust port exactly when it will maximize scavenging. If the timing is not perfect, the wave will do more harm than good. Instead of creating a low pressure area, it will produce turbulence and obstruction. But if the exhaust pipe is exactly the right length for the engine's rpm's, then the effect is dramatic.

Because it works at such a narrow rpm range, acoustical tuning is normally used only on all-out racing engines (Figure 11–14).

## Inertia Tuning

A more widely used method of exhaust tuning is *inertia tuning*. As the name implies, this approach uses the weight of the exhaust gases themselves to improve volumetric efficiency. As those gases leave the cylinder, they are moving at 200–300 feet per second. At that velocity, their inertia carries them out the exhaust pipe, even after the exhaust valve closes. Behind each of these rushes of exhaust gases, however, is a low pressure area. For when the exhaust valve has closed, the continuing rush of gases toward the tailpipe creates a partial vacuum (Figure 11–15).

**Figure 11–14.**   Because it works at such a narrow rpm range, accoustical tuning is normally used only on all-out racing engines. *Official Photo, Indianapolis Motor Speedway.*

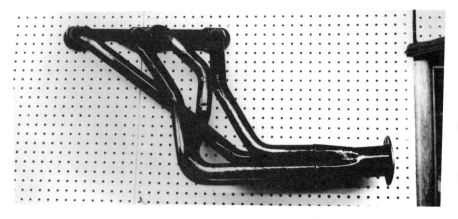

**Figure 11–15.**   Bolt-on tuned exhaust systems, called *headers*, are manufactured for most engine-chassis combinations.

The goal of inertial tuning is to have the next exhausting cylinder void its gases into this low pressure area. When this can be done, it gives the exhaust gases from the second cylinder a helpful boost that greatly improves scavenging. There are several approaches to the design of inertia-tuned exhaust systems.

**Individual Pipes.** Pipes of equal length may lead from each cylinder to a collector, or expansion chamber. Sometimes pairs of pipes, usually from cylinders 90°–130° apart, are merged before they reach the collector. A more complex design, usually used only in all-out racing, uses a different hook-up for the pipes. In this alternative, the individual pipes are still of the same length. But they are connected by cylinders 180° apart, from bank to bank, following the engine's firing order.

**Headers.** Bolt-on tuned exhaust systems called *headers* are manufactured for most engine-chassis combinations. One of these bolt-on systems adds 10–30 horsepower to most engines. With careful choice of tubing diameter and length, headers can effect dramatic improvements in both the gas mileage and power output of a stock engine.

A detailed discussion of headers is beyond the scope of this book. Generally speaking, however, a small tube diameter, longer individual pipes, or both will tune the system for maximum power and torque at the rpm ranges used in legal driving. An engine in a heavy vehicle, like a van or station wagon, needs somewhat longer tubes.

## GENERAL CONSIDERATIONS

Perhaps the most important single thing for the mechanic to keep in mind about normally aspirated engines is *that a change in any single part of the breathing system affects the operation of the rest.* Housewives and speed freaks alike are constantly being sold "miracle" devices to improve engine aspiration. When applied without making other necessary adjustments, even the more plausible of these gimmicks often make things worse. Figure 11–16 provides a useful checklist listing the factors that are most important in determining volumetric efficiency. Be sure to consider the effects on all these components, whenever you do any work on the breathing system of an engine.

The half-informed hotrodder who slips an expensive performance camshaft into his engine and expects miracles underscores this moral. Unless he matches the rest of the system to his new cam, his engine will run worse than before. And unless he matches the entire system to the rpm range he has in mind, he is wasting his money.

```
┌─────────────────────────────────────────┐
│     FACTORS USED IN DETERMINING          │
│       VOLUMETRIC EFFICIENCY              │
├─────────────────────────────────────────┤
│                                          │
│  A. Intake System                        │
│                                          │
│     1. Air filter (size)                 │
│     2. Carburetor (CFM, mixture)         │
│     3. Intake manifold                   │
│                                          │
│        a. tube length (crossectional area)│
│        b. how they are interconnected    │
│        c. manifold heating               │
│                                          │
│  B. Ports and Valves                     │
│                                          │
│     1. Size (area)                       │
│     2. Shape (length)                    │
│     3. Valve lift                        │
│     4. Valve timing                      │
│                                          │
│  C. Combustion Chamber Layout            │
│                                          │
│     1. Valve placement                   │
│     2. Compression ratio                 │
│                                          │
│  D. Exhaust System                       │
│                                          │
│     1. Manifold versus headers           │
│     2. Muffler, etc.                     │
│     3. Restrictions                      │
│                                          │
└─────────────────────────────────────────┘
```

**Figure 11–16.**

In engine aspiration, big changes do not necessarily produce big improvements. Conversely, big problems do not necessarily have big causes. A little thing like a dirty air filter, an air leak in the intake system, or even a disconnected vacuum hose can sap volumetric efficiency.

There is no other aspect of automotive technology in which it is more important for the mechanic to use his head and work systematically. If you can relate the material in this chapter to what you learned in Units 8 and 9, then you have an excellent start. Many of the self-proclaimed performance experts who hang around garages and speed shops have never bothered to do this kind of homework. Your next step should be to test your basic understanding by beginning to read and analyze for yourself the articles on aspiration and exhaust tuning that appear regularly in the trade magazines.

## SUPERCHARGED ENGINES

So far this chapter has referred to normally aspirated engines. While much of what was said is also true in the engines now to be considered, it loses its practical importance when superchargers are used. Supercharged engines do not have to breathe for themselves in the way described. Air is force-fed into them, much as an artificial respiration machine forces a paralyzed patient through the motions of breathing.

A supercharger is nothing more than an air pump, used to blow air into the engine at more than normal atmospheric pressure. For this reason, superchargers are often called *blowers,* and supercharged power plants are commonly called *blown engines.* The two most important methods of supercharging internal combustion engines are with positive displacement air pumps and turbochargers.

### The Positive Displacement Pump

The positive displacement pumps used as superchargers are designed to be driven from the crankshaft. They may be of either the lobe type or vane type (Figure 11–17). The positive displacement compressor moves a specific volume of air with each rotation, regardless of speed.

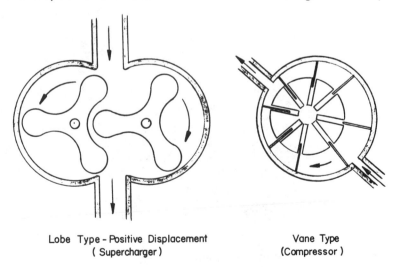

Lobe Type - Positive Displacement
( Supercharger )

Vane Type
(Compressor )

**Figure 11–17.** Two kinds of positive displacement pumps are the lobe type and the vane type.

So this kind of supercharger has the advantage of feeding the engine the same volume of charge at the same pressure even at low speeds.

However, it has two distinct disadvantages. First, crankshaft power must be used to drive it, so part of the power output it adds to the normal engine output must be used to drive itself. Second, the positive displacement pump is tied to its inherent low-speed efficiency. Such a pump, unfortunately, raises the temperature of the charge. You will learn in Unit 12 how this temperature increase can cause problems in combustion. Because of these disadvantages, positive displacement pumps are unlikely to be used in the near future as superchargers on production model engines.

## The Turbocharger

A second method of supercharging is to use a centrifugal compressor driven at high speeds by a turbine in the exhaust. Exhaust heat drives the turbocharger in much the same way it powers the compressor on the gas turbine engine we explained in Unit 3. This exhaust heat is normally wasted. So turbocharging adds nothing to the engine's load, but it adds a great deal to its volumetric efficiency. For these reasons, turbocharging is becoming common on modern gasoline- and Diesel-powered passenger cars (Figure 11–18).

**Figure 11–18.** Turbocharging adds nothing to the engine's load but adds much to its volumetric efficiency. *Courtesy of Porsche-Audi, Volkswagen of America, Inc.*

# Turbine Theory

As you know, about half the heat energy generated in a modern internal combustion engine is lost in the exhaust. It is this heat which causes exhaust gases to continue their expansion in the exhaust system. So the exhaust-gas velocity that drives the turbocharger is a heat-produced velocity. It is not, as a common misconception has it, a velocity caused by the piston movement inside the cylinders. A measurement of exhaust gas temperature on both sides of the turbine blade shows a impressive drop. A difference of 300° F (133° C) is not uncommon. This clearly demonstrates that it is the heat energy in the exhaust which drives the turbine.

For this reason, the boost in air pressure delivered by a turbocharger is proportional to the load on the engine. We can understand why if we remember that the heat which drives the turbine all originates in the combustion chamber. The burning releases the potential energy of the gasoline as heat energy and the more fuel that is burned, the more heat there will be. Since more fuel is fed into the cylinders when the engine is under load, more heat is released at that time to drive the turbine (Figure 11–19).

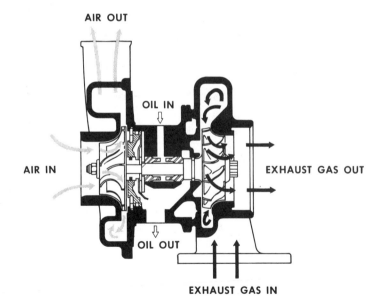

**Figure 11–19.**   Since more fuel is fed into the cylinders when the engine is under load, more heat is released at that time to drive the turbine. *Courtesy of Schwitzer Division, Wallace-Murray Corp.*

**Turbocharger Construction.** A typical centrifugal type turbocharger is a very simple machine. It consists of a centrifugal compressor and a gas turbine (Figure 11–20). The compressor has only three major parts: the impeller, the diffuser, and the housing.

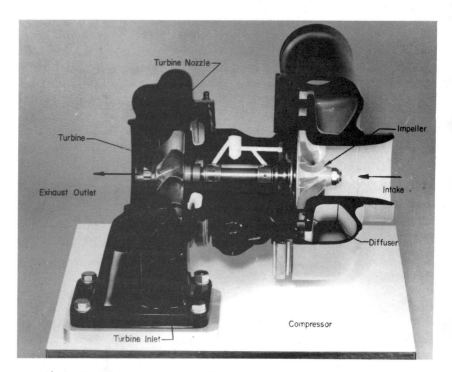

**Figure 11–20.** A typical centrifugal type turbocharger is a very simple machine consisting of a centrifugal compressor and a gas turbine. *Courtesy of Schwitzer Division, Wallace-Murray Corp.*

*The impeller,* which looks much like the fan in a vacuum cleaner, is mounted on the same shaft as the turbine. Exhaust gases sweeping through the turbine rotate it, along with the attached shaft and impeller, at extremely high speeds. The impeller throws the incoming air outward at a very high velocity.

*The diffuser* then slows the air back down again without causing turbulence. As the high-velocity air slows suddenly, it is compressed and its temperature rises.

*The housing* collects the pressurized air and routes it out of the compressor towards the combustion chamber. In some designs, the diffuser and housing are made as one unit.

It is important that the turbocharger be properly matched to its engine application. The critical factor is the rpm range at which the engine is expected to function. If the compressor and turbine are too large, turbo response will be sluggish and the maximum pressure produced will be low. On the other hand, an overly small compressor, will have to race the turbine excessively in order to pump enough air and may overheat the incoming air.

**Boost.** The amount of pressure applied to an engine's intake system by the turbocharger is called its *boost*. This term often confuses beginning mechanics because there exist two completely different methods of measuring boost. It is always important to know whether boost is being measured in pounds per square inch gauge (psig) or column inches of mercury (Hg″). Normal atmospheric pressure, as measured by the column inches of mercury in a common barometer, is 29.92 Hg″.

Sometimes it is convenient to be able to convert specifications reported in psig to Hg″ or vice versa. Since normal atmospheric pressure equals 14.7 psi and 29.92 Hg″, we can easily compute the equivalent in Hg″ of one psig.

$$29.92 \text{ Hg}'' \div 14.7 \text{ psi} = 2.03537.$$

One psig equals approximately two Hg″. If we have 40 Hg″ of boost, we actually have about 6 psig in the intake manifold.

# Turbocharger Performance

Turbocharger boost easily overcomes almost any of the breathing difficulties found in different engine designs. The volumetric efficiency of almost any engine can be raised to well over 100% by turbocharging, and under certain conditions, turbocharged racing engines may exceed 200%. It is fairly common for turbocharging to double or even triple the horsepower of an engine of a given displacement. On passenger cars, where durability and ease of operation are important requirements, boost pressures are seldom over 8 psig. But even this modest boost level is capable of increasing horsepower output by around 50% (Figure 11–21).

**Figure 11-21.** Even modest boost levels are capable of increasing horsepower output by around 50%. *Courtesy of Buick Division, General Motors Corporation.*

## Turbocharger Installation

Turbochargers may be located in the intake system either before or after the carburetor. Installations after the carburetor are said to be *downstream* and to *suck through* the carburetor. Turbochargers mounted before the carburetor are said to be installed *upstream* and to *blow* through the carburetor.

**Downstream Installation.** In this arrangement, air is pulled through the carburetor much as it is in a normally aspirated engine (Figure 11-22). The turbocharger then compresses the fuel mixture and delivers it to the cylinders (Figure 11-23). Downstream installation has the advantages of letting the carburetor meter fuel in the usual way and using the impeller to help atomize the fuel. So the fuel distribution to the cylinders is very even.

Downstream installation, however, also presents some characteristic disadvantages. The necessary lengthening of the passages from the carburetor to the cylinders may cause some lag in throttle response. The fuel may condense and drop out inside those long manifold passages. Moreover, the rapid air flow over the carburetor throttle plate may cause icing unless specially heated manifolds are used.

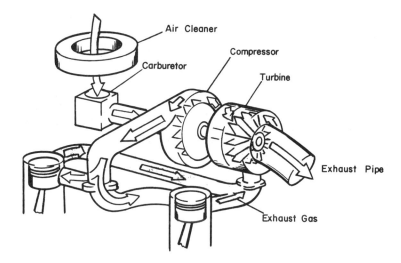

**Figure 11–22.**   In a downstream installation, air is pulled through the carburetor much as it is in a normally aspirated engine

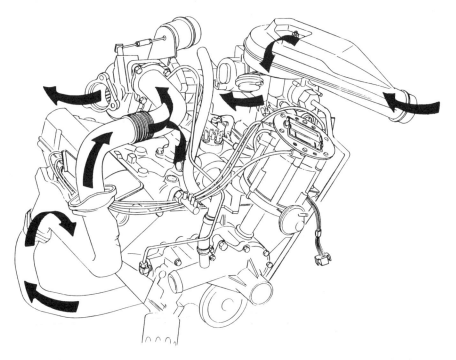

**Figure 11–23.**   Notice how compressor and carburetor are mounted close to the engine inlet manifold to reduce fuel condensation. *Courtesy of Buick Division, General Motors Corporation.*

**Upstream Installation.** By placing the turbocharger ahead of the carburetor, some of the disadvantages of downstream installation can be avoided. Icing and throttle lag are not serious problems when the turbocharger blows through the carburetor (Figure 11–24). The mounting of the turbocharger and routing of the exhaust pipes are also simplified. And this installation has the further advantage of retaining the original carburetor, intake system, and linkage.

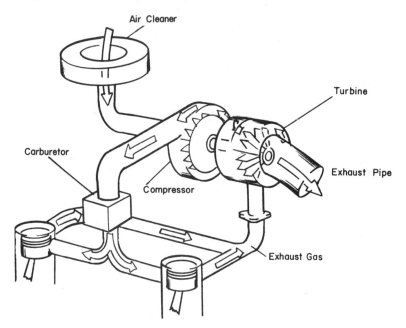

**Figure 11–24.** By placing the turbocharger ahead of the carburetor, some of the disadvantages of downstream installation can be avoided. But it then becomes necessary to make the carburetor and fuel lines airtight and to use a special fuel pump.

The most obvious disadvantage of the upstream installation is the need to make the carburetor and fuel lines air tight. Otherwise the boost pressure will cause leaks to the outside. A second disadvantage is the need for a special fuel pump. It is necessary to keep fuel pressure three to five pounds above boost pressure to insure an adequate rate of flow.

## Detonation Control

Because of the increased temperature of the fuel-air mixture in a supercharged engine, detonation control becomes important. Detonation is rapid, uncontrolled burning in the combustion chamber. In supercharged engines, it is usually caused by an overheated fuel mixture, which explodes under compression before ignition occurs. Because the peak pressure from detonation is not properly timed, it can do serious damage to the engine. (We shall say more about detonation in Unit 12 when we study the combustion process.) Just remember that, in supercharging, detonation control must always be a major consideration.

This is a caution that we extend to beginners out of our own hard-won experience. Many years ago we came back from the drag strip with a basket full of turbocharged Corvair engine. A boost of 8 psig is almost always safe but, with a production engine, one of 15 psig or higher is tempting fate.

Three general approaches to detonation control are often taken: (1) regulating boost pressure, (2) retarding spark timing, and (3) cooling the charge.

**Regulating Boost Pressure.** Boost pressure can be regulated in two ways. Some of the compressed intake charge can be bled off before it reaches the cylinders, or some of the exhaust gases can be diverted away from the turbine to slow down the rate of compression.

*Pressure control valves,* commonly called "pop-off" valves, are used to bleed off part of the compressed fuel mixture. Installed between the compressor and the engine, these valves are held closed by springs (Figure 11–25). Preset tension on these springs is such that they give way when the maximum allowable boost pressure is reached. Boost pressure then opens the valve and vents some of the pressure.

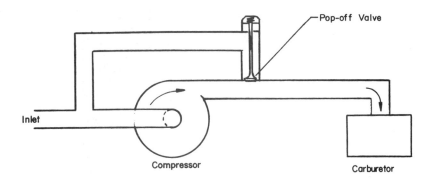

**Figure 11–25.** Pop-off valves are used to bleed off part of the compressed fuel mixture. They are installed between the compressor and the engine and are held closed by springs.

For safety, on downstream installations, the vented mixture is routed back to the compressor. On upstream installations, the pop-off valve may simply be vented to the engine compartment. Sometimes the pop-off valve is used to reduce emissions caused during closed throttle deceleration and idle. In this application the valve is opened when the closed throttle causes a vacuum in the manifold. Or the valve may be operated by either a manifold vacuum or by excessive boost pressure.

*Waste gates* are the most widely used method of regulating boost pressure. Most factory installed turbochargers use waste gates (Figure 11–26). The purpose of a waste gate is to control the flow of exhaust gases to the turbine. The gate is controlled by a diaphragm connected to the engine side of the system. When boost is low, the diaphragm routes most of the exhaust through the turbine. As boost pressure reaches the desired level, the diaphragm begins to regulate the waste gate so that turbine speed is always matched to the boost requirements of the engine (Figure 11–27).

**Figure 11–26.** Most factory installed turbochargers utilize waste gates to control the flow of exhaust gases to the turbine. *Courtesy of Buick Division, General Motors Corporation.*

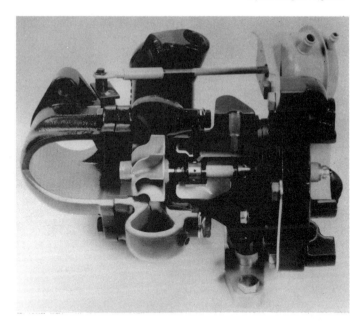

**Figure 11–27.** As boost pressure reaches the desired level, the diaphragm begins to regulate the waste gate so turbine speed is always matched to the boost requirements of the engine. *Courtesy of Ford Motor Company.*

**Retarding Spark Timing.**    Another way of reducing the chances of detonation is by delaying the spark. This lowers the peak temperature produced by combustion and gives the chamber a chance to "cool off" somewhat. A number of methods are used.

*Dual contact point distributors* are designed so that only one set of points makes contact during nonboost operation. When boost is applied, a second set of contacts is connected in series with the first set by a pressure-sensitive switch. This increases total dwell angle, thus retarding the spark timing.

*An electronic sensor system* was developed by Delco Electronics Division of General Motors for use on Buick's 1978 turbocharged V–6 (Figure 11–28). Called *Electronic Spark Control* or "ESC," this system immediately senses any vibration caused by detonation in the combustion chamber. It then feeds a signal into a mini-computer that analyzes the vibration and signals the electronic ignition distributor to delay the spark.

*Pressure retard diaphragms* are also used to retard the timing on some engines. A pressure retard diaphragm is connected to the engine just as a vacuum advance device would be hooked to a normally aspirated engine. But its working is just the opposite. It *retards* the spark when manifold pressure becomes too high.

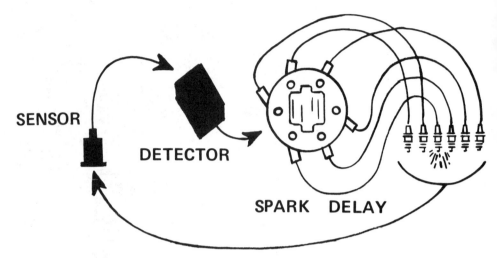

**Figure 11–28.** An electronic sensor system senses immediately any vibration caused by detonation in the combustion chamber. It then feeds a signal into a minicomputer which analyzes the vibration and signals the electronic ignition distributor to delay the spark. *Courtesy of Buick Division, General Motors Corporation.*

**Charge Cooling.** Two methods may be used to lower the temperature of the compressed charge before it enters the cylinder. One is water injection and the other is with the use of an intercooler.

*Water injection* was actually developed during World War II for use on supercharged aircraft engines. It was applied to supercharged passenger car engines as early as 1961 when Oldsmobile designed water injection into their 215 cid turbocharged aluminum V–8. It is presently used by SAAB of Sweden on their turbocharged four-cylinder power plant.

During high boost periods, when detonation is most likely, water is sprayed into the intake manifold. The heat of the charge instantly vaporizes the water. But the process of converting the water to steam uses large quantities of the excess heat energy so the intake charge is cooled to a level unlikely to cause detonation. Otherwise, the steam has little effect on the combustion process.

*An intercooler* is nothing more than a special radiator installed to cool the compressed charge before it enters the engine. The radiator may be designed to use either air or water as a coolant. Intercoolers are used in some special racing applications because of the very high boost pressures they permit. Intercoolers are also used on large Diesel trucks and industrial equipment, but presently they are not used on passenger car engines.

## THE FUTURE OF THE TURBOCHARGER

The major technical problems involved in turbocharging automotive engines were all solved by the 1960's. Almost every major manufacturer has had at least one turbocharged design in production since that time. Yet until recently Detroit has flirted with turbocharging without embracing it. This is clearly one branch of automotive technology that has been "on the back burner" for over twenty years.

Why? A number of factors were involved. Customer preference has not really favored turbocharging until recently. Blowers have made interesting conversation pieces. But with gasoline readily available at twenty-five or thirty cents a gallon, there was little economic incentive for buying a turbocharged engine. Even buyers not discouraged by the additional cost of a blown engine often hesitated because of the shortage of qualified service personnel. Most mechanics in the 1960's simply could not do justice to the careful engineering that went into a turbocharged power plant.

Now, however, the picture seems to be changing. The cost of gasoline has become increasingly important. Manufacturers are beginning to turn to supercharging to raise the horsepower output of engines that they downsized to save fuel. A case in point is the turbocharged 2.3-liter engine Ford produced for its 1979 Mustang and Capri lines (Figures 11–29 and 11–30). With only modest increases in fuel consumption, the turbocharged version raised gross engine output from 101 HP to 147 HP and torque from 122 pound feet to 154 pound feet.

**Figure 11–29.** Manufacturers are beginning to turn to turbocharging to raise the horsepower output of engines they downsized in order to save fuel. With only modest increases in fuel consumption, the turbocharged version of this engine raised gross engine output from 101 HP to 147 HP and torque from 122 pound feet to 154 pound feet. *Courtesy of Ford Motor Company.*

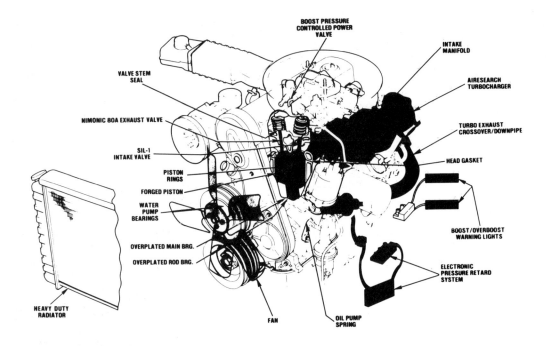

**Figure 11–30.** Effective turbocharging requires modifications of many engine systems and components. Factory installation must comply with all federal regulations and still maintain drivability, reliability, and economy. *Courtesy of Ford Motor Company.*

It now seems clear that the near future will see an increase in the number of turbocharged engines. But whether this development will be permanent or temporary remains to be seen. If the production costs of turbine-driven compressors can be lowered somewhat, turbochargers may come into widespread use as a fuel economy measure.

## REVIEW QUESTIONS

1. Supercharging increases volumetric efficiency because

   A. Air fills the engine's cylinders at higher than atmospheric pressure.

   B. Air volume is constant but density is greater.

   C. Valve overlap is reduced.

   D. Air is pre-heated.

2. Positive displacement type superchargers

    A.  Are very efficient at all speeds.
    B.  Must rotate at very high speeds.
    C.  Move the same volume of air per revolution regardless of speed.
    D.  None of the above.

3. Turbines work on the principle of

    A.  Exhaust gas velocity.
    B.  Latent heat conversion.
    C.  The expansion of hot exhaust gases.
    D.  Inertia.

4. Of the potential heat energy in a gallon of gasoline Joe says half goes out the exhaust.

    Jim says 25% is converted to mechanical energy.

    Who is correct?

    A.  Joe only
    B.  Jim only
    C.  Both are correct
    D.  Both are wrong.

5. Which device is used to control boost by controlling turbine speed?

    A.  Pop-off valve
    B.  Governor
    C.  Waste gate
    D.  Exhaust gas recirculation

6. Detonation can be prevented by

    A.  Cooling intake charge.
    B.  Reducing boost.
    C.  Retarding spark timing.
    D.  All of the above.

7. Engine driven positive displacement superchargers

    A.  Can rob up to 20% of the engine HP.
    B.  Compress the air by centrifugal force.
    C.  Do not increase charge temperature.
    D.  All of the above.

8. Most turbochargers are

    A. Valve type pumps.

    B. Centrifugal pumps.

    C. Cheap to build.

    D. Positive displacement type.

# Fuels and Combustion

The combustion process may be the last unexplored frontier in the technology of internal combustion engines. There are, after all, only two possible ways of making significant improvements in IC engines. We can improve their breathing, and we can improve their production and control of heat. You learned in Unit 11 about some of the more promising approaches to the improvement of volumetric efficiency.

In this unit, we will examine closely the nature of IC fuels, the process by which they are burned in the combustion chamber, and the most important ways now known for controlling that burning.

The future mechanics learning their trade from this text are likely to see dramatic changes in this area of automotive technology during their careers (Figure 12–1). New fuels are likely to be introduced as supplements to, or substitutions for, gasoline and Diesel oil. Experimentation now going on with new combustion chamber designs and new approaches to ignition may cause the methods now taken for granted to change radically.

But even if these things happen, the information in this unit will remain valuable to you. The chemistry and the physics of the combustion process are not going to change. Learning the basic facts presented in this chapter will do more than prepare you to work on today's engines. It will also enable you to keep abreast of developments on this most exciting frontier of the trade.

**Figure 12-1.** Mechanics beginning in the trade today may expect to see during their careers radical changes in the fuels used for IC engines and the combustion processes which burn those fuels.

## OBJECTIVES

When you have learned the material in this unit, you should be able to:

- Demonstrate, by answering appropriate questions, an understanding of the chemical make-up of gasoline and the most important processes used in refining it.
- Name fuels that could conceivably be used to replace gasoline and demonstrate, by answering specific questions, an understanding of the advantages and disadvantages of each.
- Describe what happens in the combustion chamber during the burning process.
- Explain the difference between pre-ignition and detonation, and name the common causes of each.
- Explain the working of a stratified charge ignition system.

## CONVENTIONAL HYDROCARBON FUELS

For heat to be generated in a modern internal combustion engine, oxygen must be brought into contact with a hydrocarbon fuel. The process of oxidation then turns the potential energy in the fuel into heat. The complete combustion process depends heavily upon these chemical elements: oxygen, hydrogen, and carbon. Oxygen is an extremely active gas that combines readily with a number of other substances, including hydrogen and carbon.

Hydrogen, in its pure state, is a light "burnable" gas. When burnt or oxidized, it forms the chemical compound $H_2O$, better known as water. If a surplus of oxygen is present, hydrogen oxidizes into $H_2O_2$, hydrogen peroxide. Either way, hydrogen oxidizes rapidly and gives up a large amount of heat in the process.

Carbon is a solid that exists in nature in three different forms: graphite, soot, and diamond. Graphite is a black powder often used as a lubricant for locks and other small mechanisms. When pressed into a solid, it can be used for pencil lead or for the positive pole in a flashlight battery. Common soot, or lamp black, is known to everyone. As you learned in Unit 2, it is one of the particulates in automotive exhaust which are now being studied intensively. Its presence in the air is known to constitute a health hazard, but the exact degree of risk has not been determined.

Diamond, of course, is an extremely hard stone. Gem-quality diamonds are highly valued jewels. Those of lesser quality, called *industrial diamonds*, are used as bearings and cutting instruments in a variety of applications. It is theoretically possible, under the proper conditions, to turn any form of carbon into any other, without basically altering its chemical structure.

When completely oxidized, carbon forms an inactive and harmless gas known as $CO_2$ or *carbon dioxide*. But the incomplete oxidation of carbon will produce instead CO or *carbon monoxide*. Breathing air with as little as .04 of one percent carbon monoxide can be fatal. Carbon monoxide is all the more dangerous because it is colorless and odorless. All automotive exhaust contains carbon monoxide as well as carbon dioxide. That is why it is extremely important that car engines never be run indoors unless their exhausts are properly vented to the outside. Nature gives no warning to victims being poisoned by carbon monoxide.

Neither pure hydrogen nor pure carbon is found in any quantity in nature. But both elements are contained in thousands of common everyday compounds. When they combine with each other, the compounds they form are known as *hydrocarbons*. There are literally hundreds of these hydrocarbon compounds, and almost all of them can be used as fuel. They are present in abundance in coal, petroleum, and natural gas.

At present, virtually all automotive fuel is derived from natural hydrocarbons. It takes 10,000,000 barrels of crude oil a day to supply gasoline for our nation's 149,068,000 automobiles. This is more than one-fifth of our total energy consumption. And since over half of that oil is imported, the U.S. government has become increasingly concerned over our dependence on foreign countries. Energy self-sufficiency has become a national goal of the highest priority.

Crude oil or natural petroleum consists of a wide range of hydrocarbons. The lightest of these are gases like natural gas, propane, butane, and methane. The heaviest are those used for lubricating oil and grease. In between, are a range of compounds having intermediate molecular weights and sizes. From these, we derive gasoline, kerosene, heating oil, and Diesel fuel.

# Gasoline

The gasoline pumped into cars at a corner service station is not one substance, but many. It is carefully blended from a range of liquids which can be boiled from crude oil at temperatures between 90°–425° F (32°–219° C). Many processes are involved in deriving gasoline from petroleum. But a brief look at three common methods will provide a sufficient basis for understanding the process of combustion in IC engines. The three processes to be discussed are fractional distillation, cracking, and absorption.

## *The fractional distillation process*

Fractional distillation produces, along with other petroleum products, a form of fuel known as *straight-run* gasoline. The process involves heating crude oil at increasing temperatures to vaporize, progressively, the different hydrocarbon compounds in it. The lighter, more volatile compounds boil first. They are then fed through condensers and cooled so that they return to their liquid state. Some compounds released in this process, however, do not condense. Propane and butane, for instance, remain gases unless they are compressed and kept under pressure.

By carefully regulating the condensation process, the hydrocarbons are separated, according to their boiling points, into various "fractions." Further distillation and chemical treatment are necessary to turn these fractions into finished petroleum products. Fractional distillation itself does not change the chemical structure of the various hydrocarbons. It simply separates them from each other.

## *The cracking process*

Much more gasoline can be produced from a barrel of crude oil if the heavier fractions can be *cracked* into lighter, more volatile variants

(Figure 12–2). This can be done by subjecting those so-called *heavy-end* fractions to heat or causing them to interact with other chemicals. Either method breaks some of the chemical bonds in the larger hydrocarbon molecules. In thermal cracking, the heat must be added while the heavy-end compounds are under pressure.

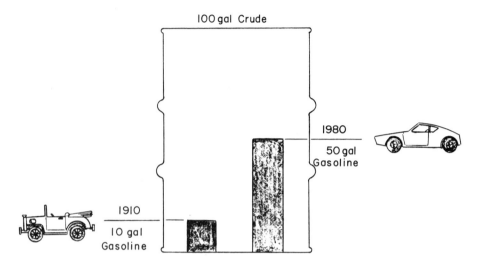

**Figure 12–2.**   Much more gasoline can be produced from a barrel of oil if the heavier fractions can be *cracked* into lighter, more volatile variants. Either heat or chemical processes can be used to crack heavy-end fractions in this way.

Most of the lighter hydrocarbons produced by cracking are suitable for use in gasoline. In fact their anti-knock values are often superior to those of straight-run gasoline. But they require further refining before they are suitable for use. Otherwise, they tend to decompose with age and to produce a varnish-like gum that clogs fuel lines and causes carburetion problems. A high percentage of the gasoline used in automobiles is produced by the cracking process.

## The absorption process

The fuel produced by the absorption process is called *casing head* or *natural* gasoline. The source of this variety of gasoline is natural gas. The gas is bubbled through a bath of heavy-end hydrocarbons which absorbs certain light-end fractions from it. Distillation of the heavy hydrocarbons  then *separates out* the gasoline. This natural gasoline, made up of very light fractions, is often blended with other gasolines to improve their vaporization.

# Characteristics of a Good Gasoline Blend

The liquid that is finally pumped into your gas tank is a carefully blended mixture of many hydrocarbon fractions. Into that mixture also have been introduced various chemical additives. Though the additives do not burn, they contribute to the combustion process in other ways. The total blend of ingredients is planned so that the resultant fuel will have several desirable characteristics.

## *Proper degree of volatility*

A liquid which evaporates easily is said to have high *volatility*. Light-end petroleum fractions have this characteristic; so they vaporize well at lower temperatures. Heavy ends require much higher temperatures. One reason for blending petroleum fractions is to ensure a fuel with the proper volatility. For volatility affects engine performance in a number of ways.

**Cold-Weather Starting.**    It is important that the final blend contain enough light-end fractions to ensure easy starting. The blends marketed at the pump vary from region to region and season to season because the exact percentage required varies with location and temperature.

**Fuel-Line Flow.**    Though the fuel should be volatile enough for easy starting, it should not vaporize too easily. So the blend must not contain too high a proportion of light-end fractions. If it does, the heat of the engine will cause them to boil inside the fuel line. This will produce pockets of gaseous vapor which cannot be pumped along the line. Then the action of the fuel pump, instead of producing a liquid flow to the carburetor, will simply expand and contract the size of the vapor bubble. This condition, known as *vapor lock*, may develop at high altitudes, even when the same blend has been working well at lower levels. Highly volatile blends also cause carburetion problems and excessive loss through evaporation.

**Mileage.**    The heavy-end fractions, those with lower volatility, possess a higher content of heat energy. Using them as generously as possible adds to fuel economy in two ways. Most important is the fact that their greater energy potential makes more BTUs available. Also, the same volatility that makes ignition of the *light*-ends easier also causes fuel loss through evaporation. But special problems are also caused by using too high a proportion of heavy-end fractions.

**Crankcase Dilution.** A blend that is too heavy will not vaporize completely, even in the cylinder. Instead, it acts as a liquid solvent and washes the film of lubrication from the cylinder wall and ring faces. It then flows past the rings and drips into the crankcase. There it dilutes the oil in the sump and progressively destroys its lubricating qualities.

The effects of this on the engine are not good. The washing of the cylinder walls causes excessive wear on the pistons, rings, and cylinders. Further down in the engine, inadequate lubrication of the bearings causes them to wear rapidly. When the thinned oil is recycled through the pump, it no longer responds well to the oil control rings. So carbon from the burning oil collects on the spark plugs and soon causes them to stop firing. Excessive smoke is usual in the exhaust of cars suffering from crankcase dilution. In some extreme cases, explosions have occurred in crankcases containing highly diluted oil. Such explosions, of course, cause catastrophic damage and fire. The goal, then, is to use enough of the heavy fractions to ensure good fuel economy, but not so much that crankcase dilution will be a problem.

Crankcase dilution is most likely to occur in cold weather. Winter driving, especially in-town, stop-and-go driving, often causes significant dilution with blends that, otherwise, would give very satisfactory service. During cold-weather warm-ups, it is normal for some cylinders to miss for a good while after an engine is started. Fuel charges fed to these cylinders may condense into raw gasoline and trickle into the crankcase. In stop-and-go driving, the engine is not operated long enough to warm it up completely. So the gasoline trapped in the crankcase does not evaporate, as it would under sustained operation. Regular checks of the dipstick, when crankcase dilution is taking place, may give the owner a false sense of security. The gasoline seepage seldom allows the oil level to drop. In fact, it is not uncommon for the engine to seem to be making its own oil, as dilution actually causes an apparent rise in the oil level (Figure 12–3).

**Figure 12–3.** When crankcase dilution is taking place, the engine may seem to be making its own oil. Gasoline seepage is often enough to cause an apparent rise in the oil level.

## *Octane rating*

Gasolines are graded according to the ease with which they ignite and the speed at which they burn. These fuel characteristics are determined in part by the blend of hydrocardons used and in part by additives. A primary function of additives is to increase resistance to detonation, or "knocking."

Until clean-air laws began requiring the use of catalytic converters on new cars in 1973, tetraethyl lead (TEL), was an important "anti-knock" additive that was routinely added to almost all blends of gasoline. By using TEL, refineries could make generous use of cheaper and more plentiful hydrocarbon fractions which otherwise would make the blend too prone to detonation. The trace amounts of lead also provided additional lubrication for the valve seats and guides.

Unfortunately, however, the effects of tetraethyl lead on the environment are not good. It is so poisonous that in its pure form it can cause death through skin contact alone. In heavy traffic, even the small amounts emitted as exhaust particulates can cause health problems. Moreover, it totally destroys the effectiveness of catalytic converters used to control emission on most new cars. The gas tank filler-necks on cars with catalytic converters are made small. They are not intended to accept the nozzles used on pumps which dispense leaded gasoline. In fact, it is illegal to put leaded gasoline into cars equipped with catalytic converters (Figure 12–4).

**Figure 12–4.** Pump nozzles dispensing leaded gasoline are not intended to fit the filler necks of cars with catalytic converters. It is illegal to put leaded gasoline into these cars.

## THE COMBUSTION PROCESS

The entire combustion process takes place in about three thousandths of a second. It begins in an engine doing 3000 rpm's, when the intake valve closes, at about 60° ABDC, and it may be considered finished by the time combustion pressure reaches its peak, at about 15° ATDC. So the whole process only lasts for about 135° of crankshaft rotation. But during this tiny fraction of time, a lot of things happen in the combustion chamber. We can understand better what happens and how it takes place if we discuss separately the three stages of the combustion process. Those stages are, in order: compression, ignition, and burning.

# Compression

As the piston moves up on the compression stroke, the temperature of the fuel mixture shoots up rapidly. There is not enough time for this heat to be dissipated to cooler parts of the engine. So the compressed mixture enters what engineers call a *pre-flame* condition. It is chemically and physically ready to burn rapidly when ignition occurs. However, a number of things can happen during compression that interfere with proper combustion.

## Combustion problems during the compression stage

If the mixture is allowed to get too hot, it will ignite on its own. This *pre-ignition,* as it is called, causes peak pressure to develop too soon, possibly even before the piston reaches TDC (Figure 12–5). Pre-ignition always upsets engine timing and causes high pressures and temperatures to develop at times when the engine is not designed to handle them. Holes are often burned in piston heads as a result of pre-ignition (Figure 12–6). In other cases, excessive heat causes the pistons to expand so much that they seize in the cylinders.

Perhaps the most familiar form of pre-ignition is the "Dieseling" which sometimes causes an engine to continue running after it is turned off. During normal operation, pre-ignition is accompanied by a characteristic pinging or knocking. This knock, however, differs from that caused by detonation. Pre-ignition causes a higher-pitched, pinging sound and is not as loud as the knocking produced by detonation. Detonation produces a much heavier, more "solid" sound.

Four important factors should always be considered whenever pre-ignition occurs. Seldom does any single one of these factors cause pre-ignition. But in combination with each other or with still other causes, all of them can be contributing causes.

**1. Compression ratio** is important because pre-ignition only occurs when the compressed mixture gets too hot. If the compression ratio is excessive, the temperature of the mixture will also be excessive. So it is important that the combustion chamber contain adequate clearance volume.

**2. The temperature of the in-coming mixture** is important, particularly on engines equipped with superchargers or pre-heaters. Even a moderate compression ratio may be too much for a mixture that has been warmed excessively before reaching the combustion chamber.

**3. The temperature of the engine** may also be a factor. Some combustion chamber designs are more liable to pre-ignition than others. Designs in which the combustion chamber is cooled with only marginal efficiency are more likely to have problems with pre-ignition.

**4. The octane of the fuel used** is obviously a factor since ignition temperature varies with octane rating. A fuel charge usually ignites spontaneously at about 1300° F (705° C), but the exact chemical make-up of the fuel is an important variable. Some blends resist pre-ignition at temperatures as high as 1600° F (872° C).

Combined with any or all of the above factors, the mechanic often finds two other causes of pre-ignition: "hot spots" and incorrect timing. A hot spot is most likely to develop in a sharp corner or around a projection such as a gasket edge or a spark plug of the incorrect heat range (Figure 12–7). A glowing piece of carbon trapped at any of these points or an overheated point in the metal itself can easily ignite a charge in the pre-flame condition. So it is best to avoid irregularities in the combustion chamber. Where this cannot be done, the other possible causes of pre-ignition must be carefully controlled. Of course, it is always important to be sure that the spark plugs used are of the proper heat range.

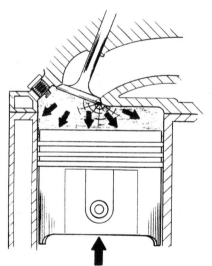

**Figure 12–5.** If the compressed mixture is allowed to get too hot, it may ignite on its own. This *pre-ignition* can be very harmful to an engine.

**Figure 12–6.** Holes like this can be burned in piston heads by pre-ignition. *Courtesy of Sealed Power Corporation.*

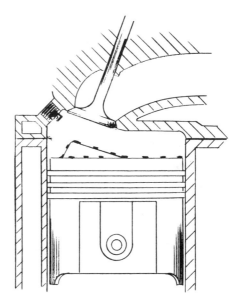

**Figure 12–7.** A common cause of pre-ignition is the development of a "hot spot" in the combustion chamber. A hot spot is most likely to develop in a sharp corner or around a projection inside the chamber.

# Ignition

From time to time, in the past few units, we have mentioned that ignition actually takes place before the piston reaches TDC on the compression stroke. The object is to reach peak combustion pressure when the piston is about fifteen degrees ATDC. So ignition must be advanced enough to allow time for most of the fuel to burn by then. The burning time for any given fuel mixture is more or less constant, therefore, the exact timing of ignition must vary with the speed of the engine.

At high rpm's, it might be necessary for ignition to occur as much as 40° BTDC. At a lower speed, the same burning time might be allowed in the same engine by ignition at or only a little before TDC.

The specific mechanisms used to advance the spark as engines speed up are usually described in texts on tune-up procedures and automotive electricity. You should be aware, however, that advancing the spark is one important way of controlling the combustion process.

A factor in determining the amount of ignition advance required is the mixture and type of fuel used. Mixtures with a high proportion of fuel are said to be *rich;* those with comparatively little fuel are *lean.* Generally speaking, lean mixtures of gasoline require more advancement of the spark (Figure 12–8). And when fuels other than gasoline are used, a totally different advancement may be required. Normally a 40° advance is sufficient for high-speed operation of a gasoline-powered engine. But special racing fuels, like nitromethane, may need an advance of as much as 80°. Although, they produce more energy, their burn rate is much slower than that of gasoline.

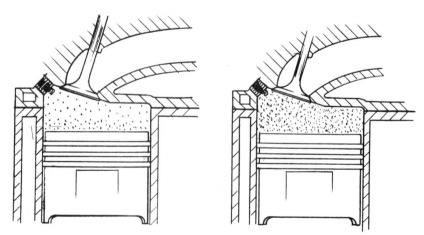

**Figure 12–8.** Because the fuel molecules are spaced further apart in a lean mixture, it takes longer for the flame to spread through the chamber. Therefore, ignition must be advanced to allow more burning time if a lean mixture is used.

# Burning

The process begun by the spark is known technically as deflagration. It is burning, of course, but it is burning of a special kind. *Deflagration* means to burn completely, rapidly, and with intense heat. Internal combustion engines depend on deflagration for their efficiency.

When ignition occurs, the spark first ignites the molecules of fuel nearest the spark plug. Heat from their burning then spreads through the combustion in a chain reaction, outward in all directions from the point of ignition (Figure 12–9). The speed of the flame front varies with the fuel, the fuel-air ratio, the temperature of the compressed mixture, and the amount of turbulence in the chamber. The flame front moves extremely fast, ranging from 50–250 meters per second.

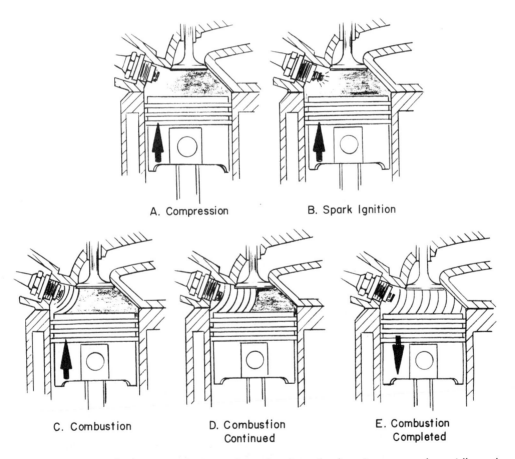

A. Compression          B. Spark Ignition

C. Combustion          D. Combustion          E. Combustion
                          Continued              Completed

**Figure 12–9.** In normal combustion, the burning proceeds rapidly and with intense heat, in a pattern known as *deflagration*. The spark first ignites the fuel molecules nearest the plug. Then the flame front moves outward in all directions.

**Detonation.** As the flame expands inside the chamber, it creates an additional source of compression for the unburnt fuel. The combustion heat creates a wave of high pressure that moves through the chamber in advance of the flame front. This expanding wave of pressure crowds the unburnt mixture against the chamber walls furthest away from the spark plug. Sometimes the additional compression is great enough to cause spontaneous ignition somewhere ahead of the main flame front. When that happens, the second flame front moves back to meet the main one. Of course, this second front is also preceded by a high-pressure wave of expanding gases. The collision of these two pressure waves releases forces which cause the heavy-sounding knock described earlier as indicative of detonation (Figure 12–10).

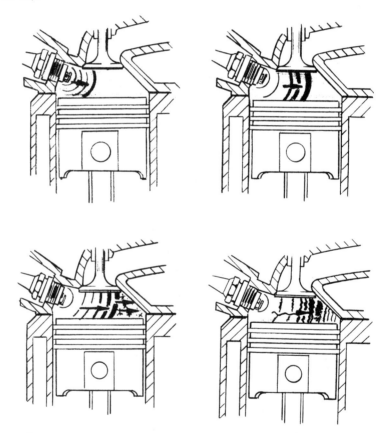

**Figure 12–10.** The expanding flame front creates a high-pressure wave which moves ahead of it through the chamber. Sometimes this high-pressure wave compresses the unburnt fuel enough to cause it to ignite spontaneously. In that case, a second flame front moves back to meet the main one. This *detonation*, as it is called, can do great harm to an engine.

Mechanics and engineers sometimes use the term *detonation* in a very general sense. In this relaxed usage, the term is used to refer to both pre-ignition and detonation, without distinguishing between them. But in careful trade talk, it is useful to be clear about the difference. Technically, pre-ignition is pinging that occurs because the mixture ignites spontaneously during compression. Detonation is knocking caused *after* ignition by the development of a second flame front. Both are forms of uncontrolled burning that can do great harm to an engine. Therefore, it is important that both pre-ignition and detonation be prevented.

**Controlling Detonation.** When Sir Harry Ricardo explored the causes of detonation, in 1921, he identified four important factors in detonation control: (1) the location of the spark plug, (2) the temperature of the mixture, (3) the amount of turbulence in the chamber, and (4) the ignition temperature of the fuel used. It was in order to control these four factors that Ricardo began experimenting with different combustion chamber designs (Figure 12–11).

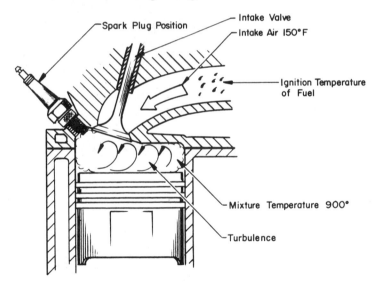

**Figure 12–11.** These four factors are always important in controlling detonation. Often more than one factor will be found contributing to the cause of detonation in a given engine.

**Spark plug location** is important, Ricardo found, because it affects the total burning time. He discovered that the spark should occur at the point which will give the flame front the shortest distance to travel as it sweeps through the chamber. This limits the time available for pressure to build in the wave preceding the flame front. It also reduces the time that the unburned mixtures, technically called *end gases,* are exposed to high temperatures.

Ricardo also found that it works better to place the spark plug near the exhaust valve, which is likely to be the hottest part of the combustion chamber. Igniting the mixture near the exhaust valve, therefore, starts the burning where it is hottest. Thus the gases most likely to detonate are burned first, in controlled deflagration. Another advantage of placing the spark plug near the exhaust valve is that, in most designs, this allows the plug to be cooled by each fresh intake charge. It is also cleaned by the surge of high-pressure exhaust gases rushing over it on each exhaust stroke (Figure 12–12).

**Figure 12–12.** Ricardo found that placing the spark plug near the exhaust valve helped to control detonation. Combustion would then begin where the gases were hottest and spread to the cooler gases.

**Mixture temperature** is obviously an important factor in controlling detonation. So Ricardo tried various ways of controlling it. One thing he found was that the end gases stay cooler if they are exposed to a relatively large surface area. That is, a fairly large area of the chamber walls should be in contact with the end gases. This part of the combustion chamber is called a *quench area.* As increasing pressure and heat from the flame front heats up the end gases, the quench area comes into play. Its larger surface area allows it instantly to dissipate some of that heat to cooler parts of the engine. This helps keep the temperature of the end gases below their ignition point and thus lessens the likelihood of detonation (Figure 12–13).

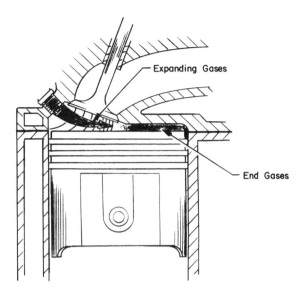

**Figure 12–13.** Detonation is less likely if the combustion chamber design includes a *quench* area. A quench area serves to keep end gases cooler by giving them a relatively large surface area through which they can release heat.

**Turbulence** also helps prevent detonation by mixing and spreading any hot exhaust gases left in the chamber after the exhaust valve closes. Unless thoroughly mixed, a small puff of very hot exhaust gases could easily cause detonation. So that is one advantage of turbulence.

Another is that it tends to sweep unburned fuel out of the quench area and mix it into the new fuel charge. Some molecules of unburned fuel are left there after almost every combustion stroke. If allowed to remain, they condense into liquid and dilute the lubricating oil. Turbulence prevents this, keeps the fuel vaporized, and—usually at the next ignition—burns it.

Ricardo also found that turbulent mixtures burn faster. Since faster burning reduces the time in which end gases are exposed to rising pressures and temperatures, this is an important gain. Rapid combustion reduces the chance of detonation.

To create turbulence, Ricardo designed into combustion chambers places known as *squish areas*. A squish area is nothing more than a place where the roof of the chamber angles downward to a very low point. At this point, very little piston clearance is left, but elsewhere in the chamber, the clearance is much greater. If you have ever stepped barefooted on a wet bar of soap, then you already know how these squish areas work. As the weight of your foot started down on the smooth edge of the soap, the bar literally shot out from under foot (Figure 12–14). The reason for that acceleration was that, with your heel planted on the floor, the angle beneath your foot functioned like a squish area. It applied the greatest force at the point of the angle. And this caused the soap to move sideways, out to where it would have more room and less pressure.

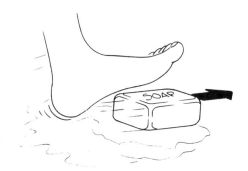

**Figure 12–14.** The principle of a squish area can be understood by understanding what happens when you step on a bar of wet soap. As the weight of your foot comes down, the bar literally shoots out of the angle formed by your heel towards the open space ahead.

The same principles of physics work in the squish area of a combustion chamber (Figure 12–15). The piston whizzing up the cylinder traps gases between the piston head and the chamber roof. Its effect on those gases is similar to the effect of your foot on the soap. The gases start to squish sideways away from the tip of the angle. Not being solid, however, the gases do not shoot out in a straight line like the bar of soap. Instead, they swirl outward in all directions, stirring and mixing the quieter gases as they do so. That swirling, stirring, and mixing of course, is the turbulence that Sir Harry was trying to produce.

In other combustion chambers, "tricks" are sometimes used to create turbulence. The direction or the manner in which the incoming charge is brought into the chamber is sometimes planned to cause swirling (Figure 12–16). In other designs, the shape of the piston head has been made irregular for the same purpose. As far as the prevention of detonation is concerned, it really does not matter how the turbulence is produced.

**The ignition temperature of any fuel,** as you already know, is connected closely with its resistance to detonation. In Ricardo's time, high octane fuel was unavailable; no matter how well the combustion chamber was designed, its compression ratio was limited to about 6:1. With refining improvements and the widespread use of tetraethyl lead, the fuels of the fifties and sixties became much more knock-resistant. Engines with compression ratios as high as 13:1 easily avoided problems with detonation. But with recent limitations on the amounts of TEL used and nitrous oxide emissions permitted, compression ratios have lowered again. With present fuels and regulations, a ratio of about 8:1 seems to be the practical limit. Experience has shown that Ricardo generally was correct in considering the ignition point of fuel to be important in preventing detonation.

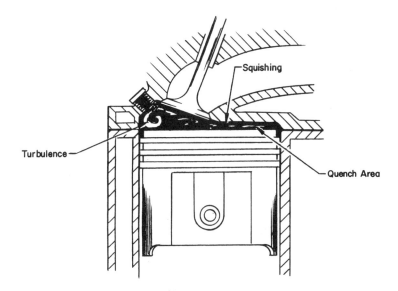

**Figure 12–15.** In the combustion chamber, the piston zipping up the cylinder traps the air in an angle, much as your foot trapped the soap. So the gases squish sideways to escape the angle. In this way, turbulence is introduced into the chamber.

**Figure 12–16.** Numerous "tricks" are used to cause turbulence in the combustion chamber. This heart-shaped BMC chamber is an example.

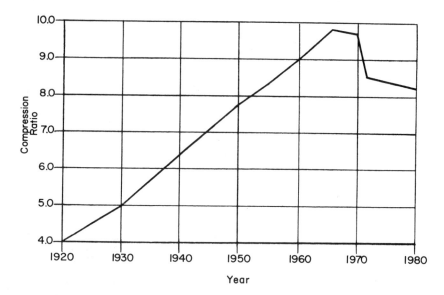

**Figure 12–17.** This graph shows how representative compression ratios increased as gasoline became better and then declined abruptly with the advent of emissions controls in the 1970's.

## COMBUSTION CHAMBER DESIGNS

You know from your reading of Unit 8 that the two basic designs of combustion chambers are the wedge-shaped and the hemispheric.

### Wedge-Shaped Designs.

Wedge-shaped designs have advantages in cost, simplicity, and turbulence (Figure 12–18). The most common way of creating a wedge-shaped chamber is simply to use a flat-topped piston and cast the wedge into the head. When this is done, both valves are placed side by side in the "high-roofed" area of the wedge. The spark plug is located between the valves. Sometimes, the axis of the valves is angled slightly to improve breathing and increase turbulence.

In other wedge-shaped designs, the roof of the chamber, in the cylinder head, is flat. But the cylinder bores are not at right angles to the deck surface that supports the head (Figure 12–19). So the piston approaches the cylinder head at an angle, and the squish area is formed by the angle of the piston head. In this design, the combustion chamber is, in reality, located in the block instead of the head.

**Figure 12–18.**   The wedge-shaped combustion chamber is cheap, simple, and very efficient in the creation of turbulence.

**Figure 12–19.**   Some engines use angle-bored cylinders so that they can get the advantages of a wedge shape in a chamber that is located completely in the block. Since the piston approaches the head at an angle, it forms a squish area on the "high" side.

# Hemispheric Designs

Hemi-head chambers do not make much use of either squish areas or quench areas. Their big advantage is the central location of the spark plug. This gives the flame front a short route in all directions. In other regards, hemispheric chambers do not offer much control over combustion. Their advantages comes from the superior breathing efficiency they make possible.

## General Observations About Combustion Chamber Design

Other things being equal, combustion is better in a chamber with the following design features:

**Proportionately Little Surface Area.**   When the chamber is considered as a whole, its volume should be large in proportion to its total surface area. If the walls and roof of the chamber present more surface than necessary, heat energy will be lost unnecessarily through those surfaces.

**Adequate Quenching.**   Though the *total* surface inside the chamber should be kept to a minimum, the end gases must not be trapped in a small corner. The part of the chamber where the end gases are burned must have enough surface area to provide adequate quenching.

**Sufficient Space for Valves.**   The valves should be large enough to get the fuel mixture in and out of the chamber rapidly. So the chamber must have space for valves that are large enough to ensure reasonable volumetric efficiency.

## STRATIFIED CHARGE COMBUSTION

As the technological race described in Unit 3 began to heat up, in the early and mid-1970's, some experts declined to join it. Or at least, they refused to search immediately for an engine that might supersede the traditional IC engine. Instead, they directed their search toward the combustion chamber and reconsidered the deflagration process. Since then, some of them have introduced changes that provide much better management of the burning. The result has been to lower emissions without using the usual add-on equipment and to increase gas mileage significantly. These results were obtained by using *stratified charge combustion*.

What, exactly, is stratified charge combustion? Essentially, it is just a method of burning fuel-air mixtures of different ratios in different areas of the combustion chamber. Typically, a small amount of rich mixture is ignited first. The resulting flame front then moves outward and ignites a very lean mixture elsewhere in the chamber. This makes it possible to burn a mixture so lean that it could not even be ignited by a spark plug. And the combustion proceeds slowly and smoothly, burning the fuel completely with minimum risk of pre-ignition or detonation.

Interestingly enough, the stratified charge is not really a new concept. Some of Nicholas August Otto's nineteenth-century patents claimed utilization of stratified charges. Ricardo experimented with stratification in the 1920's and, in 1922, patented a design with two intake valves and a pre-chamber. You will recognize these features when you work on some of the "latest" engines described in this unit.

One reason stratified charges are so attractive is economic conservatism. Progress in this direction demands no revolutionary technology or huge outlays of capital. So almost all major car manufacturers are researching the possibilities of stratification. Those efforts that seem promising are all variations of two basic designs: the pre-chamber design and the single-chamber design.

## Pre-Chamber Stratification

The first stratified charge system to be marketed in the U.S. was Honda's CVCC. As early as 1975, EPA fuel consumption tests showed that the 1700-pound Honda got 27 mpg in city driving and 39 mpg on the highway (Figure 12–20).

**Figure 12–20.** The first stratified charge system marketed in the United States appeared in Honda's "Civic." In 1975, EPA tests showed that the 1700-pound Honda got 27 mpg in city driving and 39 mpg on the highway.

In this design, an extremely lean mixture is drawn into the main combustion chamber in the usual way. At the same time, a separate induction system supplies a rich mixture to an adjoining pre-chamber.

Honda and some other manufacturers use a special, tiny intake valve which supplies a rich charge through a special carburetor barrel. This valve operates off a special lobe on the camshaft. Some other designs inject fuel at high pressure into the pre-chamber, much as fuel is injected in Diesel engines. The spark plug, located in the pre-chamber, ignites the rich mixture there. Then the flame front from this deflagration sweeps through the connecting passage and ignites the lean mixture in the main chamber (Figure 12–21),

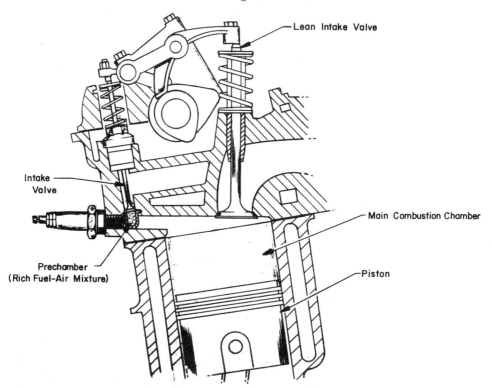

**Figure 12–21.** Honda and some other maufacturers use a second intake valve to supply a rich charge to the pre-chamber.

Pre-chamber stratification seems to work well. It is not adversely affected by engine speed and mixture variations. Engines of this type can run on mixtures as lean as 20:1. This, in turn, means that a surplus of oxygen is always available during combustion and very little carbon monoxide (CO) is formed. The slower burning keeps peak pressures and temperatures lower, so nitrogen oxides ($NO_x$) are not excessive. And the more complete burning greatly reduces emissions of unburned hydrocarbons.

## Single-Chamber Stratification

Another method of getting mixtures of differing richness into the combustion chamber at the same time makes it possible to dispense with the pre-chamber. In this method, stratification is induced in the main chamber. To do so, fuel is injected directly into the chamber using a method that creates a considerable amount of controlled turbulence. It is this turbulence which causes the stratification. The proper kind of turbulence depends heavily on three things: (1) the location of the spark plug, (2) the location and direction of the fuel injection, and (3) the velocity of air flow in the chamber.

A system using these principles is now being developed for the U.S. Army by Texaco (Figure 12–22). Called the Texaco controlled-combustion system (TCCS), it uses a fuel injector much like those used on Diesel engines. The injector is positioned so that the fuel charge is immediately blown over the spark plug, which fires just as injection begins (Figure 12–22A). While the spark continues, a flame front develops downstream from the plug and remains more or less stationary throughout the combustion process (Figure 12–22B). After the spark is discontinued, fuel injection continues to mix fuel into the swirling air. Thus the fuel is blown to the flame (Figure 12–22C). When injection ends, the end gases continue swirling toward the flame until combustion is complete (Figure 12–22D).

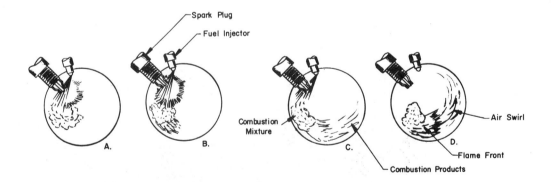

**Figure 12–22.** Texaco's experimental "controlled-combustion system" uses a fuel injector much like those on Diesel engines. The fuel is sprayed over the spark plug just as ignition occurs (A). Injection and spark both continue until a flame front is well established "downstream" from the plug (B). Then the spark is discontinued, but injection continues to feed fuel into the swirling air until maximum power is reached (C). Then injection ceases, but the swirling air continues to feed the flame front until all fuel is burned (D). This is only one of several systems for stratifying combustion with a single chamber.

When perfected, the TCCS design should operate efficiently with any injectable fuel. It is not sensitive to the octane rating of its fuels. And regulating the length of the fuel injection provides an easy control over speed and power. As with pre-chamber stratification, combustion takes place in the presence of excess oxygen. So harmful emissions are greatly reduced.

Many other projects are under way, to explore the potential of stratification. The two systems described here were chosen not because they are exceptional, but precisely because they are so representative. While some experts work to improve combustion by modifying the combustion chamber, however, others are approaching the problem differently. They are searching for newer and better fuels.

## UNCONVENTIONAL FUEL SOURCES

Of the numerous fuels which, theoretically, could be produced from domestic raw materials, the overwhelming majority suffer from one drawback: They could not be mass-produced and marketed without a major overhauling of our industrial chemistry, our technology, and our existing transportation and distribution system. No such fuel seems likely to become important to the automotive industry in the foreseeable future. So we shall confine our discussion to fuels which could be introduced with minimum technological disruption. And we shall ignore any fuels which are unlikely to be made environmentally safe or, in time, produced at a competitive price.

**Figure 12–23.**   Fuels which can be produced and distributed by existing systems have a real competitive advantage.

# Coal Gasoline

Since coal is composed of hydrocarbon compounds, it is possible to refine gasoline from coal. By the 1930's, the Germans had developed an elaborate industrial chemistry based on the hydrocarbons in coal. But the advent of cheap oil caused that technology to lose out in price competition. Even with recent rises in petroleum prices, coal gasoline has not regained its comparative cost efficiency.

Moreover, coal gasoline causes some special problems with emissions. It generally contains trace amounts of heavy metals which are poisonous but which do not present a problem in gasoline refined from petroleum. Coal gasoline also contains more nitrogen; so it is higher in nitrous oxide emissions. On the other hand, coal gasoline is compatible with virtually all existing IC engines. If ways could be found to produce it cheaply and burn it cleanly, it could conceivably become a practical fuel. But at present other fuel alternatives appear to offer more advantages.

# Methanol

Methanol is a form of alcohol that has been used for years as a racing fuel. It can be made either from coal or plant products. Its BTU content is only about half that of gasoline. It does not ignite easily in cold weather as it is comparatively low in volatility. Nor can it be mixed with most other automotive fuels. An additional disadvantage is the high aldehyde content in ethanol exhaust, which is greater than that produced by conventional gasoline.

However, methanol has superior knock resistance. Engines burning straight methanol can easily achieve compression ratios of 13:1 without danger of detonation.

# Ethanol

A form of alcohol which is relatively free of the disadvantages of methanol is grain alcohol or ethanol. Ethanol is fermented from plant products in much the same way that whiskey is distilled. But the raw material does not have to be grain. Ethanol can be produced from corn stalks, harvest chaff, grass clippings, or even organic garbage (Figure 12–24).

During fermentation, yeast is used to break down the sugars in the plant material. The sugars are turned into ethanol and carbon dioxide, and the fermented mash is distilled to extract the ethanol. The plant products used as raw material for the production of ethanol are called *bio-mass*. Many experts believe that fuels produced from bio-mass may provide the best long-range solution to our energy needs. Bio-mass is a *renewable* source which makes productive use of waste materials and by-products from existing sources. Ethanol has about two-thirds of the BTU content of conventional gasoline. It is conceivable that alcohol-based hydrocarbons could, in time, become a competitor to, or a substitute for, petroleum-based fuels.

**Figure 12–24.** Grain alcohol has a theoretical advantage because it comes from a renewable source. But its BTU content is lower than that of gasoline and it is, at present, costly to produce.

| HEAT VALUES OF FUELS | |
|---|---|
| *Fuel* | *BTU per lb* |
| Hydrogen | 51,605 |
| Gasoline | 21,400 |
| Diesel #2 | 19,650 |
| Butane | 17,300 |
| Propane | 15,500 |
| Alcohol Ethyl | 13,160 |
| Alcohol Methyl | 10,250 |
| "TNT" | 6,500 |

**Figure 12–25.**

# Gasohol

Ethanol can be blended with petroleum gasoline to produce a fuel popularly called "gasohol." Blends using 10-15% ethanol are being marketed on an experimental basis in some states. Some owners report better mileage and performance when burning gasohol. We know of no evidence that shows conclusively whether or not those claims are fact. There is no question, however, but that widespread use of gasohol could reduce U.S. petroleum consumption by as much as 12-15%.

# Liquified Petroleum (LP) Gas

When the subject of alternative fuels comes up, so does the subject of LP gas. Properly called "liquified petroleum gas," LP gas may actually be propane, butane, or almost any combination of the two. Stored under moderate pressures, LP gas turns into a liquid, but it vaporizes naturally at normal atmospheric pressure. LP gas has been used to fuel certain types of IC engines for years (Figure 12–26). Conversion kits for use in changing trucks and passenger cars over to LP gas are presently available.

**Figure 12–26.** LP gas has been used to fuel certain types of IC engines for many years. But LP gas is itself a petroleum product. So its widespread use would not alleviate the oil shortage.

Certain individuals, conceivably, may at times benefit from making such conversions. But it is important to realize that use of LP gas cannot alleviate our present energy shortage. LP fuels, like gasoline, are derived from natural petroleum. And they, like gasoline, would soon run short if their use as automotive fuel became widespread.

Nobody can say at present what fuels will power the cars of the twenty-first century. It seems likely that liquid fuels and IC engines will be major competitors in the industry at least until then. And it is possible that twenty-five years from now, when we look back, we will see that automotive history was shaped more by today's search for new fuels than by present efforts to replace the internal combustion engine.

## REVIEW QUESTIONS

*Objective Questions*

1. Gasoline is

    _____ A.  Almost pure alcohol, except for its additives
    _____ B.  Produced only from crude oil
    _____ C.  The only pure hydrocarbon fuel now used in IC engines
    _____ D.  Blended from different petroleum fractions

2. Straight-run gasoline is produced by

    _____ A.  Fractional distillation
    _____ B.  Thermal cracking
    _____ C.  Absorption
    _____ D.  Omitting additives

3. Natural gasoline is produced

    _____ A.  From coal and/or shale
    _____ B.  By simply boiling crude oil and condensing its vaporized fractions
    _____ C.  By bubbling natural gas through heavy-end hydrocarbons
    _____ D.  By combining straight-run gasoline with coal gasoline

4. The three most important elements in automotive engine combustion are

_____ A. Oxygen, hydrogen, and diamond

_____ B. Oxygen, hydrogen, and carbon

_____ C. Carbon, hydrogen peroxide, and oxygen

_____ D. Water, soot, and oxygen

5. Carbon is no longer a harmless chemical when it is found in

_____ A. Carbon dioxide ($CO_2$)

_____ B. Graphite (C)

_____ C. Carbon monoxide (CO)

_____ D. Alcohol ($C_2H_5OH$)

6. Oswald says, "A good fuel blend must have a certain amount of volatility so that it will ignite easily in cold weather."

Oliver says, "A good blend needs volatility in order to make sure that the fuel vapor locks securely in the combustion chamber."

Who is correct?

_____ A. Oswald only

_____ B. Oliver only

_____ C. Neither Oswald nor Oliver

_____ D. Both Oswald and Oliver

7. If a dipstick shows over-full on a car that is being subjected to stop-and-go cold-weather operation, this may be a sign of

_____ A. Excessive volatility

_____ B. Vapor lock

_____ C. Evaporation

_____ D. Crankcase dilution

8. The octane rating of a fuel blend is a measure of

_____ A. The number of octanes contained in one ounce

_____ B. The number of different hydrocarbons used in the blend

_____ C. The amount of crankcase dilution that can be expected from using it

_____ D. The blend's resistance to detonation

9. In an engine running at 3000 rpms, the entire combustion process lasts for about how many degrees of crankshaft rotation?

_____ A.  15°
_____ B.  135°
_____ C.  60°
_____ D.  280°

10. Peak combustion pressure should be reached when the piston is about

_____ A.  15° BBDC
_____ B.  15° BTDC
_____ C.  15° ATDC
_____ D.  15° ABDC

11. Paul says, "The actual burning time for a charge of a given amount and given fuel-air ratio does not vary with engine speed."

Pauline says, "Ignition must be advanced at higher engine speeds in order to allot more degrees of crankshaft rotation to the combustion process."

Who is correct?

_____ A.  Paul only
_____ B.  Pauline only
_____ C.  Neither Paul nor Pauline
_____ D.  Both Paul and Pauline

12. A fuel-air mixture which contains relatively little fuel and much air is said to be

_____ A.  Lean
_____ B.  Turbulent
_____ C.  Rich
_____ D.  Deflagrated

13. Milliard says, "A squish area is designed into some combustion chambers to cause turbulence."

Mortimer says, "A quench area is used to extinguish deflagration after the exhaust valve opens."

Who is correct?

_____ A. Milliard only
_____ B. Mortimer only
_____ C. Neither Milliard nor Mortimer
_____ D. Both Milliard and Mortimer

14. The best definition of a stratified charge ignition system is

_____ A. A combustion chamber designed to burn blended fractions of stratified carbohydrons

_____ B. A combustion chamber which has a pre-chamber connected to the main chamber and cam-operated fuel injection system

_____ C. A system designed so that fuel mixtures of different ratios can be burned in different parts of the combustion chamber

_____ D. An organized list of the advantages of stratification in present-day automotive technology

15. No saving of petroleum would follow if large numbers of cars and trucks began to burn

_____ A. Gasohol
_____ B. LP gas
_____ C. Methanol
_____ D. Ethanol

16. Will says, "One big disadvantage of methanol is that it does not mix well with conventional hydrocarbon fuels."

Bill says, "The overwhelming majority of the new fuel sources which are theoretically possible would require major technological upheavals before they could be introduced for widespread use."

Who is correct?

_____ A. Will only
_____ B. Bill only
_____ C. Neither Will nor Bill
_____ D. Both Will and Bill

17. The big advantage of ethanol as a potential source for fuel to power U.S. cars is

_____ A.  It blends easily with coal gasoline

_____ B.  It can be produced from bio-mass, which is a renewable source

_____ C.  It has a higher BTU content than gasoline

_____ D.  It is not a hydrocarbon fuel and, therefore, is not in short supply

18. Fred says, "The term *pre-ignition* is often used by mechanics and engineers to include both pre-ignition and detonation."

Ed says, "In careful trade talk, the term *pre-ignition* is used to describe a second flame front which develops after ignition and moves back to meet the main flame front."

Who is correct?

_____ A.  Fred only

_____ B.  Ed only

_____ C.  Neither Fred nor Ed

_____ D.  Both Fred and Ed

19. "Pinging is usually caused by

_____ A.  Pre-ignition

_____ B.  Detonation

_____ C.  Stratification

_____ D.  Deflagration

20. It is better if the spark plug is placed
    1.  At the point which will give the flame front the shortest route to the intake valve
    2.  Near the exhaust valve

_____ A.  (1) only

_____ B.  (2) only

_____ C.  Neither (1) nor (2)

_____ D.  Both (1) and (2)

# Engine Lubrication
# and Cooling

The lubrication and cooling systems of a modern automotive engine have more in common than you might suspect. Mechanically, both systems are extremely simple, at least in comparison with other engine assemblies, but both are vitally important to efficient engine operation. In fact, some experts estimate that as many as one-half of all major engine repairs are made necessary because of failures in the cooling system. Along with the dramatic improvements in lubricants discussed in this chapter have come new and important sources of engine trouble. Every mechanic, therefore, should have a good understanding of engine lubrication and cooling.

If you are inclined to feel that these subjects are less interesting than some other aspects of engine theory, you are only partly right. You will learn in this chapter about new lubricants, which may in time revolutionize our industry. And you will learn about polymerization, which, under certain conditions, suddenly solidifies lubricating oil and disables engines. The importance of the lubrication and cooling systems is too great for the mechanic ever to take them for granted. It is amazing how interesting a cooling system becomes when a man discovers that he ruined a $2,000 engine by installing a $4.00 thermostat upside down. Learning and remembering the material in this unit is essential to a complete understanding of gasoline-powered IC engines.

# OBJECTIVES

When you have completed this unit, you should be able to do the following:

- Demonstrate, by answering specific questions, a knowledge of the abbreviations used to mark various classifications of motor oil and of the use recommended for each classification.
- Explain the purpose and function of each of the following:
    1. Lubricant viscosity
    2. Multi-viscosity oils
    3. Detergent oils
    4. Lubrication
    5. Molybdenum
    6. Foam reducers
    7, Pour point depressant
- Name four functions of lubricating oils.
- Name four advantages of synthetic lubricants.
- Explain what causes polymerization and what can be done to correct it.
- Select the correct lubricating oil and specify the correct service interval for specific vehicles, given conditions under which they might be operated.
- Explain the working principles of both air and liquid cooling systems.
- Identify, in photographs or drawings, various cooling system components.
- Demonstrate, by answering specific questions, knowledge of the operation of the various components in a liquid cooling system.
- Explain the function of various coolant additives.

By the time you have accomplished these objectives, it will be clear that the functions of the lubrication and cooling systems are not completely separate. You will be reminded that the lubricating oil helps to cool the engine. And you will see that it cannot even perform its lubrication function if the cooling system allows the engine to over-heat. So the two systems are highly dependent upon each other.

# ENGINE LUBRICATION

The function of the oil pump and the means by which oil is circulated through the engine were explained in Unit 6. But there is much more to know about lubrication than we could even hint at at that time (Figure 13–1). In fact, we could not even mention all the important functions performed by the lubricating oil, so we will begin this discussion by doing that.

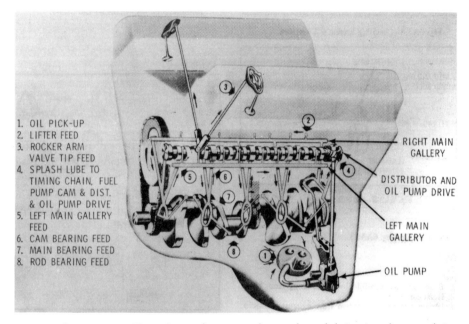

1. OIL PICK-UP
2. LIFTER FEED
3. ROCKER ARM VALVE TIP FEED
4. SPLASH LUBE TO TIMING CHAIN, FUEL PUMP CAM & DIST. & OIL PUMP DRIVE
5. LEFT MAIN GALLERY FEED
6. CAM BEARING FEED
7. MAIN BEARING FEED
8. ROD BEARING FEED

RIGHT MAIN GALLERY

DISTRIBUTOR AND OIL PUMP DRIVE

LEFT MAIN GALLERY

OIL PUMP

**Figure 13–1.** There is much more to know about lubrication than can be guessed from glancing at the components of the lubricating system. *Courtesy of Chevrolet Motor Division, General Motors Corporation.*

## FUNCTIONS OF ENGINE LUBRICANTS

One or two of the functions of lubricating oil were mentioned earlier. Let's review them briefly. In Units 6–8, when you read about basic lubrication theory, your primary attention was on bearings and rings. Now you will have an opportunity to concentrate on learning about lubrication and lubricants.

# Reduction of Friction

You probably remember from Unit 6 how a film of oil reduces friction between metal parts. We said then that oil molecules tend to fill the valleys on rough metal surfaces. You will remember that a thin film of oil separates the metal peaks and keeps them from actually contacting each other. Oil molecules in this layer roll smoothly over each other, like tiny bearings, and eliminate friction between the metal surfaces. If the lubrication system is functioning perfectly, the only friction in the engine is the result of the oil molecules rubbing against each other. This friction within the lubricant itself is called *viscous friction*.

The term *viscosity* refers to the thickness of the oil. Viscous friction, therefore, is directly related to oil thickness. The oil must always have enough viscosity to keep a lubricating film between metal surfaces. But if it is thicker than necessary, it will cause needless viscous friction.

Viscous friction is also related to something else you learned in Unit 6. On pages 157–159, in order to help you understand what goes on inside main bearings, we explained the lubrication of rotating shafts. We said that, after the shaft builds speed, its rotation keeps it literally floating on oil inside the bearing. The technical name for that kind of action is *hydrodynamic lubrication* (Figure 13–2). The explanation we gave was based on pioneering research by a scientist named Osbourne Reynolds. Reynolds' studies of hydrodynamic lubrication were conducted in 1886, only ten years after Otto developed his first IC engine.

**Figure 13–2.** The lubrication of rotating shafts inside bearings is an example of *hydrodynamic lubrication*. About 100 years ago, Osbourne Reynolds found that oil viscosity was the most important factor in hydrodynamic lubrication.

Reynolds found that oil of insufficient viscosity would not sustain the proper hydrodynamic lubrication. In simpler terms, the film of oil beneath the shaft would thin out and allow the metal "peaks" to drag against each other. On the other hand, excessively thick oil produced excessive viscous friction. Even when exactly the right lubricant is chosen, some viscous friction is always present. Viscous friction is the price that the engineer must pay for protecting the moving parts of an engine. But it is a bargain price because the same lubricant that produces viscous friction is preventing wear-causing friction between the important parts themselves.

# Cooling

As the oil circulates through the engine, it picks up heat from the hotter parts and carries it to cooler points. So it acts as a coolant as well as a lubricant. Of course, some of this heat is created by viscous friction between moving parts, but the lubricating oil also dissipates combustion heat. And in doing so, it ensures the survival of the most important parts of the engine. The piston, for instance, is exposed to some of the highest temperatures in the engine. Without a constant spray of oil to cool its inside surface, it would soon exceed its design temperature and fail.

As the heated oil drains into the engine sump, it releases some of its heat to the cooler oil pan. In turn, the pan gives up heat to the still cooler air blowing past it. In some engines, oil is pumped through special heat exchangers and allowed to cool by releasing heat to the outside air or to the engine coolant.

# Absorption of Engine Shocks

We mentioned in Unit 6 that combustion loads on connecting rod bearings can exceed two tons (1,814 kg.). Not only does the hydrodynamic action within the bearings protect the rotation of the crankshaft from friction, it also provides a cushion to absorb the force of this hammering by the reciprocating parts. Without the support of the lubricant, the shock of these forces on the crankshaft would soon destroy the engine.

# Sealing the Combustion Chamber

Oil sprayed on the cylinder wall works with the compression rings to provide a gas-tight combustion chamber. By filling microscopic irregularities in the metal surfaces and creating a lubricating film, the oil makes it difficult for combustion gases to escape past the rings. The exact means used to get the correct amount of oil into the right places were described in Unit 7. But it is well to remember that sealing the combustion chamber is another important function of the lubricating oil.

## Cleansing

Still another important function of the lubricant is to act as a cleansing agent. As it circulates, the oil washes off and carries away various substances that might cause excessive wear or harm to the engine. Dirt, carbon, microscopic bits of metal, and other waste material are picked up and held in suspension. When the oil reaches the sump, the heavier material settles to the bottom of the oil pan. The oil pick-up screen traps the larger of the remaining particles. Finally, the oil filter removes the rest of the solid contaminants.

## CHARACTERISTICS OF LUBRICATING OIL

Interestingly enough, the greatest demand on an engine lubricant is not the hydrodynamic lubrication of the bearings. That is a vitally important function, but it could be performed quite well by many liquids of the same viscosity. In terms of simple lubrication, the greatest demand is made at the point where the valve lifter rides on the camshaft lobe. The highest unit pressures in the engine exist at that point of contact. So it is important that, in addition to the correct viscosity, the oil have enough cohesion to maintain a film of lubrication, even under that extreme pressure. It must also have enough "cling" to keep it on rapidly moving parts despite the inertial forces which tend to sling it off.

To perform its many functions and meet the various operational demands made upon it, lubricating oil must be carefully blended of many ingredients. These ingredients are chosen in order to give the finished lubricant a number of important characteristics.

## Viscosity

It is particularly important that the oil retain the proper viscosity in all kinds of weather and at all stages of engine operation. In cold weather, an oil that is too thick may cause so much viscous friction that the engine will not start. Normally, the viscosity of oil will change with temperature. In fact, some oils become so thin at high temperatures that they are unable to maintain hydrodynamic lubrication. So it is important to know the accepted means of measuring viscosity and reporting. The standard markings give you essential information when you need to choose the correct lubricant for a given operating condition.

**Measuring Viscosity.** Essentially, viscosity refers to the thickness of an oil. Viscosity is measured by determining the time required for a given amount of oil to flow through a hole of a given size at a specified temperature. The Society of Automotive Engineers, in rating an oil, may measure viscosity at either or both of two temperatures: 0° F (−18° C) and 210° F (98.9° C). When viscosity is tested at 0° F (−18° C), the viscosity number is followed by the letter W. Thus an oil marked SAE 10W indicates testing under those cold-weather conditions. When oil has been tested at 210° F (98.9° C), no letter is used, so an oil marked SAE 50 indicates that the oil showed a viscosity of 50 at 210° F (98.9° C).

**Multi-Viscosity Oils.** Petroleum chemists have developed additives that are blended into oil to improve its viscosity. The purpose of these viscosity improvers is to decrease viscosity when the oil is cold and increase it at high temperatures. This causes the oil to flow better in cold weather and lubricate better when it is hot.

Oils with these characteristics are known as *multi-viscosity* lubricants. Sometimes they are also called *multi-weight* or *multi-grade* oils. Rating a multi-grade oil at 10W–30 indicates that, at 0° F (−18° C), it performs like a regular 10W oil. But at 210° F (98.9° C), the same blend performs like an oil with a viscosity rating of 30.

# Pour Point

Another important characteristic of a lubricating oil is its *pour point*. This is the lowest temperature at which the oil will remain liquid. At temperatures below its pour point, an oil will turn into a jelly and lose its capacity for hydrodynamic lubrication. Standard blends of oil often contain special additives called *pour point depressants*. These additives keep the lubricant liquified at somewhat lower temperatures.

# Flash Point

Volatile hydrocarbons begin to boil off when a lubricant is heated too far beyond its proper operating temperature. At some point, usually when the oil reaches the vicinity of 300° F (149° C) these vapors become strong enough to ignite if exposed to a flame. The temperature at which that happens is called the *flash point* of that particular oil. The flash point is another important characteristic of a lubricant because its operating range is limited to temperatures between its pour point and its flash point.

## CAUSES OF OIL DETERIORATION

During normal engine operation, a number of processes have harmful effects on lubricating oil. That is why it should be changed regularly, even though little is consumed.

## Oxidation

At any given moment, a tiny part of the oil in the engine is being exposed to temperatures above its flash point. The coating at the top of the cylinder walls and on the ring faces, for instance, is exposed to temperatures of about 800° F (427° C). And temperatures well above the flash point of oil are common on the underside of the piston, which is cooled by the oil. These elevated temperatures cause the hydrocarbon molecules to become unstable. So they join with oxygen molecules in various combinations. The result is the accumulation almost everywhere in the engine of varnish, tar, and other heavy hydrocarbons. In normal operation, not enough of these are formed to cause problems, when engine temperatures are normal and oil is changed regularly. But sustained operation at high temperatures or neglect of regular maintenance can make the cumulative effects of oxidation a cause of rapid wear.

## Acid Formation

Along with high-temperature oxidation come other harmful chemical reactions. As the oil deteriorates, some of the molecules created by the hydrocarbons and additives join with water vapor. Water vapor is often present in the crankcase as are trace amounts of sulfur and other chemicals. In combination with sulfur and water, the deteriorated hydrocarbons can easily form acids, and acids, which always tend to corrode metal, are especially hard on bearings. For this reason, manufacturers blend various additives into lubricating oil to neutralize acids or prevent their formation. They also use *corrosion inhibitors*, which displace water from metal surfaces so that oil can cling to them and provide better protection from acids.

## Sludge Formation

Sludge is formed when water mixes with engine oil. Water can enter the crankcase either as a combustion by-product or through the breathing system. When it does, the churning of the engine parts helps blend it into the oil. As this happens, the mixture turns into a brown sticky substance with the consistency of whipped cream. Sludge formation reduces the amount of oil available for lubrication and interferes with the free flow of oil through the lubrication system (Figure 13–3).

**Figure 13–3.** When water mixes with engine oil, it forms a sticky brown sludge.

This particular form of oil deterioration is most likely to occur during cold weather stop-and-go driving. Cars operated for longer periods warm up thoroughly and evaporate most of the water from the crankcase before it can do harm. This evaporation does not take place when a car is driven only on short trips. So it is important that oil be changed frequently when cars are operated in this fashion.

## Polymerization

A rarer but most dramatic form of oil deterioration is called *polymerization*. This problem first came to light in the early 1970's when emissions control devices began requiring new cars to run hotter. The higher temperatures, combined with the then-customary 6000 miles between oil changes and a certain common set of driving habits, were enough to cause polymerization.

Typically, polymerization would afflict the owner of a 1968-1975 automobile who normally drove only on in-town stop-and-go errands. If such an owner decided to drive on a long summer vacation trip without changing oil, he was unwittingly setting himself up for polymerization. After several hours of high-speed interstate driving, he might stop for a leisurely meal. While he was eating, he would never dream of the catastrophe taking place inside his engine.

As the engine cooled, after that sudden changeover to sustained high-temperature operation, the lubricating oil underwent an amazing transformation. It solidified. It turned from a liquid blend of oil, acid, and sludge into a rubbery plastic with the consistency of peanut butter (Figure 13-4). In most cases, the engine could not be cranked. When the first cases turned up, those engines had to be disassembled to remove the polymerized oil.

**Figure 13-4.**   Under certain conditions, the liquid blend of oil, acid, and sludge in a crankcase can suddenly solidify into a rubbery plastic with the consistency of peanut butter. This polymerization process renders the engine inoperable until the solidified lubricant is dissolved with special chemicals.

Special chemicals are now available to dissolve oils which have been polymerized, either by heat (as just explained) or by antifreeze leakage, which can also be a cause. The chemical used to dissolve polymerized hydrocarbon lubricants is *ethylene glycol monobutyl ether.*

---

**CAUTION:** This chemical is highly toxic. When using it, do not touch it with your bare skin, and do not breathe its vapors.

---

# Oil Dilution

We have already discussed various forms of crankcase dilution. Both dilution with water, which causes sludge and contributes to polymerization, and dilution with gasoline contribute to the deterioration of the lubricant. With the exception of the stop-and-go winter driving mentioned in Unit 12, oil dilution by gasoline is most likely to be caused by one of three things: (1) failures in the fuel system, (2) faulty ignition, and (3) worn rings and/or valves. Fuel-system failures commonly involve malfunctioning of the carburetor or fuel pump. Ignition difficulties may be nothing more serious than faulty timing or a fouled plug. The part that worn rings and valves can play in this kind of dilution was detailed in Unit 9. A mechanic should always remember that significant oil dilution is always harmful and can at times be dangerous. In extreme cases, engines in which the oil was greatly diluted by gasoline have exploded.

# Ingredients and Ratings of Lubricating Oils

Earlier in this unit, we explained the functions of viscosity improvers, pour point depressants, oxidation inhibitors, acid neutralizers, and corrosion preventers. Each of these additives is extremely important for engines which need the protection it offers. But the above list does not include all the commonly used additives.

# Other Additives

We feel compelled to mention, in particular, three other kinds of additives.

**Detergents.** The purpose of a detergent is to prevent the formation of sludge and carbon deposits. It attaches itself to the dirt particle and acts as a solvent. Often it succeeds at loosening the bond between carbon particle and metal. When that happens, the particle breaks loose, and the oil stream carries it away to the sump or oil filter.

**Dispersants.** A different kind of additive, called a *dispersant* is often used in combination with a detergent. The purpose of the dispersant is to hold dirt particles in suspension in the oil. It combats their natural tendency to join together and coagulate into deposits, which attach themselves to the engine.

**Foam Reducers.** As the crankshaft churns in the crankcase, it tends to cause the oil to form tiny bubbles. This *aeration,* as it is called, interferes with proper lubrication. Foam cannot support hydrostatic lubrication or even provide an effective lubricating film. Nor can it flow well through the lubrication system. So special additives called *foam reducers* are used to increase the surface tension of the lubricant. This rise in surface tension increases the tendency of the oil molecules to cling to each other and thus increases resistance to aeration.

## Oil Service Ratings

In addition to the viscosity numbers explained earlier, oil is also rated according to its *service designation.* The American Petroleum Institute (API) developed the system of service designations now used in the industry. The purpose of these ratings is to indicate the extent of the loadings, stresses, and adversities an oil can be expected to withstand. The API service designation is marked on each can, along with the SAE viscosity rating (Figure 13–5). This information is essential to the mechanic, who is often called upon to choose the proper lubricant for a given set of operating conditions. So you should make a special effort to learn and remember the API service designations. There are five ratings used to classify lubricants for gasoline engines and four different designations for Diesel lubricants.

**API Ratings for Lubricants Used in Gasoline-Powered Engines.** All lubricants intended for use in gasoline-powered engines have the letter "S" prefixed to their API designations. The designation of the lubricant itself is then indicated by one of the letters A through E. Generally, "A" indicates the bottom of the scale. That is, "D" and "E" lubricants can perform adequately under much more adverse conditions than A-rated lubricants. "B" and "C" lubricants are rated between the extremes. It is a good idea to learn the significance of API ratings in more detail. For that, the descriptions below are helpful.

*SA* oil is, essentially, straight mineral oil containing few if any additives. It is intended for use in utility engines subjected only to very mild operating conditions.

*SB* oil is also intended for use under comparatively mild conditions. It offers somewhat more anti-scuffing protection than SA oil and contains oxidation preventatives and acid neutralizers. SB oils are similar to state-of-the-art oils used in the 1930's.

*SC* lubricants are intended for use in passenger cars and light trucks built before 1967. They contain additives which protect engines with hydraulic lifters from camshaft wear, corrosion, sludge formation and carbon build-up.

*SD* is the designation used for oils blended to meet the requirements of passenger cars and trucks built between 1968 and 1971. At the temperatures found in those engines, they provide adequate protection in usage of the severest kind.

*SE* oils were formulated to meet the special high-temperature needs of passenger cars and trucks manufactured in 1971 and later. They provide essentially the same protection as SD oil. But they resist oxidation better at high temperatures.

**Figure 13–5.**   The API service designation is usually printed near the SAE viscosity rating on each can of oil.

**API Ratings for Lubricants Used in Diesel Engines.** Instead of the prefix "S," which identifies oils intended for gasoline engines, Diesel lubricants use the prefix "C." And as with gasoline-engine lubricants, the ratings progress upward beginning with the least efficient lubricants, which are rated "A." However only four designations are used for Diesel lubricants. So the greatest amount of protection available to a Diesel engine is found in an oil rated "CD."

It is important to remember, when choosing a lubricant, that its SAE viscosity rating and its API service designation are of equal importance. Always make sure that both are appropriate for the use you have in mind.

## SPECIAL LONG-INTERVAL OILS

For new-model passenger cars operated under mild conditions, manufacturers are now recommending oil changes at one-year or 7500 mile (12,070 km) intervals. To meet the requirements imposed by these longer service periods, oil companies have greatly improved their lubricants. By using special additives, they have produced oils which far surpass the requirements for an API SE rating. The additives used by some companies are metallic sulfides of molybdenum, graphite, or tungsten. Perhaps the most widely accepted of them is the additive *molybdenum disulfide* ($MoS_2$).

Molybdenum disulfide or "moly" is well established as an additive for greases. Millions of pounds of moly greases are used in the U.S. each year. Some of those greases are as much as 50% $MoS_2$. In molybdenum oils, however, the $MoS_2$ used is only about 1% of the total weight. But this small amount of molybdenum additive greatly extends the oil's capacity to withstand high pressures (Figure 13–6).

During operation, the suspended molybdenum is said to bond chemically with the metal surfaces of the engine. This, of course, fills in the microscopic holes and smoothes out the surfaces. And the lubricating film produced by $MoS_2$ is reported to resist pressures exceeding 500,000 psi. Considerable research is being done on oils using $MoS_2$ as an additive, both by major oil companies and by independent testing laboratories. The outcome of this research cannot now be predicted. But current evidence seems to indicate that $MoS_2$ additives can increase gas mileage by about 4 or 5% and can significantly reduce engine wear. Car manufacturers do not yet recommend the longer intervals between oil changes advertised by manufacturers of these special oils. If the findings of recent research are not reversed by further investigation, however, less frequent changes may become standard.

Drain intervals as high as 75,000 miles have been claimed in Diesel engines using some varieties of molybdenum oils.

**Figure 13–6.** Use of molybdenum disulfide as an additive greatly extends an oil's capacity to withstand high pressures. *Courtesy of International Molybdenum*

## SYNTHETIC OILS

In the "long-life" oils just described, most of the gain in performance is due to the metallic additives. The oil itself continues to be a high-quality, petroleum-based lubricant. This is not the case with the synthetic oils which were introduced to the automotive industry in the late 1970's. These oils come to car owners not from oil wells but from laboratories. Technologically, they are, in every sense of the term, test-tube babies.

Even though they are still in an early stage of commercial development, we feel that these "infants" merit discussion, for two reasons. First, their advantages over conventional lubricants are already winning them widespread acceptance in the industry. Second, they are likely to find increasing use as the petroleum shortage becomes more pressing.

**Figure 13–7.** Though still comparatively expensive, modern synthetic oils have so many advantages that many car owners are willing to pay more for them. Developed for use by the military, these lubricants have performed well in a variety of abusive conditions. *Courtesy of International Molybdenum.*

## History and Background of Synthetic Oils

Despite the recency of their commercial availability, synthetic oils themselves are not a new development. They were created by the Germans during World War II. And they have long been used by the military under a variety of abusive conditions. Both gasoline and Diesel engines have been lubricated with synthetic oils and operated in the arctic winter. Jet engines oiled with the same synthetics have subjected them to extremely high temperatures. So the new development in the latter 1970's was commercial rather than technological. It was then that synthetics became available to the average car owner at a price which was reasonably competitive with the cost of petroleum-based lubricants. This does not mean that, quart for quart, the current prices of the two oils are anywhere near equal. The synthetics still cost three to four times as much as petroleum-based oils. But, considering their undeniable advantages, many car owners now feel them to be worth the difference.

## Advantages of Synthetic Oils

To justify such an extreme price differential the advantages of synthetic oil must be considerable. And they certainly are, though experts are not yet in complete agreement about their true significance.

**Better Gas Mileage.** The synthetics are inherently more "slippery" than petroleum-based lubricants. This slipperiness, described in proper technical language as a "low coefficient of friction" greatly reduces the amount of energy lost due to friction. The result is an improvement in gas mileage, with some drivers claiming gains as high as 10%.

**Longer Service Life.** At present, vehicle manufacturers recommend the use of synthetic oils only if the standard oil-change procedures are followed. But manufacturers of synthetic oils claim that the new lubricants will stand up for 25-50 thousand miles. Some even claim 100,000 mile service intervals. These claims for synthetic lubricants are supported by extensive research, much of it conducted by independent testing laboratories. So it seems probable that synthetic oils do have a somewhat longer service life than petroleum-based oils.

**Better Cold Weather Service.** Since they have extremely low pour points, the synthetics create much less viscous friction in very cold weather. So starting is much easier and lubrication better, especially during warm-up.

**Superior Lubrication at High Temperatures.** Petroleum-based oils begin breaking down at about 250° F (121° C) and reach their flash point at around 300° F (185° C). Synthetic oils resist oxidation and polymerization at much higher temperatures. In fact, they withstand temperatures up to 600° F (316° C) without significant deterioration.

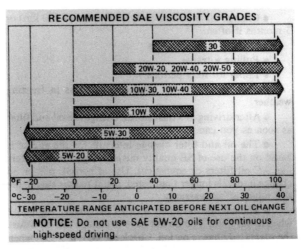

**Figure 13–8.** This table shows the recommended SAE viscosity grades for use at different temperature ranges. *Courtesy of Chevrolet Division, General Motors Corporation.*

**Lower Oil Consumption.** The superior heat resistance of synthetic oils suggests, correctly, that they have less volatility. Less oil is lost through evaporation, and overall oil consumption is lower.

## Disadvantages of Synthetic Oils

The two most obvious disadvantages of synthetic lubricants involve their cost and their lack of compatibility with petroleum-based oils. As long as their cost remains three or four times that of natural petroleum oils, they are not likely to replace conventional lubricants. And the fact that they cannot be mixed with one another nor with petroleum-based oils is a further disadvantage.

## Types of Synthetic Oils

Three general types of synthetic lubricants are now being marketed: (1) esthers, (2) polyglycols, and (3) synthesized hydrocarbons.

**Esthers.** Compounds known as esthers are created when certain types of acid are allowed to react with certain alcohol-based chemicals. Synthetic oils composed of esthers have proven compatible with many of the same additives used in conventional lubricants. Esthers can be derived either from animal or vegetable oils, i.e., either from substances like tallow or soybean oil.

**Polyglycols.** The oldest and cheapest of the synthetics are the polyglycols. They are also exceptional in that they are partially derived from alcohols found in natural petroleum. Polyglycols are made from chemicals known as propylene oxides and butyl alcohols.

**Synthesized Hydrocarbons.** Most common among the synthetic oils now being made available to the public are the synthesized hydrocarbons. Though most of those now marketed are still made from crude oil, present technology can make them from coal. The base for synthesized hydrocarbon lubricants is created by polymerizing certain hydrocarbon molecules known as olefins. The lubricant can then be built up almost molecule by molecule. So it can be tailored to give maximum performance in its intended application.

# ENGINE COOLING

The function of the cooling system is to maintain the intended operating temperature of the engine at all times. It must do this despite changes in weather, speed, or other operating conditions. Among other things, this means that the cooling system must bring the engine to design temperature as quickly as possible after starting. Then it must maintain this temperature without ever allowing it to be exceeded. In liquid-cooled engines, the cooling system also provides heat for the passenger compartment. In some vehicles, it may assist in cooling oil in the automatic transmission or even in the engine.

## AIR-COOLED SYSTEMS

The essential features of air-cooled systems were detailed in Unit 8, so only a little more must be said about them in this chapter.

Air-cooled engines use an engine-driven fan to force outside air across the cooling fins you learned about in Unit 8. On motorcycles and recreational vehicles, the fan may not be necessary, but forced air cooling is always used for automobile engines.

**Figure 13–9.**  A VW air-cooled engine with its shrouds and fan assembly removed.

Special metal covers, called *shrouds,* surround the engine parts to be cooled. The fan forces air inside the shrouds, where attached metal parts called *deflectors* come into play. The deflectors keep the air moving through the shroud and direct it towards the parts to be cooled (Figure 13–10).

**Figure 13–10.** During the operation of an air-cooled engine,metal shrouds direct air supplied by an engine-driven fan over the cooling surfaces of the engine.

Precise temperature control is difficult to achieve in an air-cooled engine. The most common method of control uses a temperature-sensitive bellows to control either the amount of air admitted to or escaping from the system. Problems with odor and the danger of carbon monoxide poisoning prevent heating the passenger compartment with the air that cools the engine. Heat exchangers in the engine's exhaust system usually serve this function.

## LIQUID-COOLED SYSTEMS

Modern liquid-cooled systems are pressurized and use engine-driven centrifugal water pumps to circulate coolant. In addition to the coolant passages in the cylinder head and block, which were described in Units 5 and 7, the cooling system consists of ten parts. It is not necessary to discuss each of these components in detail. But we will list them to help you remain aware of the complete system as you read about its more important parts. The complete system includes the

- Coolant
- Water pump
- Hoses
- Thermostat
- Radiator
- Pressure cap
- Fan
- Coolant recovery system
- Temperature gauge or warning light
- Heater core

The most important of these components are shown in Figure 13–11.

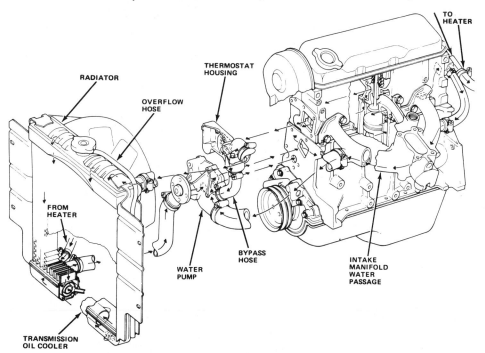

**Figure 13–11.** The most important components in a liquid cooling system can be seen in this diagram. *Courtesy of American Motors Corporation.*

## Coolant

The coolant commonly used in modern liquid-cooled engines is a mixture of pure water and ethylene glycol alcohol. The ethylene glycol improves the performance of the water as a coolant in several important ways. Added in the correct proportion, ethylene glycol lowers the freezing point and raises the boiling point. In combination with the proper additives, it also resists the tendency of water to corrode metal, and suppresses foaming (Figure 13–12).

**Figure 13–12.** A 50-50 mixture of water and ethylene glycol alcohol makes an ideal coolant. The "antifreeze" protects against freezing to −34° F (−37°C), raises the boiling point, and resists the tendency of water to corrode metal.

All these modifications are important contributions to cooling efficiency. The lower freezing point protects the block and head from damage often caused by the expansion of freezing coolant. The higher boiling point enables the coolant to transfer heat more efficiently. And the added resistance to corrosion and foaming help prevent damage from *cavitation*. Cavitation is a unique kind of corrosion which attacks the water pump housing. It is caused by a combination of factors.

One of those factors is the partial vacuum which is formed inside the water pump during normal operation. Near the impeller blades, which shove the water through the system, a localized low-pressure area builds up. This is caused by the fact that the blades are moving water out of the pump faster than it is flowing in. In this small low-pressure area, therefore, the boiling point is lowered. For that reason, minute vapor bubbles form in great numbers. They burst, of course, when they strike the water pump housing, which they do at great speed.

Over a period of time, this constant bombardment of the metal housing erodes it. In water pumps in which the impeller and housing are made of different materials the process may be accelerated. Sometimes this causes a slight acidity, which is often sufficient to cause very rapid erosion. Housings of zinc and aluminum are especially susceptible to damage from cavitation. In extreme cases, the erosion can penetrate the housing and destroy the water pump.

A 50% mixture of water and antifreeze is commonly recommended. This is sufficient to prevent freezing at −34° F (−37° C). Coupled with the pressurization of the system, it enables the coolant to reach 264° F (128° C) before boiling.

| %Ethylene Glycol by Volume | Freezing Point | Boiling Point (with 15 psi) |
|---|---|---|
| 33 | 0°F(−18°C) | 259°F(126°C) |
| 40 | −12°F(−25°C) | 261°F(127°C) |
| 50 | −34°F(−37°C) | 264°F(129°C) |
| 60 | −52°F(−46°C) | 269°F(131°C) |
| 70 | −85°F(−65°C) | 275°F(135°C) |

**Figure 13–13.** This table shows the performance of various mixtures of ethylene glycol alcohol and water.

# Water Pump

Usually, the centrifugal water pump is driven by a V–type belt, which is turned by a pulley attached to the vibration dampener (Figure 13–14). Inside the pump, a steel or cast-iron impeller is pressed onto one end of a steel shaft. The shaft is supported by sealed, pre-lubricated roller bearings. Sometimes, as in the pump shown in Figure 13–15, ball bearings are used in addition to roller bearings. These roller bearings, in turn, are pressed into an aluminum or cast-iron pump housing. Notice in Figure 13–15 that a small drain hole is located in the housing between the rear bearing and the shaft seal. The purpose of this "weep" hole is to allow seepage to escape so that it will not puddle there and eventually cause deterioration in the bearings. The water pump seals prevent leakage around the rotating shaft. During operation, the antifreeze solution acts as a lubricant for these special seals.

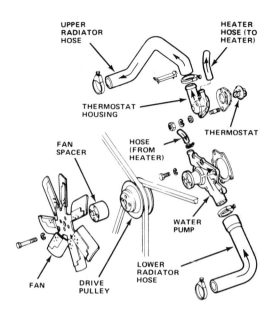

**Figure 13–14.** Usually the water pump is driven by a V-type belt which is turned by a pulley attached to the engine's vibration dampener. The other cooling system components are clearly shown. *Courtesy of American Motors Corporation.*

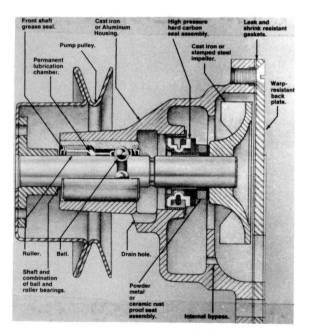

**Figure 13–15.** Inside the pump, the impeller shaft is supported by sealed, pre-lubricated bearings. *Courtesy of TRW Corporation.*

## Hoses

Coolant is routed to and from the heater core and radiator by rubber hoses. The purpose of these hoses is to provide flexible connections between the engine block and the parts of the cooling system mounted on the chassis. Radiator hoses may have the necessary curves molded into them or may be corrugated so that they are easily bent (Figure 13–16). Both types are made of synthetic rubber and reinforced with textile cord. Manufacturers of some flexible hoses reinforce the rubber by laminating into it coiled spring steel wire. This prevents the hose from collapsing when bent. Hoses molded for use on the lower radiator connection usually have reinforcing springs installed inside them. This reinforcement prevents their collapse from the suction of the water pump.

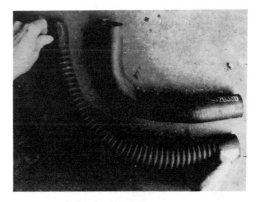

**Figure 13–16.** Radiator hoses may have the necessary curves molded into them or they may be corrugated so that they are easily bent.

Heater hoses are manufactured in continuous lengths of flexible multi-layered hose that are reinforced with textile cord. The outer layer of protective rubber guards the inner layer from damage by abrasion, oil, and engine heat. That inner layer, which contacts the coolant, is made of a softer rubber compound more resistant to decomposition at high temperatures (Figure 13–17).

## Thermostat

The termostat controls the operating temperature of the engine by controlling the flow of coolant from the block to the radiator. The thermostat contains a temperature-sensitive pellet that closes a restricting valve while the coolant is below the engine's normal operating temperature (Figure 13–18). As long as this valve is closed, the coolant simply recycles through the engine. (See Figure 13–11.) But when the coolant reaches normal operating temperature, the pellet contracts and opens the valve (Figure 13–19). The coolant is then allowed to flow through the radiator before returning to the block. In this way, the thermostat allows for quick warmup and provides overall temperature control.

**Figure 13–17.**   Heater hoses are manufactured in various designs. The outer layer of rubber guards the inner layer from damage. The inner layer, made of a softer rubber compound is more resistant to decomposition at high temperatures.

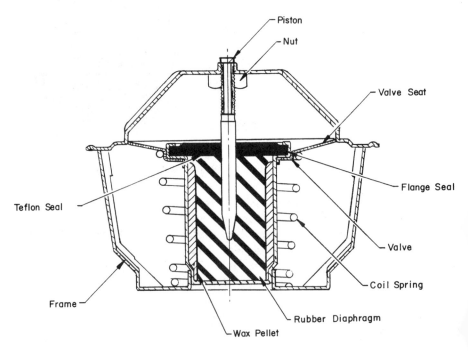

**Figure 13–18.**   The thermostat contains a temperature-sensitive pellet which opens and closes a restricting valve. The valve remains closed until the coolant reaches normal operating temperature.

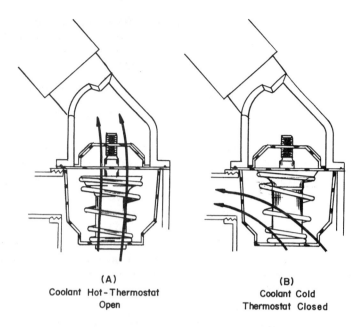

(A)
Coolant Hot - Thermostat
Open

(B)
Coolant Cold
Thermostat Closed

**Figure 13-19.** After the engine warms up, the pellet contracts and opens the valve (A). When the engine is shut off and allowed to cool, the valve closes again (B).

Thermostats are normally marked, to indicate the operating temperature at which they open. They are also marked to indicate their proper position when installed. It is important that a thermostat not be installed upside down. An engine should not be operated without a thermostat except during testing and servicing. Doing so causes prolonged warmups, poor fuel vaporization, and excessive crankcase condensation. These conditions lead quickly to oil dilution, sludge formation, and engine damage. An engine should always be equipped with an operable thermostat of the proper temperature range.

Older cars were equipped with thermostats designed to maintain coolant temperatures of 160°–180° F (71°–82° C). Today's cars have thermostats designed to keep temperatures between 195°–205° F (91°–96° C).

## adiator

The automotive radiator is a variety of heat exchanger. Its function is to dissipate the heat removed from the engine by the coolant. It does this by releasing that heat into the surrounding air. To accomplish this, the radiator is constructed of many small tubes each of which has many cooling fins bonded or soldered to it. As the coolant flows through the tubes, it surrenders part of its heat to the cooling fins. At the same time, the cooling fins, which are parallel to the vehicle's line of forward motion, direct air over the tubes. Air moving through the radiator absorbs heat both from the cooling fins and from the tubes. The increased surface area provided by the fins ensures a more efficient exchange of heat.

Radiator tubes and fins are usually made of brass or copper. But aluminum, steel, or steel and brass radiators are used in some applications. The tubes and fins just described comprise the radiator *core*. The core is positioned between two tanks, one of which is the coolant *inlet* tank and the other, the coolant *outlet* tank.

The location of these two tanks determines the basic design of the radiator. A radiator with the inlet tank on the top and the outlet tank on the bottom is called a *downflow* radiator (Figure 13–20). Coolant enters the top tank and flows downward through the core into the outlet tank at the bottom. The other common design places the inlet and outlet tanks on opposite sides of the core. In this design, the coolant flows horizontally, across the core (Figure 13–21). So this kind of cooling system is said to have a *crossflow* radiator. A big advantage of the crossflow radiator is that it allows the designer to use a much lower hood profile.

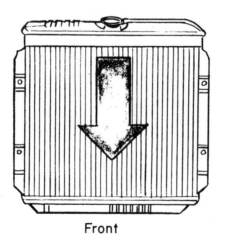 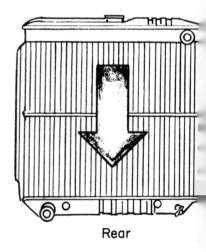

Front        Rear

**Crossflow**

**Figure 13–20.** In a downflow radiator, coolant enters the inlet tank at the top and flows downward through the core into the outlet tank at the bottom.

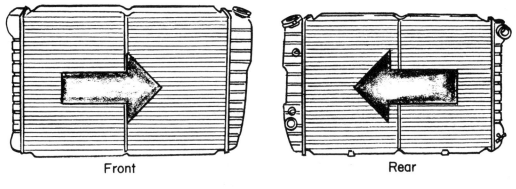

Front                               Rear

Crossflow

**Figure 13–21.** Cross-flow radiators have their inlet and outlet tanks on opposite sides. So the coolant flows horizontally through the core. This design allows the manufacturer to use a lower hood profile.

The radiator cap and filler neck are normally located on the inlet tank. The outlet tank contains a draincock, which is used—along with a draincock in the block—to remove or exchange coolant. It may also contain an oil-to-coolant heat exchanger on vehicles equipped with automatic transmissions.

## Radiator Pressure Cap

Modern cooling systems commonly operate at pressures about 14 psi (96.5 kpa) above the pressure of the normal atmosphere. The boiling point of the coolant is raised about 2.5° F (.2° C) by each pound (kilopascal) imposed above normal atmospheric pressure. So instead of boiling at 212° F (100° C), a system that is pressurized by 14 psi will resist boiling up to 247° F (120° C).

Maintaining the proper pressure on the coolant is the function of the radiator pressure cap (Figure 13–22). The cap is equipped with two valves: (1) a pressure relief valve, and (2) a vacuum relief valve. The pressure relief valve is spring-operated and is designed to open if the pressure in the system exceeds a preset level. This serves to minimize damage in the event of overheating. The vacuum relief valve opens to allow outside air pressure to equalize the pressure in the system during cooldown. This is necessary because—after an initial surge in temperature when the engine is first shut off—the cooling engine creates a vacuum inside the cooling system. The radiator cap also prevents loss of coolant while the car is moving and keeps impurities out of the cooling system.

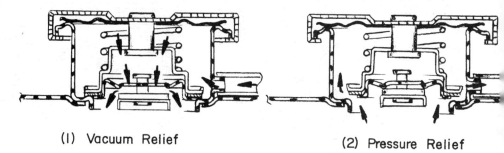

(1) Vacuum Relief                    (2) Pressure Relief

**Figure 13–22.**  The radiator pressure cap maintains the proper pressure on the coolant. For this purpose, it is equipped with two valves: (1) a vacuum relief valve, and (2) a pressure relief valve.

# Fan

The fan may either be attached to the outer end of the water pump shaft or mounted separately. If attached to the water pump shaft, it is driven from the crankshaft. If mounted separately, it is usually driven by an electric motor.

Fans mounted on water pump shafts pull air through the radiator. This is particularly advantageous at low road speeds and when the car is standing still. At higher speeds the motion of the vehicle serves to force air over the cooling fins. Two types of fans are designed to be driven by water pumps. One, known as the fixed-type fan, operates whenever the engine is running, and its speed varies directly with the speed of the engine. Fixed-type fans have 4 to 7 blades and are attached to the water pump by spacers. The purpose of the spacer is to increase cooling efficiency by positioning the fan close to the radiator.

CROSS FAN              POWER FLEX FAN              THERMO CLUTCH FAN

**Figure 13–23.**  Fixed-type fans have 4 to 7 blades and are attached to the water pump by means of spacers designed to position them close to their radiators. *Courtesy of Pontiac Division, General Motors Corporation.*

The second type of fan, which is mounted on the water pump, uses a temperature-controlled fluid coupling between the fan and water pump. The coupling is sensitive to both temperature and torque, so it automatically increases and decreases the speed of the fan to maintain proper cooling.

To accomplish this, a thermostatic coil in the fluid coupling reacts to the temperature of the air flowing through the radiator. The thermostatic coil controls the flow of a special silicone fluid inside the coupling. It is the action of this silicone fluid that controls the speed of the fan and keeps it proportional to the amount of cooling needed by the engine.

**Figure 13–24.** A special silicone fluid inside this coupling is controlled by a thermostatic coil, which reacts to the temperature of the air flowing through the radiator. The action of the silicone fluid adjusts the speed of the fan to the cooling needs of the engine.

Driving the fan consumes some of the horsepower produced by the engine. But the fluid coupling minimizes that power drain by connecting the fan only when it is needed. The resulting economy is noticeable in highway driving. A further advantage of minimizing the operation of the fan is noise reduction; that too is noticeable in fans mounted with fluid couplings. A similar control is achieved over the operation of an electrically driven fan by a temperature-sensitive switch located in the radiator.

**Fan Shrouds.** Plastic or sheetmetal rings are often mounted around the sides of the radiator and fan. Called *fan shrouds*, these rings form a kind of wind tunnel to channel air through the radiator. They increase cooling efficiency and are an integral part of the cooling system. It is important that they always be replaced after an engine repair (Figure 13–25).

**Figure 13–25.** Plastic or sheet metal rings are often used as shrouds to channel air through the radiator. They are an integral part of the cooling system and should always be replaced when removed.

> **CAUTION:** Broken fan blades have killed mechanics on numerous occasions. It is not wise to stand in line with the fan when the engine is running. It is also good practice to inspect the fan blades before starting an engine. Beginning mechanics should be especially cautious because the fan is invisible when the engine is running. Students who value their fingers should remember that a turning fan blade forgives no mistakes.

## Coolant Recovery System

Some vehicles are equipped with an auxiliary system designed to recover coolant that might be lost during *hot soak*. Hot soak occurs just after an engine is shut off. When the ignition is switched off, the water pump stops circulating the coolant, but the engine is still hot. So with the cooling action stopped, the temperature of the coolant rises rapidly. If the coolant becomes too hot, the pressure relief valve in the radiator pressure cap will open and allow coolant to escape through the overflow tube.

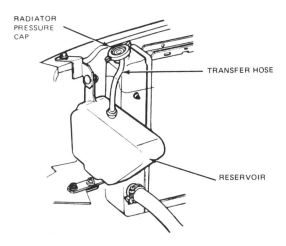

RADIATOR
PRESSURE
CAP

TRANSFER HOSE

RESERVOIR

**Figure 13–26.** A coolant recovery system prevents loss of coolant if the pressure relief valve opens during heat soak. Instead of flowing onto the ground, the coolant goes into the reservoir. Later, when the engine cools, the resulting vacuum in the radiator opens the vacuum valve in the radiator cap and draws the coolant in the reservoir back into the system. *Courtesy of Ford Motor Company.*

The coolant recovery system consists of a hose running from the overflow tube to the bottom of a special tank. Instead of spilling on the ground, any coolant being voided drains into this tank. Then later, when normal engine cooling creates a vacuum in the cooling system, the vacuum valve in the radiator cap opens. But before outside air can reach the area of the vacuum, it must force the coolant in the recovery tank back into the cooling system. Only when the tank is almost empty is air admitted directly into the radiator.

These, then, are the major components in the engine's cooling system. It only remains for us to watch them in operation, to be sure that we understand how they work together as a system (Figure 13–27).

## Cooling System Operation

Let us begin with the engine running and the water pump circulating coolant. One point not yet mentioned is the speed with which coolant flows through the system. A typical automotive water pump is capable of circulating 2000–6000 gallons per hour. On an in-line engine, the pump feeds coolant directly into the water jackets around the cylinders. From there, it travels up through openings in the head gasket and through passages in the head which surround the combustion chambers and valves. Meanwhile, it is flowing back towards the front of the engine. Until normal operating temperature is reached, the thermostat remains closed, and the coolant is recycled into the engine block. When the thermostat opens, the coolant is allowed to flow into the radiator.

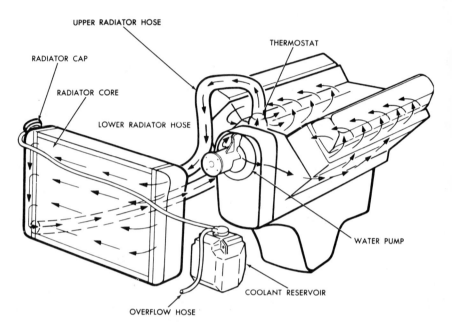

UPPER RADIATOR HOSE

THERMOSTAT

RADIATOR CAP

RADIATOR CORE

LOWER RADIATOR HOSE

WATER PUMP

COOLANT RESERVOIR

OVERFLOW HOSE

**Figure 13–27.** By studying this diagram, it is possible to see how all components in the cooling system contribute to the cooling of the engine. *Courtesy of Cadillac Division, General Motors Corporation.*

Before following it on that journey, though, let's go back a bit and change our beginning assumption. What difference would it have made if we had set out to describe the cooling of a V–type engine? Essentially, it would have made no difference, except that the cooling process just described would have to be shown operating simultaneously in both banks of cylinders. On V–type engines, coolant is pumped into the water jackets in both cylinder banks at the same time. It flows through the jackets, around the cylinders, and up through holes in the gasket into the water passages in both heads. There, it flows around the combustion chamber and valves, then into passages at the front of the heads which carry it through the intake manifolds to the thermostat. At some point on this return trip, some of the coolant is routed through a hose to the heater. Usually, the heater's intake hose is connected to one of the cylinder heads or intake manifolds. After being forced through the heater core, the coolant is fed back through another hose to the water pump. Either a manual or vacuum-controlled valve may provide control over the flow of coolant to the heater. In the V–8, as in the in-line engine, coolant is recirculated through the engine until the thermostat opens.

When that happens, regardless of the design of the engine, the coolant is allowed to flow to the inlet tank of the radiator. Then it passes through the core and is cooled. Both air drawn through the radiator by the fan and air forced through it by vehicular movement contribute to the cooling. The latter is sometimes called *ram air flow*. Ram air flow is usually sufficient at highway speeds, but the help of the fan is necessary at slower speeds.

After cooling, the antifreeze passes through the hose into the water pump. It is then ready to begin the cycle anew.

## REVIEW QUESTIONS

*Objective Questions*

1. For a Diesel engine that is to be subjected to very heavy loadings, which oil would you recommend?

_____ A.  SA
_____ B.  SD
_____ C.  CB
_____ D.  CD

2. William says, "The pour point of an oil is the lowest temperature at which the oil will remain liquid."

Wilber says, "The flash point of an oil is the temperature at which it provides the fastest possible lubrication."

Who is right?

_____ A.  William only
_____ B.  Wilber only
_____ C.  Neither William nor Wilber
_____ D.  Both William and Wilber

3. Which of the following are functions performed by the lubricating oil?

 1. Cooling important parts
 2. Supporting moving parts
 3. Sealing the combustion chamber
 4. Cleansing the engine

 _____ A.  1, 3, and 4 only
 _____ B.  1, 2, and 3 only
 _____ C.  2, 3, and 4 only
 _____ D.  All four

4. 1. Pour point depressants
   2. Detergents
   3. Oxidation inhibitors
   4. Acid neutralizers
   5. Foam reducers
   6. Extreme pressure
      lubricants

Sigmund says that all the substances listed above function as dispersants.

Simon says that all the substances listed are commonly used as additives to *antifreeze*.

Who is correct?

 _____ A.  Sigmund only
 _____ B.  Simon only
 _____ C.  Neither Sigmund nor Simon
 _____ D.  Both Sigmund and Simon

5. Ishmael the Eskimo discovered one winter morning that his car would not start. Which of the following is the most likely cause of his difficulty?

 _____ A.  Viscous friction
 _____ B.  Polymerization
 _____ C.  Hydrodynamic lubrication
 _____ D.  Oxidation

6. Thad says that viscosity is not a particularly important factor in maintaining hydrodynamic lubrication.

Theo says that the SAE viscosity rating and the API service rating should be considered of equal importance in selecting a lubricant.

Who is correct?

_____ A. Thad only

_____ B. Theo only

_____ C. Neither Thad nor Theo

_____ D. Both Thad and Theo

7. Which kind of oil is most likely to exceed the minimum standards for the highest API service designation?

_____ A. SAE 20W API CC

_____ B. Aereated

_____ C. Synthetic

_____ D. Polymerized

8. Jean says, "Esthers, polyglycols, and synthesized hydrocarbons are varieties of synthetic oils."

Jeanette says, "Molybdenum disulfide is one of the most important of the new additives used in extreme pressure lubricants."

Who is right?

_____ A. Jean only

_____ B. Jeanette only

_____ C. Neither Jean nor Jeanette

_____ D. Both Jean and Jeanette

9. Cavitation

_____ A. Helps bring the coolant to normal operating temperature quickly

_____ B. Causes corrosion of water pumps

_____ C. Injures careless mechanics

_____ D. Forces more air through the radiator to increase cooling efficiency

10. Neil says, "Cooling fins are used on the heads of air-cooled engines."

Norm says, "Cooling fins are used between the tubes of radiators."

Who is right?

_____ A.   Neil only

_____ B.   Norm only

_____ C.   Neither Neil nor Norm

_____ D.   Both Neil and Norm

11.  The best way to describe ethylene glycol alcohol is to say that it improves engine coolant by

_____ A.   Lowering the freezing point

_____ B.   Raising the boiling point

_____ C.   Increasing its efficiency in transferring heat

_____ D.   Doing all of the above

12.  Lee says, "A *heat soak* condition is most likely to exist in an engine during efficient highway operation."

Lou says, "Bubbles play no part in cavitation."

Who is right?

_____ A.   Lee only

_____ B.   Lou only

_____ C.   Neither Lee nor Lou

_____ D.   Both Lee and Lou

13.  A *weep hole* is most likely to be found

_____ A.   In a radiator cap

_____ B.   In a water pump housing

_____ C.   On the intake tank of a radiator

_____ D.   At the top of a coolant recovery tank

14.  Peter says, "Shrouds are used to guide air flow around air-cooled engines and also to channel air from the fan through the radiator on liquid-cooled engines."

Paul says, "The fan shrouds on liquid-cooled engines are not important and may be left off if it is more convenient to do so."

Who is correct?

_____ A.   Peter only

_____ B.   Paul only

_____ C.   Neither Peter nor Paul

_____ D.   Both Peter and Paul

15. The coolant recovery system is connected to the

_____ A. Intake manifold

_____ B. Heater hose

_____ C. Overflow hose

_____ D. Water pump

UNIT

# 14

# The Diesel Passenger Car

Most of what you have learned so far in this book applies to small Diesels as well as to gasoline engines, but not everything does. In this unit, we will discuss the construction and operational details of the Diesels currently being used in passenger cars. You will also learn about some innovations that make Diesel engines more practical for passenger cars. And you will see that the unique advantages of the Diesel now lead some experts to expect its widespread use in the remaining decades of this century (Figure 14–1).

**Figure 14–1.** Diesel passenger cars, like this 1979 Peugeot 504 station wagon, are becoming more popular with American drivers. *Courtesy of Peugeot Motors Inc. U.S.A.*

By the end of the 1970's, the U.S. government was pressing car manufacturers for immediate improvements in fuel economy and emissions control. Consequently, many manufacturers began to turn to the Diesel, at least for a short-term solution. Its greater fuel economy is undeniable. Averages of 30–50% better than those of comparable gasoline-powered engines are common. Its emissions of the pollutants which were regulated by law in the late 1970's are significantly lower. Claims are also made for its greater longevity and lower maintenance costs.

These advantages no doubt explain why the IC engines used in certain other applications are almost always Diesels. The American farm, for instance, is almost completely "Dieselized." Nearly 80% of the self-propelled farm machinery now being manufactured is Diesel powered. With the exception of passenger cars, the Diesel has long been king of the transportation industry. Almost all heavy trucks today are driven by Diesel power plants. So are most buses. In railroading and barge freight, Diesels long ago nudged steam power completely out of the picture (Figure 14–2).

**Figure 14–2.** Many kinds of transportation have been completely "Dieselized" for a long time.

It does not seem likely, at this point, that they will dominate the passenger car market as completely—at least for very long. But unless governmental restrictions on nitrous oxide and particulate emissions become stricter, it is almost a certainty that mechanics will be working on more small Diesels in the next quarter century. The information in this unit will help prepare you to take advantage of those new opportunities.

## OBJECTIVES

When you have completed this unit you should be able to do the following:

- Explain the basic operation of the four-stroke Diesel engine.
- Demonstrate, by answering appropriate questions, an understanding of the advantages and disadvantages of the Diesel, as a passenger car power plant.
- Explain, with the aid of appropriate diagrams, the functioning of the major components and combustion chamber designs used in modern high-speed Diesel engines.
- Demonstrate, by answering appropriate questions, an understanding of three Diesel injection systems.
- Demonstrate, by answering specific questions, familiarity with the differences between gasoline and Diesel oil combustion.

## DIESEL FUNDAMENTALS

As with all ingenious ideas, the concept of the Diesel engine seems simple—once somebody else explains it. Air is compressed in a chamber until it becomes extremely hot. A quantity of fuel is injected and immediately ignited by the heat of the compressed air. A piston assembly operates as in a conventional engine, and power output is controlled by varying the volume of fuel injected. These, in a nutshell, are the principles conceived, just before the turn of the century, by the German engineer Rudolf Diesel (Figure 14–3). Since 1897, when he introduced his first "Diesel-cycle" engine, all engines employing these principles have borne his name.

By 1922, the French car manufacturer Peugeot had built an experimental passenger car which was Diesel powered. In 1936,

Mercedes-Benz, in Germany, marketed the first production-model Diesel car. That 1936 Mercedes-Benz 260D surprised everyone, even its builders, by gaining quick popularity as a taxicab. Since then, the popularity of Diesel-powered passenger cars has not been overwhelming, but it has been constant. Diesel-powered cars have steadily developed and flourished in almost every industrialized nation in the world. But their development has never been pursued with more purpose and intensity than right now.

**Figure 14–3.** Rudolph Diesel, a German engineer, introduced his first Diesel cycle engine in 1897. *Courtesy of The Bettman Archive*

At the time this chapter was written, in late 1979, General Motors was the only American manufacturer building Diesel-powered passenger cars (Figure 14–4). And their Diesel car production amounted to only 4% percent of their total output. General Motors predicts, however, that, by 1985, 25% of their passenger car output will be Diesel powered.

Both American and European manufacturers have begun producing a new generation of small Diesel engines designed especially for passenger cars. These new Diesels differ from previous ones in several important respects. They are lighter and higher "revving", so they perform better. Many of them have evolved from successful gasoline-powered engines. Consequently, much of the tooling and machinery needed for their production was already in existence. This means that the new generation of Diesels can be priced more competitively than any previous Diesel.

**Figure 14–4.** For a long time, General Motors was the only American manufacturer building Diesel-powered passenger cars. But GM experts correctly predicted a rapid increase in Diesel sales. It remains to be seen whether they will also be correct in their prediction that 25% of GM's passenger car output will be Diesel-powered by 1985.

## The Volkswagen Diesel: A Typical Example

Volkswagen's development of a successful Diesel engine based on the design of a current gasoline-powered engine is an excellent example of the trend mentioned above. The gasoline-powered version of the VW Diesel was a commercial success in its own right. In fact, it was chosen by two American manufacturers to power their own small cars. We are, of course, referring to the Volkswagen SOHC "Four," which is used in both the Dodge Omni and Plymouth Horizon (Figure 14–5).

VW's little Diesel seems to be so representative of the emerging trend that we shall use it as our example. All the details cited in the following review of Diesel fundamentals can be found in the VW "Rabbit" engine. Like most passenger car Diesels, the VW uses a combustion chamber with an adjoining pre-chamber. In this respect, it resembles the combustion chambers you learned about in Unit 12, when we discussed stratified charge systems. The VW pre-chamber is spherical in shape, so a swirling air flow is introduced, which improves combustion. Figure 14–6 shows how it works.

**Stroke I: Air Intake.** The toothed timing belt turns the overhead camshaft and causes it to open the intake valve. Meanwhile, the piston moves downward in the cylinder. This increases the volume and lowers the pressure in the chamber. So normal atmospheric pressure, outside the engine, forces in a full charge of fresh air. At this point in the Diesel cycle, no fuel is present in the combustion chamber.

**Figure 14–5.** Like other recent Diesel engines intended for use in passenger cars, VW's Rabbit "C" is based on the design of a successful gasoline engine. The gasoline-powered original was the Volkswagen SOHC "Four." *Courtesy of Volkswagen of America.*

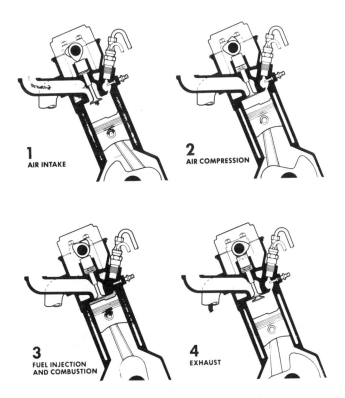

**Figure 14–6.** The four strokes of the Diesel cycle are well illustrated by these diagrams of the combustion chamber of a VW Rabbit engine. Notice the use of a pre-chamber to increase swirling. *Courtesy of Volkswagen of America.*

Stroke 2: Air Compression.  With both valves closed, the piston moves upward and compresses the trapped air into a space 23.5 times smaller than before. This makes the air extremely hot. Its maximum temperature of 1650° F (900° C) is far above the flash point of Diesel fuel.

Stroke 3: Fuel Injection and Combustion.  With the piston nearing TDC and the air temperature nearing its maximum, a mist of Diesel fuel is injected into the spherical pre-chamber. The hot air ignites the fuel, and the resultant burning immediately expands the mixture and carries the flame front into the cylinder. By this time, the piston has passed TDC, and the expanding combustion gases give it a power impulse as it starts downward.

Stroke 4: Exhaust.  When most of the combustion energy is spent, the exhaust valve opens, and the hot gases begin to rush out. The piston moves upward, shoving out the remaining gases. Then the exhaust valve closes and the intake valve opens. As the piston starts down again, the Diesel cycle begins anew.

## Constant Pressure Combustion

Less obvious than the Diesel's ignition by compression is its constant-pressure combustion process, which is another important advantage of the Diesel. In gasoline engines, with the fuel and air compressed together, combustion is very rapid. By the time the piston nears BDC on the power stroke, the compression forces have already peaked and begun to subside. But in the Diesel, combustion is slower and the power output more even. To understand why, let us look again at the Diesel cycle. Having no throttle to restrict its air flow, the Diesel can fill its cylinders to their maximum volumetric ability. So the Diesel takes in proportionately more air. Then, with its 23.5:1 ratio, it subjects the air to greater compression.

When fuel is ignited, the pressure in the chamber builds to about 1600 psi (113 ksc). So, for the fuel to enter at all, it must be sprayed at a pressure greater than 1600 psi (113 ksc). It is important to understand that the injection continues for a while even after combustion pressure has built. As the piston starts downward in the cylinder, injection and combustion proceed at about the same pressure. The result is that the piston is followed down the cylinder by a more or less continuous power impulse. This is why Diesel power output is generally smoother and less jerky than the power impulses from gasoline-powered engines. It is an additional advantage of the Diesel's fuel injection process.

# BASIC PRINCIPLES OF FUEL INJECTION

The Diesel cycle depends on precise control of the fuel entering the combustion chamber. This is the means used to control the speed and power output of the engine. For this reason, the fuel injection pump is the very heart of a modern Diesel engine (Figure 14–7).

**Figure 14–7.** The injection pump is the heart of the modern Diesel engine. *Courtesy of GMC Truck Division, General Motors Corporation.*

Its function is to deliver exactly the right amount of fuel at exactly the right time in exactly the right form. The amount of fuel must be exactly measured to correspond to the load on the engine. The timing must be exact in two ways. First, the injection must begin at precisely the right point in the Diesel cycle. Second, the injection should continue for an exactly determined period of time. And finally, to promote proper combustion, the fuel must reach the chamber in the form of a fine spray. The injection pumps which ensure that these requirements are met are driven by the engine itself. There are three general types.

## In-Line Injection Pumps

For years, European manufacturers have used a variety known as an *in-line* injection pump (Figure 14–8). Inside the in-line pump is a small camshaft which activates individual plungers (Figure 14–9). Each plunger feeds fuel to one cylinder (Figure 14–10). The timing of the injection and volume of discharge are controlled by a special governor. When the driver wishes to change speed or power, his control changes are fed first into this governor, which adjusts fuel input accordingly.

**Figure 14–8.**   For years, European manufacturers have used *in-line* injection pumps like this one. *Courtesy of Robert Bosch Corporation.*

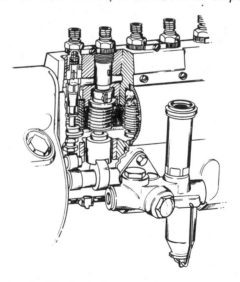

**Figure 14–9.**   Inside the in-line type injection pump is a small camshaft which activates an individual plunger to feed fuel to each cylinder.

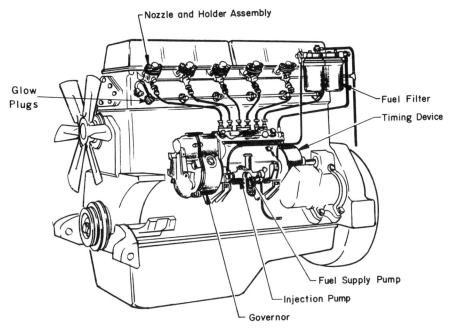

**Figure 14–10.**    Installed on an engine, the entire injection system looks like this.

## Distributor-Type Pumps

Another kind of injection pump uses a rotating distributor (Figure 14–11). Instead of an individual plunger for each cylinder, this system uses a single high-pressure pump. The pump delivers the correct fuel allotments directly into a rotating distributor. As with the electric spark on a conventional gasoline engine, the distributor feeds fuel injections to cylinders in the proper firing order.

## Individual Plunger/Injector Valve Pumps

The type of injection pump commonly found on the large American-built Diesels used to power big trucks employs a constant-pressure pump and individual injector valves. The injector valves are located above each cylinder (Figure 14–12).

The subject of Diesel fuel injection is both interesting and important. But an extensive treatment is necessarily beyond the scope of this text. Our goal in this chapter is to provide sufficient orientation to enable you to judge for yourself the extent to which your general knowledge of IC engines does and does not apply to Diesels. This discussion of the basic principles of fuel injection should, however, alert you to the variety of considerations and possibilities involved. Understanding those things, you can proceed more intelligently as you learn more about Diesels.

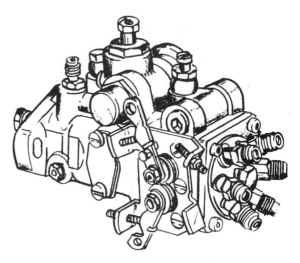

**Figure 14-11.** Some injection systems use a rotating distributor with a single high-pressure pump. The pump delivers metered fuel allotments to the distributor, which feeds the cylinders in the proper firing order.

**Figure 14-12.** On some large Diesels used to power American-built trucks, a constant-pressure pump feeds individual injector valves located above each cylinder.

One important thing to remember is that, regardless of the injection system used, the objective is always the same. The ability to deliver an accurately metered quantity of fuel to the cylinder at exactly the right time is the key to Diesel efficiency. To accomplish this timely delivery, all three kinds of pumps use three subsystems. These almost universally used subsystems include a governor, a pump timing device, and injection nozzles.

**Governor.**   Since it has no throttle, the Diesel engine is capable of almost instant acceleration. It is so responsive, in fact, that no human driver could control it without mechanical or electronic assistance. So a governor is used in the Diesel passenger car to relay some of the driver's commands and ensure smooth responses by the engine.

The mechanical controls commonly used with truck and passenger car engines are not the true variable devices usually referred to by the term *governors*. Diesel governors are more accurately described as *partial-load* or *limited-speed* controls. They serve mainly to prevent over-speeding and to maintain proper idle. This type of governor allows the gas pedal to control fuel input directly during an appropriate range of speeds. Once the engine is accelerated above idle, the governor only cuts in when the engine overspeeds. This makes Diesel response feel more like that of a gasoline engine.

The mechanical governor consists of a set of flyweights that are rotated at the speed of the pump (Figure 14–13). Precisely calibrated springs act against the flyweights as centrifugal force causes them to be "slung" outward. The faster the engine turns, of course, the more the flyweights move outward. Their movement is transmitted by linkage to the fuel control rod in the injection pump. In this way, the movement of the flyweights increases and decreases the amount of fuel injected. Also built into the governors of many injection pumps are torque control systems. These systems increase fuel quantity when the pedal is depressed and engine speed remains low, as would be the case when the vehicle was laboring up a hill or under heavy load.

**Pump Timing Devices.**   Diesel injection, like spark ignition, must be advanced as engine speed increases. As in the Otto-cycle engine, the purpose of this advance is to provide enough burning time to enable combustion pressure to peak just after the piston passes TDC. This adjustment is made by a centrifugal advance mechanism similar to those used on gasoline-powered engines. Unlike the governor, this timing device does not alter the amount of fuel being injected. It only controls when injection begins.

**Injection Nozzles.**   The fuel injected into the pre-chamber must be aimed in the proper direction and vaporized into the proper kind of spray. These are the functions of the injector nozzle (Figure 14–14). The design of the injector nozzle must be matched to both the size of the engine and the shape of the combustion chamber.

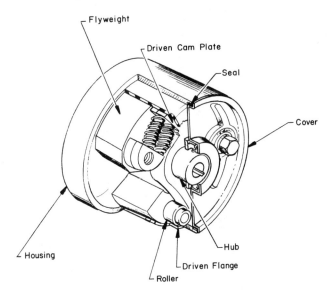

**Figure 14–13.** The mechanical governor consists of a set of flyweights which are rotated at the speed of the pump. The faster the pump rotates, the more they swing outward against the tension of their retaining springs. It is this movement of the weights that controls the amount of fuel injected.

The injector nozzles used in most passenger cars receive fuel from the injection pump through connecting high-pressure lines at 1000-2000 psi (80-140 bar). This pressurized fuel acts against a special part of the injector needle known as the *piston area* (Figure 14–15). The resulting hydraulic pressure, pushing on the piston area, overcomes the spring pressure that keeps the needle closed between fuel injections. When the needle lifts off its seat, the pressurized fuel is allowed to squirt through the nozzle. This injection continues as long as the pressure from the pump exceeds the spring pressure in the nozzle. So the time required to inject a given amount of fuel is determined by two things: (1) the amount of pump pressure, and (2) the length of time that pressure remains great enough to lift the needle.

## Aneroid Compensators

Some injection systems use an additional component called an *aneroid compensator*. An aneroid is a special metal bellows shaped a little bit like an accordion. It can expand or contract according to changes in

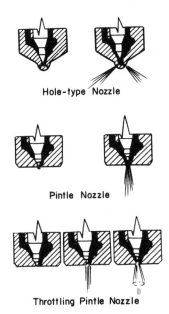

Hole-type Nozzle

Pintle Nozzle

Throttling Pintle Nozzle

**Figure 14–14.** The design of the injector nozzle must be matched to both the size of the engine and the shape of the combustion chamber.

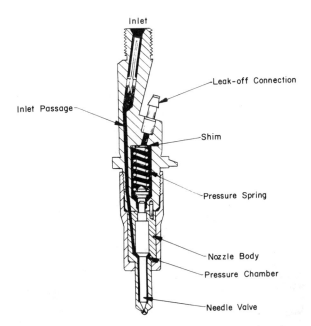

**Figure 14–15.** When the pressurized fuel pushes on the piston area of the needle with sufficient force, the needle lifts off its seat and fuel is injected. After injection, the spring pressure exceeds fuel pressure. So the needle is re-seated.

the surrounding air pressure. In a way, it is like a barometer; it senses and reacts to changes in pressure.

Aneroids may serve more than one function. One end of the bellows acts through linkage on the main fuel control rod in the injection pump. This connection enables the aneroid to adjust fuel injection automatically to compensate for changes in altitude. As altitude increases, atmospheric pressure decreases. So the bellows expands and thus acts on the fuel control rod, which reduces the amount of fuel injected.

In turbocharged engines, the aneroid is connected so that boost pressure will act on the bellows. When boost pressure increases, the aneroid collapses and allows more fuel to be delivered. Some fail-safe device is usually included in such turbocharged systems to protect the engine from overboost, in case the turbocharger's waste gate fails.

## Diesel Combustion Chambers

The shape of the combustion chamber is just as important in a Diesel as in an Otto-cycle engine. Not only does it affect the power output and emissions levels, as it does in a gasoline engine, but it also affects the noise level of the Diesel. There are, in fact, four major design-types for Diesel combustion chambers. Our explanation will be clearer if we divide them into two groups: (1) open-chamber designs, and (2) separate-chamber designs.

## Open-Chamber Designs

In open-chamber designs, the actual shape of the chamber is usually formed by the shape of the piston head. Fuel is injected directly into the main combustion chamber.

**Direct-Injection Chamber.**   One variety of open chamber, known as the direct-injection chamber, is shown in Figure 14–16A. Such a design gives maximum power and economy. But it produces objectionable levels of noise and pollution. Perhaps for these reasons, the direct injection chamber is not presently used in passenger cars.

**MAN-M Chamber.**   The so-called MAN-M type of chamber is a spherical hollow in the head of the piston (Figure 14–16B). This shape greatly reduces the noise of the Diesel at idle but does little to reduce emissions.

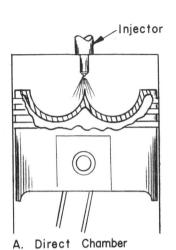

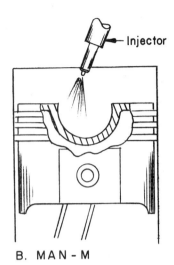

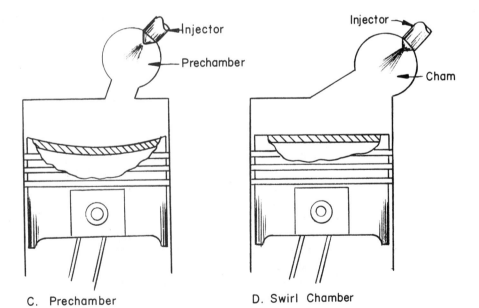

**Figure 14–16.** Figures A and B present open-chamber designs for Diesel combustion chambers. C and D show the two common separate-chamber designs.

## Separate-Chamber Designs

One of the two most common separate-chamber designs utilizes a pre-chamber. The other, uses a similar space, which is connected to the main chamber by a much larger passage and is properly called a swirl chamber.

**Pre-chamber.** Use of a pre-chamber (Figure 14–16C) almost always lowers power output and fuel economy by 10–15% from the levels achievable with an open chamber. But engines with pre-chambers run quieter and produce less pollution. When equipped with glow plugs, as they usually are, they start easier.

Glow plugs are, in effect, miniature electric heaters used to warm the air near the injection nozzle. Their added heat ensures that the temperature of the compressed air will exceed the flash point of Diesel oil, even in cold weather. Glow plugs are also used in other kinds of combustion chambers.

**Swirl Chamber.** The swirl chamber design offers the benefits of a pre-chamber and provides even better control over emissions (Figure 14–16D).

An additional benefit of these separate-chamber designs is that they tend to dampen somewhat the sharp pressure build-up found with open-chamber designs. This makes it possible for the block, pistons, and crankshaft to be made somewhat lighter.

## DIESEL FUEL

Theoretically, Diesel engines can be designed to burn almost anything from powdered coal to soybean oil. But automotive Diesels normally use petroleum-based fuels blended from fractions known as *middle distillates*. These are the fractions that boil from crude oil after gasoline but before lubricating oil. They are very similar to kerosene or home heating oil. But the special requirements of Diesel injection systems make it unwise to burn any grade of fuel not recommended by the manufacturer. The common grades of Diesel fuel are No. 1 and No. 2.

The viscosities of the two grades are different, so they are not interchangeable. An unwarranted change in viscosity may adversely affect the injection pump. Too thin an oil may not lubricate the pump adequately; too thick a fuel may not pump properly (Figure 14–17). Fuel viscosity also affects the pattern of the spray discharged by the injection nozzle. A fuel that is either too thick or too thin is not likely to atomize properly. Whether it leaves the nozzle as large droplets or vaporizes too completely, it will distort the rate of combustion.

**Figure 14–17.** The viscosities of the two grades of Diesel fuel are different. So it is important not to burn fuel not recommended by the manufacturer. Using fuel of the wrong viscosity may adversely affect the injection pump.

## Cetane Number

Just as the "knock" resistance of gasoline is rated in octanes, the comparable qualities in Diesel fuel are rated in *cetanes*. The lower a fuel's cetane number, the higher the temperature necessary to ignite it. When low cetane fuel is injected, part of it may not ignite. This unburned fuel can accumulate in the combustion chamber, and a later compression stroke may raise the temperature high enough to ignite it. The resulting "bang" produces abnormal pressure waves in the compression chamber, which can be heard as an audible knock. Fuels with high cetane ratings will ignite completely upon injection and produce a properly timed pressure to act evenly on the piston.

## TURBOCHARGED DIESELS

For a number of reasons, turbocharging is likely to improve the performance of a Diesel more than it would that of a comparable gasoline-powered engine. It is true that the Diesel must be strengthened and made heavier to withstand the higher pressures of turbocharging. It is also true that the Diesel's rpm's must be kept lower so that inertial forces, generated by those heavier parts, do not damage the engine. But the Diesel, by its very nature, is relatively free of the problems with detonation which plague supercharged gasoline engines. Moreover, a turbocharged Diesel operates with excess air at near-maximum volumetric efficiency. So the fuel injection can be tailored to provide peak thermal efficiency through a wide range of operating modes.

Though putting turbocharged Diesel engines into passenger cars is a recent trend, the idea of turbocharging Diesels is by no means new. Cummins Diesel entered a turbocharged Diesel race car in the 1952 Indianapolis 500. In the try-outs, despite its size and weight disadvantages, the "turbo Cummins" broke existing track records and won the pole position. In the race itself, the turbocharged Diesel developed mechanical problems and failed to finish. Soon afterwards, auto club rules were changed to make it ineligible for further competition. But it had proved, during its brief outing at the track, that turbocharged Diesel performance was competitive with that of gasoline engines. Cummins and others began to offer turbocharging on their large truck and industrial Diesels (Figure 14–18). And by the 1960's turbocharged Diesel trucks were common on American highways.

**Figure 14–18.** In the 1952 Indianapolis 500, the Cummins turbocharged Diesel proved that Diesel performance was comparable to that of spark ignition engines. *Official photo, Indianapolis Motor Speedway.*

To understand why turbocharging is so beneficial to a small Diesel engine, we have only to remind ourselves of the Diesel's weight problem. You probably remember from Unit 3 that a Diesel is likely to weigh more than a gasoline engine of equal displacement, and because of its low rpm's, it will usually develop 30–50% less power. These are important disadvantages for passenger car engines. With turbocharging, the power-weight ratio of the Diesel becomes comparable to that of a gasoline engine. This enables the Diesel's higher thermal efficiency and the higher BTU content of Diesel fuel to give the Diesel a significant edge in fuel economy.

## MODERN DIESEL-POWERED PASSENGER CARS

Perhaps the best way to get a sense of what is happening in this exciting area of automotive technology is to look at some of the newer Diesel-powered passenger cars. We will take a brief look at three.

### The Mercedes-Benz Turbocharged Five-Cylinder Diesel

In 1978, Mercedes-Benz introduced the first turbocharged Diesel passenger car. It was based on their unusual but popular five-cylinder 183 cid (3000 cc) Diesel passenger car engine. The turbocharged version develops 43% more horsepower but weighs only 7% more (Figure 14–19). The gain in performance was great enough to allow Mercedes-Benz to offer Diesel power in their large, 4000 pound (1765 kg) passenger car models for the first time.

**Figure 14–19.** In 1978, Mercedes-Benz introduced the first turbocharged Diesel passenger car. The turbocharged version of this 300 SD engine develops 43% more horsepower with only a 7% gain in weight. *Courtesy of Mercedes-Benz of North America.*

With turbocharging, it became necessary to strengthen and redesign some components. To withstand the higher cylinder pressures, a specially hardened, or *nitrided*, crankshaft was used, and a new type of oil-cooled aluminum piston was designed. The wrist pins were enlarged and the connecting rod bearings modified. The head gasket sealing surfaces were also redesigned, and sodium-cooled exhaust valves were introduced. The existing lubrication system was augmented with a larger oil pump, an oil cooler, and a redesigned oil filter.

For its turbocharger, Mercedes chose the AIResearch TA 0301, with its waste gate adjusted to limit boost to about 11 psi (75 kpa). The waste gate is sized so that it produces maximum boost at 2000 rpm and bleeds off excess exhaust gases at higher speeds.

Figure 14–20 shows a cutaway view of the cylinder and head of the Mercedes 300 SD. Valves on the five cylinders are operated, through followers, by a single chain-driven, overhead camshaft. Notice particularly the removable pre-chamber and the glow plug, which enters the pre-chamber from the side, near the injector nozzle. The Mercedes 300 SD seems to be very near state-of-the-art engineering. It should give the economy expected of a Diesel along with performance and smoothness typical of gasoline engines.

**Figure 14–20.** The Mercedes 300 SD combustion chamber has a removable pre-chamber. The glow plug enters this pre-chamber from the side near the injector nozzle. *Courtesy of Mercedes-Benz of North America.*

# The Oldsmobile Diesels

A considerably larger Diesel has been developed in the U.S. by engineers at the Oldsmobile Division of General Motors. Reportedly very cost effective, this V–8 Diesel promises to give excellent fuel economy when installed in full-sized passenger cars and light trucks (Figure 14–21). This Oldsmobile Diesel is also based on the design of an existing gasoline engine—the Olds 350 cid V–8. Though the Diesel shares almost no major components with its gasoline-burning forerunner, dimensional similarities were preserved. So the Diesel can be manufactured on existing assembly lines. The Oldsmobile Diesel uses removable, stainless steel pre-chambers and a distributor-type fuel injection pump. It weighs about 100 pounds more than the comparable Otto-cycle engine (Figure 14–22).

**Figure 14–21.** Cadillac's V-8 Diesel is also based on the design of a successful gasoline engine. In this case, the "model" was the Olds 350 cid V-8.

During its first year of manufacture, General Motors installed 177,000 Diesel 350 V–8's in Oldsmobile and Cadillac passenger cars and half-ton Chevrolet trucks. Since it has no throttle, this Diesel—like most others—develops very little manifold vacuum. So a special pump, driven from the engine camshaft, is necessary in order to supply vacuum for the various pneumatic accessories. The power brakes are hydraulically boosted from the power steering pump.

**The Oldsmobile 260 cid Diesel V–8.** Oldsmobile also produces an almost identical 260 cid Diesel, also a V–8. The smaller version has only a 3.5 inch cylinder bore, as opposed to the 4.067 inch bore of its larger cousin. Instead of the 125 horsepower produced by the 350 cid, the 260 develops 90.

The Diesel-powered passenger cars now manufactured in America are, by almost any standards, quite refined. They offer the luxury car buyer the economy of a Diesel engine in a vehicle that is, in all regards, acceptable to his or her tastes.

**Figure 14–22.**    The Olds V-8 Diesel weighs about 110 pounds more than the comparable Otto-cycle engine. *Courtesy of GMC Truck Division, General Motors Corporation.*

**The Volkswagen 1.5 Litre Four-Cylinder Diesel.**    Pursuing a different kind of excellence, Volkswagen engineers set out, in 1975, to exploit fully the advantages of the Diesel's constant pressure. Their goal was to maximize fuel economy and control over the peak pressures developed in the engine. What they came up with was the so-called "Rabbit" Diesel engine, which we cited as an example earlier in this unit.

Volkswagen, like the other developers of passenger car Diesels, began by studying the design of one of their successful gasoline engines. For this they selected their four-cylinder SOHC engine. And they made only the modifications actually required by the "Dieselization" of their gasoline version (Figure 14–23). In this case, they succeeded in retaining many common parts and production processes.

Only minor modifications were necessary in the water jackets of the gasoline engine block. So both blocks can be manufactured on the same machining lines (Figure 14–24). More changes were required in the SOHC aluminum cylinder head. Where the spark plugs had been on the gasoline engine, Volkswagen installed removable swirl chambers and injectors. Special cast reinforcements in the "Dieselized" head provide extra strength and redirect the flow of the coolant. In the Diesel, it is especially important that the area around the swirl chamber be thoroughly cooled. So the water passages in the head of the Diesel are quite different. Yet both heads can be produced from the same mold. Specially designed pistons are used in the Diesel. Their com pression ring grooves are cast in place, as are special steel struts used to control expansion caused by the Diesel's higher operating temperatures.

**Figure 14–23.** For their successful Rabbit, VW "Dieselized" their four-cylinder SOHC. *Courtesy of Volkswagen of America.*

The timing of the intake valves was adjusted so that they open later and close earlier. This slight change tends to raise the compression ratio and reduces the risk of a piston-valve collision. Because the distribution-type injection pump is lighter and smaller as well as cheaper, VW chose it over an in-line pump. The use of a mechanical injection advance unit and a mechanical governor makes the VW Diesel respond much like a gasoline engine. And because the cogged timing belt also drives the injection pump, it is made stronger and heavier.

More recently, Volkswagen engineers, using many of the same concepts, have converted the five- and six-cylinder gasoline engines currently used in VW/Audi cars. The resulting mid-size Diesels are supposed to be installed in VW's new line of passenger cars and trucks. They will also be made available to other European car manufacturers, for possible installation in their vehicles.

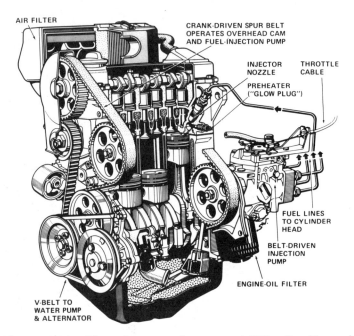

**Figure 14–24.** Like other manufacturers of "Dieselized" gasoline engines, Volkswagen produced, in its 1.5 litre Diesel, a design which could be manufactured on the same machining lines. *Courtesy of Volkswagen of America.*

## REVIEW QUESTIONS

*Objective Questions*

1. The speed and power output of a Diesel engine are controlled by

    _____ A.  The amount of fuel injected

    _____ B.  The throttle

    _____ C.  Linkage between the glow plugs and the waste gate

    _____ D.  The cetane rating of the fuel

2. Jim says, "Cetane is a measure of the viscosity of Diesel fuel."
   Joe says, "The cetane rating of Diesel fuel is comparable to the octane rating of gasoline."
   Who is correct?

   _____ A.   Jim only
   _____ B.   Joe only
   _____ C.   Both Jim and Joe
   _____ D.   Neither Jim nor Joe

3. Which kind of Diesel injection pump has an internal camshaft?

   _____ A.   Distributor type
   _____ B.   Individual plunger/injector valve type
   _____ C.   Aneroid type
   _____ D.   In-line type

4. The purpose of the governor on a Diesel engine is to

   (1) Maintain proper idle
   (2) Prevent overspeeding

   _____ A.   (1) only
   _____ B.   (2) only
   _____ C.   Both (1) and (2)
   _____ D.   Neither (1) nor (2)

5. Sid says, "One purpose for an aneroid on a Diesel engine is to compensate for changes in fuel cetane."
   Sam says, "Sid is correct, and that is the only purpose for the aneroids used on passenger cars."
   Who is right?

   _____ A.   Sid only
   _____ B.   Sam only
   _____ C.   Both Sam and Sid
   _____ D.   Neither Sam nor Sid

6. With what mechanism on a gasoline engine is the pump timing device of the Diesel most comparable?

   _____ A.   Ignition advance
   _____ B.   Timing belt
   _____ C.   Valve overlap register
   _____ D.   Oil control rings

7. Will says, "Glow plugs have long been used in the gasoline-powered engines for American passenger cars"

Bill says, "The purpose of glow plugs is to warm the air near the injector nozzle."

Who is correct?

———— A.   Will only
———— B.   Bill only
———— C.   Both Will and Bill
———— D.   Neither Will nor Bill

8. How many common grades of Diesel oil are commonly used?

———— A.   2
———— B.   3
———— C.   4
———— D.   5

9. The difference between No. 1 and No. 2 Diesel oil is chiefly a matter of

———— A.   Lubricating power
———— B.   BTU content
———— C.   Viscosity
———— D.   Coefficient of friction

*Questions of Recall and Application*

1. Name, in order, the five events of the Diesel cycle and explain what happens during each.

2. From the list below select the appropriate name for each of the Diesel combustion chambers pictured at the top of the next page and write it in the space beneath the picture.

Aneroid
MAN-M
Direct injection
Pre-chamber
Waste gate
Swirl chamber
Hemisphere

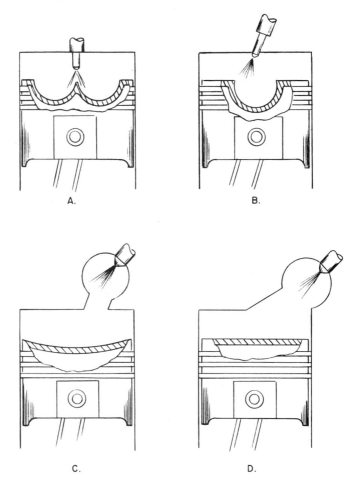

A.   B.

C.   D.

3. In the illustration on page 448, find each of the named parts. Write the number of each part in the space before its name.

_____ Injection nozzle
_____ Glow plug
_____ Injection pump
_____ Governor
_____ Fuel filter

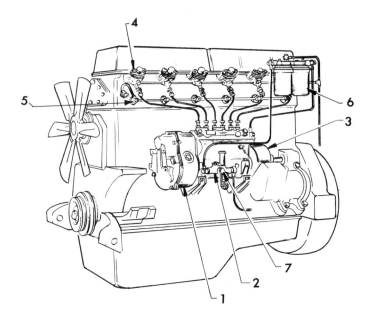

4. Explain how Diesel combustion differs from gasoline combustion. Which burns faster? Which burns more completely? Why?

5. Explain why the power output of a Diesel engine is generally smoother and less jerky than that of an Otto-cycle engine.

# The Future Is Now

Much has happened in the automotive industry during the fifteen months it has taken us to write this book. Not all of these developments have been good for the industry. But none that we know of diminish in any way the opportunities open to a well-trained automotive mechanic. Moreover, virtually every important happening was anticipated in our discussion of the state of the industry at the beginning of this text.

To us, the biggest surprise has been the unexpected rapidity with which the predictions we made in Units 1–3 are being fulfilled. To observe this, however, gives us less than a full measure of pleasure. Indeed, we would be happier today as American citizens and as human beings, if we had been less successful as prophets over a year ago.

When we wrote, in Units 1–3, about the energy crisis, we were painfully aware that the overwhelming majority of Americans doubted the reality of such a crisis. The long lines and social disruptions caused by the 1973 oil embargo had already faded from memory. And though its price had climbed steadily, plenty of gasoline seemed to be available. Polls showed that Americans blamed the shortage of the early 1970's on "politics" and the "greed" of the oil companies. They simply did not believe the energy shortage was real.

This general scepticism worried us a little. It was not that we felt qualified to deny that politics and greed might have somehow been involved. It was only that we knew, on the basis of hard statistical evidence, that an increasingly severe shortage of oil loomed ahead. And if students reading our text were to understand our reasoning about the industry, it was important that they accept the reality of that oil shortage. Surely the events of the past year have demonstrated that reality.

## THE ENERGY CRISIS—AGAIN

Several factors combined to produce what is now being called the great gasoline shortage of 1979. The most frequently mentioned cause was an unexpected civil war in Iran, which suddenly cut American oil imports by two billion barrels a day (Figure 15–1). Though this was only a small percentage of our total imports, the cutback had an immediate impact on the daily lives of Americans. Nothing could have more dramatically proven what we said in Unit 1 about the importance of the automobile to America's economy.

**Figure 15–1.** The energy crisis of 1979 began early in the year when record winter cold created such a shortage of heating oil that businesses were forced to shorten hours and schools were closed to save energy. Later in the year, when civil war in Iran interrupted the flow of imported oil, an acute gasoline shortage developed. *Reprinted with permission from* The Courier-Journal *and* The Louisville Times.

The effect of the cut, added to other sharp price increases by the oil-producing nations, raised the price of imported crude oil by 40% in less than a year. Resulting price increases added an additional 2% to our national rate of inflation. This was enough to topple an already tottering economy into a recession that put an estimated 800,000 people out of work. And it was enough to change overnight the purchasing and driving habits of American consumers. Many people had only shrugged when told that Europeans were paying $1.60–$2.80 per gallon for gasoline. But their interest became keen in the late spring and early summer when they saw their own expenses increase by 25% in about three months.

But worse than the price increase was the ever-present question of availability. For a time, it was not safe to assume that one could buy gasoline at any price. Again, as in 1973, motorists spent hours in line at service stations. Sometimes, waiting vehicles ran out of gas and had to be pushed through the line to the pump. Tempers flared. Fights among waiting drivers were common, and at least one fatal shooting occurred after someone attempted to cut into a line. Almost all stations closed on Sundays. In some states, drivers could only buy gasoline on alternate days, depending on whether their license numbers were odd or even. Travelers planned their routes with an ear to the radio, listening to "gasoline-watch" announcements.

These afflictions did not last long, it is true. In less than two months, they ran their course. By then the political situation had stabilized in Iran, and the oil-producing countries had voted another price increase. So gasoline became available again, at the unheard of price of a dollar a gallon. As this book goes to press, accusations are again being made—as they were in the early 1970's—that American consumers were made to suffer more than necessary. Again, governmental ineptitude and oil company manipulations are being blamed for making the shortage worse. But the aftermath this time differs in one important way from that which followed the 1973 boycott. For the first time, opinion polls show that most Americans now believe that the energy crisis is real.

## The Turn to Economy Cars

The impact of this changed perception on the automotive industry has fulfilled several of our earlier predictions with almost dazzling rapidity. When we predicted a growing emphasis on fuel economy in Unit 1, we did so in the certainty that the *long-term* growth of the industry depended on it. But we were acutely aware of popular articles reporting on the "comeback" of the big car. Manufacturers who had done a minimum of "down-sizing" were doing quite well, especially with their larger vehicles. American small cars, on the other hand, were not doing as well as expected. But the 1979 fuel shortage changed all that.

Suddenly, the total sales of America's "big three" car manufac-turers dropped by 20%, and that overall plunge only tells part of the story. Sales skyrocketed on virtually all kinds of small cars. In the first four months of 1979, small car sales shot up by 29%. Foreign manufac-turers of subcompacts, like Datsun and Toyota, reported record sales. In this country, American Motors, which had anticipated an earlier switch to the small car, found a silver lining in the cloud. In May, they announced that they were expanding production by 25% to meet the growing demand for small cars. This announcement came at almost the same time the manufacturers of big cars were feeling the pinch. On almost consecutive days, Chrysler announced the layoff of 13,500 workers, Ford laid off 5,000, and General Motors reported another cutback in its big-car production.

## The Question Mark Over Chrysler

Chrysler Corporation was hurt worst. Their steadily declining sales in the late 1970's, coupled with the impact of inflation, had left them particularly vulnerable to such an unexpected shift in the market. So did their popular image. American consumers, largely unaware of Chrysler's forward-looking engineering achievements, tended to view all their products as gas-guzzling luxury cars. Alarmed Chrysler officials publicly confessed that the corporation was in serious financial trou-ble. Without massive government assistance, they said, Chrysler could not survive.

Responsible officials began studying what it would mean for one of the big three auto manufacturers to fold when the country was already entering a recession. Their findings underscored, as few things could, the central position of the automobile in the American economy.

A preliminary government report, released just as this book went to press, showed that over 100,000 Chrysler employees would be ren-dered jobless. Among the numerous smaller companies whose chief function is to supply parts to Chrysler, many would undoubtedly go bankrupt. Ignoring that possibility, however, the report focused on the number of jobs that would be lost because of cutbacks caused by a Chrysler failure. The estimates were that 180,000 jobs would be lost in supplying companies, 100,000 more in Chrysler dealerships, and 12,000 others in the freight and other related industries. So a total of 292,000 workers outside of Chrysler would be affected.

With the loss of these jobs would come a staggering loss of tax revenues at all levels. Instead of the $500 million paid in taxes on the income from those jobs, the Federal Government would find itself with additional expenses. Unemployment benefits and welfare payments due the workers would exceed $30 million a week or $1.5 billion in a year. An estimated 241,000 Chrysler customers would be expected to purchase imported cars instead. This would increase U.S. imports by another $1.5 billion and further upset our balance of payments on the world market.

At home, the impact would not be spread evenly. Rather, it would hit some communities with devastating force. The expectation is that school and city budgets, property values, and retail trade would all be severely affected in these cities:

- Detroit, Michigan
- Kokomo, Indiana
- New Castle, Indiana
- Fostoria, Ohio
- Belvidere, Illinois
- Newark, Delaware
- Syracuse, New York
- Huntsville, Alabama
- Windsor, Ontario, Canada

The probability is that the small town of New Castle, Indiana, would be completely shut down. And Detroit—one of the nation's largest cities—would have its economic base destroyed for years to come.

As this is written, it is not yet certain whether Chrysler will, in fact, receive the aid it needs. Present discussion centers on the possibility that the government might extend "less than one billion dollars" of aid in the form of loan guarantees. But the very fact that such governmental assistance is being considered, in a free enterprise economy, is significant. It shows widespread realization that the economic fate of the country is intertwined with the fate of the automotive industry. The sudden shift to small cars—whether or not this particular stampede proves to be permanent—validates our expectation. The long-term growth of the industry must be directed towards manufacturing smaller cars with more efficient engines.

## The Emergence of the Diesel

Along with the 1979 rush to smaller cars came another boom that we had predicted. As gasoline supplies tightened, the Diesel engine suddenly became the darling of car buyers.

The Volkswagen, Oldsmobile, and Mercedes-Benz Diesels discussed in Unit 14 sold faster than they could be supplied. Diesel car sales in April, 1979, tripled those of the previous April. In August, newspaper reports mentioned an ongoing Diesel development project at Ford, in cooperation with Cummins Diesel. By then, this new demand had remained strong through at least one shortage of Diesel fuel, and Oldsmobile was still reporting that they could not manufacture Diesels fast enough.

The news media no doubt helped to create this boom. Newspaper and magazine features made the public aware of advances in Diesel technology. Wire service news stories followed the progress of the "Moodymobile" on its publicity-seeking trip from Daytona Beach to Washington. The Moodymobile was a 1979 Mercury Capri with a turbocharged Perkins Diesel engine, similar to those used in Alpha Romeo cars. Named after master mechanic Ralph Moody, who tinkered with its Perkins engine and drive train, the Moodymobile averaged eighty-four miles per gallon. When the so-called "wonder car" arrived in Washington, senators and congressmen heaped praise upon it. Coming as it did in the midst of a gasoline drought, this publicity focused the attention of the lay public on the Diesel. So in the short run, as we predicted, the Diesel is gaining in popularity. It is now clear that American consumers will not categorically reject passenger cars powered by Diesels.

## Particulate and NOx Standards for Diesels

However, all this does not add up to a certainty that the Diesel is the engine of the future. The Environmental Protection Agency (EPA) has now proposed limits on those particulate and nitrous oxide emissions we mentioned in Unit 3. Though not yet backed by the force of law, the proposed standards have drawn public expressions of consternation from auto manufacturers. Especially distressing to them are the proposed limits on particulates.

The new standards allow a maximum of 0.6 grams per mile in 1981 cars but reduce the allowable level to 0.2 grams per mile for 1983 and later models. It is easy to see why the manufacturers are concerned. Emissions for current GM Diesels range from 0.78 to 1.02 grams per mile. Those of Mercedes-Benz cars are 0.45 to 0.83 grams per mile. And those of the VW Rabbit are about 0.23 grams per mile.

The proposed standards, coupled with the government's increasingly tough mileage requirements, have Diesel manufacturers in a bind. Detroit spokesmen have asserted flatly that enforcement of these requirements would kill the Diesel for use in anything larger than subcompacts. A spokesman for Mercedes-Benz accused the new standards of being an "insurmountable engineering requirement." The Council on Wage and Price Stability, another governmental agency, publicly declared the proposed requirements to be too stringent and too expensive. It is still too soon to predict which view will prevail. But it is clear that an intensive effort is under way to gain some relaxation of the proposed standards. It is clear also, as we wrote in Unit 3, that the continued viability of the Diesel hinges on this decision.

## CONTINUED CONCERN OVER AIR POLLUTION

The indications are that it will not be easy to convince the government to accept more air pollution. On the day that we began this chapter, the air in Louisville, Kentucky, was found to be unhealthy at a near-record level. A few days later, smog over Los Angeles reached its worst density in twenty-four years. Citizens were advised to stay indoors and avoid exercise. It is clear, as we wrote in Units 1–3, that air pollution is becoming a factor of greater and greater importance in deciding public policy.

**Figure 15–2.** The immediate economic advantages of relaxing emissions standards must still be weighed against the resulting health hazards. Smog over Louisville, Kentucky, and Los Angeles, California, reached near record levels while this chapter was being written. *Reprinted with permission from* The Courier-Journal *and* The Louisville Times.

To be sure, oil refineries won some temporary relaxations of the limitations on the amount of lead used during the worst of the gasoline shortage. And car manufacturers did recently win a two-year delay in the enforcement of the 1981 emission standards for a few selected cars. But this was far less than the blanket postponement requested by the six manufacturers. All in all, the realities of air pollution are becoming obvious to everyone, and despite temporary delays and exemptions, those realities are sufficient to make low emissions an inescapable requirement for automotive engines. The eventual winner of today's automotive sweepstakes is certain to be an engine with much cleaner exhaust.

## HINTS OF TECHNOLOGICAL PROGRESS

Every book must have an end, but progress in automotive technology, as you saw in Unit 2, does not. So it is impossible to conclude a text like this without being aware of the exciting possibilities which could not be discussed in it. A basic text must, after all, focus on the realities of the industry. So except for the early chapters, we have reported what already has come to pass and what seems reasonably certain to materialize in the near future. We do not, however, wish to leave completely unmentioned certain other developments. The true significance of numerous little pockets of progress can only be guessed at today. And there are many more of them than we can possibly list. But because this aspect of the trade is so fascinating to us, we want at least to introduce you to it. Somewhere in today's field of automotive research are planted the seeds of the future.

It is conceivable that by 1990 a text like this will not be complete without a unit on variable displacement engines. Engineers at Eaton Corporation's Engine Components Division are now trying to revive an idea that was long believed dead. In theory, variable displacement engines depend on a very simple principle: automobile engines need their full power only during acceleration and hill-climbing. So fuel consumption and emissions could both be lowered by a reliable mechanism for deactivating some cylinders most of the time. During those rare periods when full power was needed, the "extra" cylinders could provide added displacement. A twelve-cylinder touring car engine used this principle in 1916. But the idea seemed to die the following year when its manufacturer, the Enger Motor Car Co., went out of business. It may be that today's effort will suffer the same fate. Or it may be that dollar-a-gallon gasoline now heralds the coming of variable displacement.

You probably remember from Unit 3 that the commercial development of both gas turbine and Stirling engines is effectively blocked by the high cost of required ceramic parts. But there is reason to believe that this situation may change. An article in the August 1979 issue of *Automotive Engineering* reports that genuine progress is being made in the development of ceramic materials. New molding and machining methods are making it possible to lower the cost of ceramic components. The article concludes by observing that the rapidly-rising prices of alloy metal will soon make ceramics a cheaper alternative. When that happens, the authors predict, the profits and savings from production volume will then make it possible to reduce the cost of ceramic parts dramatically.

Such a development would obviously put the gas turbine and Stirling engines back in the race. Moreover, it just might open up new vistas in Diesel technology. Research conducted by Cummins Engine Company and the U.S. Army has recently studied the role of ceramics in Diesels. The investigators conclude that no ceramic now available can meet all the requirements of the Diesel. But thinking ahead to the time when such materials become available, they have experimented with an *adiabatic* Diesel. An adiabatic engine is one which operates without gain or loss of heat. In other words, adiabatic engines are uncooled. Using high-performance ceramic parts, it should actually be possible to create an adiabatic engine which also operates *without lubrication*. We are not yet ready to predict that you will one day work on engines without cooling and lubrication systems. But neither can we deny the possibility outright.

What we can do, in closing, is to encourage you to get the most out of what you have learned in this text. For you will be limiting your opportunities if you allow your training to end here. If you have studied this text carefully, you have a good beginning. But if you are serious about a career in automotive technology, you should realize that it is only a beginning. Only if you take steps to keep informed and to get the right kind of experience can you be sure of reaching your own goals.

Keeping informed is the easy part. Numerous professional and trade magazines are available to let you know what is going on in your field. If you have been studying this book as a text for an organized course, your instructor has probably already acquainted you with these. If not, you can learn about them in a number of ways. Perhaps the easiest way is to ask your employer. He probably subscribes to some himself. And it cannot hurt for him to know that you plan to keep yourself informed. You can also ask at virtually any trade school or automobile dealership. The important thing is to select two or three good periodicals that you enjoy. Then make a point of reading them regularly. You will be amazed, in two or three years, at the advantage this gives you over others who are less motivated or less methodical.

It goes without saying that you should read any technical leaflets and bulletins given you by your employer. And whenever possible, take advantage of every opportunity for in-service training. Employers often conduct such training programs themselves or pay tuition for their workers at nearby technical schools and community colleges. Any mechanic who takes the trouble to find out about such opportunities will find it comparatively easy to stay informed. Moreover, by doing so he will ensure his advancement in the surest possible way: he will be making himself more and more valuable as an employee.

Our last bit of advice is that you try to decide, at least in general terms, what your goal is going to be. Do you just like to work *on* cars? Or would you be just as happy working *with* cars, perhaps as a service manager or owner of your own business? If you prefer the simpler life of an employee, what kind of employer offers the job you would most like to have? Would you fit in better working with the big Diesels at a bus or trucking company? Or would you be more content working as a line mechanic at a specialized dealership? It is understandable if you do not yet know the answers to these questions.

But it is a good idea to begin pondering them now. There is an important advantage to choosing your long-range goals fairly early in your career. Doing so enables you to set about getting the *right kind* of experience to help you reach that goal. In a specialized technology like automechanics, a *lot* of experience is not always enough. A lot of *good* experience is not always enough. Only *appropriate* experience counts. So plan, whenever possible, to get the experience that matches your goal. We hope that, when you decide, you find that your goal involves automotive engines. If it does, we feel sure that what you have learned from this text will speed your progress towards it.

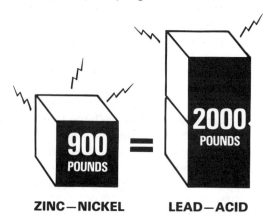

**ZINC—NICKEL          LEAD—ACID**

**Figure 15–3.**  Late in 1979, General Motors announced a "long-elusive breakthrough" in the technology of zinc-nickel oxide batteries. It is not yet clear whether this is the needed breakthrough we described in Unit 3. But it is obviously a major step towards a practical electrical car. As the above chart shows, General Motor's new battery weighs less than half as much as an equivalent lead-acid battery and takes up only half as much space. *Courtesy of General Motors Research.*

**Figure 15–4.** The greatly reduced size and weight of GM's new zinc-nickel battery leaves room to spare in this modified Chevette. The 30,000 mile life of these lighter batteries may be enough to put the electric car back in the automotive sweepstakes. "We still have a tremendous amount of development to do," GM President E.M. Estes told newsmen, "but we've cleared a major technological obstacle to our plans to begin offering electric-powered vehicles in the mid-1980's." *Courtesy of General Motors Research.*

**Figure 15–5.** Instead of the 2000-pound lead-acid battery pack in the foreground, electric cars can now be powered as well by the 900-pound zinc-nickel pack being displayed by the two Delco Remy engineers, Ralph L. Corbin (left) and William B. Wylam (right). As predicted in Unit 3, GM expects its first electric-powered vehicle to be either a small car for urban and commuter use or a delivery van for use in downtown areas. *Courtesy of General Motors Research.*

# Index